THE COLLECTOR'S ENCYCLOPEDIA OF

GRANITE WARE

COLORS, SHAPES AND VALUES

BOOK 2

by

Helen Greguire

COLLECTOR BOOKS
A Division of Schroeder Publishing Co., Inc.

The current values in this book should be used only as a guide. They are not intended to set prices, which vary from one section of the country to another. Auction prices as well as dealer prices vary greatly and are affected by condition as well as demand. Neither the Author nor the Publisher assumes responsibility for any losses that might be incurred as a result of consulting this guide.

Cover designed and photographed by Frederick Greguire III

Items on Front Cover:

Top Center; Coffee boiler, blue and white large swirl. "Columbian Ware." Extremely rare color, near mint condition, **$415.00.**

Top Left; Teakettle, black and white large swirl. Extremely rare color and shape, near mint condition, **$495.00**

Top Right; Berlin-style kettle with matching granite lid. Green and white large swirl. "Emerald Ware." Rare color, near mint condition, **$325.00.**

Bottom Left; Milk can with matching granite cover. Cobalt blue and white large swirl, Rare color, shape and size, near mint condition, **$795.00**

Bottom Center; Syrup, dark green and white large swirl, "Chrysolite." Extremely rare color and shape, mint condition, **$1,495.00.**

Bottom Right; Coffee biggin. Reddish brown and white large swirl. Rare color, shape and size, good plus condition, **$525.00.**

Printed by IMAGE GRAPHICS, INC., Paducah, Kentucky

I dedicate this book to all the people who in many ways offered their help as well as the loan of their granite ware to be photographed, and to all the people who helped to make Book I an instant success.

From the Author

Several years have passed since the introduction of my first book, *The Collector's Encyclopedia of Granite Ware*, which was an instant success.

I give thanks to Collector Books and the Schroeder Publishing Company, who did a great job in publishing and promoting the book. I also give special thanks to all the people who bought my book. Without all of you my book could not have been a success.

I would now like to present to you *The Collector's Encyclopedia of Granite Ware: Colors, Shapes, and Values*, Book 2. The new book features full page color plates with most categorized by color and/or manufacturer. In Book 2 you will find another large selection of colors, shapes, and rarities, and cross collectibles along with various pieces of literature including catalogues, posters, and advertisements.

Although the majority of the pieces shown in Book 2 were not shown in Book I, it was necessary to include some of the pieces from Book I to make a section clear.

Also included in this book are measurements, as well as a current and complete price guide.

Once again thank you for your support and enthusiasm.

Granitely,
Helen Greguire

ACKNOWLEDGMENTS

With the completion of this book I would like to take time to acknowledge and thank all the people who took the time and effort to give a word of encouragement when I needed one to go on.

Along with the people who wrote complimentary letters, loaned me their choice pieces of granite ware, copied and sent literature, these people helped bring this book forth.

A special thanks to my family: my husband Fred, who once again helped in the construction needed; my son Fred, who photographed this book, and spent many hours helping to organize the book; my daughter-in-law, Val, who helped set up the displays; my daughter Mary Lou Prince, son-in-law Paul Prince, and granddaughter Paula Jean Prince for the loan of their granite ware. Carol Viterise, once again thank you for your great expertise in typing and Phillip Daily, for your special assistance.

Last but not least my sincere thanks to the following: Delores Dolge, Roxanne Nelson, Rocki and Jacquie Rasmussen, Dr. Mark Edwards, Jim and Kathy Breeding, Muriel DeFrank, Lewis DeFrank, Arthur G. Fraser, Mary Ann and Stan Szambelan, Jay and Joan Smith, Betty and Bob Smith, Brenda Hutto, Sharon Latka, Vikki and Gary Davis, Rose Schleede, Jane Mandel, Virginia Southern, Suzanne Berger, Bob and Linda Hughett, Alison Hughett, Laurae Hartsock, Steve Smith, Elaine Roselli, Jerry Kelly, Dolores Lombard, George and Virginia Hamblin, Evelyn Welch, Sandrea Lukasiak, Fred and Elaine Hadfield, Skip and Jody Capan, Donald Mann, Ruth Van Kuren, Angel Diaz.

TABLE OF CONTENTS

Introduction 7

What is Granite Ware?...8

Pattern and Color Descriptions 9

Enameling Types 10

Is Age Determined by Construction? 10

How to Determine the New Granite Ware...11

Popularity Helps to Determine Desirability...12

How to Clean and Preserve Granite Ware..12

Granite Ware's Future..13

Measurements 13

Pricing Information 14

Section 1: Labeled Pieces and Advertising..16

Section 2: Catalogues, Advertising & Historical Items. 36

Section 3: Blue and White...48

Section 4: Standard Sizes Compared to Miniatures, Salesman's Samples,
             and Individual Serving Sizes..120

Section 5: Pink & White, Aqua Green & White, Lava Ware,
             Yellow & White, & Redipped 128

Section 6: Gray 140

Section 7: Red and White 160

Section 8: Solid White and White with Colored Trim 176

Section 9: Solid Colors and Solid Colors on Cast Iron.........................184

Section 10: Brown and White..208

Section 11: Recreational and Household Items....................................218

Section 12: Metal Trimmed Pieces, White Metal, Nickel Plate,
             Quadruple Silver Plate, etc 226

Section 13: Shaded...232

Section 14: Relish Pattern 248

Section 15: Chrysolite 254

Section 16: Chicken Wire Pattern and Snow on the Mountain. 262

Section 17: End of Day 270

Section 18: Emerald Ware 288

Section 19: Decorated 296

Section 20: Child's Items, Miniatures, and Salesman's Samples 310

Section 21: The Hunt Goes On!...350

Section 22: Gathering and Convention Commemoratives and Related Items...376

INTRODUCTION

With this book I have used different categories, in comparison to Book I, such as grouping companies, as well as colors when possible, that are closely related. I did this so you could see the different shades of colors. I have been asked why I don't do a color chart. From my point of view, and as you can see by this book, it would be almost impossible. While photographing the pieces that we thought were identical in color to the naked eye, the camera picked up the different shades. What you think is one shade of color is another in disguise. Lighting also affects the colors.

Even though the manufacturer intended to produce a specific color or shade, many variables affected the finished product, such as weather conditions, area of production, as well as period of production.

Measurements are another feature I have included in this book, as I felt they are very important to most people. Some collectors are in search of a certain size, which could complete a set or setting, or it could be just an individual piece. Measurements are useful when buying a piece over the phone. Size is important because it is a major factor in pricing a piece. Compare a coffee pot that measures 4" to the top of the cover knob with 1 cup capacity, to a coffee pot that is 5½" tall and holds 1½ cups, in the same color and condition. Most of the 5½" coffee pots are mistaken for 1 cup coffee pots, when in reality they hold 1½ cups. Although both sizes are rare and would demand a premium price, the smaller pot would demand the higher price of the two.

In Book I, *The Collector's Encyclopedia of Granite Ware,* there is a section entitled "The Hunt Goes On," which was a very popular part of the book. So once again in this book, I have included this section, which shows my recent finds as well as other people's recent finds. I hope this will encourage all of you people out there to seek out that special piece. Even though this book is not meant to be a reference book on the companies and/or history of granite ware, I have included a number of pieces that are marked, labeled, dated, or embossed, along with literature, catalogues, and illustrations. In conclusion I sincerely hope that the enthusiasm that was shown for Book I will carry over and further the interest of one of America's most popular collectibles, granite ware.

WHAT IS GRANITE WARE?

To make granite ware, single or multiple coats of enamels were adhered to different metals with a high degree of heat to produce a glasslike finish. Some of the metals used in these pieces were cast iron, steel, and aluminum.

Granite ware was often advertised as "Pure, Acid Proof, and Strong in Use." It could also be subjected to quick temperature changes with no ill effects. Most advertisements made no mention of the chipping that could occur with rough handling. Many pieces of granite ware were intended for utilitarian use, which helped to make everyday work easier, because granite ware did in fact "Clean Like China," as some of the ads stated. Granite ware was also less expensive than some of the kitchen wares of that time, and added beauty and color to the surroundings.

When the granite ware industry began, the rivalry was fierce, with every company trying to outdo the other. Most of these artisans were highly skilled and very secretive about their enameling processes. Because of this secretiveness, some of the enameling processes were never revealed and went to the grave with their inventor. In the early 1800's the granite ware industry was still in its infancy, however by the 1900's the industry was in full-swing. Like any industry many companies were short lived because of hard times and bad business sense, as well as catastrophes such as fire. When a small company had a fire they usually were devastated because they did not have enough financial backing to rebuild. The remaining companies continued to produce thousands of pieces daily.

Many pieces or sets of granite ware were sold as "trade pullers" or "profit makers." These usually consisted of a whole set at one price, or a whole grouping of shapes at one low price for each piece. An example of this would be regular 75¢ items selling for 39¢ as a special. Some of the leaders of the industry such as the LaLance and Grosjean Manufacturing Company of New York, New York, The St. Louis Stamping Company, St. Louis, Missouri, The Columbian Enameling and Stamping Company, Terre Haute, Indiana, The Bellaire Enameling Company, Bellaire, Ohio, The Strong Manufacturing Company, Sebring, Ohio, the Vollrath Company of Sheboygan, Wisconsin, were involved in a battle to outdo each other in production as well as price.

Today, there are very few enameling companies here or abroad, and most companies are phasing out enameled products in favor of items made with today's newer technologies.

You may not be seeing a lot of new granite ware, but just visit any antique show, or shop, or talk to an avid collector and I can assure you that the old granite ware is alive and very well.

PATTERN AND COLOR DESCRIPTIONS

Pattern and color descriptions refer to the predominant pattern and/or color, e.g. chicken wire pattern, end of day color.

Swirl – Marbled or ribbon-like effect. Can be small, medium, or large.

Mottled – Can be small, fine, medium, or large.
Small Mottled – Small sponge-like effect.
Fine Mottled – Smaller version of small mottled.
Medium or Large Mottled – The color is more flowing thus predominates; in comparison with the lighter background.

Spatter – A splash effect.

Speckled – A flecked effect.

Snow on the Mountain – Usually heavy coats of white enamel applied over contrasting color giving the white a lumpy effect.

Confetti – Looks exactly like colored paper confetti.

Relish – Looks exactly like pickled relish but comes in a number of colors.

Chicken Wire – Looks like chicken wire. The wire effect is usually the predominant colored part.

Feathered – Looks like feathers.

Checkered – Squared-type pattern.

Redipped – Colors applied over original color by the factory. The reason for the change may have been the lack of popularity of the original color, or the company may have wanted to experiment with another color variation. Often on redipped pieces the original factory color can be seen slightly through the redipped color. Sometimes when a piece is chipped, the original factory color can be seen clearly.

Solid Color – One overall color outside. It can be a light or dark shade, sometimes with a white or other color inside. It may be trimmed in another contrasting solid color.

Shaded – Gradual lightening of solid color.

End of Day – Combination of three or more colors, usually one color is more predominant. End of day can have a pattern with a number of colors in the veining, or it may have a swirl or mottled effect. This could have been a company's unique way of using leftover colors at the end of a day's production.

Decorated – Various decorations, applied to the piece. Decorations may be in the form of decals, enameling in high relief, or impressed enamel decoration. Various metals may also be used for trimmings, such as pewter, e.g. pewter lids, bands spouts, bottoms and feet of teapots or coffee pots, or cast iron handles on various items.

Lettered Pieces – Name and usage of piece such as "Bread." These may be in different languages. Another example of lettered pieces is a child's ABC plate. The letters can also be embossed.

Predominant Color – The predominant color is named first throughout the book when a color description is given.

ENAMELING TYPES

Single Coat of Enamel

Two Coats of Enamel

Three Coats of Enamel – Results in very high quality. (Some companies even boast of using four coats or more.)

Porcelain – A form of enameling usually found on kitchen table tops, appliances, and advertising signs, very often in white. Porcelain may also be applied over a ceramic-type base for such purposes as stoppers.

IS AGE DETERMINED BY CONSTRUCTION?

Most of the pieces I have seen that are rivetted are old. But rivets alone do not determine age. Some companies, in order to advertise a better quality product, felt that seams and extra bends in a certain area gave it more strength and appeal. Other companies advertised seamless ware, because they felt the seams would rust first, which they usually did.

Another factor determining age is when a piece has the company, brand name, and a date fired into the granite ware.

Construction of certain types of handles, knobs, spouts, and covers, (e.g. weld handles, wood handles, wood and spun knobs, and hinged covers) along with the shape of the piece itself, helps to determine age. The older pieces are usually heavier.

HOW TO DETERMINE THE NEW GRANITE WARE

Paper labels on granite ware are one good source of age information. Some of the new pieces have the name of the place where manufactured (e.g. Made in Hong Kong) lightly stamped on the bottom instead of fired into the enamel like the older granite ware. Generally, the newer pieces are of lighter weight and the texture of the granite ware seems to be applied thinly.

On some new granite ware, the swirl colors are applied both inside and out. Colors to watch for include red and white swirl, yellow and white swirl, blue and white swirl, brown and white swirl, brown and white mottled, green and white swirl, combination orange and red swirl, and a gray mottled (like a large relish pattern which was made in Romania.)

In the red and white swirl, I have seen the mugs swirled on the outside only, and on both sides. The ones with the white inside are generally from the 1950's. This 1950's era red and white swirl has a black outline blending into the red swirl. After the 1950's, the red and white does not have this blending, and the red coloring is not as deep. On the other hand, the turn-of-the-century "old" red and white swirl also has a black blending into the red swirl. The main differences are that the "old" red and white swirl is usually very heavy, is white on the inside, and has more coats of enamel (e.g. triple coated with rivetted handles and spout and a hinged cover.)

Some newer blue and white swirl has been, and still is, coming out of Hong Kong (C.G.S. International Inc. of Miami, Florida is the distributor). The coffee pot I have with this label looks like it might have been stamped out all in one piece except for the cover. Again, the cover is not hinged to the coffee pot. The piece is very lightweight.

There is also solid color enamel ware being made today that is heavy. I saw a colander in the solid red trimmed in black, but it had a modern look about it.

Some of the shapes made in newer granite ware are mugs, large wash basins, plates, sectioned plates, soup plates, large trays, coffee pots, teapots, utensils, colanders, handled butter melters, tumblers, cups and saucers, sugars and creamers. These were made from the 1950's to the 1970's, and some are still being made today.

One of the best ways to sum this up is to check out stores and outlets in your area for what is being made today. Try to seek out experienced collectors when in doubt. When you are buying from a person you don't know, ask that person to mark your sales slip guaranteeing the item or items you have purchased as old.

POPULARITY HELPS TO DETERMINE DESIRABILITY

Certain items are more popular among collectors for one reason or another. It could be for the color, shape, size, or rarity of a particular piece. Some of the most popular items in granite ware are coffee pots, teapots, and coffee biggins because these may be found in wide variety of colors, shapes, and sizes.

Hanging items such as dippers, muffin tins, and spoons are also popular because many collectors have only limited space to display their granite ware. Most of all, the rare pieces of granite ware are always at the top of the popularity list.

HOW TO CLEAN AND PRESERVE GRANITE WARE

If a piece is greasy and dirty, I first spray it with oven cleaner. I leave this on at least five or six hours or until I see the black grease start to roll off. I then rinse it with very hot water to remove the dirt and grease. If a lot of dirt and grease is still left on the piece, I spray it again and leave it as long as needed. Then I rinse it in hot water again. After rinsing clean, use a hot soapy water to wash it thoroughly. Wash again with hot soapy water. Rinse again and dry thoroughly, leaving all covers off or open to fully dry.

You should never use a metal object to pick off burnt-on foods, because it could cause chipping. Also, never hold a piece by the handle while cleaning because you could loosen or break the handle.

If a piece has a tin cover or other types of metal, its not advisable to get the oven cleaner on the metal because it has a tendency to give the metal a spotty look. Also, wooden parts, painted or unpainted, should be covered with plastic because it will remove the paint when spraying with oven cleaner. Another word of caution, steel wool pads with or without soap, or scrubbies should not be used because they could scratch the finish.

To clean the tin covers, I usually use fine, dry steel wool. After cleaning, I spray with an aerosol furniture wax and polish it.

It is not advisable to use a cleaner that contains lye for cleaning the inside of tea kettles or other items to remove lime deposits. If it gets on the finish, it will destroy the shine. Usually vinegar will soften the lime deposits if left to soak overnight or longer.

The last step is to spray the piece with a wax polish. This usually gives it a good shine and protects it from rusting. *Caution:* Do not spray wax on pieces that you intend to use.

Granite Ware's Future

Granite ware has reached new heights as I predicted it would in Book 1. Is it any wonder with granite ware's offerings of brilliant colors and outstanding design that it has become increasingly popular among collectors, as well as being featured in movies, antique and decorating magazines, and cook books? With this number of collectors and enthusiasts it is not surprising that the demands for granite ware have more than tripled in just this short time.

Many more regional granite ware clubs have formed, and our National Graniteware Society maintains a strong support of members along with newsletters and an annual convention each year.

People from all over the country gather together for this annual convention. The convention includes registration and a commemorative item, workshops, room sales, and also features "Avenue of the States" with it's beautiful displays of granite ware from many States. These displays could feature the theme chosen for the year by the Graniteware society, or one could choose one's own theme. Also following is the member's auction and banquet, and then with a fond farewell we all look forward to next year's convention.

So as you can see with all the excitement and intrigue following granite ware and the people associated with it, there is no doubt granite ware collecting is here to stay for many generations to come.

For further information on your area, contact: The National Graniteware Society, P.O. Box 10013, Cedar Rapids, Iowa, 52410. For further information in New York State, contact the author.

Measurements

Height is determined most times from top to bottom. Example: Coffee or teapots are measured to the top of the cover knob, handle, or finial. Even though a cover does not add to the holding capacity of a coffee or teapot, most of the time collectors purchasing a pot want to know the height including the cover knob, handle, or finial. This is important because a collector may have a certain shelf or area a piece will fit in. Originally coffee or teapots were sold for their holding capacity, but to today's collectors size is usually more important. This is the reasoning for measuring pots to the top of the cover knobs.

Also items that have an added base, pedestal, or foot are measured in height rather than depth because the base, pedestal, or foot does not add to the holding capacity.

Diameter is measured across the widest point of a round piece. For example if the piece has a squatty shape the diameter dimension is measured across the squatty portion which is the largest section of the pot. Otherwise on a conventional pot the diameter is usually measured across the bottom of the pot.

Length is measured across the longest dimension. Handles are not normally included in this dimension with the exceptions of the measurements of spoons, dippers, ladles, and skimmers. Old company catalogues do not include handles in their measurements.

Width is determined by the piece's widest dimension. Example, if a baking pan measure 14" wide at the top and only 12" at the bottom, the top width is the size used.

PRICING INFORMATION

With the ever increasing demands in granite ware, fortunately or unfortunately granite ware has shown a rise in price. But anything that has a great demand and is popular for collecting and decorating is inclined to do so.

What I will try to achieve in pricing the granite ware in this book is an approximate price for each item even though different areas of the country and abroad demand different prices. Many factors help to determine the price. Some of these include condition, rarity, color, shape, size, age, popularity, dates, types of marks or labels and cross collectibility.

Condition is of prime importance when setting up any price guide. Granite ware is more likely to be found in "Good Plus" condition, meaning all sides should be quite presentable with no more than minor chipping. The piece should also have a good shine to the finish. A pinhole in the bottom could be permissible. The same condition holds for all metal and wood parts. We must remember that granite ware was made to be utilitarian. It was both used and abused. This is why I chose to base this guide on "Good Plus" condition.

Even harder to find and commanding a premium over "Good Plus" condition are those "Near Mint" items. They can have limited tiny chips, and again must have a good shine to the finish. All metal and wood parts must be in similar condition. "Mint" pieces are not often found. By "Mint" I mean like new, including all metal and wood parts. When these "Mint" pieces do surface, they command the largest additional premium of all over "Good Plus." It should be noted that items found in poorer condition than "Good Plus," that is anything lacking at least one good display side, having lots of rust or holes, and lacking a good shine to the finish, fall into a category which leaves it to the discretion of each buyer as to what he or she feels they should pay.

Rarity is determined by availability of a particular color, shape, or size. Certain colors were originally made in very limited quantities. A good example of this is "Old" Red and White Swirl. Shape and size play a very important part in pricing too. Smaller, larger, longer or shorter than usual, or different shapes such as squatty, straight-sided, pedestalled bases, footed or any other shapes not often seen in a particular item, help to increase an item's value.

Popularity can also have a very important effect on the pricing and saleability of an item. Pieces can be popular for one reason or another, such as color, shape or size. Certain items are always highly sought after such as coffee and teapots, granite ware which can be easily hung for display, miniatures and children's pieces. Dates stamped, embossed or marked on pieces can make a great difference in their value. The type of other marks or labels are also important. Many collectors look for a manufacturer's name or place of manufacture. Additional information on a label, such as color or the name of a particular line, can be most important when it comes to collecting or researching.

Last but not least, cross collectibility adds a degree of importance to granite ware. If a piece has advertising on it for a World's Fair, it then belongs in the advertising category, and is of particular interest to World's Fair collectors as well.

In summary, my personal opinion is that granite ware is only worth what you or anyone else is willing to pay for it. The prices listed in this book are meant to be used as a guide. In an effort to bring you the closest price on an item, I have compiled price lists from all over the country, going auction prices, antique show prices, dealers' prices, and private sale prices. I have also discussed prices that have been actually paid for granite ware with hundreds of collectors. I feel prices paid over two years ago to be out of date!

My main purpose in trying to reach an appropriate figure is not to outprice granite ware for beginning collectors. On the other hand, I want to give the reader a realistic idea of granite ware prices. If a collector after reading this book was to see a piece of granite ware for sale at a high price, he or she might well pass it up if the book had quoted an unrealistic lower price. Remember, suggested prices in the book are based on "Good Plus" condition unless otherwise stated. I have to decline to assume any responsibility for losses incurred by purchasers or users of the book.

Special Note: Once again I would like to point out the condition of a piece is very important. Example, mint condition as opposed to good plus condition makes a big difference in pricing as well as collecting, because most people strive to collect pieces in the best possible condition. When a piece is extremely rare it sometimes is excepted for its condition until another can be found in better condition. Most often this piece will also bring a premium price, because of its extreme rarity, and this piece could turn out to be a one of a kind.

Mint Condition – No chips and a good shine to the finish, also all metal and wooden parts should be mint.

Near Mint Condition – Limited tiny chips and a good shine to the finish. Also, all metal and wooden parts should be near mint.

Good Plus Condition – All sides should be quite presentable with minor chipping and a good shine to the finish. Also, all metal and wooden parts should be in good plus condition. A pinhole in the bottom could be permissible.

Complete sets add 15% more, meaning it should have all its parts including covers. Also labeled, marked, dated or embossed pieces usually demand a higher premium.

Rarity of a piece is determined by a particular color, shape or size. Some colors are more popular than others and are readily sought after. For example, a muffin pan in any size, in "Columbian Ware," in large blue and white swirl is an extreme rarity. Also if this same piece were labeled, marked, dated, or embossed it would demand an even higher price.

Marked, labeled, dated, or embossed pieces are highly sought after by collectors because it helps collectors identify a particular color, size, number of coats of enameling, manufacturer, and/or the period in which it was produced. Sometimes these pieces only identify the company and the place of manufacture, others may identify the color, company, and date, as well as the size and the number of coats of enamel applied to the piece. Size could be a number or capacity of the piece, for example, 1½ cups. These pieces usually demand a premium price as opposed to a piece with none of the above.

Popularity of certain items is often an important factor when making a purchase.

SECTION 1
LABELED PIECES AND ADVERTISING

Row 1:
1. **Teapot,** 8" high, 5¼" bottom diameter, gray large mottled. Labeled "Cream City Gray Ware 101 Acid Resisting, Cleans like China, Geuder Paeschke & Frey Co. Manufacturers, Milwaukee, U.S.A." Mint, **$235.00.**
2. **Pudding Pan,** deep, 2" deep, 5¼" top diameter, gray large mottled. Labeled "La Fayette Quality Ware, Made In U.S.A. The Moore Enameling & MFG. Company, West Lafeyette, Ohio." Mint **$50.00.**
3. **Coffee Biggin,** squatty shape, 4 pieces, cover, biggin, spreader & squatty teapot. 9" high including biggin, 5" diameter, cream bottom section with black trim & handle, black biggin. Labeled on biggin "Porcelain Enameled, No Metallic Taste, Coffee Drip. Also Instructions For Making Drip Coffee." Pot labeled "Lisk De Luxe Enameled Ware. Lisk Manufacturing Co. Ltd. Canandaigua, New York," red tag reads "Lisk Deluxe Super Quality Enameled Ware. This Utensil Will Help To Modernize Your Kitchen. Extra Heavy Steel Base. Gives Greater Durability. Chrome Plated Copper Cover. Beautiful Non-Tarnish Finish. Triple Coated Enamel. Famous Lisk Quality Cleans Like China." Mint, rare shape & size, **$285.00.**
4. **Pudding Pan,** shallow, 1¾" deep, 6⅞" top diameter, gray large mottled. Labeled the same as No. 2 on this row. Mint, **$50.00.**
5. **Cream Can,** 7¼" high, 4¼" bottom diameter, gray large mottled. Labeled "Made In The U.S.A. By Savory Inc. No 71 LF-476." Seamed 4 piece body, tin cover. Mint, **$195.00.**

Row 2:
1. **Covered Berlin-style Kettle,** 6½" high, 8" diameter, blue & white large mottled, white interior, black trim & wood bail, enameled wire ears. Labeled "The Stewart Company, Bellaire, Ohio, U.S.A. No. 0 Cost Sell." Mint, **$295.00**
2. **Tart Pan,** 1" deep, 6" diameter, gray medium mottled. Labeled the same as No. 2 & 4 on Row 1. Mint, **$50.00.**
3. **Milk Pan,** 3" deep, 13¼" diameter, blue & white large mottled, white interior, black trim. Labeled the same as No. 1 on this row. Mint, **$180.00.**
4. **Covered Chamber Pot,** 6½" high, 9½" diameter, blue & white fine mottled, chamber pot has white interior, cover is blue & white fine mottled on both sides, black trim, seamless body, riveted handle. Labeled "Lisk" "Four Coat Enamel Ware Sold By Ellsworth's Bargain Store, 65 Main Street, Batavia, N.Y." Good plus, **$240.00.**

Row 3:
1. **Covered bucket,** 5" high, 4⅝" diameter, blue & white fine mottled, black trim & ears, seamless body, wire bail. Labeled "Exclusive-Distinctive. Enameled Ware No. Juniata. Cost—Sell." Also label pictures a bell. Mint, **$195.00.**
2. **Measure,** 2¾" high, 2⅜" bottom diameter, gray large mottled, seamed body, riveted handle. Labeled "Durability Quality Safety, Oriole Ware B.S. & E. Co. Cost—Sell. No. Maryland, No. Co. Balto." Near mint, rare shape & size, **$485.00. Note:** I believe B.S. & E. Co. stands for Baltimore Stamping & Enameling Company, Baltimore, Maryland.
3. **Coffee Pot,** 7½" high, 4⅝" bottom diameter, apple green, darker green trim, tangerine interior, light gray coffee basket, glass knob. Embossed "Even Spray." Labeled "Vollrath Ware Apple Green, Harmonizing Color. The Vollrath Co., Sheboygan, Wis., U.S.A. Registered U.S. Pat. Off. Copyrighted 1929 By T.V. Co." Mint, rare color, shape & size, **$195.00.**
4. **Measure,** 4¾" high, 3½" diameter, gray large mottled, seamed body, weld handle. Embossed "1Pt. Liq'd. U.S. Standard." Labeled "Nesco pure greystone enameled ware trademark registered U.S. Patent Office, Made In The U.S.A. Patented July 20, 1909, Dec. 9, 1912." Mint condition, **$365.00.**
5. **Shallow Pie Plate,** ¾" deep, 8" diameter, green & white large swirl, dark blue trim. Labeled "Emerald Ware No. 8, Shallow Pie Plate. Cost—Sell At. The Strong Enamel Co., Bellaire, Ohio." Mint, rare color, **$195.00. Note:** The label is in the shape of a shield.

Row 4:
1. **Dust Pan,** 14" overall length, 12¾" width, American gray large mottled. Labeled "Haberman's Steel Enameled Ware. Haberman Mfg. Co. Pat. Oct. 9, 1894 No. 30 Dust Pan." Also in a diamond is a teakettle. Good plus, rare shape, **$575.00.**
2. **Saucer,** ¾" deep, 6¼" top diameter, blue & white large mottled, blue trim, white interior. Labeled "Tulip" "Guaranteed, Pure. Safe. Superior Ware. Quality Trade Mark. Made By Geuder Paeschke & Frey Company, Milwaukee." Mint, **$155.00.**
3. **Dough Bowl,** 5½" deep, 14" diameter, blue & white fine mottled, white interior, black trim. Labeled "Lisk's Warranted Enameled Steel Ware Lisk Trademark The Lisk Manufacturing Co. Limited, Canandaigua, New York." Mint, rare shape & size, **$185.00. Note:** This is one of the largest bowls I have seen.
4. **Oval Platter,** 1⅛" deep, 8⅜" wide, 12" long, gray large mottled. Labeled "Iron City." "Durable—Absolutely Pure Easy To Clean As China. Cost—Sell Reg. App. For Federal Enameling & Stamping Company, Pittsburgh, PA." Mint, **$165.00.**

Row 1:

1. **Lipped Preserving Kettle,** 5" deep, 10¾" top diameter, blue & white, white interior, black trim & wooden bail, large swirl. Labeled "Azure Enamelware. Acid Proof, The Belmont Stamping & Enameling Co., New Philadelphia, Ohio." Mint, **$275.00.**

2. **Custard Cup,** 2" deep, 3½" top diameter, white trimmed in black. Labeled "Vollrath Since 1874 Trademark, Reg. U.S. Pat. Off. Original & Exclusive Manufacturers of Vollrath Ware, The Vollrath Co., Sheboygan, Wis., U.S.A." Mint, **$40.00.**

3. **Measure,** 4½" deep, 3¾" top diameter, white trimmed in black. Marked inside from 2 ozs. to 16 ozs. Label same as the custard cup on this row. Mint, **$65.00.**

4. **Measure,** 5¼" deep, 4¾" diameter, white trimmed in black. Marked inside 2 ozs. to 32 ozs., also, 1pt., 1qt. Labeled "The Vollrath Co. Since 1874, Sheboygan, Wis." Mint, **$65.00.**

5. **Measure,** 6¾" deep, 5¾" diameter, white trimmed in black. Marked inside 4 ozs. to 64 ozs. Labeled. Mint. **$65.00.**

Row 2:

1. **Coaster or Ash Tray,** ¾" deep, 3" top diameter, solid maroon. Labeled "This Is A Suporcel Superior Porcelain Enameled Metal Product. Reg. Trademark. The porcelain coaster & ash tray with its base of Armco enameling iron will not rust, peel, fade or burn & will resist acid & alcohol stains. For cleaning, use any soap or soap powder. M'F'R'D' By Porcelain Metals Inc., L.I. City." Mint, rare shape, **$75.00.**

2. **Coaster or Ash Tray,** Solid green. Same size & labels as the first one on this row. Mint, rare shape, **$75.00. Note:** These are part of a set of four, the others being solid orange & solid blue.

Row 3:

1. **Oval Lunch Box with Food Insert,** 7¼" high including insert, 9¼" long, 6½" wide, gray, medium mottled. Labeled "Victor Gray Ware. Guaranteed Absolutely Pure S.F.E. Co." Good plus, **$295.00.**

2. **Coffeepot,** 9" high, 6" bottom diameter, light blue & white, large swirl. Labeled "Azure. The Belmont Stamping & Enameling Company, New Philadelphia, Ohio." Good plus, **$350.00**

3. **Teakettle,** 7¼" high, 9¼" bottom diameter, solid red, solid cobalt blue inside, black trim & wooden bail. Labeled on the cover "Everbrite Covers With Bakelite Knob. Chromium Plated. Sanitary, Durable, Easy to Clean." Label on teakettle "Gloria. Triple Coated. M21. Beautiful, Durable, Easy to Clean." Mint, **$275.00.**

Row 4:

1. **Bread Slicer,** 7½" high, 11½" long not including the bread board, white trimmed in red. Labeled "Prima Emaille Qualitats Fabrikat. Messer. Rostfreier Stahl." Embossed On Slicer "M. 190." Slicer has adjustments for thin or thick bread slices. Clamp on the side is for fastening slicer to table top. Back board is hinged to drop down for loaf of bread. Near mint, **$255.00.**

2. **Cup & Saucer,** cup 2¼" deep, 4½" top diameter, saucer 1⅛" deep, 5¾" diameter, gray & white, medium mottled. Labeled "Pearl Enameled Ware." Made in Canada by General Steel Wares Limited. Both pieces mint, **$125.00.**

3. **Water Pail,** 8⅛" deep, 10" diameter, blue & white, fine mottled, dark blue trim, black wooden bail. Labeled Turquoise Blue Pearl-Agate Ware, L & G Mfg. Co. Note: L & G. Mfg. Co. This label stands for the Lalance & Grosjean Manufacturing Company, Woodhaven, New York. Mint, **$185.00.**

Row 1:

1. **Checkerboard Table Advertising Coca-Cola,** 29" high table top, 29½" x 29½", white with red & white checkerboard, also, around the outer edge of the table top are 4 advertisements "Disfrute" "Coca-Cola," "Marca Reg." also "Disfrute La Chispa De La Vida." Good plus, extremely rare shape, **$825.00**.

2. **Piedmont Advertising Fold-Up Chair, advertising enamel insert** 10¼" high, 11¼" wide, cobalt blue & white lettering on both front & back advertising "Smoke Piedmont The Cigarette Of Quality." On each wooden side rail of the chair is marked in black letters "Piedmont Cigarettes." Good plus, rare shape, **$175.00.**

3. **Piedmont Advertising Fold-Up Chair advertising enamel insert** 10" high, 10⅞" wide, cobalt blue with white lettering on both front & back advertising "For Cigarettes Virginia Tobacco Is The Best. Piedmont. The Virginia Cigarette." On each wooden side rail of the chair is marked in black letters "Piedmont Cigarettes." Mint, rare shape, **$195.00.**

Advertising Catalogues and some of the colors and shapes illustrated in them.

Row 1:

1. **Covered Bucket,** 7¼" high, 6½" diameter. An exquisite blend shading from a deep sea green to a delicate moss green, white interior. "Shamrock Enameled Ware. Made in the United States. Triple coated of Superb Quality, Acid Proof, & Remarkably Durable. Novell Shapleigh Hardware Co. St. Louis, Sole distributors for this ware. Trade mark Reg. U.S. Pat. Off." Mint, rare color, **$190.00. Note:** The illustration of the Shamrock Ware label. This ware today is generically called "Shaded" granite ware.

2. **Novell–Shapleigh Hardware Co. Loose Leaf Catalogue,** 5¾" thick x 11½" long & 10½" wide. Copyrighted 1910. Features color as well as black & white photos of thousands of items. Granite ware was illustrated in color with shapes & prices. This catalogue was expandable, in that it allowed updates & revisions. This catalogue was used by the dealer & because of the wholesale pricing was not shown to the buying public. A catalogue of this magnitude is priceless when it comes to the wealth of knowledge it offers. Good plus, **$795.00.**

3. **Gravy or Sauce boat** (½ pint), 8½" x 3¾" x 2½". Seamless body, beaded handle, beautiful blue mottling on pure white, white lined interior. "Triple Coated Blue Diamond Enamel Ware. Made in the United States, Novell–Shapleigh Hardware Co." **Note:** Notice the illustration of the Blue Diamond Ware label. It is a diamond ring through the shape of another diamond. Also note: "Price per dozen–$13.50. There are 6 dozen per case, each case weighing 55 pounds, with $15.00 shipping." Generically this ware is referred to as large blue & white swirl, or Iris Ware. Near mint, extremely rare color & shape, **$1,150.00.**

Row 2:

1. **Lee Manufacturing Company Premium House Catalogue,** Chicago 1915, 1¼" thick x 8" wide & 10¼" long. Illustrates premiums given for selling their goods. Used the honor system because both the goods & the premiums were shipped together. Good plus, **$265.00. Note:** Notice the illustration of blue & white triple coated granite ware. The entire set was given for selling a $15.00 order. It also states "This is a first quality triple coated granite ware & everybody knows how expensive this fine blue & white enamelware is at the store & will appreciate this wonderful value." The opposite page illustrates a gray granite enamelware set. This set was given as a premium for selling a $12.50 order. It states "This set was made for us by one of the largest gray enamelware manufacturers in the United States & is known as the "Ware that wears." It is not seconds but guaranteed to be strictly first grade enamelware & will give entire satisfaction." There are numerous pages of granite ware illustrated in this premium house catalog, including High Grade Sanitary Pure White enamelware unbreakable, made of white enameled steel. New Turquoise Blue, Azure Marble Enamel ware, was one of the goods they sold. They claimed it was "made of the finest grade American sheet steel, triple coated with new turquoise blue enamel–sanitary, acid proof, high gloss finish. Much superior to ordinary enamelware which chips & peels." A vegetable dish which was 10½" x 7½" x 2¼" was priced at 75¢. Note: 12 pieces of this ware was $10.85, which included vegetable dish, large 8 qt. size kettle, 17 qt. dishpan, 3 piece cereal cooker, 2 qt. pudding pan, child's chamber pot (no cover), & 4 sizes of mixing bowls. That was not inexpensive back in 1915, yet they gave the set of 12 pieces as a premium for selling a $15.00 order.

2. **Coffee Boiler,** 11¼" high, 9¾" diameter, light blue & white wave type mottling with white interior, black trim & handle, seamed body, rivetted ears & strap handle, also wire bail handle. Near mint, rare color, **$365.00. Note:** This is the generic description of this coffee boiler, & it resembles the pattern in the catalogue. I feel this is the same type of enamelware.

Row 3:

1. **Swing Kettle with Patent Textile Fabric Filters & Spirit Lamp.** Swing kettle, 9¼" high, 4¾" diameter, gray medium mottled with white metal mountings & protection bands. Patent Perfection Granite Ironware. Spirit lamp frame measures 15" tall x 7½" diameter. Mint, extremely rare shape, **$1,275.00.**

2. **1892 Manning, Bowman & Co. Catalogue** with color & black & white illustrations of Perfection Granite Ironware, Decorated Pearl Agateware, & also chafing dish outfits, five o'clock teas, porcelain lined coffee urns, etc. Price list included. Measures 14" tall x 11" wide. Good plus, **$595.00.**

3. **Teapot,** 9¾" high, 5½" diameter. Patent Decorated Pearl Agateware, patented June 5, 1883. Registered January 13, 1885. White metal mountings & protection bands. No. 8450 Series R decoration. White porcelain inside. Mint, rare colore & shape, **$395.00.**

Row 1:
1. **Creamer,** 4⅝" tall, 3⅝" diameter, gray large mottled seamless bottom, white metal upper body & protection band. Top section is engraved with an oriental scene on the front & a sugar cane design on the back. Near mint, rare shape, **$225.00.**
2. **Sugar,** 4⅜" tall, 3⅝" diameter, gray large mottled seamless bottom, white metal upper body & protection band. Top section is engraved the same as #1 in this row. Near mint, rare shape, **$225.00.**
3. **Syrup,** 5¾" tall, 3⅝" diameter, gray large mottled seamless bottom, white metal upper body & protection band. Top section is engraved the same as #1 in this row. Near mint, rare shape, **$495.00.**

Row 2:
1. **1892 Manning Bowman & Co. Catalog** with color & black & white illustrations of Perfection Granite Ironware, & decorated Agateware. Catalog also shows chafing dish outfits, (five o'clock teas,) porcelain lined coffee urns, etc. Price list is included. 14" x 11". Good plus, **$595.00.**
2. **Teapot,** 9¼" high, 6" diameter, gray large mottled seamless bottom, white metal upper section & protection band. Upper section engraved with an oriental design on the front, a sugar cane design on the back. Near mint, rare shape, **$225.00. Note:** Notice the similarity in the catalogue #1 Row 1 of "The Good Evening" tea set, the engraved design & the shape of the teapot are the same, but notice the different shape of the handle & the cover. It is believed that these companies bought different shaped mountings for their wares from other distributors that were less expensive or possibly of a better design. Companies were always looking for ways to improve their wares because of competition.

Row 3:
1. **Measure,** 9⅝" high, 6¾" diameter, gray large mottled. Embossed "1 Gal. Liq'd." Labeled "Royal Granite National Enameling & Stamping Co. Nesco, Nesco Is Everywhere." Mint, **$235.00.**
2. **Advertising Pot Luck Souvenir,** 3¼" high, 2" diameter. From the St. Louis Exposition, by the "National Enameling & Stamping Co." manufacturers of "Royal Granite Steel Ware." Illustrating their wares along with illustrations of the factory, photos of Napoleon Bonaparte, who sold Louisiana to the U.S.A. in 1803, & President Thomas Jefferson. Near mint, extremely rare shape & size, **$155.00.**
3. **Covered Bed Pan,** 4" tall tapering down to 1⅛" tall, 19" long, 13½" wide, gray large mottled. Labeled "Nesco Royal Granite Enameled Ware, Nescoware Is Everywhere." Mint, **$95.00.**
4. **Teakettle,** 6½" high, 9¼" diameter, dark gray medium mottled, seamed bottom & spout, wooden bail. Labeled, "Savory Sterling Enameled Nickeled Steel Ware, Newark, N.J. Made In U.S.A. Reg. U.S. Pat. Off." Near mint, **$215.00.**

Row 1:

1. **Catalogue #21,** Coonley Manufacturing Co., Cicero, Il., Manufacturers of Enameled Ware, Tin Ware, & Galvanized Ware. Manufactured "Austral" blue & white ware. Finish "A." "Cling Steel Ware, Extra durable guaranteed first quality. Finish "C." Crystal white & white ware. Shows a picture of a raccoon's head on the label. The only date in the catalogue is obtained from listing of the freight rates: April 9, 1915. Good plus, **$295.00.**

2. **Egg Dish,** 4⅞" diameter, 1¼" deep. **Note:** This shape is in the Coonley Manufacturing Co. Catalogue. I believe this is their "Austral" blue & white large mottled ware. This ware is triple coated. Pure white inside with black trim & handle. This is referred to by collectors as a small fry pan. Also note the list price of $3.00 per dozen. Near mint, extremely rare size, rare color, **$295.00.**

3. **Advertising Bottle Holder,** 11¾" long, 3" back width. The section that holds the 3 cream bottles is 3⅛" wide. Each bottle cutout is 2½" deep, 2" wide. White with dark blue. Advertises "Onondaga Milk Producers Co-op Ass'n Inc. Burnet Ave, Syracuse, N.Y. Phone 2-0103. Marked on the back "Sanitary Sevor Trademark. Springfield, Ohio. Pat Appl'd For." Good plus, rare shape, **$165.00.**

4. **Card of E-Z Mend-RS,** 6" long, 4" wide, includes 4 different size E-Z Mend-RS & reamer wrench. "Patented. Nov 12, 1935, Bullis Mfg, Co, Inc. Amsterdam, N.Y." Near mint, **$25.00.**

5. **Box of Mendets,** ¾" deep, 4" long, 1⅝" wide. Includes instructions on how to apply Mendets. States that "10¢ will save $10.00" by repairing your own wares. Also includes 3 pkgs. of 3 mendets & 1 wrench. "Collette Mfg, Co. Amsterdam, N.Y. Pat Dec 18, 1906." Good plus, **$29.00.**

6. **Mendets Box** used for advertising & displaying in stores. Includes box of Mendets. 9" high, 2½" deep. 6⅜" wide, 8¼" long. Advertising "10¢ & 25¢ Per Package of Mendets, Mends without the use of heat, solder, cement, or rivets, will fit any surface. Cheap, Neat & Simple. Mends tin, copper, brass, sheet metal, all cooking utensils & rubber goods. Collette Mfg. Co. Amsterdam, N.Y. U.S.A., Collingwood, Ont, Canada, Sydney N.S.W. Australia." Good Plus, rare shape, $155.00.

Row 2:

1. **Card of Mendets,** 6" high, 4" wide. Includes 3 different size metal mendets with lock gaskets, screws, nuts & metal wrench. "10¢ saves $10.00, Mendets a Patent Patch. Trade Mark Reg, U.S. Pat. Off." Good plus, **$20.00.**

2. **Box of Peck's** (soft metal rivets), ¼" deep, 5" long, 2⅞" wide. Includes a number of different size rivets, & reaming tool. Claimed to repair aluminum, iron, enamel, & tin. "Tested & Approved by Department of Household Engineering, Good Housekeeping Institute, 1919. Made by E.E. Peck Co. Medina, N.Y. U.S.A." Good Plus, **$20.00.**

3. **Advertising Ash Tray,** 1¾", 5½" bottom diameter. Cobalt blue with white advertising. "Pfaudler." Near mint, **$55.00.**

4. **Manning Bowman & Co. 1892 Illustrated Catalogue & Price List For Perfection Granite Ironware, Decorated Pearl Agateware,** 11⅜" wide, 14" long. This company had factories in Meriden, Conn. Their salesroom was at 57 Beekman Street, New York. Catalogue advertises chafing dish outfits, five o'clock teas, porcelain lined coffee urns, etc. This company won the Centennial Medal in Philadelphia in 1876 & the Grand Gold Medal in Paris in 1878. Good Plus, **$595.00.**

5. **Card of Stars,** 3⅞", 3⅞". Includes 5 metal "Stars" disks, screws, nuts, & wrench. Manufactured "Sapoline Co. Ltd. Walkerville, Ontario." Good, **$15.00.**

6. **Pickle Stand, or castor.** 9" tall, 3¼" diameter. Blue decorated with apple blossom pattern. White interior. Mint, extremely rare color, shape, size, **$1,850.00. Note:** illustration on bottom left hand corner of the page in the Manning, Bowman & Co. catalogue.

Row 3:

1. **Advertising Sign,** shaped like a bag of cement, 25¼", 17". Light gray & white with black & red lettering. Advertising "Canada Cement & Company Limited, Montreal, Portland Cement, Canada, Sold Here." **Note:** This sign hung in front of the place of business & has the message on both sides. Good plus, rare shape, **$215.00.**

Row 1:

    1. **Covered Chamber Pot,** 6½" tall, 8⅞" diameter, blue & white large swirl, white interior, black trim & handle, seamless body. Labeled "Azure Enamelware Acid Proof the Belmon Stamping & Enameling Co., New Philadelphia, Ohio." Good plus, **$255.00.**

    2. **Wash Basin**, 3⅜" deep, 12" diameter, white decorated with gold bands inside & out, black trim, brass eyelet for hanging. Labeled "Lisk Warranted No. 2. Lisk's Four-Coated Enameled Steelware, Canandaigua, New York. The lisk Manufacturing Co. Limited." Good plus, **$60.00.**

    3. **Milk or Buttermilk Kettle,** 9½" high, 6¼" diameter, white with black trim & handle. Bakelite cover knob. Labeled "U.S. Standard 3Qt. Enameled Ware Manufactured By United States Stamping Co., Moundsville, W. VA., U.S.A." Good plus, **$130.00.**

Row 2:

    1. **Pudding Pan**, 2¾" deep, 8⅜" diameter, brown & white medium mottled. "Onyx Triple-Coated Steel Enameled Ware. Purity & Durability Guaranteed. 18 Extra Deep Pudding Pan. Columbian Enameling & Stamping Company, Terre Haute, Indiana." Their guarantee reads "We Guarantee Quality, Purity & Durability Unexcelled 'Onyx Ware.' The housekeeper requires in the kitchen the best grade of Enameled Ware at a moderate cost. It is a waste of money to buy so-called imported wares at an extremely high price or the many miscellaneous brands of unknown value mostly worthless. 'Onyx Ware' Stands the test, & we guarantee it to please you. It costs no more than poor ware. Look for the 'Onyx' label before buying. Columbian Enameling & Stamping Company." Mint, **$65.00.**

    2. **Cup**, open handle, 2¼" deep, 4¼" diameter, white with black trim & handle. Labeled "Lisk Flintstone, 712, Porcelain Enameled Ware Lisk-Savory Corporation, Canandaigua, N.Y." Mint, **$35.00.**

    3. **Sauce Pan**, ribbed sides, 3¾" deep, 7½" diameter, cream with green trim & handle, seamless. Labeled "Leader, Easy To Clean As China Sanitary Durable Pure Enameled Ware." Mint, **$60.00.**

    4. **Funnel**, 4" long, 3¾" diameter, gray medium mottled. Labeled "Sterling Gray, Enameled Ware, Special coated Aluminum Absolutely Pure Not Affected By Fruit Or Vegetable Acids, Trade Mark, The Central Stamping Co., N.Y. Patented Sept. 2, 1902, Apr 26, 1904, Nov. 8, 1904." Mint, **$65.00.**

    5. **Hanging Soap Dish**, 3½" back height, 4¼" wide, 6⅜" long, blue & white large mottled inside & out. Labeled "Seal Of Purity 60 Soap Dish, Extra Quality Ware." Mint, **$255.00.**

Row 3:

    1. **Pudding Pan**, ribbed sides, 3" deep, 10⅜" diameter, cream with green trim, eyelet for hanging. Labeled "Oriental Durable Absolutely Pure, Easy To Clean As China, Reg. App. For." Mint, **$50.00.**

    2. **Milk Can**, 9" high, 5¼" bottom diameter, gray large mottled, seamed body, wooden bail. Labeled "Nesco-Royal Granite Enameled Ware. Nesco Ware Is Everywhere. copyright by National Enameling & Stamping Co. Inc., Patented July 20, 1909, Feb 14, 1911." Mint, **$175.00.**

    3. **Coffeepot**, 7¾" high, 5¼", bottom diameter gray medium mottled, seamed body, rivetted tin cover, weld handle. Labeled "Old Holland" Durable, Easy To Clean As China, Porcelain-Steel Sanitary Ware, Federal Enameling & Stamping Co. Pittsburgh, PA." Near mint, **$135.00.**

    4. **Wash Basin**, 2½" deep, 11" top diameter, dark gray large mottled. Labeled "Hoosier Gray Columbian Made. No 228 Economical Enameled Ware. Columbian Enameling & Stamping co. Inc., Terre Haute, Ind., Made In U.S.A." Mint. **$85.00.**

Row 1:
1. **Candlestick,** 1¾" high, 5⅛" diameter, solid red with white neck and navy blue trim. Embossed "Columbian Terre Haute." Note: This could be a promotional giveaway for Columbian Enameling & Stamping Company's factory built in Terre Haute, Indiana in 1902. Good plus, extremely rare color, shape, size, **$395.00.**
2. **Oval Foot Tub,** 4⅛" deep, 13" wide, 17¼" long, cream with green trim, eyelet for hanging. "Danahy-Faxon. Buffalo, Owned & Operated" (This was a grocery chain in the Buffalo NY area.) Mint, **$185.00.**
3. **Pitcher,** 6½" deep, 5" diameter, white with flecks of blue, black trim with a Bakelite-type handle advertising its use for different liquids. Marked "G.H.C. ©." (General Housewares Company.) Good plus, **$70.00.**

Row 2:
1. **Coaster,** ¼" deep, 3½" diameter, olive green & white large mottled, dark blue trim, white interior. Marked "The Enterprise Enamel Co., Bellaire, O." Near mint, extremely rare color & shape, **$235.00. Note:** It is hard to show you both sides of the advertising pieces, so I try to show it to the best advantage.
2. **Advertising Coaster,** ⅜" deep, 4" diameter, blue & white large swirl, dark blue trim, white interior. Marked very faint in a double circle "Norvell-Shapleigh Hdw. St. Louis, Distributors Blue Diamond Ware." Near Mint, extremely rare color & shape, **$275.00.**

Row 3:
1. **Ashtray,** ⅜" deep, 4½" diameter, gray medium mottled, red lettering. "Cream City Gray Ware. H.M. Hillson Company. Somerville, Mass." Near mint, **$225.00. Note:** This was one of the wares that Geuder, Paeschke & Frey Co., Milwaukee, Wis. made in the 1900's. H.M. Hillson Company were the distributors.
2. **Oval Scalloped Tray,** ½" deep, 3" wide, 4" long, dark blue enamel on cast iron, no enameling on the underside. Embossed "Enduro Enamel, Wincroft Stove Works, Middletown, PA." Near mint, rare shape & size, **$175.00.**
3. **Carnation Malted Milk Container,** 9½" high, 6" diameter, white decorated with red, green & black trim brass, nickel-plated cover. Marked "Carnation Malted Milk, Malted Milk, Carnation Company, Oconomowoc, Wis., Seattle, Wash., U.S.A., For Contented Customers." Mint, Extremely rare color, shape & size, **$795.00.**
4. **Paperweight,** 3½" high, 2⅝" bottom diameter, light gray, enamel on cast iron. Embossed "Your Warm Friend, Thatcher, Boilers, Ranges, Furnaces." Good plus, rare shape, **$155.00.**
5. **Ashtray,** ½" deep, 4¾" diameter, light green center, black lettering, red with light blue, yellow & dark blue flowers, cream indentations, underside black. Marked "Ceramic Color & Chem. Mfg. Co., New Brighton, PA." In the center is what appears to be a vessel marked "Wenning Ceramic Colors, Trade Mark." Good plus, **$165.00.**

Row 4:
1. **Nesco Pot Scraper,** 3½" high, 2⅞" wide. Good plus, extremely rare shape, **$695.00. Note:** This is not granite ware but it is a related advertising item. Enamel paint on metal. Marked "Nesco Pot & Pan Scraper. The Nesco boy with his Royal Granite Enameled Ware. They might imitate the Ware but they can't imitate the Wear." On the other side is marked "A curve or point to fit anywhere in the pots or pans" shows the Nesco Boy in a diamond with "Nescoware is Everywhere. Nesco, Registered in U.S. Patent Office, Royal Granite Enameled Ware. Buy & Use Always Royal Granite Enameled Ware. It's easy to Clean & Long Lasting. The Standard in Kitchen Utensils For Over 25 Years."
2. **Lapel Pin,** ⅞" diameter, light beige with a light green stippled background. Shows a shaded brown coffee pot. Marked with an S over an R and "Norvell-Shapleigh HDW. Company, St. Louis, Stewart-Rozwood Enameled Ware." Paper label on back marked "Bastian Bros. Co., Mfgs. of Ribbon Metal & Celluloid Novelties, Rochester, N.Y." Mint, Extremely rare color, shape, size, **$265.00. Note:** This is not granite ware but it is a related advertising item.
3. **Match Holder,** 1⅝" high, ¾" wide, 2⅜" long, aluminum. **Note:** This is not granite ware but a related advertising item. Marked on the front "Royal Granite Enameled Ware." In a diamond is the Nesco Boy & the words "Nesco, Registered in the U.S. Pat. Office, National Enameling & Stamping Co." Marked on back "Panama Pacific Exposition, San Francisco 1915." On the top edge is marked "Compliments of National Enameling & Stamping Company U.S.A." Mint, rare shape, **$225.00.**

Row 5:
1. **Ashtray,** ½" deep, 7¾" diameter, white, red & cream, with black embossed advertising for the Whirlpool Appliance Co. Near mint, rare color, **$155.00. Note:** The **W** under the Whirlpool. I assume this is the logo. End of Day.
2. **Pie Plate,** 1⅜" deep, 10" top diameter, black with white flecks "General Housewares Corporation Commitment to Excellence. 1984" with what appears to be an eagle. Mint, **$55.00.**
3. **Columbia Name Plate,** 2" high, 10¼" long, light gray. Near mint, **$55.00. Note:** I believe this was attached to something, possibly a cook stove. It has a bolt & nut on each end.
4. **Findlay Plate,** 1" deep, 7⅜" diameter, solid red front, black lettering advertising "Findlay" & also showing the items used for curling, a game played in Canada. The reverse side is black with white "Findlay of Carleton Place, Canada, Ranges-Furnaces." Mint, **$125.00.**

SECTION 1: LABELED PIECES AND ADVERTISING

Row 1:

1. **Ashtray**, 1" deep, 4⅝" diameter, red with black embossed advertising. "Polar Ware," made by The Polar Ware Co., Sheboygan, Wisconsin. Mint, rare color, **$185.00. Note:** They made white ware with black trim in 1924. In 1928 they made colors.
2. **Polar Bear**, papier-maché, 7½" high, 4¾" wide, 14⅝" long, white with black embossing advertising "Polar Enameled Ware." Circa 1924. Good plus, extremely rare shape & size, **$695.00.**
3. **Ashtray**, 1" deep, 4⅝" diameter, white with black trim & embossed advertising "Polar Ware." Mint, **$155.00.**

Row 2:

1. **Spatula**, 3⅛" wide, 4⅝" long, 12¼" long, black with white embossed lettering, rivetted handle. Good Plus, **$95.00.**
2. **Horse Spoon Rest**, 1½" deep, 8¼" long, solid black on a cast iron base, 3 molded feet, hook on back. Made by Prizer Stove Co., Reading, PA as premium in the 1920's. Mint, extremely rare shape, rare color, **$235.00. Note:** See No. 5 on this row.
3. **Trade Card**, 5½" long, 3⅜" wide, advertising "Ironclad Enameled Iron Ware," reverse side reads "The Housekeepers Delight, Handsome, Durable, Perfect. Complete line in stock at Nelson's 5¢ Store, 928 Elm Street, Manchester, N.H." Near mint, **$25.00. Note:** Their trade mark, the submarine, is on the left.
4. **Salesman's Sample Sink**, 1" deep, 3¾" wide, 4¾" long, solid white on a cast iron base, nickel-plated faucets. Embossed on the underside "Lenox Standard." Mint, rare shape & size **$475.00. Note:** It is believed that salesman's sample items were carried by traveling salesmen.
5. **Advertising Horse Spoon Rest**, 1½" deep, 8¼" long, solid black on cast iron base, 3 molded feet, hook on back. Mint, extremely rare shape & size, **$295.00. Note:** Made & embossed on the back by "Prizer Stove Co.," Reading, PA as an advertising premium for the Unity Stove Co., New York, NY. This is the only horse spoon rest I've seen with embossed advertising.
6. **Test Bucket**, 4" deep, 5¼" diameter, rivetted spout on the bottom ¾" long, ¾" diameter, cobalt with gold "Marschall Rennet Test. Manufactured By Chr Hansens Laboratory, Little Falls, NY." Interior is white with 0-10 measurements. Good plus, **$85.00. Note:** used in cheesemaking.

Row 3:

1. **Menders**, large 1" diameter, medium ¾" diameter, small ¾" diameter. Card comes with 8 menders & 1 reamer wrench. Made in Newark, NJ by the Metal Goods Mfg. Co. Good, **$18.00.**
2. **Trade Card**, 4¼" long, 3" wide advertising "Granite Iron Ware is 'all the gossip'." Reverse states "Granite Iron Ware is without a peer, & its growing popularity is such that no home is thoroughly equipped without a full supply of these wares. If you are in favor of cleanliness, healthfulness & economy use the Granite Iron Ware. A word to the wise is sufficient. For sale by S.M. Benjamin Bargain House, 178 East Main St., Rochester, NY." Good plus, **$25.00.**
3. **Trade Card**, 5¼" long, 3¼" wide advertising "Granite Iron Ware, copyright 1884 'Polly Put The Kettle On'." Reverse states "The Best Ware Made for the Kitchen. Manufactured only by St. Louis Stamping Co., St. Louis, Mo. For Sale Everywhere." Good plus, **$28.00.**
4. **Tappan Range Serving Tray**, ¾" deep, 8¾" wide, 18" long, black embossed with white decorations & the Tappan Man, white exterior. Recessed molded handles. Mint, **$110.00.**
5. **Trade Card**, 4¼" long, 3" wide advertising "Granite Iron Ware." Reverse is blank. Good plus. **$25.00.**
6. **Trade Card**, 4⅞" long, 2⅞" wide advertising "Granite Iron Ware." Reverse is blank. Mint, **$25.00.**
7. **Trade Card**, 4⅞" long, 2⅞" wide advertising "Granite Iron Ware." "Don't care if I do fall. The pitcher won't break." Reverse side "Manufactured only by St. Louis Stamping Co., St. Louis, Mo., For Sale Everywhere." Mint, **$28.00.**

Row 4:

1. **Deluxe Oven Thermometer**, with recipe file box, cards & recipes. Thermometer, 5¼" high, 2½" bottom diameter, white with a vitreous enameled scale, glazed pottery base made by Taylor Instrument Co., Rochester, New York. Mint, **$75.00. Note:** Original price was $3.25 each.
2. **Match Holder**, 1¼" deep, 1⅝" wide, 2⅝" long, solid green. Marked "Crawford Ranges." The match holder is on a cast iron base, has 4 molded feet. Near Mint, rare shape **$115.00.**
3. **Salesman's Sample Hairdresser's Sink**, 1¾" high, 3⅜" x 3⅜" top diameter, light solid green on a cast iron base. Good plus, rare shape & size, **$235.00.**
4. **Agate Cookbook**, 6⅛" x 4⅝", advertises the durability & cleanliness of "Agate Iron Ware." Also showing many shapes & sizes along with recipes & a picture of the factory. Fifth edition. It is not dated but others that were dated in the 1880's showed these same items. This cookbook was given compliments of W.F. Horton & Son, Lyndonville, NY. Good plus **$225.00.**

Row 1:

1. **Mother's Oats Cardboard Container,** Manufactured by The Quaker Oats Company of Chicago, Ill., U.S.A. Good plus, $20.00. Note: I'm showing this container so you can see what the next item on this row was used for.

2. **Quaker Oats Container Storage Cover,** 1⅛" deep, 5⅜" top diameter. Fine mottled dark blue. Labeled "Quaker Reg. U.S. Pat. Off." Near mint, rare shape, **$110.00. Note:** This cover was used for storing Quaker Oats after the cardboard cover was removed. This was one of their attempts to keep food more sanitary.

3. **Combination Pan,** 4¼" deep, 11½" long, 8" wide, large mottled green. Labeled "5-in-1 Combination Pan for The Ice Box & The Stove + Makes Housekeeping Easier. Baking Pan Storage Pan. Restores Garden Freshness. Baking Pan, Double Roaster. Chilling Gelatin, Frozen Desserts, Etc. Five Uses In One Pan. Made by Republic." Near mint, **$125.00.**

4. **Bowl,** 2½" deep, 6" diameter, large mottled, blue & white, white interior. Labeled "U.S. Standard Quality Enameled Ware. United States Stamping Co., Moundsville, W.VA." Mint, **$100.00.**

5. **Convex Water Pitcher,** 6½" to top of lip, 5" middle diameter, large mottled gray. Labeled "Double Coated Puritan. No.__ Guaranteed Chemically Pure. Cost__ Sell 25¢." The 25¢ is written in pencil on the label. Mint, rare shape, **$235.00.**

Row 2:

1. **Coffeepot,** 6¾" high to top of knob, 6½" bottom diameter, cream with black trim & handle, white interior. Labeled "Kook King Vollrath Ware. Quality Guaranteed Finest since 1874 Vollrath Company. Sheboygan, Wis." Marked on the bottom "Kook King Ware, K.C. The Vollrath Co., U.S.A." Circa 1920. Mint, **$115.00.**

2. **Cup,** 2" deep, 4¼" diameter, light blue & white, large mottled, white interior. Labeled "S.M.P. Diamond Ware The Sheet Metal Products Co. of Canada Ltd." Near mint, **$130.00.**

3. **Pudding Pan,** 3¼" deep, 11¾" top diameter, light blue & white, white interior, large mottled. Labeled "Republic Metalware Co., Chicago-Buffalo, NY. Niagara Enameled Ware. Size 6. Cost Number. Sell. This Label A Guarantee Of Quality." Label also shows a picture of Niagara Falls. This piece also has a paper label guarantee. "Guarantee: We guarantee each piece of Enamel Ware to contain four coats of Enamel of absolute purity & freedom from all injurious substances. It is also guaranteed against imperfections resulting from ordinary usage & will not chip or scale from exposure to heat. The Republic Metalware Co." Mint, **$165.00.**

4. **Butterdish,** 3½" high, 4¼" inside diameter, 7⅝" bottom diameter including collar base, solid yellow, black trim & knob. Labeled "Fabrique Par Patemail Garanti Au Feu, Tital Gosselies Belgique." Label shows a person carrying what appears to be a cooking vessel over his head. Mint, rare shape, **$245.00.**

5. **Teakettle,** 5" high, 5⅜" diameter, white with black trim & handle. Labeled "Special Enameled S Ware, United States Stamping Co., Moundsville, W.VA., U.S.A." Mint, **$70.00.**

Row 3:

1. **Cuspidor,** 3¾" deep, 7¼" top diameter, dark blue & white inside & out, large mottled. Labeled "Scotch Granite. Acid Proof. U.S. Quality Guaranteed, United States Stamping Co., Moundsville, W.VA, Cost__ Sell__ No. 20, Made In U.S.A." Good plus, **$255.00.**

2. **Pudding Pan,** 3" deep, 10½" top diameter, white decorated with a light blue scallop design. "Bonnie Blue." Made in the U.S.A. by Nesco. Part of label shows the Nesco Boy, Nescoware. Mint, **$130.00.**

3. **Forceps Jar,** 7⅝" deep, 2½" top diameter, white trimmed in black. Labeled "J. Jones Specialized Hospital Surgical Ware, Forceps Jar No. 8, The Jones Metal Products Company, West Lafayette, Ohio, U.S.A." Mint, **$45.00.**

4. **Child's Potty,** 3¾" deep, 6½" top diameter, gray, large mottled. Labeled "EL-AN-GE, Mottled Gray Ware." Also in an oval is labeled "Absolute Safety Guarantee, Pat. Off., L & G Mfg. Co." Mint, rare size, **$125.00.**

SECTION 2
CATALOGUES, ADVERTISING & HISTORICAL ITEMS

Row 1:

1. **LaLance & Grosjean Mfg. Co. Advertising,** 4½" x 5¾", "You can insure yourself against poison by looking for the tradename on the bottom, & buying Lalance & Grosjean Mfg. Co. Products." Mint, **$25.00.**

2. **King Manufacturing Co. Premium Catalogue,** No. 26, St. Louis, MO. 8½" x 5¾", pictured on this page is a 10-piece blue & white enameled ware set, given as a premium for selling $16.00 worth of their products. Also pictured is a blue & white enameled ware bucket & a 12qt. dishpan given as a premium for each $2.00 sale of their products. A number of pieces of graniteware are pictured. The catalogue has no date, but I believe that it dates around 1915. Good plus, **$225.00.**

3. **1950 Federal Enameling & Stamping Co. Advertisement,** 6¼" x 4¾", pictures white pieces trimmed in red, & advertising Federal Vogue Enameled Ware with Titanium. It states that titanium was added for lasting whiteness & long wear. Good plus, **$25.00.**

Row 2:

1. **Envelope with the Granite Ironware Mark,** 3½" x 6¼", Stamped St. Louis Stamping Co. St. Louis, Mo. Good plus, **$20.00.**

2. **Granite Ironware Trade Card.** 4¼" x 2¾". Entitled "The Two Orphans." Reverse reads "Granite Ironware is light, handsome, and wholesome. The best ware made." Good plus, **$25.00.**

3. **Granite Ironware Trade Card.** 2¾" x 4⅛", advertises "The Best Ware Made For The Kitchen, For Broiling, Baking, Boiling, Preserving." Good plus, **$25.00.**

4. **Folded Booklet.** Folded measures 3½" x 6". Open measures 12" x 10". Advertising "Nesco Kerosene Ranges & Stoves" in the different sizes available. I would date this booklet in the 1920's. The National Enameling & Stamping Company, Milwaukee, Wisconsin. Good plus, **$35.00.**

5. **Granite Ironware Trade Card,** 4¼" x 2¾" advertises "This Trademark on Every Piece." Also "Chas. W. Collins, Crockery & House Furnishing Goods, No. 27 North Main St. Cortland, NY" Good plus, **$25.00.**

6. **Granite Ironware Trade Card,** 2¾" x 4¼". Pictures a boy carrying a gray mottled cocoa dipper with wooden handle, & the girl is carrying an oval gray mottled, butter kettle. Good plus, **$25.00.**

Row 3:

1. **1924 Nesco Advertisement,** from the *Saturday Evening Post.* 10⅝" x 13½". Advertising the "Nesco Perfect Oil Cook Stove." Notice the advertisement for the gray mottled refrigerator bowl. It says "Send 15¢ & your dealers name, & we will send you this handy, covered refrigerator bowl made of clean, durable 'Nesco Royal Granite Enameled Ware.' Good plus, **$25.00.**

2. **Agate Ironware Trade Card,** 2¾" x 4". Pictures people dancing around an Agate Ironware gray mottled teapot with iron handle, & also a lady placing a crown over the cover knob. "The Crowning Triumph." Good plus, **$30.00.**

3. **Granite Ironware Trade Card,** 2⅞" x 4¼". Pictures a girl showing another girl a Granite Ironware cover & handled kettle. Good plus, **$30.00. Note:** On the Granite Ironware patent mark is shown a gray mottled kettle with spout & metal bail.

4. **Granite Ironware Trade Card,** 2¾" x 4¼", advertising "Palmer Hardware Co. 429 East State St. Rockford, Ill." Good plus, **$30.00. Note:** These trade cards were given to customers, or mailed to customers to advertise the manufacturer of the granite ware, & also the place where it was sold.

5. **1920 Advertisement** of "C-Ruso Gray Enameled Ware," 9½" x 7½". Pictures a number of gray mottled pieces as well as the price for individual pieces or by the dozen. Good plus, **$25.00. Note:** Kettles with wood grips were 10¢ more than the kettles without.

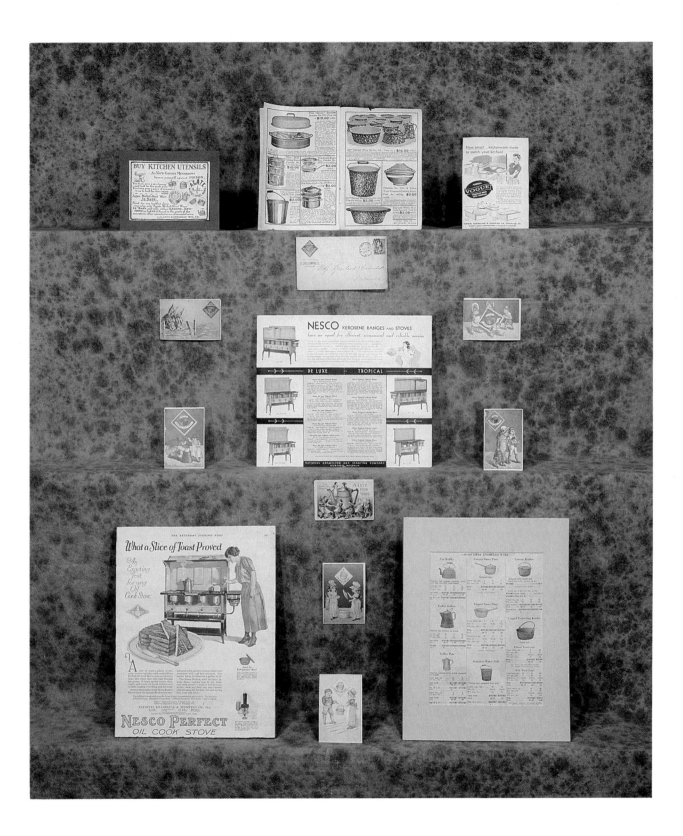

Row 1:

1. **Matthai - Ingram Co. Illustrated Catalog,** 8" x 5½" from Baltimore, MD U.S.A. I would date this catalog from the late 1800's. They were the manufacturers of Greystone Enameled Ware. This catalog also pictures the Matthai - Ingram factory & its floor plan that covered an area of over 10 acres. They also made sheet metal goods that included coffee & teapot spouts, handles, bottoms, & trimmings, & enameled teapot handles & knobs. Good plus, **$250.00.**

2. **1925 NESCO Advertisement,** 13¾" x 10¾". Advertising "Royal Enameled Ware, National Enameling & Stamping Co., Inc. Milwaukee, Wis." It states that one burner burns 25 hours on a gallon of kerosene. These stoves could be purchased with the oven that sat over the burners for baking. The top back section was optional. Good plus, **$40.00.**

3. **Lalance & Grosjean Manufacturing Co. Illustrated Catalogue** from March 1, 1884, 5¾" x 4¾". Pictured are some of the gray mottled wares that they made & sold. This company won the highest centennial award in 1876 & also the Grand Gold Medal at the Paris Exposition of 1878. Good plus, **$250.00**

Row 2:

1. **1915 Lee's Premium Catalogue,** 10⅜" x 8", illustrating the many items that were given for selling a certain amount of their goods. These premiums included granite ware, including New Blue Turquoise. This ware was solid blue trimmed in black. The catalogue also pictures a blue & white triple coated enamelware 12 piece set that was given as a premium for selling a $15.00 order. They were also jobbers for this ware. Good plus, **$265.00.**

2. **1923 Nesco Royal Granite Enameled Ware Advertisement,** 13¾" x 10¾". Pictures a number of pieces of gray large mottled Royal Granite Enameled Ware. Also pictures a little sauce pan, with this statement: "To introduce the famous ware into your home, we'll send you this handy little sauce pan, if you'll send us your dealer's name & a dime to cover postage & packaging. National Enameling & Stamping Co. Inc. Advertising Department. Section Y Milwaukee, Wis." Good plus, **$40.00.**

3. **Central Stamping Co. Advertisement,** 11½" x 8". Pictures their plant in Newark, NJ. "Manufacturers of 'Sterling' Aluminum Enameled Ware. A 2 coated gray ware which has a fine gloss finish & is warranted absolutely pure. Also 'Alba' Enameled Ware, a pure white lined ware, the outside is white corrugated with blue; edges & handles black. All of our enameled wares are full sizes & full weight, & are absolutely pure." Good plus, **$25.00.**

Row 3:

1. **1920 Advertisement for "Cruso" Gray Enameled Ware,** 9½" x 7½". Pictures a number of gray mottled pieces. Good plus, **$25.00. Note:** I find it interesting that the bed pans came complete with the cover, whereas the chamber pots did not. Instead the cover was bought for 15¢.

2. **Hibbard, Spencer, Bartlett, & Co., Chicago Advertisement,** 9½" x 7½". "'Hibbard' Ivory with green trim. Ware of Quality–3 coats carefully selected–on heavy steel shapes–Improved patterns." Good plus, **$25.00.**

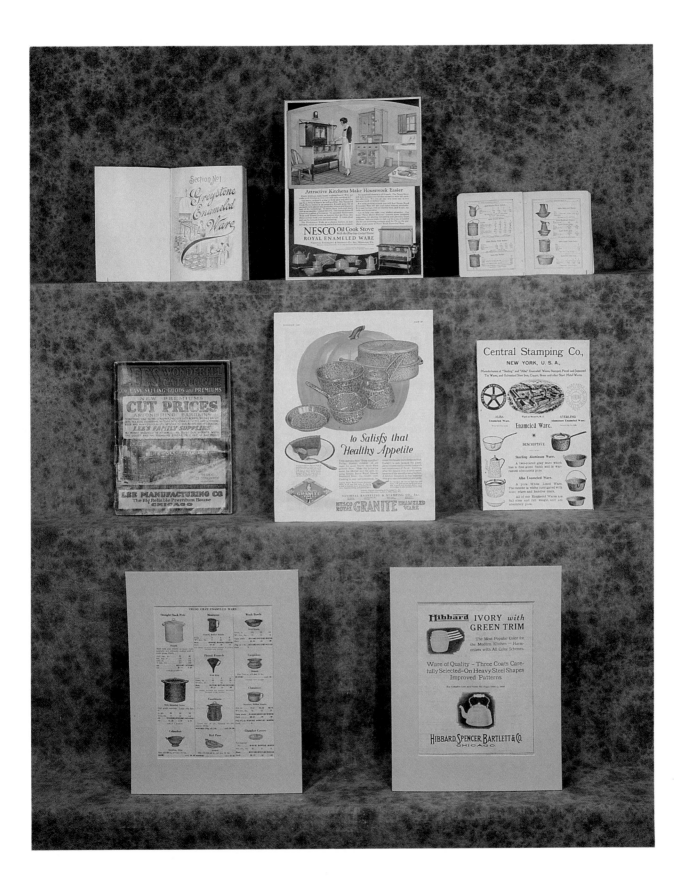

Row 1:

1. **1920's Lisk Manufacturing Company "Limited" Catalogue, No. 27,** Canadaigua, NY, 7½" x 5¾". Illustrated picture of "Lisk" better quality enameled ware. Good plus, **$295.00.**
2. **1920's Reed's Flintstone Enameled Ware Catalogue,** Reed Manufacturing Co. Newark, NY, 9¼" x 6¼". Illustrations of turquoise blue roasters, water pails, wash basins, seamless cocoa dipers, sauce pans, kettles, & many more pieces. Their logo was "Better Take Heed & Buy Matchless Reed." Good plus, **$295.00.**
3. **1920's Reed Manufacturing Company Catalog,** No. 27, Newark, NY, 7½" x 5¾". Illustrates dark imperial color, which is black with white flecks. Both Reed & Lisk Manufacturing Companies were famous for their self basting roasters. Good plus, **$295.00.**

Row 2:

1. **1939 Lisk Manufacturing Co., Ltd. 50th Anniversary Catalog,** 12" x 9¼". From a modest beginning in 1889 Lisk Mfg. Co. had completed 50 years of distinctive service to the retailers of this country. Illustrated are pieces of Flintstone Ivory Enameled Ware. Also shown was the Black Top, & the Imperial line which was the black with white flecks. "Lisk Stainless" three coat acid resisting, solid white enameled ware. Special anniversary prices listed. Mint, **$240.00.**
2. **1928 Lisk Price Booklet,** list "E" limited from Canadaigua, NY plant, 6¼" x 3½". Features Lisk Fancy Teapots with enameled hinged cover, made in Alice blue, white, red, yellow, orange, & green. Price for the 1qt. was $14.40/doz., the 1½qt. was $15.60/doz. Their motto was "Run no risk – Be sure it's LISK." Good plus, **$45.00.**
3. **1889 Grandma Garnet's Household Hints,** 7¼" x 5". "Geuder Paeschke & Frey company, Milwaukee, U.S.A." Back cover marked "Cream City Ware. Milwaukee G.P. & F. Trade Mark. Cream City Ware Never Disappoints." Inside cover reads "A valuable little book designed to aid housewives in every department of household work." Explains the art of setting a table, how to purify foods, keep the kitchen sanitary, reduce the coal bill, & keep the cellar wholesome. Pictures a number of "Cream City" Garnet Ware. Good plus, **$295.00.**
4. **1909 Republic Metalware Company Catalog,** No. 73, 10¾" x 8½". This company was established in 1836, & incorporated in 1905. This catalogue illustrates goods manufactured & sold by the Republic Metalware Co. of Buffalo, Chicago, & New York, successors to Sidney Shepard & Co., Buffalo & New York & Sidney Shepard & Co., Chicago. They made Niagara Enameled Ware, a delicate turquoise with uniform mottling of fine white lines. The inside was pure white. They also made Steel Gray & Hearthstone wares, as well as Savory roasters, Buffalo Steam egg poachers, with water pan, rack, 2 sets of 5 egg cups (deep, shallow), cover. Good plus, **$250.00.**

Row 3:

1. **1920's United States Stamping Co. Catalogue,** #7, Moundsville, WV, 9⅛" x 6¼". "Victoria" Blue & white mottled effect with black rims & handles, lined with acid resisting white enamel. "Royal blue," deep royal blue with white mottling. These wares are advertised as 3 coats of enamel on heavy steel. "Scotch" granite was royal blue stippled with white, "an exceedingly tough & durable ware." "Azure" was a blue & white marble effect with black rim & handles. This company also made hospital ware including individual service sets, feeding cups, sponge bowls, needle boxes & so on. Good plus, **$295.00.**
2. **Manning Bowman & Co. Perfection Granite Iron Ware & Decorated Pearl Agateware Illustrated Catalogue** with price list, 14" x 11¼". This catalog illustrates the many colors, shapes, & sizes of these products & their prices. The larger pieces were $1.00 extra or more depending upon the work required for special orders. This character of work can only be entrusted to a skilled & expensive order of workmanship. White metal mountings & protection bands were nickel or silver plated which was the customer's choice. The silver plate cost $5.25 & the nickel plate was $4.50. Good plus. **$595.00.**
3. **1915 Coonley Manufacturing Company Catalog,** No. 21, Cicero, Il, 9" x 6". Manufacturers of "Austral" blue & white ware, medium mottled with white interior, triple coated. "Cling Steel Ware" is a light green with large white mottling inside & out. "Crystal" white & "White" ware are pure white with deep blue trim, triple coated wares. Label pictures a raccoon. This company also made roasters in "Jet Black" enamel with fine white spray, dark brown enamel with large white spray, & turquoise blue with white interior. Good plus, **$295.00.**

Special Note: Anyone lucky enough to have catalogues or other advertising should cherish them because they are a wealth of undisputed information. The search is well worth while. Catalogues are priced according to the amount of information shown & described in them along with the colors. Example: A catalogue that has colored photos would cost more than one in black & white. A complete catalogue on only granite ware would be worth more than one that shows other items as well.

Row 1.

1. **1876 Perfection Granite Ironware Trade Poster,** 21¾" x 15½". Illustrates a number of their metal trimmed Perfection Granite Ironware pieces in gray large mottled. It states that "The Granite Coating is an insoluble glaze, vitrified under an intense heat, & receives its mottled finish from a liberal mixture of Iron Oxide. The material being a non-conductor of heat & cold, this ware is especially & equally valuable for keeping beverages at either extreme of temperature. In the Perfection Granite Ironware they offer vessels absolutely faultless for preparing & serving in a state of purity the highly prized beverages of the table." Near mint, **$200.00.**

Row 1.

1. **1915 Coonley Manufacturing Company Trade Poster,** 21¼" x 15½". Illustrates a number of shapes & sizes that were sold as trade & profit makers. Most of the items surrounding the 39¢ special were sold by the dozen. Example, soup ladles were 65¢ a dozen, miner's dinner pail with food compartment on top, & coffee in bottom, 4qt. size, were $4.50/doz. All these items were blue mottled on the outside & pure white inside. Each piece was wrapped & labeled. Good plus, **$200.00. Note:** The 39¢ special insert. These items were sold by the 3 doz., 9 doz. costing $3.25 on special, which were regularly 75¢ each. Their factory was located in Cicero, IL. Their sales office was located at 139 N. Clark Street, Chicago, IL.

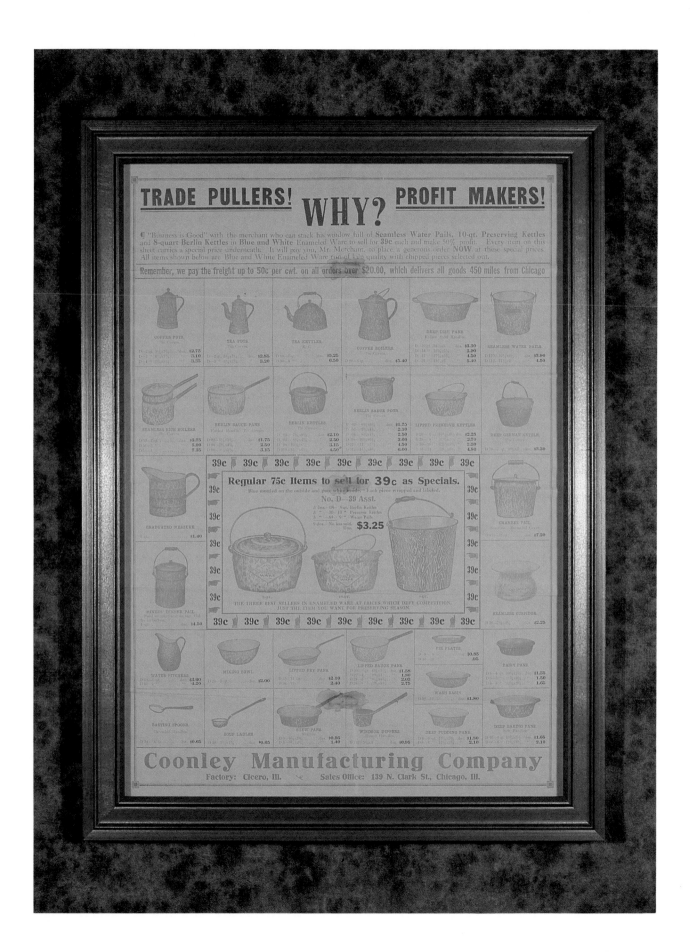

Row 1:

1. **1902 Coronation Mug,** 2⅞" deep, 3" diameter, white with brown trim, rivetted handle & seamless body. Commemorates the 1902 coronation of Edward VII of England with the royal coat of arms and royal mottoes, "Dieu et Mon Droit" and "Honi Soit Qui Mal Y Pense." Near mint, extremely rare shape, **$215.00.**

2. **1902 Exhibition Mug,** 2⅞" deep, 3" diameter, white, decorated & trimmed in gold relief, rivetted handle & seamless body. Commemorates the "Cork" international exhibition of 1902. Near mint, extremely rare shape, **$215.00.**

3. **1904 World's Fair & Exposition Mug,** 2¾" deep, 2⅞" diameter, white, decorated & trimmed in gold. Commemorates the 1904 World's Fair, St. Louis, & the Louisiana Purchase Exposition. Pictures a 1903 United States map, "Napoleon," St. Louis, Mo. U.S.A., & an emblem of an eagle & script reading "E Pluribus Unum, Jefferson." Map of Louisiana Purchase 1803. Marked across the map; "Province of Louisiana Ceded By France in 1803. Centennial celebrated at St. Louis 1903." Bottom Marked "Elite Austria, Norvell-Shapleigh Hardware, St. Louis, Mo. copyright 1903 by Rothschild, Meyers, & Co." Near Mint, extremely rare shape, **$195.00.**

Row 2:

1. **1837–1897 Commemorative Tumbler,** 3⅝" deep, 3" diameter, white, decorated & trimmed in brown. Commemorating Queen Victoria, from 1837 to 1897. Shows two emblems: "The Queen's Earliest Resolve. I will be good," & "Borough of Derby 20th June 1897 Sir Thomas-Roe Kt, Mayor." Good plus, extremely rare shape, **$175.00.**

2. **1848–1898 Commemorative Tumbler,** 4" deep, 3⅜" diameter, white decorated with gold relief bands. Commemorates "Franz Joseph King of Austria 1848 to 1898." Good Plus, extremely rare shape, **$175.00.**

3. **1901 Commemorative Tumbler,** 3⅝" deep, 3" diameter, white, decorated with gold relief band. Commemorating the wedding of Queen Wilhelmina of the Netherlands to Duke Hendrik in 1901. Around the top of the tumbler is marked "Per Aspera Ad Astra Je Maintiendrai." Part of this mark is not visible because as you can see the crown covers it up. Good plus, extremely rare shape, **$175.00.**

Row 3:

1. **1837–1897 Commemorative Tumbler,** 3¾" deep, 3⅜" diameter, white, decorated with gold relief bands. Shows a picture of the queen from 1837 & also from 1897. Good plus, extremely rare shape, **$175.00.** **Note:** This has a different decoration than the tumbler on Row 2 of this page.

2. **1898 Commemorative Tumbler,** 4½" deep, 3¼" diameter, white, decorated with gold relief bands. Commemorating the accession to the throne of the Netherlands by Queen Wilhelmina in 1898 with an emblem on the back side that reads "Je Maintiendrai." Marked on the bottom in an oval "H. Berk & Zoon Kampen." Good, extremely rare shape, **$175.00.**

3. **1837–1897 Commemorative Tumbler,** 3⅞" deep, 3⅜" diameter, white, decorated with gold relief bands. Commemorating the Queen from 1837 to 1897. This is another version of tumbler in Row 2 which shows a picture of the Queen in 1897. This tumbler also shows a picture of the Queen in 1837. Good plus, extremely rare shape, **$175.00.**

Note: There is a variation of size & designs for this type of tumblers, more than likely because they were made by different companies. These tumblers & mugs are exceptionally well made & are also a cross collectible because of their historical value.

SECTION 3:
BLUE AND WHITE

Row 1:

1. **Graduated Measuring Cup,** 2⅛" deep, 3¼" diameter, 1 cup. Lavender cobalt blue & white medium swirl with white interior. Rivetted strap handle. Good plus, extremely rare color, shape, size, **$800.00. Note:** In the design of this measuring cup, the four graduated sections each equal ¼ cup.

2. **Grocer's Scoop,** 2⅜" deep, 6⅝" wide, 8¾" long not including the handle. Cobalt blue & white large swirl with white interior. Rivetted seamed tubular handle with closed end. Good, extremely rare color, shape & size, **$345.00**

3. **Shoe Horn,** 7" long, 1⅞" wide. Cobalt blue & white large swirl both front & back. Has eyelet for hanging. Near mint, extremely rare color, shape & size, **$2,450.00**

Row 2:

1. **Teapot,** 5¾" high, 4⅝" diameter. Brilliant cobalt blue with white veins, "chicken wire pattern" with white interior. The lip of the cover that fits down inside the teapot has a spring action that holds the cover secure while pouring. Marked "Patent." The bottom of the pot is marked with a lion standing with his front paws on a coffee pot. Good plus, **$135.00.**

2. **Oblong Covered Soap Dish,** 2⅜" to top of the cover knob. 4" wide, 6" top length. Cobalt blue & white large mottled inside & out. White perforated insert. Good plus, extremely rare color, shape, size, **$1,400.00.**

3. **Coffee Flask,** 4½" to top of the screw on metal cover, 3½" bottom diameter. Dark cobalt blue & light blue with white flecks. Seamless body. Near mint, extremely rare shape and color, **$350.00.**

Row 3:

1. **Water Pitcher with flared top,** 8¾" tall, 6½" diameter at the widest point. Cobalt blue & white medium swirl with white interior. Black rivetted handle & trim. Seamless body. Good plus, extremely rare shape, **$375.00. Note:** The unusual shape of this pitcher with its flared top & no pouring lip.

2. **Covered Canister,** 6⅝" tall, 4½" diameter. Cobalt blue & white large mottled with white interior & dark blue trim. Seamless body. Good plus, rare color, **$300.00.**

3. **Covered Chamber Pail,** 11¼" tall, 10½" diameter. Cobalt blue & white large swirl with white interior. Rivetted ears. Black wooden bail handle & seamed body. Near mint, **$300.00.**

Row 1:

1. **Oblong Bread Pan,** 3" deep, 4¾" wide, 9¾" long, cobalt blue & white large mottled, white interior, seamed ends. Near mint, rare color & shape, **$345.00.**

2. **Syrup,** 7½" high, 3⅝" diameter, dark cobalt blue & white large swirl, white interior. "Azurelite" made by the Enterprise Enamel Company, Bellaire, Ohio. Near mint, extremely rare color & shape, **$895.00.**

3. **Turk's Head Turban Style Muffin Pan,** 1¼" deep, 7½" wide, 14½" long, cobalt blue & white large mottled, white interior. Near mint, extremely rare shape, **$1,450.00.**

4. **Measure,** 3½" high, 3" diameter, cobalt blue & white large swirl, white interior, black trim, rivetted spout & handle. Near mint, rare color, shape & size, **$595.00.**

5. **Cream Can,** 7¼" high, 4¼" diameter, cobalt blue & white medium swirl, white interior, black trim & wooden bail, seamed body & neck. Mint, rare color & size, **$495.00.**

Row 2:

1. **Percolator Funnel,** 7⅝" long, 4¼" diameter without attached rivetted collar. Upper portion & rivetted collar are cobalt blue & white large swirl, funnel & interior are white with cobalt blue trim. Good plus, extremely rare color & shape, **$595.00.**

2. **Coffeepot,** 10" high, 6¾" diameter, cobalt blue & white large swirl, white interior, black wooden handle & trim. Matching cover has a ribbed design. Mint, **$365.00.**

3. **Round Fluted Mold,** 2¼" deep, 4¾" diameter, cobalt blue & white large swirl, white interior. Near mint, extremely rare color, shape & size, **$435.00.**

4. **Bean Pot,** (cracker or biscuit jar). 7" to top of cover knob, 6⅞" diameter, cobalt blue & white large swirl, white interior, black handles & trim. Good plus, extremely rare color & shape, **$525.00. Note:** This item has been called by today's collectors a Bean Pot, Cracker Jar or Biscuit Jar. I have found no information as to what it is for sure. If anyone has seen an ad identifying this piece, I would appreciate a copy of it.

Row 3:

1. **Oval Bread Pan,** 3⅜" deep, 8½" wide, 11" long, lavender cobalt blue & white large swirl, white interior, cobalt blue trim. Good plus, rare color & shape, **$225.00.**

2. **Cuspidor,** 2 piece, 5" high including cover, 11¼" top diameter with cover, 8⅜" bottom diameter, cobalt blue & white large swirl, white interior, cobalt blue trim. Good plus, **$425.00.**

3. **Fudge Pan,** ¾" deep, 6½" wide, 9½" long, lavender cobalt blue & white large swirl, white interior, cobalt blue trim. Good plus, rare color, **$195.00.**

Row 4:

1. **Oblong Baking Pan,** 2¼" deep, 10⅞" wide, 17" long including handles, cobalt blue & white large swirl, white interior, black trim, molded handles. Near mint, rare color, **$265.00. Note:** This is the smaller version of the one pictured in Book 1.

Row 1:
1. **Pedestal Fruit Bowl,** 7½" high, 8" top diameter, 6⅜" bottom diameter, cobalt blue and white large mottled, white interior. Near mint, extremely rare shape and size, **$975.00.**
2. **Mug,** 3⅛" deep, 3⅞" diameter, cobalt blue and white, large swirl, black trim, white interior. Near mint, **$95.00.**
3. **Scale Tray,** ½" deep, 9" diameter, cobalt blue and white large mottled, white interior. Labeled "N.E. & S.Co. Badger Enameled Ware No." **Note:** Marked in pencil on the label is the selling price of 20¢. This could be a product of National Enameling and Stamping Company. Mint, rare color and shape, **$695.00.**
4. **Measure,** 3⅜" to top of the lip, 2⅞" bottom diameter, cobalt blue and white large mottled, black trim and handle, white interior, applied lip and rivetted handle. Good plus, rare color and size, **$365.00.**
5. **Teapot,** 10" high to top of cover knob, 6½" bottom diameter, cobalt blue and white large mottled, white interior, black wooden handle, knob and trim. Near mint, **$335.00.**

Row 2:
1. **Footed Bread Raiser,** 11" high including cover, 17¼" top diameter handles not included, cobalt blue & white medium mottled, white interior. Good plus, rare color, **$325.00.**
2. **Graduated Lipped Dry Measure,** 5" high to top of the lip, 4½" diameter, cobalt blue & white large mottled, white interior, black trim & handle. Good plus, rare color & shape, **$295.00.**
3. **Oval Butter Kettle or Carrier,** 7" high to top of cover knob, 9¼" long, 7½" wide, cobalt blue & white medium mottled, white interior, black trim, metal strap handle. Good plus, rare color, **$425.00.**

Row 3:
1. **Water Boiler,** 10¼" high including cover, 15¼" wide, 31¼" long, cobalt blue & white large swirl, white interior, on the back side of the boiler is a hole 3" diameter. Top cover is hinged. Good plus, extremely rare color, rare shape & size, **$495.00. Note:** I have been told these were used on the side of a wood burning cook stove to heat water for household use.

Row 1:

1. **Milk Can,** 9" tall, 4⅞" diameter, cobalt blue & white large swirl with white interior, black trim, handle, & ears, seamed body, wooden bail & matching cover. Near mint, rare color & size. **$795.00.**
2. **Candlestick,** 2¼" tall, 4¾" diameter, cobalt blue & white large swirl, inside & out. Black trim has finger ring with flat thumb rest for carrying. Good plus, extremely rare color, shape & size, **$1,100.00**
3. **Covered Bucket,** 7¾" tall, 7½" diameter, cobalt blue & white large swirl, white interior, wire bail handle, seamless body. Good plus, rare color, **$295.00.**

Row 2:

1. **Teapot,** squatty shape, 5⅞" tall, 4⅝" diameter, cobalt blue & white medium swirl, white interior with black trim, handle, & wooden knob, rivetted handle, seamless body with seamed spout. Near mint, extremely rare color, shape & size, **$1,200.00.**
2. **Muffin Pan,** each cup ¾" deep, 3" top diameter, overall measurement 1" deep, 7¼" wide, 10⅝" long, cobalt blue & white large mottled inside & out. Near mint, extremely rare color, shape & size, **$1,250.00.**
3. **Coffee Biggin,** including pot, tin biggin, spreader & cover, 8½" tall, 3⅞" diameter, cobalt blue & white large mottled with white interior & black trim, rivetted handle & seamed body. Good plus, extremely rare color, shape & size, **$1,150.00.**

Row 3:

1. **Teakettle,** 7½" tall, 10¼" diameter, cobalt blue & white large mottled with white interior black trim, ears, & wooden bail, seamed body & spout. Good plus, rare color, **$375.00.**
2. **Mug,** 2⅝" deep, 3⅞" diameter, cobalt blue & white large swirl, white interior with dark blue trim & handle, seamed body & rivetted handle. Good plus, **$95.00.**
3. **Oval Platter,** 1¼" deep, 12¾" wide, 16¼" long, cobalt blue & white large mottled, white interior with dark blue trim. Good plus, rare color, **$295.00.**

Row 4:

1. **Bidet,** 4" deep, 11⅝" wide, 18⅝" long, cobalt blue & white large mottled with white interior. Good plus, rare color & shape, **$295.00. Note:** This is a vessel that is used in sitz baths. Sometimes it's found with the metal or wood framework that holds the bidet.

54

Row 1:
1. **Muffin Pan,** 1" deep, 7¼" wide, 14¼" long. Each cup measures ¾" deep, 3" diameter, lavender cobalt blue & white medium swirl with white interior & black trim, eyelet for hanging. Near mint, extremely rare color, **$595.00.**

Row 2:
1. **Covered Sugar Bowl,** squatty-shaped, 6¼" tall, 4½" diameter, cobalt blue & white medium swirl with white interior, black trim, rivetted roll shaped handle, seamless body. Good plus, extremely rare color & shape, **$1,250.00.**
2. **Candlestick,** 2¼" tall, 5⅛" diameter, cobalt blue & white large swirl inside & out. Finger ring with thumb rest. Good plus, extremely rare color, shape & size, **$1,100.00.**
3. **Teapot,** "Belle" shape, 7" tall, 4⅜" diameter, cobalt blue & white large swirl with white interior, black trim & rivetted handles. Good plus, rare color & shape, **$900.00.**

Row 3:
1. **Syrup,** 5⅝" tall, 3⅛" diameter, cobalt blue & white medium swirl with white interior, rivetted handle, seamed bottom. Good, rare color & size, **$495.00.**
2. **Coffeepot,** straight sided, 8½" tall, 5¾" diameter, dark cobalt blue & white large swirl with white interior & black rivetted handle, seamed body. Good plus, extremely rare color, shape & size, **$525.00.**
3. **Measure,** 4½" tall, 3¾" diameter, cobalt blue & white large mottled with white interior, cobalt blue trim, rivetted handle & seamed body. Good plus, rare color, shape & size, **$550.00.**

Row 4:
1. **Teakettle,** 7¼" tall, 9½" diameter, blue & white medium swirl with white interior, black wooden bail handle & trim. Notched rivetted ears prevent the handle from dropping onto the teakettle, which keeps the handle cool for pouring. Seamed spout & bottom. Good plus, rare color, **$395.00.**
2. **Covered Chamber Pail,** 12" tall, 10¾" diameter, cobalt blue & white large mottled with white interior, cobalt trim, seamless body, wooden bail handle with black rubber ring in the center. This rubber ring prevents the handle from chipping the chamber pail. Labeled "Royal Blue, Acid Proof. U.S. Quality Guaranteed, United States Stamping Co. Moundsville, WV. Made In The United U.S.A." Near mint, **$425.00.**
3. **Coffee Biggin,** including pot, biggin, & cover, 10⅛" tall, 3⅝" diameter, cobalt blue & white large swirl with white interior, cobalt blue trim, seamless body. Good plus, rare color, shape, & size. **$725.00 Note:** The inside edge of the biggin has a spring that holds a cloth bag for the coffee. It also holds the biggin secure in the top of the pot.

Note: The different shades & variations of the cobalt blue & white on this page.

56

Row 1:

1. **Syrup,** squatty shape, 7¼" tall, 4¼" diameter, blue & white large swirl, white interior, cobalt blue handle, seamed body, rivetted handle. Flip top cover is brass with nickel plating. Good plus, extremely rare color, shape & size, **$850.00. Note:** I believe this is "Blue Diamond Ware" triple coated ware pictured & advertised in Norvell-Shapleigh's 1910 catalogue, made in the United States, distributed by Norvell-Shapleigh Hardware Co., St. Louis. This color is generically termed "Iris" today.
2. **Advertising Coaster,** ⅜" deep, 4" diameter, blue & white large swirl, white interior, cobalt blue trim, triple coated. Advertising "Blue Diamond Ware" Norvell-Shapleigh Hdw., St. Louis, also distributors of Blue Diamond Ware. Near mint, extremely rare color & shape, **$275.00. Note:** Advertising is faint.
3. **Oval Platter,** 1" deep, 10⅞" wide, 14" long, blue & white large swirl, white interior, cobalt blue trim. Blue Diamond Ware. Near mint, rare color & shape, **$365.00.**
4. **Coaster,** ⅜" deep, 4" diameter, blue & white large swirl, white interior, cobalt blue trim, triple coated. Blue Diamond Ware. Mint, extremely rare color & shape, **$275.00. Note:** The different swirling on the coasters on this row. That's why I chose to show them together.
5. **Molasses Pitcher,** 6¼" tall, 3½" diameter, blue & white large swirl, white interior, cobalt blue trim & handle, triple coated, rivetted handle & spout, seamless body. Cover has spun knob & covered spout. Near mint, extremely rare color, shape & size, **$950.00. Note:** This style molasses pitcher is pictured in the Norvell-Shapleigh 1910 catalogue & advertised as "Blue Diamond Ware."

Row 2:

1. **Gravy or Sauce Boat,** (½ pint) 8½" x 3¾" x 2½", blue & white large swirl, white interior, cobalt blue trim & handle, triple coated, seamless body, rivetted handle. Near mint, extremely rare color & shape, **$1,150.00. Note:** This style gravy boat is pictured in the Norvell-Shapleigh 1910 catalogue & advertised as "Blue Diamond Ware."
2. **Colander,** 5" high, 9¾" top diameter not including handles, blue & white large swirl inside & out, cobalt blue trim & handles, rivetted handles, triple coated. Blue Diamond Ware. Near mint, rare color, **$350.00.**
3. **Tea Steeper,** 4½" tall, 4¼" diameter, blue & white large swirl, white interior, cobalt blue trim & handle, rivetted spout & handle, seamless body. Blue Diamond Ware. Good plus, rare color, **$375.00.**

Row 3:

1. **Pitcher & Bowl.** Pitcher, 10" to top of the lip, 7⅛" diameter at the widest point, rivetted handle, seamless body. Bowl, 4⅛" deep, 14¾" top diameter, both pieces blue & white large swirl, white interior, cobalt blue trim. Blue Diamond Ware. Near mint, rare color, 2 pieces, **$1,850.00**
2. **Flat-Top Roaster,** 7½" tall, 11¾" wide, 17½" long not including the handles, blue & white large swirl, white interior, cobalt blue trim & handles, seamless body, rivetted handles. Insert, 1⅞" deep, 10⅝" wide, 16⅛" long, white with cobalt blue trim & handles. Good plus, rare color, **$350.00. Note:** The metal steam vent that covers the hole in the top of the flat cover can be swung to the side to vent the steam out of the roaster before the cover is raised, thus preventing a person from burning their hands or face. Blue Diamond Ware.

Special Note: I believe the pieces pictured are Blue Diamond Ware because the color & swirls as well as some of the shapes are so similar to the Blue Diamond Ware pictured in the 1910 Norvell-Shapleigh Catalogue.

Row 1:

1. **Teapot,** 9" tall, 5¾" diameter, blue & white large swirl, white interior, cobalt blue trim, seamless body. Blue Diamond Ware. Good plus, rare color, **$395.00.**
2. **Wash Basin,** 3¼" deep, 11¾" diameter, blue & white large swirl, white interior, cobalt blue trim. Blue Diamond Ware. Near mint, rare color, **$165.00.**
3. **Coffee Boiler,** 11½" tall, 8⅝" diameter, blue & white large swirl, white interior, cobalt blue trim, seamed body, rivetted ears & side handle, wire bail. Blue Diamond Ware. Good plus, rare color, **$285.00.**

Row 2:

1. **Custard cup,** 2⅛" deep, 4¼" diameter, blue & white large swirl, white interior, cobalt blue trim. Blue Diamond Ware. Good plus, rare color & shape, **$115.00.**
2. **Cream Can,** 7¾" tall, 4" diameter, blue & white large swirl, white interior, cobalt blue trim, rivetted wire ears & wooden bail. Blue Diamond Ware. Near mint, rare color, shape & size, **$675.00.**
3. **Egg Plate,** 1¾" deep, 9" diameter, blue & white large swirl, cobalt blue trim & rivetted handles. Blue Diamond Ware. Good plus, rare color, **$210.00.**

Row 3:

1. **Oval Platter,** 1½" deep, 14¼" wide, 18" long, blue & white large swirl, white interior, cobalt blue trim Blue Diamond Ware. Near mint, rare color & size, **$360.00.**

Row 1:
1. **Coffeepot,** 9¼" tall, 5¾" diameter, blue & white wavy mottling, white interior, black trim & handle, seamed body. Near mint, rare color, **$375.00.**
2. **Coffee Boiler,** 10½" tall, 8" diameter, blue & white wavy mottling, white interior, black trim & handle, seamed body, rivetted spout & strap handle, wire bail. Near mint, rare color, **$360.00.**
3. **Water Pitcher,** 9" tall, 5" diameter, light blue & white wavy mottling, black trim & handle, seamless body. Mint, rare color & shape, **$575.00.**

Row 2:
1. **Windsor Dipper,** 2¾" deep, 5" diameter, light blue & white wavy mottling, white interior, black trim & rivetted handle with eyelet for hanging. Good plus, rare color, **$115.00.**
2. **Pie Plate,** ⅞" deep, 8½" diameter, light blue & white wavy mottling, white interior, black trim. Near mint, rare color, **$110.00.**
3. **Covered Bucket,** 6" tall, 6" diameter, light blue & white wavy mottling, white interior, black trim & ears, seamed body, wire bail. Near mint, rare color, **$245.00.**

Row 3:
1. **Coffeepot,** 8" tall, 5¼" diameter, light blue & white large swirl with a ribbon effect, white interior, black trim & handle, seamed body. I believe this is Azure Ware. Near mint, rare color, **$385.00. Note:** I chose to use this piece in this photo because of its unique up & down design in the wavy mottling & also for comparison to other designs on this page.
2. **Milk Can,** 8¾" tall, 4⅞" diameter, light blue & white wavy mottling, white interior, black trim, seamless body, rivetted ears, wire bail. Distributed by The Lee Manufacturing Co., Chicago. Mint, rare color & shape, **$650.00.**
3. **Coffeepot,** 9" tall, 5¾" diameter, blue & white wavy mottling, white interior, black trim & handle, seamed body, rivetted handle. Near mint, rare color, **$375.00. Note:** How the pattern differs in design from the others on this page.

Row 4:
1. **Coffee Boiler,** 11¼" tall, 9¾" diameter, light blue & white wavy mottling, white interior, black trim & handle, seamed body, rivetted ears & strap handle, wire bail. Near mint, rare color, **$360.00.**

Note: On all the pieces shown on this page, the pattern varies drastically from one side to the other side of the piece. Also note the different shades of blue.

Row 1:
1. **Measure,** 9⅞" tall, 6½" diameter, lavender blue & white large swirl, white interior, black trim, seamed body. Good plus, rare color, **$395.00.**
2. **Water Carrier,** 12½" tall, 8½" diameter, lavender blue & white large swirl, white interior, black trim, rivetted handle, ears & foot, seamed spout, seamless body. Good plus, extremely rare color, shape & size, **$950.00. Note:** This was used for carrying cold or hot water. When carrying hot water the closed cover helped to keep the water hot.
3. **Coffeepot,** 10½" tall, 7" diameter, lavender blue & white large swirl, white interior, black trim, seamed body. Good plus, rare color, **$295.00.**

Row 2:
1. **Covered Berlin-Style Kettle,** 7¼" tall, 9½" diameter, lavender blue & white medium swirl, white interior, black handles & trim, seamless body, rivetted handles. Good plus, **$210.00.**
2. **Creamer,** 5" tall, 3¾" diameter, lavender blue & white large swirl, white interior, black trim & handle, seamless body. Good plus, extremely rare color, rare shape, **$425.00.**
3. **Cream Can,** 8" tall, 4" diameter, lavender blue & white medium swirl, white interior, black trim, seamless body. Near mint, rare color, **$295.00.**
4. **Funnel,** squatty shape, 5½" tall, 5⅞" diameter, lavender blue & white large swirl, white interior, black trim & handle. Near mint, rare color, **$135.00.**
5. **Mixing Bowl,** 4" deep, 9¾" diameter, lavender blue & white large mottled, white interior, black trim. Good plus, **$55.00.**

Row 3:
1. **Cuspidor,** 4¼" tall, 10⅝" bottom diameter, 2 piece, lavender blue & white large swirl, white interior, with black trim around the bottom edge. Good plus, rare color & shape, **$295.00.**
2. **Pie Plate,** 1" deep, 9⅞" diameter, lavender blue & white large mottled, white interior, black trim. Good plus, **$65.00.**
3. **Flat Hook-Handled Dipper,** 15½" long, 2¼" deep, 4½" diameter, lavender blue & white, white interior, black trim & handle, seamless body, rivetted handle. Near mint, **$115.00.**
4. **Oval Roaster,** 8" tall, 11⅞" wide, 17¼" long not including handles, 2 piece lavender blue & white large swirl inside & out, black trim & handles, perforated attached foot, bottom of the roaster's interior is rounded. The attached perforated foot keeps roaster from coming in direct contact with the heat, thus preventing food from burning & sticking on the bottom of the roaster. Good plus, rare color & shape, **$375.00.**

Row 4:
1. **Oblong Baking Pan,** 2" deep, 8⅜" wide, 13½" long not including handles, lavender blue & white large swirl, white interior, molded handles, eyelet for hanging. Mint, **$120.00.**
2. **Fry Pan,** 2" deep, 9⅞" diameter, lavender blue & white large swirl, white interior, black trim & handle. Good plus, rare color, **$210.00.**
3. **Oblong Baking Pan,** 2" deep, 8¼" wide, 9½" long not including handles, lavender blue & white large swirl, white interior, molded handles, eyelet for hanging. Good plus, **$95.00.**

Note: This color is referred to as lavender blue because the blue has a light lavender cast.

Special Note: I believe all the pieces on this page are "Columbian Ware."

Row 1:

1. **Double Boiler,** 7¼" to top of the cover knob including the insert, 6⅝" diameter, blue & white large swirl with white interior, black trim & handle, seamed body. Near mint, extremely rare color, **$395.00.**

2. **Oblong Baking Pan or Stove Pan,** 1¾" deep, 8¾" wide, 10¼" long not including the molded handles, blue & white large swirl with white interior, black trim & molded handles, eyelet for hanging. Good plus, extremely rare, **$260.00. Note:** These pans were referred to as stove pans or baking pans because they were useful on the stovetop as well as in the oven.

3. **Bowl,** 2¼" deep, 5⅞" diameter, blue & white large swirl, white interior & black trim. Good plus, extremely rare color, **$130.00.**

4. **Cuspidor,** 4⅝" deep, 8⅜" diameter, blue & white large swirl with white interior & black trim, seamed body. Near mint, extremely rare color, rare shape, **$575.00.**

Row 2:

1. **Graduated Dry Measure,** 4⅛" deep, 4½" diameter, blue & white large swirl with white interior, black trim & handle. Good plus, extremely rare color & shape, **$480.00. Note:** There are 4 unmarked rims that are meant to equal a certain size measurement.

2. **Cream Can,** 7¼" tall, 4¼" diameter, blue & white large swirl, white interior, black trim & ears, wooden bail handle, seamed body. Good plus, extremely rare color, rare shape, **$895.00.**

3. **Coffee Biggin,** including pot, tin biggin, spreader, & cover, 8¾" tall, 4¼" diameter, blue & white large swirl with white interior, black trim & handle. Good plus, extremely rare color shape & size, **$1,500.00**

4. **Molasses Pitcher,** 5½" tall, 4¼" diameter, blue & white large swirl with white interior, black trim & weld handle. Good plus, extremely rare color, shape & size, **$1,600.00. Note:** Sometimes molasses pitchers are called syrups by today's collectors. Some old trade catalogues refer to them as molasses pitchers.

Row 3:

1. **Coffeepot,** 8½" tall, 5⅝" diameter, blue & white large swirl with white interior, black trim, knob & handle, seamed body. Good plus, extremely rare color, **$360.00.**

2. **Funnel,** 4½" tall, 3¼" diameter, blue & white large swirl with white interior, black trim & handle, seamed body. Near mint, extremely rare color, rare size, **$200.00**

3. **Cuspidor,** 5" high, 11⅜" diameter. Bottom section is blue & white large swirl with white interior & black trim. Cover is white with black trim. Good plus, extremely rare color, **$395.00.** These are also called hotel cuspidors.

4. **Pudding Pan,** 3¼" deep x 9⅝" diameter, blue & white large swirl with white interior & black trim. Good plus, extremely rare color, **$195.00.**

Row 1:
1. **Coffeepot,** 11" tall, 6½" diameter, blue & white large swirl, white interior, black trim & handle, seamless body. Near mint, extremely rare color, **$395.00.**
2. **Biscuit Sheet,** 11" long, 8½" wide, biscuit size ¹⁄₁₆" deep, 2¼" diameter, blue & white large swirl, white interior, black trim. Holds 12 biscuits. Near mint, extremely rare color, shape & size, **$2,100.00.**
3. **Oval Dinner Bucket with Food Insert,** 7½" tall to top of cover knob including food insert, 6¾" wide, 9" long, blue & white large swirl, white interior, black trim & ears, seamless body. Near mint, extremely rare color, shape & size, **$595.00.**

Row 2:
1. **Teapot,** 8½" tall, 5¾" diameter, blue & white large swirl, white interior, black trim, handle & knob, seamed body. Mint, extremely rare color, **$475.00.**
2. **Covered Bucket With Matching Cover,** 5½" tall, 6" diameter, blue & white large swirl, white interior, black trim, ears & knob, black wooden bail, seamed body. Mint, extremely rare color, **$300.00.**
3. **Coffeepot,** 7½" tall, 4¾" diameter, blue & white large swirl, white interior, black trim, handle & knob. Mint, extremely rare color, **$425.00.**

Row 3:
1. **Milk Can,** 10½" tall, 7¼" diameter, blue & white large swirl, white interior, black trim, wooden bail, seamed body. Good plus, extremely rare color, rare shape, **$785.00.**
2. **Oblong Tray,** ¾" deep, 11⅛" wide, 15⅝" long, blue & white large swirl, white interior, black trim, Good plus, extremely rare color, rare shape, **$415.00.**
3. **Coffee Boiler,** 10½" tall, 9" diameter, blue & white large swirl, white interior, black trim, handle & knob, wooden bail, seamed body. Near mint, extremely rare color, **$415.00.**

Special Note: Even though some of these pieces vary in color & shape, it is believed that when a color formula was applied in a different factory environment other than the original factory, the enameling was affected by materials used from that area as well as weather conditions. The application of the enamels and the type of finish could also be a factory worker's own creation. The shapes also vary because many times pieces were purchased for enameling from other companies. I believe all these pieces pictured are "Columbian Ware."

Row 1:

1. **Milk Can,** 8¾" tall, 5⅛" diameter, blue & white large swirl with white interior, black wooden bail & trim, seamed body. Good plus, extremely rare color, rare shape, **$800.00. Note:** "Lock tin lid" refers to grooves on the tin lid that fit into the indentation on the neck of the milk can to lock it in place.

2. **Muffin Pan,** overall dimensions 1" deep, 11⅜" wide, 14½" long. Each cup measures ⅞" deep x 3¼" diameter, blue & white large swirl, white interior, black trim, seamed body. Good plus, extremely rare color, shape & size, **$1,850.00**

3. **Cuspidor,** 3⅞" tall, 6⅞" diameter, blue & white large swirl, white interior, black trim, seamed body. Good plus, extremely rare color, rare shape, **$495.00.**

4. **Milk Can,** 11½" tall, 6¾" bottom diameter, blue & white large swirl with white interior, black trim, seamed body. Good plus, extremely rare color, rare shape, **$785.00. Note:** This is not the original cover because it does not have the side grooves to lock it into the indentations on the neck of the milk can.

Row 2:

1. **Covered Casserole,** 4¾" tall, 8¾" diameter, blue & white large swirl with white interior, black cover knob, trim, & handles, seamless body. Near mint, extremely rare color & shape, **$485.00. Note:** Hole in cover for ventilation.

2. **Farmer's Mug,** 4½" deep, 4¼" diameter, blue & white large swirl with white interior, black trim & handle, seamless body. Good plus, extremely rare color, **$265.00.**

3. **Plate,** 1" deep, 9" diameter, blue & white large swirl with white interior & black trim. Good plus, extremely rare color, **$155.00.**

Row 3:

1. **Oval Platter,** 1" deep, 10½" wide, 13⅞" long, blue & white large swirl with white interior & black trim. Good plus, extremely rare color & shape, **$375.00.**

2. **Teakettle,** 7½" tall, 9" diameter, blue and white large swirl with white interior, black cover knob, trim, and ears, wooden handle, seamed body. Good plus, extremely rare color & shape, **$575.00.**

Row 4:

1. **Oblong Baking Pan,** 2⅛" deep, 9⅝" wide, 14" long not including the molded handles, blue & white large swirl, white interior & black trim. Good plus, extremely rare color, **$450.00.**

2. **Muffin Pan,** overall dimensions ⅞" deep, 7⅜" wide, 14¼" long. Each cup measures ¾" deep, 3⅜" diameter, blue & white large swirl, white interior & black trim. Good plus, extremely rare color, shape & size, **$1,850.00.**

Row 1:

1. **Water Pitcher,** 9" tall, 4" diameter, blue & white large swirl, white interior, black weld handle & trim, seamless. Good plus, extremely rare color, **$525.00.**
2. **Cup,** 2¾" deep, 3⅞" diameter, blue & white medium swirl, white interior, black trim & handle. Good plus, extremely rare color, **$90.00.**
3. **Oval Tray** 1" deep, 11¼" top width, 14" long blue & white large swirl, white interior, black trim. Good plus, extremely rare color and shape, **$325.00.**
4. **Child's cup,** 2¼" deep, 2⅞" diameter, blue & white large swirl, white interior, black trim & handle. Good plus, extremely rare color and shape, **$175.00.**
5. **Teapot,** 9¾" high, 6⅞" diameter, blue & white large swirl, white interior, black trim & handle, seamed body & spout. Good plus, extremely rare color, **$380.00.**

Row 2:

1. **Preserving Kettle,** flared shape, 6⅛" deep, 8¾" diameter, blue & white large swirl, white interior, black trim & ears, seamless. Good plus, extremely rare color, rare shape, **$485.00. Note:** This has been called a "Small Pail" by today's collectors.
2. **Dipper,** cup shape, 2⅜" deep, 4¼" diameter, blue & white large swirl, white interior, black trim & handle with hook & eyelet for hanging. Near mint, extremely rare color, **$215.00.**
3. **Tea Strainer,** ¾" deep, 4" diameter not including handle, blue white large swirl inside & out, screen bottom. Near mint, extremely rare color, rare shape, **$255.00.**
4. **Hanging Soap Dish,** 3⅝" back height, 4" wide, 6¼" long, blue & white large swirl inside & out. Good plus, extremely rare color, **$245.00.**
5. **Coffeepot,** 9¼" tall, 6¼" diameter, blue & white large swirl, white interior, black trim & handle, seamed body. Good plus, extremely rare color, **$340.00.**

Row 3:

1. **Milk Can,** 11" tall, 6⅜" diameter, blue & white large swirl, white interior, black ears & trim, seamless body, wire bail, matching cover. Good plus, extremely rare color, rare shape, **$825.00.**
2. **Berlin-Style Kettle** with matching cover, 11¼" tall, 14¼" diameter, blue & white large swirl, white interior, black handles & trim, seamless body. Good plus, extremely rare color, rare size, **$425.00.**
3. **Water Pail,** 8⅜" deep, 10" diameter, blue & white large swirl, white interior, black trim & ears, wooden bail, seamless body. Mint, extremely rare color, **$225.00.**

Special Note: I believe all these pieces are Columbian Ware because they all seem to have similar characteristics, such as the depth of color, swirls & trim plus the construction of the pieces including, cover, knobs, handles & ears.

Row 1:

1. **Handled Strainer,** 2½" deep, 6⅝" diameter, light blue & white large mottled with white interior, rivetted handles, fancy perforated bottom & sides. Handle has eyelet for hanging & kettle hook. Good plus, rare color & shape, **$315.00.**

Row 2:

1. **Teapot,** 5½" tall, 3½" diameter, blue & white large swirl with white interior, black weld handle & trim, seamed body. "Columbian Ware" Columbian Enameling & Stamping Company. Good plus, extremely rare color, shape & size, **$985.00.**

2. **Triangular Sink Strainer,** 2½" high, 7¾" wide, 9¾" long, blue & white medium swirl with white interior, perforated bottom & fancy perforated sides. Good plus, extremely rare color & shape, **$360.00. Note:** The bottom of the strainer has 3 attached ring feet.

3. **Covered Bucket,** 5¼" tall, 4¾" diameter, light blue & white large swirl with white interior, black trim & ears, wire bail. Good plus, **$195.00.**

Row 3:

1. **Pitcher & Bowl,** 11¼" tall, 6¼" diameter, blue & white large mottled with white interior, black trim & handle. Bowl measures 3½" deep, 13¾" diameter, blue & white large mottled with white interior, black trim, eyelet for hanging. Both, near mint, rare shape, 2 pieces, **$850.00.**

2. **Soup Ladle,** 1½" deep, 3⅞" diameter, light blue & white large mottled with white interior, black rivetted handle & trim. Near mint, rare shape, **$65.00.**

3. **Water Pitcher,** 11½" tall, 8" diameter, blue & white large swirl with white interior, black weld handle & trim. "Columbian Ware" Columbian Enameling & Stamping Co. Mint, extremely rare color, shape & size, **$1,350.00**

Row 4:

1. **Stew Pan,** 3⅛" deep, 10⅛" diameter, blue & white medium swirl with white interior, black rivetted handles & trim. Near mint, extremely rare color, rare size, **$210.00.**

2. **Stew Pan,** 2½" deep, 7¾" diameter, light blue & white dapple-type mottling with black rivetted handle & trim. Good plus, extremely rare color, **$180.00.**

3. **Windsor Dipper,** 3⅝" deep, 6½" diameter, blue & white large mottled with white interior, black tubular handle & trim. Good plus, **$120.00.**

Row 1:
1. **Rice or Farina Boiler,** 6½" to top of the cover knob including the insert, 6" diameter. Insert, 4½" to top of the cover knob, 6⅜" diameter not including the ears, blue & white large swirl, white interior, black trim, ears & handle, seamless body. Near mint, extremely rare shape, **$485.00.**
2. **Pump or Bellboy Pitcher,** 8¼" tall, 6" diameter, blue & white large spatter that has a splash effect, white interior, black trim, bottom tipping handle & wooden bail, seamless body. Mint, extremely rare color, shape & size, **$895.00. Note:** This type of pitcher gets its name because it was used by bellboys in hotels. It was also used in homes with the kitchen pump.
3. **Teapot,** 8¼" tall, 5⅞" diameter, blue & white large spatter splash effect, white interior, black trim & handle, seamed top section. Good plus, extremely rare shape & size, **$595.00. Note:** This straight-sided teapot is very unusual in shape & hard to find.

Row 2:
1. **Measure,** 8⅞" tall, 5¼" diameter, blue & white, large swirl, white interior, blue trim, seamed body. Good plus, rare color, **$295.00.**
2. **Covered Berlin-Style Kettle,** 9¾" tall, 12" diameter, blue & white large swirl, white interior, black trim & riv-etted ears, wire bail, seamless body. Good plus, **$210.00.**
3. **Pie Plate,** 1¼" deep, 10¾" diameter, blue & white large swirl, white interior, black trim. Good plus, **$95.00.**

Row 3:
1. **Butter Churn,** Floor Model, Dasher Type with Storage Cover, 19" tall, 10⅜" diameter, blue & white large swirl, white interior, black trim & handles, seamed body. Near mint, extremely rare color, shape & size, **$2,500.00. Note:** This type of churn also has a handled wooden dasher & a wooden cover that has a hole in the center for the dasher handle to fit through. I chose to show this one with the matching storage cover because the one pictured in Book 1 shows one with the wooden cover & dasher. Most people don't real-ize that the churn could come with a storage cover.
2. **Chamber Pail,** 12" tall, 10½" diameter, blue & white large swirl, white interior, black trim & wooden bail, seamless body. Near mint, **$210.00. Note:** The outer edge of the cover is designed to fit down into the chamber pail's top edge to prevent the cover from slipping off while carrying, and make it airtight.

Row 1:

1. **Pitcher & Bowl,** Pitcher, 7½" tall, 5¼" diameter, blue & white large mottled, black trim & handle, white interior. Near mint, rare shape. Bowl, 2¾" deep, 10⅜" diameter, blue & white large mottled, white interior, black trim. Mint, rare shape, 2 pieces, **$795.00.**

2. **Fry Pan,** 1⅞" deep, 10¼" diameter, blue & white large mottled, white interior. Good plus, **$175.00.**

3. **Mug,** 2⅞" deep, 3⅜" diameter, blue & white large mottled, white interior, black trim & handle. Near mint, **$65.00.**

4. **Milk Can,** 10¾" tall, 5" diameter, blue & white large mottled, white interior, black trim & wooden bail, seamless body. Near mint, **$495.00.**

Row 2:

1. **Hanging Soap Dish,** 2⅜" back height, 3¾" wide, 5¼" long, blue & white large mottled outside, white interior. Mint, rare color, **$225.00.**

2. **Covered Berlin-Style Kettle or Handled Bean Pot,** 4¾" high, 6⅛" diameter at the widest point not including handle, blue & white medium swirl, white interior, black handles & trim, seamless body. Mint, rare shape & size, **$240.00.**

3. **Coffee Biggin,** 9¾" high to top of the cover knob including the biggin, 5⅛" diameter, blue & white large swirl, white interior, blue trim, seamed body. Near mint, extremely rare color & shape, **$495.00. Note:** The Coffee Biggin consists of four pieces: cover, biggin, spreader, coffeepot.

4. **Coffeepot,** 9½" tall, 6½" diameter, blue & white large swirl, white interior, black trim, seamed body. Mint, **$165.00.**

5. **Lipped Preserve Kettle,** 3¼" deep, 7" diameter, blue & white large swirl, white interior, black trim, handles & wooden bail, seamless body. Mint, **$155.00.**

Row 3:

1. **Teakettle,** 8" high, 7¼" diameter, blue & white large swirl, white interior, black trim & ears, wooden bail, seamed body. Good plus, rare color & size, **$295.00.**

2. **Teakettle,** 7½" high, 9" diameter, blue & white large swirl, white interior, black trim & ears, wooden bail, seamed body. Good plus, rare color, **$295.00.**

3. **Teakettle,** 7" tall, 8" diameter, blue & white large swirl, white interior, black trim ears & wooden bail. Near mint, rare color, **$325.00.**

Row 1:

1. **Covered Convex Kettle or Saucepan,** 7½" tall, 10¼" diameter, blue & white large mottled, white interior, black trim & handles, seamless body, rivetted handles. Near mint, **$265.00.**
2. **Camp or Mush Mug,** 4⅜" deep, 6" diameter, blue & white wavy mottling, white interior, black trim & handle, seamless body. Mint, rare color, shape & size, **$175.00. Note:** On the bottom of the mug is a raised center, 3¾" in diameter.
3. **Oblong Pudding or Vegetable Dish,** 2¾" deep, 9¾" wide, 13¼" long, blue & white large mottled, white interior. Near mint, rare color, shape & size, **$235.00.**
4. **Covered Steamer Insert,** 6" tall, 7⅜" diameter, 6⅞" diameter, blue & white large mottled, black trim & handles. Bottom of the steamer is perforated. Near mint, rare shape, **$195.00. Note:** I believe this is meant to fit into the top of another pan for steaming foods.
5. **Cream Can,** with matching granite cover, 7½" tall, 4¼" diameter, blue & white large mottled, white interior, black trim & wire ears, wire bail, seamless body. Good plus, **$525.00.**

Row 2:

1. **Convex Sauce Pan,** 5¼" deep, 10" diameter, blue & white large mottled, white interior, black trim & rolled flat handle. Good plus, **$165.00.**
2. **Mixing or Serving Bowl,** 3¾" deep, 10" diameter, blue & white large mottled, white interior, black trim. Near mint, **$115.00.**
3. **Coffee Boiler,** 10½" tall, 9⅝" diameter, blue & white large mottled, white interior, black trim, wire ears & handle, black wooden bail, seamed body. Mint, **$285.00.**

Row 3:

1. **Oblong Baking Pan,** 2½" deep, 11" wide, 15¾" long, blue & white large mottled, white interior, black trim & handles. Imprinted heart-shaped bottom. Near mint, rare shape, **$275.00.**
2. **Handled Skimmer,** 13¾" long, including 4⅝" skimmer diameter, blue & white medium mottled, black handle. Near mint, rare color, **$185.00.**
3. **Spoon,** 13" long, including handle, 2⅜" spoon diameter at the widest point, blue & white large mottled, white interior, black handle. Good plus, extremely rare shape, **$110.00.**
4. **Round Miner's Dinner Bucket,** 10" high to top of the cover handle, 7¾" diameter, blue & white large swirl, white interior, black trim, ears & wooden bail. Good plus, extremely rare color & shape, **$535.00. Note:** The dinner bucket consists of three pieces — cover, insert, and bottom section.

Row 1:

1. **Teapot,** 8" tall, 4¾" diameter, blue & white large mottled, white interior, black trim & handle. Near mint, **$265.00.**

2. **Flat-Handled Dipper,** dipper size 2¼" deep, 5" diameter, blue & white large mottled, white interior, black trim & handle. Good plus, **$75.00.**

3. **Fry pan,** 2¼" deep, 11¼" diameter, blue & white large mottled, white interior, black rolled handle with eyelet for hanging. Near mint, **$235.00. Note:** The edges of the handle have been rolled over to give the handle more strength. The metal used in this fry pan is heavy steel.

4. **Mug,** 2⅞" deep, 3½" diameter, blue & white large mottled, white interior, black trim & handle. **$65.00.**

5. **Straight-Style Spaghetti or Potato Kettle,** 6¾" high, 9¼" diameter not including the spout blue & white large swirl, white interior, blue trim, back-tipping handle, wooden bail, seamless body. Good plus, rare shape, rare color, **$325.00. Note:** The bail handle is designed to hold cover secure when handle is raised for draining.

Row 2:

1. **Cuspidor,** 4⅛" tall, 7¾" diameter, blue & white medium swirl, white interior, black trim, seamed body. Good plus, **$265.00.**

2. **Teakettle,** 7½" tall, 7¼" bottom diameter, blue & white medium swirl, white interior, black trim & ears, wooden bail, seamless body. Good plus, rare color & size, **$310.00.**

3. **Covered Berlin-Style Kettle or Handled Bean Pot,** 5½" tall, 6¼" diameter, blue & white large swirl, white interior, black handles & trim. Mint, rare shape & size, **$240.00**

Row 3:

1. **Coffee Boiler,** 11¾" tall, 9¾" diameter, blue & white medium swirl, white interior, black trim, seamed body. Mint, **$285.00.**

2. **Cup,** 1¾" deep, 4¼" diameter, blue & white medium swirl, white interior, black trim. Near mint, **$110.00.**

3. **Tea Steeper,** 4½" tall, 4½" diameter, blue & white medium swirl, white interior, black trim. Mint, **$235.00.**

4. **Convex Water or Milk Pitcher,** squatty shape, 6⅛" tall, 5¼" diameter, blue & white large swirl, white interior, seamless body. Mint, extremely rare shape & size, **$365.00.**

5. **Muffin Pan,** twelve cup, overall measurements 1" deep, 14¾" long, 10¾" wide; each cup measures ⅞" deep, 3⅛" top diameter, blue & white large mottled, gray interior, eyelet for hanging. Good plus, extremely rare color, shape & size, **$1,450.00**

Row 4:

1. **Wash Bowl or Basin,** 3⅝" deep, 13¾" diameter, blue & white large swirl, white interior, black trim, eyelet for hanging. Near mint, **$125.00. Note:** This bowl is meant to go with a wash set that includes several pieces.

Row 1:
1. **Wash Basin,** 2⅝" deep, 10¼" top diameter, blue & white large spatter with white interior & black trim with eyelet for hanging. Good plus, **$125.00.**

Row 2:
1. **Teapot,** squatty shape, 5" tall, 4⅝" diameter, blue & white medium mottled with white interior, black trim, seamless body, seamed spout, & rivetted handle. Near mint, rare color, shape, & size, **$265.00.**
2. **Bread pan with seamed ends,** 3" deep, 6" wide, 11½" long, light blue & white large mottled with white interior & black trim. Good plus, rare color, **$295.00. Note:** Each end of the bread pan has been seamed onto the pan.
3. **Cream Can,** 7" tall, 4⅜" diameter, blue & white fine mottled with white interior & cobalt blue trim, & black wooden bail handle. Near mint, **$185.00. Note:** The body of this cream can is put together with seams in five different places. Seamed bottom, middle, lower section of neck, & upper section of neck.

Row 3:
1. **Measuring Cup** with graduated ¼ cup measurements, blue & white medium mottled with white interior. Rivetted handle, seamed body & bottom. Good plus, rare color, **$145.00.**

Row 4:
1. **Rice or Farina Boiler,** 6¼" to top of the ring handle, including insert, 5⅞" diameter, blue & white large swirl with white interior & black trim, ears, & handle, seamless body. Good plus, extremely rare shape, **$395.00. Note:** there is another rice or farina boiler in this section on page 77 Row 1 that shows different shaped ears on the insert, as well as a different pattern of swirl.
2. **Measure,** 3⅜" to top of the rivetted lip, 3⅛" diameter, blue & white medium mottled with white interior, black trim & rivetted handle, seamed body. Good plus, rare shape, **$195.00.**
3. **Covered Bucket,** 4⅞" tall, 5" diameter, blue & white large wavy mottling with white interior, black trim & ears, wire bail, seamless body. Good plus, rare color & size, **$265.00.**

Row 5:
1. **Footed Bread Raiser,** 9" tall, 14⅜" diameter, blue & white large mottled with white interior, blue rivetted handles & trim, rivetted foot. Good plus, rare color, shape & size, **$495.00.**
2. **Coffee Boiler,** 12" tall, 9⅝" diameter, blue & white large mottled with white interior, black trim, handle, & wooden bail, seamed body. Near mint, **$265.00.**

Row 1:
1. **Milk Can,** 11" tall, 6½" diameter, blue & white large swirl with white interior, black trim, seamed body & black wooden bail handle. Good plus, **$525.00.**
2. **Cup,** 2" deep, 4¼" diameter, blue & white large mottled with white interior, black trim & handle. Mint, **$110.00.**
3. **Oval Dish Pan,** 5" deep, 12¾" wide. 16⅞" top length not including the handles, blue & white large mottled with white interior, dark blue trim & handles. Near mint, **$270.00.**
4. **Cup,** 1⅞" deep, 4⅜" diameter, blue & white large swirl with white interior, rivetted ring handle. Good plus, **$75.00.**
5. **Water Pitcher,** 9¾" tall, 6⅜" diameter, blue & white large swirl with white interior, black trim & handle, seamless body. Good plus, **$265.00.**

Row 2:
1. **Covered Bucket,** 5¾" to top of the cover knob, 5⅞" diameter, blue & white large swirl with white interior, black trim & ears. Wire bail handle & rivetted ears. Near mint, **$225.00.**
2. **Double Boiler,** matching granite cover. 7½" to top of the cover knob including the insert, 6⅛" bottom diameter. Blue & white large swirl with white interior & black trim. Seamless body. Near mint, **$295.00.**
3. **Muffin Pan,** 6 cup, each cup 1" deep, 3⅛" top diameter, overall measures 1¼" deep, 7⅜" wide, 10¾" long. Blue & white large swirl, white interior, with eyelet for hanging. Near mint, **$1,500.00.**

Row 3:
1. **Round Handled Dishpan,** 5⅛" deep, 17¾" diameter not including the handles, blue & white large mottled with white interior, medium blue rivetted handles & trim. Good plus, **$135.00.**
2. **Water Pail,** 8⅞" deep, 11¼" diameter, blue & white large mottled with white interior, black trim, ears, & wooden handle. Near mint, **$195.00.**

Row 1:

1. **Teapot,** 9" tall, 5½" diameter, blue & white large splash-type mottling, white interior, black trim & handle. Near mint, **$265.00. Note:** The large mottling with a splash effect is on a number of the pieces on this page. This type mottling is referred to by collectors as "Splash-Type Mottling."

2. **Cup & Saucer,** cup 2⅝" deep, 4" diameter; saucer, ⅞" deep, 6" diameter. Cup & saucer are blue & white large splash-type mottling, white interior, black trim. Good plus, 2 pieces. **$135.00.**

3. **Coffeepot,** 10½" tall, 6½" diameter, blue & white large splash-type mottling, white interior, black trim & handle. Good plus, **$210.00.**

4. **Bowl,** 2¼" deep, 5¼" diameter, blue & white large splash-type mottling, white interior, black trim, Mint, **$60.00.**

5. **Convex Water Pitcher,** squatty shape, 8⅜" to top of lip, 6" diameter, blue & white large splash-type mottling, white interior, black trim, seamless. Near mint, **$395.00. Note:** this is a good example of the splash effect in large mottling. It looks like the enamel was just thrown at the piece, giving it the splash effect.

Row 2:

1. **Deep Stew Pan,** 2" deep, 9" diameter, blue & white large splash-type mottling, white interior, black handle & trim, rivetted handle. Near mint, rare color, **$195.00. Note:** Most stew pans do not have a pouring lip. They are straight-sided with a rolled rim. Some are shallow, others are deep.

2. **Shallow Stew Pan,** 1⅝" deep, 6⅝" diameter, blue & white large splash-type mottling, white interior, black trim & handle. Good plus, rare color, **$195.00.**

3. **Fry Pan,** 1⅝" deep, 9¼" diameter, blue & white large splash-type mottling, white interior, black trim & handle. Good plus, rare color, **$175.00. Note:** The pouring lip on the left side of the fry pan. Also, note how the side of the fry pan is flared.

Row 3:

1. **Pudding Pan,** 1⅞" deep, 5¾" top diameter, blue & white large mottled, white interior, black trim, Mint, **$60.00.**

2. **Colander,** footed, 3½" deep, 9½" top diameter not including handles, blue & white large splash-type mottling, white interior, black trim & handles. Good plus, rare color, **$265.00.**

3. **Tea Strainer,** ¾" deep, 4" diameter not including the handle, blue & white large splash-type mottling inside & out, screen bottom. Near mint, rare color & shape, **$220.00.**

Row 4:

1. **Coffeepot,** 7½" high to top of the cover knob, 4¾" bottom diameter, blue & white wavy mottling, white interior, black trim, seamed body. Good plus, rare size, **$295.00.**

2. **Covered Bucket,** with matching granite cover, 6½" high to top of cover knob, 6" diameter, blue & white large splash-type mottling, white interior, black trim & ears, seamed body. Near mint. **$225.00.**

3. **Coffeepot,** 7½" to top of cover knob, 4⅝" bottom diameter, blue & white large splash-type mottling, white interior, black trim, weld handle, seamed body. Near mint, rare size, **$320.00.**

Row 5:

1. **Handled Dishpan,** 5" deep, 14½" top diameter not including handles, blue & white large splash-type mottling, white interior, black rivetted handles & trim. Good plus, **$145.00.**

Row 1:

1. **Muffin Pan,** 9 cup, overall measurements 1" deep, 10¾" square. Each cup measures ⅞" deep, 3" top diameter. Light blue & white large mottled inside & out, eyelet for hanging. Near mint, extremely rare color, shape & size, **$1,600.00.**

2. **Mug,** Camp or Mush, 5⅝" deep, 6⅞" top diameter, blue & white medium mottled, white interior, black weld handle & trim. Good plus, rare color & shape, **$165.00.**

3. **Candlestick or Chamberstick,** 1¾" high, 5⅝" diameter, lavender blue & white large swirl with white underside, round finger ring for carrying. Good plus, extremely rare color, **$535.00.**

4. **Sugar Bowl,** 6¼" tall, 4¾" diameter, light blue & white swirl with white interior, black trim, rivetted handles, seamed body. Good plus, extremely rare shape, **$795.00. Note:** Even though this piece resembles a sugar bowl, both handles have been applied to the same side of the piece. Just what the intended use for this piece was is a mystery to me. It would be interesting to hear from you out there what your opinion is on this piece & its intended use.

Row 2:

1. **Funnel,** squatty shaped, 5¾" to top of the spout, 5¼" top diameter, blue & white large swirl with white interior, black trim & handle. Seamed spout. Good plus, **$165.00.**

2. **Covered Bucket,** with matching granite cover. 5½" tall, 6⅛" diameter, blue & white large mottled with white interior, black trim & ears, wooden bail, seamless body. Good plus, rare color & shape, **$200.00.**

3. **2 handled Egg Plate or Pan,** 1" deep, 6¼" diameter, blue & white large mottled with white interior, black trim & handles. Good plus, **$245.00.**

Row 3:

1. **Covered Berlin-Style Sauce Pan,** with matching granite cover. 8" tall, 10¼" diameter, blue & white large swirl with white interior, dark blue trim, & tubular handle. Good plus, rare shape, **$175.00.**

2. **Milk Pan,** 3¼" deep, 9" diameter, blue & white medium mottled with white interior. Good plus, rare shape, **$155.00. Note:** The sides of this milk pan are slanted in comparison to a pudding pan. Also notice the side pouring lip.

3. **Coffee Biggin,** includes the pot, biggin, spreader & cover, 10¾" to top of the cover knob including biggin. 5¼" diameter, blue & white large mottled with white interior & black trim. Near mint, rare color & shape, **$495.00.**

Row 4:

1. **Thumb Scoop,** 6¼" long, 2⅞" wide, blue & white inside & out with traces of light gray throughout the white, rivetted handle. Near mint, extremely rare color, shape & size, **$675.00.**

2. **Grater,** 13⅜" long, 4⅞" wide, blue & white medium mottled, rivetted handle & feet. Near mint, rare color & shape, **$400.00.**

3. **Grocer's Scoop,** 10" long, 4⅝" wide, blue & white large mottled. Semi-covered top seamed to bottom part of the scoop. Tubular, closed end seamed handle applied to bottom section of the scoop; handle has eyelet for hanging. Near mint, extremely rare color, shape & size, **$895.00.**

Row 1:

1. **Measure,** 9⅝" tall, 6⅝" diameter, light blue & white, medium swirl, white interior, black trim, rivetted spout & handle. Mint, rare color, **$285.00. Note:** Collectors refer to this color as powder blue & white.
2. **Soup Ladle,** 13⅜" long, 3⅝" diameter, blue & white medium swirl, white interior, black trim & handle. Mint, **$75.00.**
3. **Tube cake mold,** 8 sided, 3½" deep, 8" diameter, light blue & white large swirl, white interior, black trim, Good plus, rare color & shape, **$285.00.**
4. **Milk Can,** with matching granite cover, 11¼" tall, 5¾" diameter, light blue & white large swirl, white interior, light blue trim, seamless body, wooden bail. Near mint, rare color & size, **$525.00.**

Row 2:

1. **Bread Pan,** 3" deep, 6" wide, 11½" long, light blue & white large mottled, white interior, black trim, seamed ends. Good plus, rare color, **$395.00.**
2. **Coffee pot,** 8½" tall, 4⅝" diameter, light blue & white large swirl, white interior, black trim. Good plus, **$165.00.**
3. **Bread Pan,** 3" deep, 4½" wide, 9¾" long, light blue & white large mottled, white interior, black trim, seamed ends. Good plus, rare color, **$395.00.**

Row 3:

1. **Candlestick or Chamberstick,** scalloped style, 1⅞" tall, 6" diameter not including the handle, light blue & white large swirl, with finger ring & thumb rest. Good plus, rare shape, **$595.00.**
2. **Lipped Sauce Pan,** 3" deep, 7" diameter, light blue & white medium mottled, white interior, black trim & handle. Good plus, **$65.00.**
3. **Round Roaster,** 2-piece, 5¾" tall, 11¾" diameter not including handles, light blue & white large swirl, white interior, black trim & handles. Mint, rare color, **$195.00. Note:** This is referred to as a self-basting roaster. The steam forms drops of moisture on the indentations on the cover & they drop back onto the food being cooked. The bottom section of the roaster has grooves where liquids can accumulate, thus preventing foods from sticking or burning.
4. **Covered Berlin-Style Kettle or 2-handled bean pot,** 7¼" tall, 9", light blue & white large mottled, white interior, black-trim & handles, seamless body, rivetted handles. Near mint, **$195.00.**

Note: The pieces on this page are all classified in the light blue & white category even though the shades of blue vary slightly.

Row 1:

1. **Round Miner's Dinner Bucket,** 7¼" tall, 6⅜" diameter, blue & white medium mottled, light gray interior with fine blue flecks, wooden bail. Food tray insert is missing. Good plus, rare shape, **$265.00. Note:** The tops of the ears slant down so they do not interfere with the food tray insert when it's placed into the top.

2. **Double Boiler,** 8½" high to top of the cover knob including insert, 7" diameter, blue & white large mottled, light gray interior with fine blue flecks, black trim & handles, rivetted handles, seamless body. Good plus, **$265.00.**

3. **Teapot,** 8⅜" tall, 5⅜" diameter, blue & white medium mottled, light gray with fine blue flecks, rivetted handle, seamed body. Good plus, **$235.00.**

Row 2:

1. **Teapot,** squatty shape, 5¼" tall, 4¾" diameter, blue & white medium swirl, white interior, black trim & handle, rivetted handle, seamless body. Near mint, rare shape & size, **$265.00.**

2. **Bread Plate,** ¾" deep, 6¼" diameter, blue & white large mottled, gray interior, black trim. Good plus, rare size, **$95.00.**

3. **Oil Stove Teakettle,** 4¾" tall, 8¾" diameter, blue & white large mottled, white interior, seamed body, wooden bail. Good plus, extremely rare color, rare shape, **$325.00. Note:** This style teakettle with the flared bottom was designed for the oil stove to help conserve fuel & prevent the flames from blackening the teakettle sides.

4. **Dessert Plate,** ⅞" deep, 7" diameter, blue & white large mottled inside & out, black trim. Good plus, **$75.00.**

5. **Lipped Sauce Pan,** 2⅝" deep, 5¾" diameter, blue & white large mottled, bluish gray interior, fine blue flecks, rivetted handle. Good plus, **$75.00.**

Row 3:

1. **Chamber Pot,** 5⅛" deep, 8" diameter, blue & white large mottled, blue trim & handle, white interior, seamless. Good plus, **$135.00.**

2. **Slop Bucket,** 9½" tall, 10¼" diameter, blue & white medium mottled, white interior, dark blue trim, black wooden bail. Near mint, rare shape, **$195.00. Note:** The rim of the bucket has a recessed edge that the cover fits down into to prevent the cover from slipping off the bucket.

3. **Oblong Bed Pan,** 2⅛" deep, 10¾" wide, 15⅞" long, blue & white large mottled inside & out, black trim. Good plus, rare color, **$115.00. Note:** The bottom of the bed pan has six molded round indentations that protrude to form round feet.

Row 1:
1. **Coffeepot,** 9½" tall, 6½" diameter, grayish blue & white large mottled inside & out with black trim & handle, seamed body. Good plus, **$165.00. Note:** The pieces on this page have a light gray cast, giving the colors a subdued look. I believe the pieces pictured are "Scotch Granite" from the U.S. Stamping Co., Moundsville, West Virginia.
2. **Fry Pan,** 1⅞" deep, 9⅞" top diameter, grayish blue & white large mottled inside & out with black handle & trim. Good plus, **$140.00.**
3. **Oblong Pudding or Vegetable Dish,** 2" deep, 7" wide, 9⅜" long, grayish blue & white large mottled inside & out with black trim. Good plus, **$120.00.**
4. **Fry Pan,** 1½" deep, 8⅞" diameter, grayish blue & white large mottled inside & out with black handle & trim. Good plus, **$140.00. Note:** I chose to show these 2 fry pans so you could see the mottling on the outside as well as the mottling on the inside, and to illustrate some of the different sizes the fry pans were made in.

Row 2:
1. **Covered Bucket,** with matching granite lid, 7" tall, 6¾" diameter, grayish blue & white large mottled inside & out, seamless body with wooden bail handle, black trim & ears. Near mint, **$175.00.**
2. **Berlin-Style Sauce Pan,** with matching granite lid, 6¼" tall, 8" diameter, grayish blue & white large mottled inside & out, seamless body, black tubular handle & trim. Good plus, **$165.00.**
3. **Cream Can,** with matching granite cover, 7½" tall, 4" diameter, grayish blue & white medium swirl inside & out with black trim & ears, wooden bail, seamless body. Good plus, **$265.00.**

Row 3:
1. **Funnel,** squatty shape, 3¾" high to the top of the spout, 4" diameter, grayish blue & white large mottled inside & out with black handle & trim. Near mint, **$165.00.**
2. **Flared Dipper,** 3⅛" deep, 5½" diameter, grayish blue & white large mottled inside & out. Mint, rare color & shape, **$125.00. Note:** This dipper does not have the black trim like the other pieces on this page, but the coloring & the mottling are very similar. This piece could be questionable whether it is "Scotch Granite" or not. This is what makes it interesting when you group together what you believe is the same color combination & possibly the same manufacturer.
3. **Funnel,** squatty shape, 5" tall, 6" diameter, grayish blue & white large mottled inside & out with black handles & trim. Good, **$140.00. Note:** The U.S. Stamping Co., Moundsville, WV advertised that "Scotch Granite" was "Acid Proof" & as far as claims went acids from fruits & such were known to affect the finest of Granite Ware.

Row 1:
1. **Covered Butter Dish,** 3½" tall, 7⅛" diameter, blue & white medium mottled, white interior. Near mint, extremely rare color, shape & size, **$500.00.**
2. **Syrup,** 7¾" tall, 4" diameter, blue & white large mottled with white interior, black rivetted handle, seamless, body. Near mint, Rare color & shape, **$595.00.**
3. **Covered Sugar Bowl,** squatty-shaped, 5" tall, 4¼" diameter, blue & white medium mottled inside & out, black trim & rivetted handles, seamless body. Near mint, extremely rare shape, rare color, **$550.00.**

Row 2:
1. **Measure,** 4¾" tall to top of the rivetted lip. 3⅝" diameter, blue & white large swirl with white interior, black trim & rivetted, strap handle, seamed body. "Columbian Ware." Near mint, extremely rare color, rare shape & size, **$725.00.**
2. **Cream Can,** 7¼" tall, 4¼" diameter, blue & white large mottled with white interior, light blue trim, seamed body with rivetted neck & ears, wooden bail. Good plus, **$475.00.**
3. **Measure,** 2⅞" tall, 2¼" diameter, blue & white fine mottled with white interior, light blue trim, seamed body, rivetted strap handle. Good plus, rare color, **$185.00.**
4. **Covered Bucket,** 5½" tall, 4¾" diameter, blue & white large mottled with white interior, black trim & ears, seamless body, wooden bail handle. Good plus **$215.00.**
5. **Cup,** 2" deep, 4" diameter, blue & white large swirl with white interior, black trim & rivetted strap handle. "Columbian Ware." Near mint, extremely rare color, **$105.00.**

Row 3:
1. **Slop Bucket,** with matching granite cover, 12¼" tall, 10" diameter, dark blue & white "up & down" unusual type swirl, dark blue trim, ears & interior, wooden bail. Labeled with 3 labels: "Samaritaine Paris," "CF 35 27/3", "Societe Francaise Des Fers Emailles Email Garanti Choix." Near mint, rare color, **$295.00.**
2. **Body Pitcher,** 13⅜" tall, 8" diameter, dark blue & white "up & down" unusual type swirl, dark blue interior, seamed body. Both pieces on this row are from the same maker. Near mint, rare color & shape, **$350.00.**

Row 1:

1. **Oblong Pudding Pan or Vegetable Dish,** 1⅞" deep, 7½" wide top, 10½" top length, blue & white medium mottled, interior light gray with fine blue flecks, black trim. Good plus, **$115.00.**
2. **Milk Can,** 9½" tall, 4¼" diameter, blue & white medium mottled, interior light gray with fine blue flecks, light blue trim, seamed body, rivetted ears, wire bail. Good plus, **$335.00.**
3. **Dog's Dish,** 3" deep, 8½" diameter including flared bottom rim, blue & white medium mottled. Good, rare shape, **$155.00.**

Row 2:

1. **Candlestick,** 2⅜" tall, 4¾" diameter, light blue & white large swirl, dark blue trim, finger ring with flat thumb rest. Near mint, extremely rare color, **$525.00.**
2. **Saucer,** 1" deep, 4¾" diameter, light blue & white medium mottled, white interior. Good plus, rare size, **$55.00. Note:** This could be a child's saucer.
3. **Sugar Bowl,** 4½" tall, 5¼" diameter, blue & white large mottled, with white interior, cover interior is also mottled. Good plus, rare shape, **$435.00. Note:** Often, the covers are mottled or swirled on the inside, whereas the body of the piece is white inside.
4. **Cup,** 2" deep, 3⅜" diameter, blue & white large mottled, white interior, dark blue trim. Good plus, **$55.00.**
5. **Hanging Soap Dish,** 3" back height, 4¼" wide, 6½" long, blue & white medium mottled. Good plus, **$145.00.**

Row 3:

1. **Plate,** 1" deep, 9¾" top diameter, light blue & white large mottled, white interior. Good Plus, **$65.00.**
2. **Spoon,** 13" long, bowl of spoon 2½" wide, blue & white large mottled, white interior, black handle. Good plus, **$55.00.**
3. **Teapot,** 10" tall, 6¾" diameter, light blue & white medium mottled, white interior, weld handle. Good plus, **$325.00.**
4. **Covered Bucket,** 4¾" tall, 4⅞" diameter, blue & white large mottled, white interior, blue trim. Good plus, **$165.00.**

Row 1:

1. **Coffeepot,** 6¾" tall, 4½" diameter, light blue & white medium swirl, white interior, black trim & handle. Good plus, **$160.00.**

2. **Tea Strainer,** 1" deep, 3¾" diameter not including the handle, blue & white medium mottled inside & out, screen bottom. Good plus, rare color & shape, **$185.00.**

3. **Percolator or Teapot with Aluminum Coffee Basket,** 9¼" tall, 5½" diameter, blue & white fine mottled, white interior, black trim, nickel-plated copper cover with glass insert, seamless body. Base of percolator is corrugated. Manufactured by Lisk Manufacturing Co., Ltd., Canandaigua, NY. Mint, rare shape, **$350.00.**

4. **Fruit Jar Filler,** 5⅛" diameter, 3" tall, blue & white medium mottled, light gray interior with fine blue flecks, black trim & handle. Good plus, rare color, **$140.00.**

5. **Measure,** 7⅜" tall, 4" diameter, blue & white medium mottled, white interior, black trim & rivetted handle, seamless body. Good, **$155.00.**

Row 2:

1. **Coffeepot,** 5½" tall, 3½" diameter, light blue & white medium mottled, white interior, cobalt blue trim, metal thumb rest, seamed body, rivetted handle. Near mint, rare color, shape & size, **$365.00.**

2. **Teapot,** 5½" tall, 3½" diameter, light blue & white medium mottled, white interior, cobalt blue trim. Good plus, rare color, shape & size, **$295.00. Note:** This pot & No. 1 on this row hold exactly 1½ cups to the top of the rim.

3. **Turk's Head Turban Mold,** 3⅞" to top of the tin cover, 8⅝" top diameter, light blue & white large mottled inside & out. Good plus, extremely rare shape, **$455.00. Note:** This is the only one of these I have seen with this type of top edge made to fit a cover.

4. **Tumbler,** 2¾" deep, 2¾" diameter, blue & white fine mottled inside & out, black trim. Near mint, rare shape & size, **$115.00. Note:** This could be a child's tumbler or a juice tumbler.

5. **Dessert Plate,** ½" deep, 6⅝" diameter, light blue & white large swirl inside & out. Good, **$40.00.**

row 3:

1. **Teakettle,** 8¼" tall, 10¼" diameter, light blue & white large mottled, white interior, seamed body, wooden bail. Good plus, **$170.00.**

2. **Soup Ladle,** 14⅞" long, bowl 1¾" deep, 4⅜" diameter, light blue & white large mottled, white interior. Good plus, **$60.00.**

3. **Covered Bucket,** with matching granite lid, 5½" tall, 6" diameter, blue & white medium mottled, white interior, dark blue trim & ears, black wooden bail & knob, seamed body. Near mint, **$195.00.**

Row 1:

1. **Muffin Pan,** 8 cup, 1½" deep, 6¾" wide, 13⅜" long. Each cup measures 1¼" deep, 2⅞" diameter, light blue & white fine mottled with white interior & cobalt blue trim. Near mint, rare color & shape, **$595.00.**

Row 2:

1. **Footed Gravy or Sauce Boat,** 4½" tall, 3⅝" wide, 8" long not including the handle, blue & white fine mottled with white interior, cobalt blue trim & handle. Near mint, rare color & shape, **$395.00.**

2. **Round Tube Cake Pan,** 2½" deep, 7¼" diameter, blue & white fine mottled with white interior, cobalt blue trim. Near mint, rare size, **$285.00.**

3. **Covered Berlin-Style Kettle,** 4⅞" tall, 6" diameter, blue & white fine mottled with white interior, black wooden cover knob & bail handle. Near mint, **$165.00.**

Row 3:

1. **Custard Cup,** 1⅞" deep, 4¼" diameter, blue & white fine mottled with white interior & cobalt blue trim. Near mint, rare shape, **$95.00.**

2. **Oblong Dinner Bucket,** including the bucket, removable, seamed coffee flask, handled cup that fits over the neck of the coffee flask, white, handled dessert tray. Self locking bail with black wooden handle. 9¾" to top of the cup including the coffee flask, 6" wide, 8¾" long, blue & white fine mottled with white interior & cobalt blue trim, seamed body & coffee flask. Near mint, extremely rare color & shape, **$595.00. Note:** The bail handle is designed to hold the cover secure when the handle is raised for carrying.

3. **Coffeepot,** 10½" tall, 6⅞" diameter, blue & white fine mottled with white interior, cobalt blue trim, seamed body. Near mint, **$245.00.**

4. **Mug,** 2⅞" deep, 2¾" diameter, blue & white fine mottled with white interior & cobalt blue trim. Near mint, rare shape, **$95.00.**

Row 4:

1. **Tart Pan,** 1⅞" deep, 5⅝" diameter, blue & white fine mottled with white interior & cobalt blue trim. Mint, **$75.00.**

Row 5:

1. **Footed colander,** 4¾" high, 11" diameter, fine mottled blue & white inside & out, cobalt blue trim & handles, fancy perforated bottom & sides. Good plus, **$165.00.**

2. **Oblong Baking Pan,** 2¼" deep, 12¾" wide, 19¼" long not including the molded handles, fine mottled blue & white with white interior, cobalt blue trim. Good plus, **$145.00.**

Row 1:
1. **Oval Fluted Mold,** 2¼" deep, 4¾" wide, 6⅛" long, blue & grayish white medium mottled, light gray interior with a fine blue flecking. Near mint, rare color, shape & size, **$435.00. Note:** Because this mold is on a light gray background, the white has a light gray effect.
2. **Oval Platter,** 1½" deep, 16¼" wide, 20½" long, blue & white medium mottled, white interior, medium blue trim. Good plus, rare shape, **$235.00.**
3. **Round Fluted Mold,** 3⅛" deep, 6½" diameter, blue & grayish white medium mottled, light gray interior with fine blue flecking. Near Mint, rare color, shape & size, **$435.00.**
4. **Oval Fluted Mold,** with wheat imprint, 2¾" deep, 6" wide, 7" long, blue & grayish white medium mottled, light gray interior with fine blue flecking. Near mint, rare color, shape & size, **$435.00. Note:** The enameling is so heavy that the wheat imprint is hardly visible.

Row 2:
1. **Coffeepot,** 7¾" tall, 4½" diameter, blue & white fine mottled, white interior, black trim, seamless body, rivetted handle & spout. Near mint, **$225.00.**
2. **Cream Can,** with matching granite lock lid, 7½" tall, 4" diameter, blue & white fine mottled, white interior, black trim, seamless body, lock cover, enameled wire ears, metal bail. Near mint, **$225.00.**
3. **Milk Can,** with matching granite lock lid, 10¾" tall, 5" diameter, blue & white fine mottled, white interior, black trim, seamless body, enameled wire ears, metal bail. Near mint, **$185.00. Note:** Lock lid has protruding sections on the rim that lock when turned onto the neck of the milk can with indentations. The difference between a milk can & a cream can is the size. A cream can usually varies from 1 pint to a quart. Anything larger is considered a milk can.
4. **Teakettle,** 5¼" tall, 6" diameter, blue & white fine mottled, white interior, wooden bail. Marked "Elite." Good, rare shape & size, **$395.00. Note:** The unusual shaped spout.

Row 3:
1. **Oval Water Carrier,** 11" high to top of the handle, 5½" wide, 7¼" long, blue & white really fine mottling, white interior, rivetted handles & spout, seamed body, two piece hinged cover that helped to keep water hot when closed. Good, rare shape & size, **$195.00.**
2. **Muffin Pan,** 8 shallow cups, overall measures 1⅛" deep, 7¼" wide, 14¼" long, blue & white fine mottled, white interior, black trim. Near mint, rare color & shape, **$625.00.**
3. **Teapot,** large squatty shape 9½" high, 5¼" top diameter with 4" bottom diameter attached metal pedestal, blue & white fine mottled, aluminum coffee basket & cover with glass insert. Pot marked "Elite." Aluminum coffee basket marked "Universal Percolator, Landers, Trary & Clark: New Britain, Conn., U.S.A. No. 11144L Grind Coffee, Medium, Fine Pat'd. May 22, 94, May 11, 97, July 12, 98, May 22, 06, July 16, 07." Good plus, rare shape & size, **$325.00. Note:** The attached metal pedestal bottom fits the smallest section of a 3 piece lid on top of a wood burning stove.

Row 4:
1. **Funnel,** squatty shaped, 4" long, 3" top diameter, blue & white fine mottled, white interior, black trim. Near mint, rare size, **$170.00.**
2. **Colander,** 3½" high, 10" diameter not including handles, blue & white medium mottled inside & outside. Good plus, rare shape, **$295.00. Note:** The foot of the colander is attached with four individual rivetted straps, leaving ⅛" space all around between the colander & the foot.
3. **Hand Skimmer,** 5¼" long, 5" wide, blue & white fine mottled, diamond perforated center. Good plus, extremely rare color & shape, **$425.00. Note:** This was used for skimming milk & other liquids.

Row 1:

1. **Pitcher,** 6½" deep, 5" diameter, blue & white fine mottled, white interior, light blue trim & handle. Marked "Elite. Austria." Good plus, rare shape, **$295.00. Note:** This pitcher was designed with the larger bottom to keep it from tipping over. This type could have been used on trains & so forth.

2. **Pie Plate,** ⅞" deep, 9" diameter, blue & white fine mottled, white interior, blue trim. Near mint, **$55.00.**

3. **Teapot,** 9" high to top of the cover knob, 6⅜" diameter, blue & white fine mottled, white interior, black trim & rivetted welded handle, fancy tin-ribbed cover, with wooden acorn knob. Good plus, **$295.00.**

4. **Fry Pan,** 1½" deep, 11" top diameter, blue & white fine mottled, white interior. Marked "Germany 613-28." Pictures a lion standing with his front paws on a coffee boiler. The coffee boiler has the letter "B" in the center. The underside of the handle is marked "D.H.G.M." Good plus, **$155.00.**

5. **Mug,** 4¾" deep, 4¼" diameter, blue & white fine mottled, white interior, black trim, rivetted handle, seamless body. Near mint, **$75.00.**

Row 2:

1. **Turk's Head Tube-Style Turban Mold,** 3½" deep, 8¾" diameter, blue & white medium mottled, interior gray with dark blue specks. Good Plus, **$295.00.**

2. **Teapot,** small squatty shape, 5" high to top of the cover knob, 3¾" diameter, blue & white medium mottled, white interior, light blue trim. Marked "38." Pictures a lion standing with his front paws on a coffee boiler. The coffee boiler has the letter "B" in the center. Good plus, rare shape & size, **$325.00.**

3. **Rice Ball,** 4¾" high, 4½" diameter, fancy perforated body, blue & white medium mottled, black trim, metal latch hinge & ring applied by brass rivets. Mint, extremely rare color, shape & size, **$595.00. Note:** This was used for boiling rice by putting rice in the rice ball then immersing it into the boiling water. There usually is a fine chain on the top ring for lifting it out of the boiling water. Rice balls come in a number of sizes; this one is the medium size. The smaller ones were also used as soap savers. The left over soap pieces were placed in the ball & immersed in the water for washing clothes.

4. **Teapot,** 6" tall, 3½" diameter, blue & white medium mottled, with blue & white medium mottled interior, black trim & weld handle. Good plus, rare shape & size, **$295.00.**

5. **Footed Melon Mold,** 3" deep, 6¼" wide, 8¼" long, blue & white medium mottled, white interior, cobalt blue trim, rolled-top edge & four little rivetted feet on the rounded bottom to keep the mold from tipping. Mint, rare color & shape, **$295.00. Note:** This mold is not meant to have a cover. The rolled-top edge has no place for a cover to fit onto.

Row 3:

1. **Double Boiler,** 7½" tall including the insert, 5¾" diameter, blue & white medium mottled, white interior, cobalt blue trim & handles, seamless. Near mint, **$215.00.**

2. **Tea Strainer,** 1" deep, 4" top diameter not including the handle, blue & white medium mottled, white interior, fancy perforated bottom. Near mint, **$195.00.**

3. **Fry Pan,** 1¼" deep, 9" diameter, blue & white medium mottled, white interior, black trim, rivetted handle. Near mint, rare shape, **$195.00. Note:** This fry pan appears to have been made from a pie plate because it has a flared rolled edge like a pie plate.

4. **Teakettle,** 5¼" tall, 6⅛" diameter, light blue & white large mottled, white interior, wooden bail. Near mint, rare color, shape & size, **$495.00.**

Row 4:

1. **Cuspidor,** 2-piece, 4½" tall, 8¾" top diameter, 9¾" bottom diameter, blue & white extra fine mottling, white interior. Near mint, **$265.00.**

2. **Chocolate or Coffeepot,** 8¾" tall, 4½" diameter, blue & white medium mottled, white interior, black trim & handle, wooden cover knob, seamless body, welded rivetted handle. Near mint, rare shape **$325.00. Note:** The larger version is shown in Book 1.

3. **Covered Bucket,** with matching granite lid, 7¼" tall, 3⅞" diameter not including ears, blue & white fine mottling inside & out, seamless body, rivetted cover handle, applied ears, wire bail. Good plus, **$155.00.**

4. **Turk's Head Tube-Style Turban Mold,** 2¾" deep, 6" diameter, blue & white, extra fine mottling, white interior, ring for hanging. Good, rare size, **$215.00.**

Row 1:
1. **Cuspidor,** 5" high, 9" diameter, blue & white medium mottled, white interior, seamless body. Good plus, **$225.00.**
2. **Bowl,** 2⅞" deep, 6" diameter, blue & white medium mottled, bluish gray interior. Good plus, **$45.00.**
3. **Dishpan,** 4½" deep, 14½" diameter, blue & white large mottled, white interior, eyelet for hanging. Good plus, **$110.00.**
4. **Custard Cup,** 2¾" deep, 4½" diameter, blue & white large mottled, white interior. Good plus, **$110.00.**
5. **Wash Pan,** 5" deep, 12¼" diameter, blue & white large mottled, white interior. Good plus, **$95.00.**

Row 2:
1. **Toothbrush Holder,** ¾" deep, 3½" wide, 8¾" long, blue & white large mottled, white interior, cobalt blue trim. Mint, extremely rare color, shape & size, **$295.00. Note:** On the bottom interior of the toothbrush holder are three indentations. The toothbrush is placed on these indentations to keep it dry after use. This holder is not meant to have a cover.
2. **Shaker,** 2½" tall, 1½" diameter, light blue & white large mottled, white interior, seamless body. Near mint, extremely rare color, shape & size, **$1,125.00. Note:** The unusual top on this shaker. It is not pierced, instead it has an individual hole that measures ⅜" x ⅜". With this cover, there are no screw-on threads for the metal cover or the metal part that is attached to the shaker. This shaker might have been used for spices or salt.
3. **Salt Shaker,** 2½" tall, 1½" diameter, light blue & white large mottled, white interior, seamless body. Near mint, extremely rare color, shape & size, **$1,125.00.**
4. **Maslin-Style Kettle,** with matching granite cover, 7" tall, 9" diameter, blue & white large mottled, white interior, blue trim, seamless body, top-tipping handle. Good plus, **$185.00.**
5. **Teakettle,** 7" tall, 9¼" diameter, blue & white large swirl, white interior, black trim & wooden bail. Good plus, rare shape & size, **$325.00.**

Row 3:
1. **Mixing or Dough Bowl,** 5½" deep, 11½" diameter, light blue & white medium mottled, white interior. Good plus, **$95.00.**
2. **Teapot,** 9" tall, 6¼" diameter, light blue & white medium mottled, white interior, seamed body. Good plus, **$195.00.**
3. **Creamer,** squatty shape, 6" tall, 3¾" diameter, blue & white large mottled, bluish gray interior, rivetted handle, seamless body. Good plus, rare color, shape & size, **$395.00.**
4. **Jelly Roll Pan,** 1" deep, 10¼" diameter, blue & white medium mottled, white interior. Near mint, **$85.00.**

Row 4:
1. **Muffin Pan,** 9 cup, 10½" x 10½", light blue & white large mottled inside & out, two eyelets for hanging. "Snow on the Mountain." Near mint, extremely rare color, shape & size, **$795.00.**
2. **Salt Box,** 10" back height, 4¼" wide, 5¾" long, light blue & white large mottled, white interior, black lettering & trim, seamed body, fancy brass hinges. Good plus, extremely rare color & rare shape, **$475.00.**
3. **Maslin-Style Kettle,** 7¾" deep, 11½" diameter, blue & white large mottled, white interior, seamless body, wooden bail, with bottom tipping handle. Good plus, **$135.00.**

Row 1:

1. **Berlin-Style Spaghetti or Potato Kettle,** 8" tall, 9¼" diameter, blue & white medium mottled, gray interior with fine blue flecks, black trim, ears & tipping handle, wooden bail. Good plus, extremely rare shape, rare color, **$395.00. Note:** The metal cover on the tapered spout is hinged to raise for draining then flip back down on the spout.

2. **Funnel,** squatty shape, 4¾" tall, 3¾" diameter, blue & white medium mottled, gray interior with fine blue flecks, seamless body, spout seamed. Good plus, rare shape, **$165.00.**

3. **Fry Pan,** 2" deep, 10⅜" diameter, blue & white medium mottled, light gray interior with fine blue flecks. Handle is reinforced with an applied steel handle that is crimped over the original handle. Steel handle is embossed "Best Steel." Good plus, **$145.00. Note:** This type metal handle is referred to as a "Cold Handle" because it keeps the direct heat off the part of the handle that is held.

4. **Plate,** ¾" deep, 8¾" diameter, blue & white, medium mottled, light gray interior with fine blue flacks. Good plus, **$85.00.**

5. **Tea Steeper or Baby Food Cup,** 5" tall, 4" diameter, blue & white medium mottled, light gray interior with fine blue flacks, black trim & handle, seamless body, rivetted handle. Good plus, **$185.00. Note:** These were used for steeping teas & warming baby food.

6. **Oblong Pudding Pan or Vegetable Dish,** 2" deep, 9⅜" width, 12¾" long, blue & white medium mottled, light gray interior with fine blue flecks, black trim. Good plus, **$115.00.**

Row 2:

1. **Lipped Sauce Pan,** 3⅜" deep, 6⅜" diameter, blue & white medium mottled, white interior, blue trim, seamless body, brass eyelet in the handle for hanging. Marked on the bottom with a lion standing with his front paws on a coffeepot. This is the trademark of the "Paragon Lion Brand Enameled Ware" made in Germany. The New England Enameling Company, Middletown, Connecticut was the exclusive distributing agent. Good plus, **$95.00.**

2. **Round Fluted Mold,** 2¾" deep, 5¾" diameter, blue & white medium mottled, light gray interior with fine blue flecks. Good plus, rare color, shape & size, **$435.00.**

3. **Boston Milk Can,** 9½" to top of the cover handle, 5½" bottom diameter, blue & white medium mottled, light gray interior with fine blue flecks, seamed body, rivetted handles, wire bail. Good plus, rare shape, **$465.00.**

4. **Oval Fluted Mold,** 2¼" deep, 4" wide, 5" long, blue & white medium mottled, light gray interior with fine blue flecks. Good plus, rare color, shape & size, **$435.00.**

5. **Colander,** footed, 4" high, 11⅜" diameter, blue & white medium mottled inside & out, blue rivetted handles & feet. Good plus, **$165.00.**

Row 3:

1. **Preserving Kettle,** 8⅝" deep, 17¼" diameter, blue & white medium mottled, light gray interior, black trim, rivetted ears, & tipping handle, wire bail, seamless body. Good plus, **$165.00.**

2. **Hanging Soap Dish with Insert,** 3⅝" back height, 4½" wide, 6½" long, soap section, 1" deep, blue & white medium mottled inside & out. Insert, ¾" deep, 4⅜" wide, 6¼" long, solid white. Near mint, **$165.00.**

3. **Hanging Soap Dish,** 4¼" back height, 3½" wide, 6" long, soap section, 1⅜" deep, blue & white medium mottled inside & out, fancy embossed back, scalloped edge. Good, **$160.00.**

4. **Preserving Kettle,** 8½" deep, 17¼" diameter, blue & white medium mottled, light gray interior with fine blue flecks, rivetted ears & tipping handle, wooden bail, seamless body. Good plus, **$165.00.**

Row 1:

1. **Plate,** ¾" deep, 10" diameter, light blue & white medium swirl inside & out. Good Plus, **$95.00. Note:** It is hard to find pieces with the mottling or swirling both inside & out.

2. **Mug,** 3" deep, 3½" diameter, light blue & white medium swirl, white interior, light blue trim, seamless. Good plus, **$55.00.**

3. **Footed Colander Deep,** 3¾" high, 11½" diameter, light blue & white large mottled inside & out, dark blue trim on the foot of the colander. Near mint, **$180.00.**

4. **Sugar Bowl,** squatty shape, 4¾" tall, 5¼" diameter, light blue & white medium swirl, white interior, seamed body. Near mint, rare shape, rare color, **$595.00.**

5. **Funnel,** 6¾" tall, 5⅞" diameter, blue & white medium mottled inside & out, black trim, rivetted wire ear for hanging, seamed body & spout. Good plus, **$145.00.**

Row 2:

1. **Footed Colander,** deep, 4½" high, 9⅛" diameter, light blue & white large mottled inside & out, dark blue trim on the foot of the colander. Near mint, **$180.00.**

2. **Triangular Sink Strainer,** 2½" high, 7⅞" wide, 10⅛" long, light blue & white large mottled, seamless. Good plus, extremely rare color & shape, **$345.00. Note:** The base has three molded feet that protrude down so the strainer does not fit flat on the surface, giving it better drainage.

3. **Footed Colander,** deep, 5½" high, 9¾" diameter, light blue & white large mottled inside & out, light blue trim on the top, dark blue trim on the foot. Good plus, **$155.00.**

Row 3:

1. **Oval Pudding or Vegetable Dish,** 1⅞" deep, 9" wide, 11¾" long, light blue & white large mottled, white interior. Good plus, **$120.00.**

2. **Stock Pot,** with matching granite lid. Straight sided, 11¾" high to top of the cover handle, 13" diameter, light blue & white medium swirl, white interior, wire bail, back-tipping handle. Good plus, **$125.00.**

3. **Double Boiler,** with matching granite cover. 7⅞" high to top of the cover handle including insert, 8⅜" diameter, light blue & white large mottled, white interior, seamless body. Near mint, **$165.00.**

Row 1:

1. **Teapot,** 9¾" tall, 6¼" diameter, blue & white large mottled, white interior, seamed body. Near mint, **$225.00.**
2. **Footed Colander,** 4¼" high, 12" diameter, blue & white medium mottled inside & out, blue trim on the foot. Near mint, **$180.00.**
3. **Spoon,** 13¼" long, 2¼" bowl width, blue & white medium mottled inside & out. Good plus, **$65.00.**
4. **Water Pitcher,** 12¼" tall, 7⅜" wide, blue & white large mottled, light gray interior with fine blue flecks, black trim & handle, seamless body, rivetted handle. Near mint, rare color & shape, **$595.00. Note:** I believe this pitcher is part of a wash set.

Row 2:

1. **Measure,** 6⅛" tall, 4¼" diameter, blue & white medium mottled, white interior, dark blue trim & handle, seamless body, rivetted handle. Near mint, rare color, **$495.00.**
2. **Funnel,** 5½" long, 4¾" diameter, blue & white medium mottled, light gray interior with fine blue flecks, seamless body, seamed spout. Good plus, rare shape, **$165.00.**
3. **Candlestick,** leaf shaped with finger ring, 2" high. Leaf section, 1⅛" deep, 6⅝" long, 6¾" wide, blue & white fine mottled inside & out, rivetted finger ring. Good plus, **$595.00.**
4. **Cream Can,** 6¼" high, 3⅛" bottom diameter, blue & white medium mottled, white interior, dark blue trim, seamless body, wire bail. Good plus, extremely rare color, shape & size, **$695.00.**
5. **Coffeepot,** 6¾" high, to top of the cover knob, 4¼" bottom diameter, blue & white medium mottled, light gray interior with fine blue flecks, black trim, rivetted handle & spout, seamed body. Good plus, **$195.00.**

Row 3:

1. **Chamber Pot,** 4¾" deep, 9⅜" diameter, blue & white large mottled, white interior with fine blue flecks, rivetted strap handle, seamless body. Good plus, **$125.00.**
2. **Salad Bowl,** 2¾" deep, 10⅝" diameter, blue & white medium mottled, white interior. Good plus, rare shape, **$145.00. Note:** Most people mistake the large salad bowl for a wash basin. The salad bowl does not have the flat outer rim or a hole for hanging that most wash basins do.
3. **Cuspidor,** 5" high, 8⅜" diameter, blue & white medium mottled, white interior, blue trim, seamless body. Good plus, **$285.00.**

116

Row 1:

1. **Teapot,** 8¾" tall, 5" diameter, blue & white large mottled, white interior, weld handle, seamed body. Near mint, **$235.00.**
2. **Spoon,** 15⅜" long, to top of the handle, 2⅜" spoon width, blue & white large mottled inside & out. Good plus, **$75.00.**
3. **Windsor-Style Pit Bottom Kettle,** 7¼" deep, 10¼" diameter, blue & white large mottled, light gray interior with fine blue flecks, rivetted ears & back-tipping handle, wooden bail, seamless body. Good plus, **$215.00. Note:** A pit bottom kettle has an extended section that fits down into the lid opening on a wood-burning stove. This heats the kettle faster.
4. **Pie Plate,** 1" deep, 9⅝" top diameter, blue & white medium mottled, white interior. Good plus, **$55.00.**
5. **Covered Bucket,** with matching granite lid, 5½" high, 5⅞" diameter, blue & white medium mottled, white interior, seamless body, wooden bail. Good plus, **$215.00.**

Row 2:

1. **Handled Sauce Pan,** with matching granite cover, 6⅝" high, 7½" diameter, blue & white large mottled, light blue trim, white interior, seamless body. Good plus, **$135.00.**
2. **Milk Can,** 7¼" high, 4⅝" diameter, blue & white large mottled, white interior, seamed body, wire bail. Good plus, **$325.00.**
3. **Water Pitcher,** 9⅜" tall, 5" diameter, blue & white large mottled, white interior, seamless body. Near mint, rare shape, **$395.00.**
4. **Boston Cream Can,** 8¼" high, 4¼" diameter, blue & white medium mottled, white interior, side strap handle, wire bail, seamed body. Good plus, **$365.00.**
5. **Straight-Style Spaghetti or Potato Kettle,** with matching granite cover, 6¾" high, 8⅜" diameter not includ-ing the spout, light blue & white large mottled, white interior, seamless body, back bottom tipping handle, wooden bail. Good plus, extremely rare shape, rare color, **$345.00. Note:** The wire bail is crimped on each end to hold the cover on while pouring. Also note the pouring spout is not meant to be covered like others pictured in this book.

Row 3:

1. **Boston Milk Can,** 11¼" high, 6⅜" diameter, blue & white large mottled, white interior, side strap handle, wooden bail. Good plus, extremely rare color shape & size, **$595.00.**
2. **Chamber Pail,** 14¼" high, 11¼" diameter, light blue & white large mottled, white interior, dark blue trim, wooden bail, seamed body. Good plus, rare shape, **$225.00.**
3. **Teapot,** 11¾" high, 7⅛" diameter, blue & white large mottled, white interior, seamed body. Good plus, **$185.00.**

SECTION 4
STANDARD SIZES COMPARED TO MINIATURES, SALESMAN'S SAMPLES AND INDIVIDUAL SERVING SIZES

I chose to compare the standard sizes to miniatures, salesman's samples & individual serving sizes so you could get a better concept of the size difference in granite ware. Also note the variations in shape & pattern designed to best suit the sizes shown. Some of the items pictured are not miniatures or salesman's samples. Instead they are individual serving size pieces. Whatever the case may be, I find it interesting and fun to compare the variations in size, shape & pattern.

Row 1:
1. **Teapot,** squatty shape, 7½" tall, 6" diameter, white decorated with a band of violets, leaves & solid reddish brown bands, metal trim & protective bands. Near mint, **$295.00.**
2. **Teapot,** 9¾" tall, 4½" diameter, metal trim, white decorated with a heron & rushes scene. Near mint, **$295.00. Note:** The unique handle decoration of flowers.
3. **Teapot,** 6" tall, 3¼" diameter, metal trim, white decorated with a heron & rushes scene. Good plus, rare size, **$550.00.**

Row 2:
1. **Teapot,** squatty shape, 5½" tall, 4½" diameter, metal trim & protective bands, white decorated with a band of violets & leaves. Inscribed on the front & back "Oakland." Near mint, rare shape & size, **$550.00.**
2. **Mush or Miner's Mug,** 4¼" deep, 6¼" diameter, brown & white large swirl, white interior, cobalt blue trim & handle, seamless body, rivetted handle. Good plus, rare color, **$325.00.**
3. **Miniature Mug,** 1" deep, 1⅛" diameter, brown & white large swirl, white interior, rivetted handle. Good plus, extremely rare color, shape & size, **$465.00.**
4. **Salesman's Sample Water Pail,** 3" deep, 3⅜" diameter, gray medium mottled, black wooden bail, seamless body, rivetted ears. Near mint, rare shape & size, **$275.00.**

Row 3:
1. **Teapot,** 6¼" tall, 4" diameter, gray medium mottled, metal trim & protective bands. Good plus, rare shape & size, **$595.00.**
2. **Teapot,** 10¾ " tall, 5⅝" diameter, gray large mottled, metal trim & protective bands. Mint, **$295.00.**
3. **Water Pail,** 9⅜" deep, 11⅞" diameter, gray large mottled, seamless body, wooden bail. Good plus, **$65.00.**

Row 1:

1. **Handled Insert & Rack,** for No. 3 on this row, 1¾" deep, 9¾" wide, 15¼" long, black & white fine mottled inside & out, metal rack, 4⅜" high, 6¾" wide, 11" long.

2. **Lisk's 50th Anniversary Catalog,** issued in 1939 by the Lisk Manufacturing Co., Canandaigua, N.Y. showing their 50th anniversary special on their line of roasters. **$240.00. Note:** This company started in business in 1889. The Lisk Company won the Gold Medal in 1904 at the World's Fair for their line of wares. One of the unusual methods they used was to spray their blue enameled finishes on last, in comparison to the methods other companies were using. Note the different colors shown. Also, the self basting enameled roasters have a damper on the cover to regulate evaporation & permit browning the roast, whereas, the drip top style does not have a damper.

3. **4-Piece Complete Roaster,** 6¾" tall, 11¼" wide, 16½" long not including handles, black & white fine mottled inside & out. Cover is embossed "Lisk." Good plus, **$85.00. Note:** This roaster has two dampers on the cover. I believe this roaster is prior to the one shown with the one damper on Row 3, No. 1.

Row 2:

1. **3-Piece Complete Salesman's Sample Oval Roaster with Handled Insert,** 3" tall, 3¾" wide, 6⅛" long not including handles, cobalt blue & white large swirl inside & out, black trim & handles, seamless body. Near mint, extremely rare color, shape & size, **$1,850.00.**

2. **Handled Insert,** for No. 1 on this row, ¾" deep, 3¼" wide, 5⅞" long, white inside & out, black trim & handles.

3. **Handled Insert,** for No. 4 on this row ⅜" deep, 3½" wide, 5⅜" long, black & white fine mottled inside & out.

4. **3-Piece Salesman's Sample Roaster,** 2⅝" high, 4" wide, 5⅝" long, black & white fine mottled inside & out, top of the cover has two metal dampers. Cover is embossed "Lisk." Mint, extremely rare color, shape & size, **$795.00.**

Row 3:

1. **2-Piece Roaster,** 8½" tall, 12" wide, 18½" long not including the handles, black & white fine mottled inside & out, metal damper on the cover. Cover embossed "Lisk." Good plus, **$60.00. Note:** This roaster has a center handle on the cover whereas No. 3 on Row 1 does not.

2. **Oval Roaster Insert,** for No. 3 on this row, 1¾" deep, 11¼" wide, 16½" long, white with black trim & handles, shell-shaped bottom.

3. **Oval Roaster,** No. 2 and 3. 8½" to top of cover handle, 12" wide, 17¼" long not including the handles, cobalt blue & white large swirl inside & out, black trim & handle, end damper on the top of the cover, wire cover locks on each end, rivetted handles & seamless body. Near mint, rare color, **$525.00.**

Row 1:

1. **Oval Roaster,** 3-piece, 7" tall, 11" wide, 16½" long not including handles, blue & white fine mottled, white interior with fine blue flecks, black trim, seamless body. The cover is embossed "Lisk." The two metal dampers on the cover have wire handles. Dampers are dated "Pat. May 2, 1911." Handle Insert, 1¾" deep, 9¾" wide, 15⅜" long, white with fine blue flecks. Manufactured by The Lisk Manufacturing Co., Canandaigua, N.Y. which was famous for these self basting roasters. Near Mint, **$160.00.**

2. **Lisk Advertisement,** 10½" long, 7¼" wide not including frame. This is a 1919 ad for the famous Lisk roaster. I believe it tells it all in this statement "Run No Risk—Be Sure It's Lisk." Mint, **$110.00.**

3. **Oval Roaster,** 3-piece, 6⅛" tall, 9" wide, 11⅝" long not including handles, blue & white fine mottled inside & out, black trim. The cover is embossed "Lisk." The two metal dampers on the cover have wire handles. Dampers are dated "Pat. May 2, 1911." Handled insert, 1⅝" deep, 7⅝" deep, 10⅝" long, white with fine blue flecks. Manufactured by "The Lisk Manufacturing Co." Near mint, rare color & size, **$395.00.**

Row 2:

1. **Salesman's Sample Roaster,** with handled insert, 2⅝" high, 4" wide, 5¾" long not including the handles, blue & white fine mottled inside & out, black trim, seamless body. The cover is embossed "Lisk." The two metal dampers on the cover that open & close when turned are not dated like the ones on the larger roasters are. Handled insert, ⅜" deep not including the handles, 3½" wide, 5⅜" long, white with black trim & rivetted handles. Mint, extremely rare color, shape & size, **$1,100.00.**

Row 3:

1. **Oval Roaster,** 3-piece, insert, 1⅞" deep not including handle, 11⅞" wide, 17⅝" long, white with fine blue flecks. Roaster, 8¾" high, 13⅜" wide, 19⅞" long not including the handles, blue & white fine mottled inside & out, black trim, seamless body. The cover is embossed "Lisk." The two metal dampers have wire handles. Dampers are dated & "Pat. May 2, 1911." Manufactured by The Lisk Manufacturing Co., Canandaigua, N.Y. Good plus, **$145.00. Note:** In Book 1 I stated that there were four different sizes of these roasters. I finally was able to get all four sizes. I photographed them all together so you could compare & see the size difference.

Row 1:

1. **Covered Bucket,** 5" tall, 3⅛" diameter, green veins of large mottling with a white lumpy effect, Snow on the Mountain, white interior, green trim, wooden bail, seamless body. Marked "Elite" Austria Reg'd," Mint, extremely rare size, **$295.00.**

2. **Covered Bucket,** 10" tall, 8½" diameter, green veins of large mottling with a white lumpy effect, Snow on the Mountain, white interior, light green trim, wooden bail, seamless body, marked "Elite" Austria Reg'd." Good plus, **$210.00.**

3. **Cuspidor,** 4" high, 7¾" diameter, blue & white large mottled, white interior, black trim, seamed body. Good plus, **$265.00.**

Row 2:

1. **Salesman's Sample Wash Basin,** 1¼" deep, 4⅜" diameter, blue & white large mottled, white interior, blue trim, eyelet for hanging. Mint, rare color, **$110.00.**

2. **Salesman's Sample Coverless Roaster,** 1⅛" deep, 4¼" wide, 6⅛" long not including handles. The inside raised well is ⅝" deep, reddish brown & white medium mottled inside & out, rivetted wire handles, seamless body. "Cream City Ware. 'Garnet', Milwaukee Geuder Paeschke & Frey Co." Good plus, extremely rare color, shape & size, **$435.00.**

3. **Salesman's Sample Advertising Cuspidor,** 1⅞" high, 3" diameter, blue & white large mottled, white interior, black trim. Advertising on inside bottom of cuspidor "United States Stamping Co., Moundsville, WV." Mint, extremely rare color, shape & size, **$850.00. Note:** This is an advertising cross-collectible because it's collectible in the cuspidor category, granite ware category & salesman's sample category.

Row 3:

1. **Wash Basin,** 2⅞" deep, 12⅜" diameter, blue & white large mottled, white interior, blue trim, eyelet for hanging. Good plus, **$120.00.**

2. **Coverless Roaster,** 2⅜" deep, 13¼" wide, 15⅞" long not including the handles. The inside raised well is 1⅞" deep, reddish brown & white medium mottled inside & out, rivetted wire handles, seamed bottom. Marked "Cream City Ware, 'Garnet,' Milwaukee Geuder Paeschke & Frey Co." Near mint, rare shape, **$165.00.**

Section 5
Pink & White, black & White, Aqua Green & White, Lava Ware, Yellow & White, & Redipped

Row 1:
1. **Teakettle,** 6¾" tall, 9" diameter, light pink & white large marbleized, white interior, black trim, ears, wooden bail, Bakelite knob, seamed body. Near mint, extremely rare color & shape, **$495.00. Note:** I believe this is a product of the Federal Enameling & Stamping Company, Pittsburgh, PA.
2. **Wash Bowl,** 3¾" deep, 13⅜" diameter, mauve pink & white large mottled, white interior, dark brown trim. Mint, extremely rare color, **$395.00.**
3. **Teapot,** squatty shape, 4¼" tall, 4⅝" diameter, mauve pink & white large swirl, cobalt blue cover, white interior, dark brown trim. Good plus, extremely rare color, shape & size, **$425.00. Note:** This is the original cover. They used many colors to accessorize the pinks.
4. **Stack Dinner Carrier,** 11¼" tall, 4¾" diameter, light pink & white large swirl, each dinner carrier measures 3" deep. The cover section measures ½" deep. When the cover is turned upright it can also be used as a serving dish. Near mint, extremely rare color, shape & size, **$795.00.**

Row 2:
1. **Coffee Carrier,** 7¼" tall, 4⅞" diameter, pink & white large swirl, white interior, cobalt blue trim, wire bail, seamed body. Good plus, extremely rare color, shape & size, **$325.00.**
2. **Teakettle,** 7" tall, 7½" diameter, solid light pink inside & out, black trim & handle, seamed body. Good plus, **$55.00. Note:** I believe this is circa 1950.
3. **Child's Wash Basin,** 2⅛" deep, 7⅞" diameter, light pink & white large mottled, white interior, bright cobalt blue trim. Good plus, extremely rare color, shape & size, **$395.00.**

Row 3:
1. **Coffee Biggin,** 10¾" tall to top of the cover knob including biggin, 5¼" diameter, deep mauve pink & white large swirl, white interior, black trim, seamed body. Near mint, extremely rare color, rare shape, **$495.00.**
2. **Two-Handled Pan,** 2¾" deep, 8¼" diameter, pink & white large mottled, white interior, cobalt blue trim. Marked "H.W. 20." Good plus, extremely rare color, **$235.00. Note:** This could be the top part of a double boiler.
3. **Teapot,** 8½" tall, 4½" diameter, pink & white large swirl, pink trim, white interior, seamed body. Good plus, extremely rare color, **$430.00. Note:** This is not the original cover.
4. **Coffee Biggin,** 14¼" tall, 5⅞" diameter, fine mottled pink & white, white interior, red trim. Coffee biggin consists of four pieces: the pot, biggin, spreader & cover. Good plus, extremely rare color, & rare shape, **$465.00.**

Special Note: Trying to get enough of the pink & white mottled or swirl to complete a single picture was quite a chore. There is only a single picture of certain colors in this book because, some colors were hard to achieve the right shade or hue in manufacturing, or it may not have been a popular color to begin with, so less of this color was manufactured. It could also be that some colors were more popular than others, such as blue & white compared to pink & white.

Row 1:
1. **Covered Bucket,** 7½" tall, 7½" diameter, black & white large swirl inside & out, black trim, wooden bail, seamed body. Good plus, extremely rare color, **$425.00.**
2. **Pudding Pan,** 3⅛" deep, 9¾" diameter, black & white large swirl inside & out, black trim, seamless body. Mint, extremely rare color, **$245.00.**
3. **Handled Sauce Pan,** 5½" tall, 6¾" diameter, black & white large swirl inside & out, black trim, seamed body. Near mint, extremely rare color, **$255.00.**

Row 2:
1. **Measure,** 5⅛" tall, 3" diameter, black & white medium mottled inside & out, seamed body, applied strap handle & lip. Embossed on the side "IPT." Also embossed on the bottom "U.S.N." Mint, **$85.00. Note:** These measures were made for military use in the United States Navy. They also come in 1 gallon & 1 quart size.
2. **Measure,** 2⅜" tall, 2¼" diameter, black & white medium mottled inside & out, seamed body, applied strap handle & lip. Embossed on the side "IGIL." Also embossed on the bottom "U.S.N." Originally sold for $1.25 each. Mint, rare size, **$135.00.**
3. **Teakettle,** 6¾" tall, 9" diameter, black & white large swirl, white interior, black trim, ears & Bakelite knob, seamed body. Near mint, extremely rare color & shape, **$495.00. Note:** I believe this is a product of The Federal Enameling & Stamping Co., Pittsburgh, PA.
4. **Bowl,** 2½" deep, 6¾" diameter, black & white large swirl, white interior, black trim. Mint, extremely rare color, **$135.00. Note:** I believe this is a product of The Federal Enameling & Stamping Co., Pittsburgh, PA.

Row 3:
1. **Double Boiler,** 8¼" tall, 5⅞" diameter, black & white large swirl inside & out, seamless body, chrome-plated cover with wooden knob. "Ebony Ware." Near Mint, extremely rare color, **$295.00.**
2. **Insulated Bottle,** 9¾" to top of the cover, 3⅛" bottom diameter, black & white fine mottled, white interior, brass screw-on cover with ring for carrying. Good plus, rare shape, **$165.00.**
3. **Fry Pan Shaped Ash Tray,** ⅞" deep, 3¾" diameter, black & white large mottled inside & out. Embossed "Wagner" on the bottom. Mint, rare color, **$85.00. Note:** These were probably given away as an advertising promotion for this company.
4. **Maslin-Style Kettle,** 7¼" tall, 8" diameter, black & white large swirl inside & out, seamless body, wooden bail. "Ebony Ware." Mint, rare color, **$265.00.**

Special Note: The black & white swirls are rare.

Row 1:
1. **Measure,** 4⅞" tall, 3⅝" diameter, aqua green & white large swirl, cobalt blue trim, white interior, rivetted spout & strap handle, seamed body. Near mint, extremely rare color & shape, **$295.00.**
2. **Oval Butter Kettle or Carrier,** 7¼" tall, 6½" wide, 8¾" long, aqua green & white large swirl, cobalt blue trim, white interior, metal strap handle with metal support piece, seamless body. Mint, extremely rare color, shape & size. **$365.00.**
3. **Muffin Pan,** 6-cup, shallow, 1" deep, 6⅞" wide, 10⅛" long, aqua green & white large swirl, cobalt blue trim, white interior. Near mint, extremely rare color, shape & size, **$650.00.**
4. **Mug, tumbler-shaped,** 5" deep, 3⅞" diameter, aqua green & white large swirl, cobalt blue trim, white interior, rivetted handle, seamless body. Good plus, extremely rare color & shape, **$85.00. Note:** A similar mug in gray is shown in the LaLance & Grosjean 1884 Catalog. They referred to it as an ice cream mug.

Row 2:
1. **Lipped Preserve Kettle,** 3¾" deep, 8" diameter, aqua green & white large swirl, cobalt blue trim, white interior, rivetted handles, seamless body with pouring lip & backtipping handle, wire bail. Near mint, extremely rare color, **$145.00.**
2. **Syrup,** 8¾" tall, 5" diameter, aqua green & white large swirl, white interior, rivetted rolled handle, nickel-plated brass top with thumb lift. Near mint, extremely rare color, shape & size, **$975.00.**
3. **Turk's Head Tube-Style Turban Mold,** 3½" deep, 8¼" diameter, aqua green & white large swirl, white interior, cobalt blue trim. Good plus, extremely rare color, **$395.00.**

Row 3:
1. **Measure,** 3½" tall, 3" diameter, aqua green & white large swirl, white interior, cobalt blue trim, rivetted spout & strap handle, seamed body. Good plus, extremely rare color, shape & size, **$295.00.**
2. **Teapot,** 6½" tall, 3¾" diameter, aqua green & white large swirl, white interior, cobalt blue trim, rivetted rolled handle. Good plus, extremely rare color & size, **$265.00.**
3. **Cup,** flared shape, 2⅜" deep, 3¾" diameter, aqua green & white large swirl, white interior, cobalt blue trim, rivetted strap handle. Good plus, extremely rare color & shape, **$95.00.**
4. **Cream Can,** 5" tall, 3½" diameter, aqua green & white large swirl, white interior, cobalt blue trim, rivetted ears, seamed body, wire bail. Near mint, extremely rare color, shape & size, **$695.00.**
5. **Creamer,** squatty shape, 4⅝" tall, 3⅜" diameter, aqua green & white large swirl, white interior, cobalt blue trim, seamless body, rivetted handle. Good plus, extremely rare color, shape & size, **$355.00.**

Row 4:
1. **Double Boiler,** 8½" tall, 9¾" diameter, aqua green & white large swirl, white interior, cobalt blue trim & handles, seamed flared bottom, rivetted handles. Near mint, extremely rare color, **$310.00.**
2. **Dessert Plate,** ⅝" deep, 6½" diameter, aqua green & white large swirl, white interior, cobalt blue trim. Good plus, extremely rare color, shape & size, **$125.00.**
3. **Water Pitcher,** 10¼" tall, 7½" diameter aqua green & white large swirl, white interior, cobalt blue trim. Mint, extremely rare color, shape & size, **$395.00.**

Row 1:

1. **Coffeepot,** 10½" tall, 6⅝" diameter, light blue & white large swirl with white interior, rivetted handle, & seamless body. Mint, extremely rare color, **$495.00.**

2. **Wash Basin,** 3¼" deep, by 12⅜" diameter, light blue & white large swirl with white interior, eyelet for hanging. Near mint, extremely rare color, **$155.00.**

3. **Tube Cake Pan,** 3⅜" deep, 10⅜" diameter, light blue & white large swirl with white interior. Good plus, extremely rare color & shape, **$395.00.**

4. **Round Tray,** ⅞" deep, 10¾" diameter, light blue & white large swirl with white interior. Good plus, rare color & shape, **$195.00.**

Row 2:

1. **Double Boiler,** 8" tall, 6⅞" diameter, dark blue & white large swirl with white interior, seamless body. Good plus, extremely rare color, **$375.00.**

2. **2-Handled Pudding Pan,** 3½" deep, 11¼" diameter, grayish lavender & white large swirl with white interior, rivetted handles. Good plus, extremely rare color, **$145.00.**

3. **Measure,** 7¾" tall, 5½" diameter, dark blue & white large swirl with white interior, seamless body. Good plus, extremely rare color, shape & size, **$495.00.**

Row 3:

1. **Fry Pan,** 2⅛" deep, 10½" diameter, grayish lavender & white large swirl with white interior, enameled on a heavy iron base. Good plus, extremely rare color, **$245.00.**

2. **Tea Strainer,** ¾" deep, 4" diameter not including the handle, screened bottom, gray & white large swirl inside & out. Good plus, extremely rare color, rare shape, **$165.00.**

3. **Water Cooler,** (3 pieces) 17¼" to top of the cover handle including the top section, 10⅜" diameter, light blue & white large swirl with white interior. Wooden bail handle with seamless body. Near mint, extremely rare color & shape, **$750.00. Note:** The top section has a stone type filter that is placed on the collar around the bottom edge of the top section. This filters and purifies the water.

4. **Fry Pan,** 2¼" deep, 11½" diameter, light blue & white large swirl with white interior, enameled on a heavy cast iron base. Near mint, extremely rare color, **$275.00.**

Note: You will notice that Lava Ware has a look all its own. The large swirl effect has a swirling inside the swirl. The Cleveland Stamping & Tool Co. of Cleveland, Ohio, is believed to be one of the manufacturers of Lava Ware.

135

Row 1:

1. **Teapot,** 8" deep, 5" diameter, yellow & white large swirl, white interior, black trim, seamed body, circa 1960, lightweight. Good plus, **$120.00.**
2. **Round Tray,** 1⅝" deep, 17¾" diameter, yellow & white large swirl on both sides, black trim, circa 1950. Mint, **$85.00.**
3. **Mug,** 3⅛" deep, 3¼" diameter, yellow & white large swirl, white interior, black trim, seamless body, circa 1950. Mint, **$50.00.**
4. **Wine Cooler,** 7½" deep, 7" diameter, yellow & white large swirl inside & out, black trim, circa 1960, lightweight. Mint, rare color & shape, **$215.00.**

Row 2:

1. **Cereal Bowl,** 2¼" deep, 4⅞" diameter, yellow & white large swirl inside & out, black trim, circa 1950, lightweight, rare shape, **$45.00.**
2. **Cup,** 2" deep, 3⅛" diameter, yellow & white large mottled inside & out, black trim, circa 1960, lightweight. Mint, **$45.00.**
3. **Oblong Stove or Fudge Pan,** 1⅛" deep, 6⅛" wide, 8¼" long, yellow & white large swirl inside & out, black trim, circa 1950. Good plus, rare shape, **$50.00.**
4. **Saucers (3),** ¾" deep, 5¼" diameter, yellow & white large mottled inside & out, black trim, circa 1960. Mint, each **$45.00.**
5. **Cup,** 2" deep, 3⅛" diameter, yellow & white large mottled inside & out, black trim, circa 1960, lightweight. Mint, **$45.00.**
6. **Tumbler,** 4" deep, 3" diameter, yellow & white large swirl inside & out, black trim, circa 1950. Mint, rare shape, **$60.00.**

Row 3:

1. **Sectioned or Divided Plate,** ⅞" deep, 11⅛" diameter, yellow & white large swirl inside & out, black trim, circa 1950. Mint, **$45.00.**
2. **Cup,** 2" deep, 3⅛" diameter, yellow & white large mottled inside & out, black trim. Circa 1960, lightweight. Mint, **$45.00.**
3. **Fry Pan,** 1¾" deep, 8⅛" diameter, yellow & white large mottled, white interior, black handle & trim, handle has been applied by screws, circa 1950. Mint, **$110.00.**
4. **Plate,** ⅞" deep, 10¼" diameter, yellow & white large swirl inside & out, black trim, circa 1950. Mint, **$40.00.**

Row 4:

1. **Mixing or Serving Bowl,** 4⅞" deep, 9¾" top diameter, yellow & white large swirl inside & out, black trim. Circa 1950. Mint, **$40.00.**
2. **Oblong Pudding or Vegetable Dish,** 2½" deep, 8¼" wide, 10⅞" long, yellow & white large swirl inside & out, black trim, circa 1930. Mint, **$165.00.**
3. **Mixing Bowl,** 6" deep, 12¼" diameter, yellow & white large swirl inside & out, black trim, circa 1950. Near mint, **$40.00.**

Note: The pieces from circa 1960 to circa 1980 are lightweight, whereas the earlier pieces seem to be of a heavier weight & the finish on the earlier pieces seem to be smoother in texture. The yellow & white, swirled or mottled pieces seem to date from circa 1930 to the circa 1980. Most of the circa 1930 teapots & coffeepots had a hinged lid & the handle was attached closer to the top of the pot.

Row 1:
1. **Muffin Pan,** 8 cup, 14" long, 7¼" wide, each cup 1½" deep, 3" top diameter, redipped brown & white large mottled inside & out. Near mint, rare color, **$285.00. Note:** This color was redipped at the factory over the original color of cobalt blue & white. When a piece is redipped at the factory with the new color, the original color can be seen slightly through the new color. Therefore, one can tell what type of swirl, mottling, or color it was originally. Also, when a piece gets chipped most often the original factory color can be seen quite clearly. The possible reasons these colors were redipped could have been the original color was not a good seller or a company may have wanted to experiment with a new line of colors. It was cheaper for the companies to use the pieces they already had in stock rather than make or buy new ones.

Row 2:
1. **Oval Pudding or Vegetable Dish,** 1½" deep, 8¼" top width, 10¼" long, redipped light lavender blue & white large swirl, white interior, black trim. Near mint, **$210.00. Note:** This color was redipped at the factory over the original cobalt blue and white. The redipped white enamel did not cover well over the original cobalt blue color.
2. **Measure,** 5½" tall, 3½" diameter, redipped brown & white large swirl over the original cobalt blue & white, white interior, seamed body & lip, rivetted handle. Near mint, rare color & shape, **$325.00.**
3. **Coffeepot,** 8½" tall, 5" diameter, redipped dark lavender & white large swirl over brown & white, white interior, black trim, rivetted handle, seamless body. Good, **$95.00. Note:** I deliberately showed this large chip so you could see how clearly the original factory color shows through the outer edge of the chip.

Row 3:
1. **Teapot,** 7½" tall, 4½" diameter, redipped dark green & white speckled over the original brown & white large swirl, gray & white mottled inside, black trim, seamless body, rivetted handle. Near mint, rare color, **$325.00.**
2. **Flat-Handled Dipper,** 14¼" long, dipper 2" deep, 4¼" diameter, redipped dark blue & white speckled over "emerald" green & white large swirl, white interior, black rivetted handle & trim, Good plus, **$75.00.**
3. **Teapot,** 8¼" tall, 4⅝" diameter, redipped brown & white large swirl over the original cobalt blue & white large swirl, white interior, seamed body, rivetted handle. Near mint, rare color, **$395.00.**

Row 4:
1. **Teakettle,** 8¾" tall, 10" diameter, redipped lavender blue with white flecks inside & out over the original brown & white large mottled, black wooden bail & knob, seamed body, rivetted ears. Good plus, rare color, **$265.00.**
2. **Coffeepot,** 11" tall, 7" diameter, redipped dark blue with white flecks over the original dark green & white "Chrysolite," white interior, black trim, seamless body, rivetted handle. Good plus, **$135.00.**

SECTION 6
GRAY

Row 1:

1. **Water Carrier,** 8" deep, 8½" diameter, gray large mottled, seamless body, pouring lip, bottom tipping handle, wooden bail. Near mint, rare shape and size, **$295.00.**

2. **Sectioned Pie Plate,** ⅝" deep, 8¾" diameter, gray medium mottled. Near mint, extremely rare shape, **$165.00. Note:** The pie plate is sectioned off into 8 recessed sections. The part where the sections are divided are recessed from the center of the pan up to the rolled edge. When a knife is inserted into the pie, it can follow the recessed section for even cutting.

3. **Water Pitcher,** 10⅝" high, 7" diameter, gray large mottled, weld handle, seamless body. Near mint, rare size, **$185.00. Note:** I believe this pitcher was part of a pitcher and bowl set.

Row 2:

1. **Hand Skimmer,** 5¼" long, 5" at the widest point, light gray medium mottled. Near mint, rare shape, **$350.00. Note:** This one is not perforated. Hand skimmers were used for skimming milk or other liquids.

2. **Hand Skimmer,** 5¼" long, 5" at the widest point, gray medium mottled, perforated center. Mint, rare shape, **$375.00. Note:** The perforations are in a diamond shape.

Row 3:

1. **Cover** for upcooker, perforated, 3" high, 6¾" diameter, gray large mottled, perforated bottom section on cover is applied by three rivets. It measures 3¼" diameter, rivetted handle. The edge of the cover flares up over the rim of the bottom section on Row 4, No 1. **Handled bottom section,** 5¼" high, 9¼" top diameter, 5½" bottom diameter, gray large mottled, seamless body, rivetted handle. Near mint, extremely rare shape, 2 pieces complete, **$325.00. Note:** Upcookers were used to boil milk and other liquids. The perforated sections in the cover kept liquids from boiling over on the stove because the boiling liquid would run back through the holes in the perforated cover.

2. **Oval Butter Carrier,** 9¼" high, 7⅝" top width, 10¼" top length, gray large mottled, seamed body, wooden cover. Marked "PAT. AUG. 21, 1888." Near mint, extremely rare color, shape and size, **$695.00. Note:** When the metal handle on the cover is pulled up it locks the metal prongs into the sides of the butter carrier. When the metal handle is pushed down, it releases the prongs to remove the cover. The wooden cover also has a recessed wooden handle to pick the cover off when the metal handle is in a down position.

3. **Scoop,** 8½" long, 2½" deep, 4⅜" wide, gray large mottled, rolled seamed edges. Good plus, extremely rare shape and size, **$265.00. Note:** This scoop does not have a handle. Instead, it is held by the covered top section.

Row 4:

1. **Handled Bottom Section** of the upcooker for the cover on Row 3, No. 1 on this page. Price is given above for both pieces.

2. **Cream Can** with matching granite lock cover, 5¾" high, 3¼" bottom diameter, seamless body, wire bail, gray medium mottled. Near mint, rare shape and size, **$225.00.**

Row 5:

1. **Bench Butter Churn,** 9⅝" high including cover, 6⅝" top width, 11⅛" top length, gray medium mottled, seamed body, metal spigot. Wooden butter paddle, 3⅛" long, 4" wide, handle is 26½" long, paddle has 12 perforations. Butter paddle is attached to the handle with wooden pegs. The handle also swings back and forth on a wooden peg that is placed through the two applied wooden pieces on the cover. Butter Churn Bench, 9¾" high, 7¼" wide, 24" long. Two pieces of wood are applied to top edges of the bench so churn can slide back and forth without tipping off the bench sideways. Near mint, extremely rare color, shape and size, **$985.00.**

Row 1:

1. **Coffee or Tea Canister,** 6" tall, 4¾" diameter, gray medium mottled, seamed body, slip-on tin lid. Near mint, extremely rare shape, **$595.00.**

2. **Coffee Basket,** stemmed, 4¾" tall, basket size 1½" deep, 2⅜" diameter, solid light gray. Good plus, rare size, **$45.00. Note:** I decided to show this coffee basket because this small size is not usually seen.

3. **Double Sauce Pan Set,** each pan 4⅝" high, 5" diameter, 9" long, gray medium mottled, seamed body, rivetted handle, tin cover, black wooden knob. Good plus, rare shape, **$295.00. Note:** These sauce pans were designed to sit on a single burner of a stove to conserve fuel.

4. **Oyster Measure,** 4⅛" deep, 3½" diameter, gray large mottled, seamed body. Embossed "1pt. liq'd." Good plus, extremely rare shape, **$255.00. Note:** Oyster measures do not have lips. These were used to dip & measure oysters from the container at the store.

5. **Oyster Measure,** 5⅜" deep, 4¼" diameter, gray large mottled, seamed body. Embossed "1qt. liq'd." Near mint, extremely rare shape, **$275.00.**

Row 2:

1. **Teakettle,** 6½" tall, 8½" diameter, light gray large mottled, seamed body & spout, rivetted ears, wooden bail. Good plus, **$195.00.**

2. **Coffee Biggin,** 5 pieces. 14¼" tall, including biggin & cover. Biggin measures 4" diameter, 5⅞" tall, gray small mottled, screen bottom, applied nickel-plated rim on top of biggin, rivetted seam the whole length of the biggin. Mint, extremely rare shape & size, **$575.00.**

3. **Spreader,** tall stemmed, 3¾" high, 3⅜" spreader diameter, gray small mottled, perforated bottom. Mint. **Note:** This spreader fits into the bottom section of the biggin.

4. **Coffeepot with Cover,** 9½" tall without biggin, 5½" diameter, gray small mottled, seamed body, applied nickel-plated rim on top of coffeepot. Coffeepot marked "Agate. Nickel-Steel-Ware L & G Mfg. Company." Mint.

5. **Spreader,** short stemmed, 1½" tall, 3⅜" diameter, gray small mottled, perforated bottom. Mint. **Note:** This spreader fits into the top recessed band on the biggin. Coffee biggin complete is 14¼" high.

6. **Teakettle,** 6½" tall, 5¾" diameter, gray medium mottled, seamed body, rivetted ears. Marked "Granite Iron Ware, May 30, 76 – July 3, 77." **Note:** These dates are 1876 – 1877. Good plus, extremely rare shape & size, **$295.00.**

Row 3:

1. **Oval Vienna Pan,** 13½" long not including handles, 6½" wide, each cup measures 1" deep, 3¼" wide, 4½" top length, gray large mottled. Each cup is rivetted together in the middle section of the Vienna pan whereas the outer edges are rolled over the wire frame. The wire frame also forms the handles. Good plus, extremely rare color, shape & size, **$495.00.**

2. **Egg Pan,** five eyes, 1¼" deep, 12" diameter, gray large mottled, each eye measures ⅝" deep, 2¾" top diameter, rivetted handle. Near mint, rare shape, **$275.00.**

3. **Grater,** 11¾" long including handle & feet, 4⅞" wide, solid dark gray. Good plus, rare shape, **$235.00. Note:** The sides of the grater are rolled around the wire frame that also forms the handle & feet. Good plus, rare shape.

Row 4:

1. **Pitcher with Ice Lip,** 7½" tall, 5" diameter, dark gray large mottled, seamless body. Near mint, extremely rare shape, **$225.00. Note:** The lip is turned up to hold the ice from coming out when the liquid is poured.

2. **Muffin or Cake Pan,** each cup, 1¼" deep by 3⅜" diameter, bottom plate that cups are rivetted to measures 4⅝" diameter, gray large mottled. Good plus, extremely rare shape, rare size, **$425.00. Note:** It is believed that this pan was used to test the mixture for the right amount of ingredients & also the oven heat before continuing to bake the rest of the mixture.

3. **Asparagus Boiler,** 7¾" tall, 7¾" wide, 11" long, gray large mottled. Marked "Extra Agate Nickel-Steel-Ware. L & G Mfg. Company." Handled insert is missing. Good Plus, **$165.00.**

Row 1:

1. **Milk Pitcher,** squatty shape, 6⅞" tall, 4½" diameter, gray large mottled, weld handle, seamless body. Near mint, **$185.00.**

2. **Coffeepot,** 11¼" tall, 7½" diameter, gray small mottled, seamed body, rivetted tubular handle. Good plus, **$165.00.**

3. **Roaster,** 5" tall, 7 diameter, gray small mottled, seamless body. Near mint, rare size, **$110.00.**

Row 2:

1. **Covered Fluted Tube Mold,** 7¼" tall, 9" diameter, gray & light gray relish-type pattern, seamed body. Near mint, extremely rare shape & size, **$595.00**

2. **Fruit Press,** 8⅝" tall, base 4⅞" wide, 9¾" long, gray & white large mottled. The press is on cast iron. Embossed on the handle "Presse Fruits. A5." Press also has two inserts for pressing different fruits. These are dark gray medium mottled. Near mint, rare shape, **$295.00.**

3. **Teapot,** 8" tall, 4⅝" diameter, gray large mottled, seamed body. Iron handle embossed "Pat. Oct. 15, 89." Teapot marked on the bottom "Granite-Iron-Ware Pat. May 30, 78 & July 11, 77." Good plus, rare shape & size, **$355.00. Note:** You might wonder how the iron handle could be patented Oct. 15, 1889 & be on a teapot patented 1878 & 1877. The reasons are this particular teapot could have had a different type handle prior to this patented iron handle. When this handle became available, companies might have thought it was more versatile, attractive or maybe less expensive than the one they were using, & therefore, continued to produce the pot with this type handle. Accessories, such as spouts, bands, covers & such, were purchased from other companies & sometimes traveling vendors.

Row 3:

1. **Fluted Funnel,** 6" long to top of the spout, 6¼" diameter, charcoal gray & white, with finger ring & seamed spout. Good plus, rare shape, **$120.00. Note:** Eighteen flutes encircle this funnel.

2. **Pus Basin,** 1¾" deep, 11½" long, 8⅝" wide, gray small mottled. Marked "Granite-Steel-Ware Pat. Oct 9, 94 & July 21, 96." Good plus, rare shape, **$135.00.**

3. **Urinal,** 4½" high, 6" wide, 10⅛" long including spout, gray large mottled, seamed body, rivetted handle. Near mint, **$95.00.**

Row 4:

1. **Fold-Up Electric Stove,** two burners, open position 4¼" high, 8½" wide not including handles, 16¼" long, solid light gray feet, white body, black wooden carrying handles. Attached brass plate reads "Red Cross Heater & Cooker Co-operative Foundry Co., Rochester, NY Volts 110 Amps 8 patented Feb. 13, 1923. Near mint, rare color, shape & size, **$295.00. Note:** When in a fold-up position, the perforations on top allow the heat to escape. The stove then serves as a heater.

2. **Flared Kettle,** 7" deep, 15¾" diameter, gray large mottled, seamless body, wooden bail. Good plus, rare shape, **$145.00.**

Row 1:

1. **Tea Steeper,** 4" tall, 3¾" diameter, gray large mottled, tin cover, rivetted handle, seamless body. Labeled "Nesco Royal Granite Enameled Ware National Enameling & Stamping Co. Nescoware Is Everywhere, Trademark Registered U.S. Patent Office, Made In U.S.A." Near mint, rare size, **$175.00.**

2. **Convex Milk Pitcher,** 6" tall, 5¼" diameter, gray large mottled, rivetted strap handle, seamless body. Marked "Granite Iron Ware, May 30, 76, May 3, 77." Good plus, **$165.00.**

3. **Coffee Flask,** 6¼ " tall, 2" wide, 4⅜" long, gray large mottled, seamed body. Labeled, "Nesco Pure Grey-stone Enameled Ware." Near mint, rare shape, **$285.00.**

Row 2:

1. **Teapot,** metal trimmed, 6¾" tall, 3¾" diameter, gray large mottled, scalloped top edge, metal protection bands, handle, spout, & cover. Near mint, rare shape & size, **$495.00. Note:** The 1892 Manning Bowman catalogue advertises a similar pot, as a ¾ pint size. It also advertises the metal mountings come in 3 different finishes: white metal $10.00 a dozen, nickel plates each $2.00, silver plate $2.50 each.

2. **Coffee Biggin,** 4 pieces including tin biggin, cover, stemmed spreader, and gray large mottled pot. 5½" to top of the cover knob not including the biggin. 3½" diameter. Pot with tin biggin measures 7⅛" to top of the cover knob. Rivetted handle & seamed body. Near mint, rare shape & size, **$435.00. Note:** The spreaders are unusual because they are stemmed together. Most of the time they are separate & each has a knob for lifting.

3. **Teapot,** 4" tall, 3⅛" diameter, light gray large mottled, applied handle, seamed spout, seamless body. Good plus, rare shape & size, **$195.00.**

Row 3:

1. **Round Miner's Dinner Bucket,** 11¾" to top of the granite cup on the cover, 7¼" diameter, gray large mottled, rivetted ears & seamed body. Granite cup fits down inside the neck of the cover. The cover fits over the top of the dinner bucket. Cup measurements are 2" deep, 3½" diameter. Wooden bail handle. Good plus, rare shape, **$295.00. Note:** In this section page 155, Row 1, No. 1 is another round miner's dinner bucket. The difference is that this one is larger & the cup is granite ware instead of tin. Also the bail handle does not lock the cover down for carrying.

2. **Teapot,** 9¾" tall, 5¾" diameter, gray large mottled, iron handle, seamed body & spout. Good plus, rare shape, **$235.00. Note:** Notice the unusual shaped bottom section of this pot. One pot like this is advertised in the "Agate" cookbook as the "Imperial" teapot with stamped bottom.

3. **Individual Muffin Cup,** 1¼" deep, 3¼" diameter, gray large mottled. Near mint, **$85.00.**

4. **Hanging Douche or Irrigator,** 9⅛" deep, 4⅛" wide not including the spout, 8" long across the back, gray large mottled, rivetted strap handle & spout, seamed body, 2 eyelets on the back for hanging. Good plus, rare shape, **$140.00.**

Row 1:

1. **Teapot,** squatty shape, metal trimmed, 7¼" tall, 6⅛" diameter, gray large mottled, metal trimmed spout handle, cover & protection bands. Mint, rare shape, **$425.00. Note:** Protection bands keep the most vulnerable area of the pot from being chipped. This type pot is shown in the 1892 Manning Bowman & Co. catalogue as "Patent Perfection Granite Ironware" with white metal mountings & protection bands. Price per dozen with white metal is $22.00, nickel plate ea. $2.75, silver plate ea. $3.25. It is also interesting to note that the 2 pint size is advertised as a coffeepot. Today's collectors call the metal trims "pewter trim." There is no mention in this catalog of pewter trim.

2. **Dinner Castor Set,** 15½" tall, 6⅜" middle diameter, base diameter 5", gray medium mottled, white metal mountings & protection bands. Five No. 15 bottles consist of two peppers, one mustard, two vinegars. Bottles are etched. The 1892 Manning Bowman catalogue advertises these dinner castors "for strength & durability, these castors excel all ware heretofore made for a similar purpose; & should the acids or mustard or vinegar come in contact with the granite enamel it will not be affected. From these handsome designs, it will be seen that the goods are therefore more desirable than those made entirely of metal." "Patent Perfection Granite Ironware." Nickel plate sold for $5.00 each, silver plate sold for $5.75 each. Mint, extremely rare shape, **$2,500.00.**

3. **Teapot,** metal trim, 10½" tall, 5½" diameter, bottom section of the pot is gray large mottled. Advertised in the 1892 Manning, Bowman catalogue as "Patent Perfection Granite Ironware" Engraved Series with seamless bottoms & protection bands. Near mint, **$295.00.**

Row 2:

1. **Mug,** 4⅛" deep, 4" diameter, light gray & white large marbleized, white interior, seamless body. Good plus, rare color, **$75.00. Note:** I have only seen the two pieces that are shown on this page in this color. I believe they were made in Germany.

2. **Rabbit Mold,** fluted, oval shape, 1⅛" deep, 2⅞" wide, 3¾" long, charcoal gray & light gray mottled inside & out with rabbit imprint. Near mint, extremely rare shape, **$245.00. Note:** This little individual mold could have been used to mold gelatin or candy.

3. **Colander,** 4¼" deep front top side, 3¾" deep on the top of each end by the handles, 10¼" wide, 11⅝" long not including handles, gray medium mottled, seamed body, perforated on the sides & bottom. Good plus, rare shape, **$135.00. Note:** This colander, as you can see by the measurements & picture, appears to have an oval shape on the upper section. I don't know whether it was an attempt to make an oval colander or if it just came out that way. However, it is an unusual shape.

4. **Measure,** 3½" tall, 2⅞" diameter, gray large mottled, seamed body & lip, weld handle. Embossed "¼ qt. Liq'd." Near mint, rare size, **$235.00.**

5. **Covered Berlin-Style Kettle,** 5" tall, 5¾" diameter not including handles, light gray & white large marbleized, white interior, seamless body. Good plus, rare color, shape & size, **$140.00.**

Row 3:

1. **Oval Tureen,** 10½" tall, 13" wide, 16¼" long not including handles, gray large mottled, seamless body. The dome-shaped cover has a cutout on the rim's outer edge where the handle of the ladle fits. Good plus, rare size, **$195.00. Note:** This is an unusually large tureen.

2. **Handled Ladle,** 12¼" long, 3⅜" ladle diameter, charcoal gray & light gray medium mottled. Near Mint, rare shape, **$110.00. Note:** This ladle is not perforated & it is flat. This is only the second one of these I have seen. I still don't know what its purpose was. It could possibly be for scooping dumplings or such out of the broth.

3. **Double Boiler,** 11¾" tall including the insert, 9¼" diameter, gray medium mottled, seamless body, wooden bail handles. Both sections marked "L. & G. Mfg. Co." Good plus, **$115.00.**

Row 1:

1. **Oblong Tray,** ⅝" deep, 9½" wide, 13⅜" long, gray large mottled. Marked "L & G Mfg. Co." Near mint, **$135.00.**

2. **Eight-Sided Strainer with Handle,** 4" deep, 8¼" across the top, gray large mottled. The drain pan is attached to the three spatula-shaped feet. Good plus, rare shape, **$275.00. Note:** We have illustrated the other two varieties in this shape, the difference in this one is that it has an eyelet for hanging.

3. **Pump or Bellboy Pitcher,** 8¼" tall, 6¼" diameter, gray large mottled, rivetted two piece ears & tipping handle, black wooden bail handle, seamless body. Good plus, extremely rare shape & rare color, **$395.00.**

Row 2:

1. **Elliptical Funnel,** 5¾" tall, 4⅝" diameter, gray large mottled, rivetted strap handle, & seamed body. Good plus, **$65.00.**

2. **Flat Skimmer,** handled, perforated, 12" long to top of the handle, 3½" diameter, dark gray. Marked "Extra Agate Nickel-Steel-Ware. L & G Mfg. Co." Near mint, rare size, **$70.00. Note:** L & G Mfg. Co. is the logo for the Lalance & Grosjean Manufacturing Company.

3. **Convex Water Pitcher,** 6½" tall, 5½" diameter, gray medium mottled, seamless body with applied fancy handle. Good plus, rare shape, **$195.00.**

4. **Spoon,** 11¾" long to top of the handle, 2⅜" wide, gray medium mottled. Marked "Extra Agate Nickel-Steel-Ware." Near mint, **$45.00.**

5. **Grocer's Scoop,** 9¼" long including the handle, 5¼" wide, gray large mottled, tubular open end seamed handle. Handle is applied to the body of the scoop by three rivets. Good plus, rare shape, **$145.00.**

Row 3:

1. **Large Dipper,** 2⅝" deep, 6⅛" diameter, large mottled gray, seamless body, rivetted handle. Near mint, **$65.00. Note:** This dipper resembles a sauce pan with a long handle.

2. **Muffin Pan,** 12 cups, each cup measures 1¼" deep, 2¾" diameter. Overall measurements are 9½" wide, 12½" long. Gray large mottled. The underside of this muffin pan has straps that hold the cups in place. Embossed "Agate Seconds." Good plus, rare shape & size, **$185.00.**

3. **Teakettle with Insert,** 6½" tall, including the insert, 8½" diameter, gray large mottled, rivetted handles on teakettle & insert. Teakettle has seamed body & black wooden bail handle. Good plus, **$195.00.**

Row 1:

1. **Teakettle,** 4⅝" tall, 7⅛" diameter, light & darker gray relish type pattern, seamed body. The aluminum spout cover has a slit in the outer top side, so when the teakettle is boiling it makes a whistling sound. A small chain is attached to the aluminum spout cover & back to the handle. Good plus, **$170.00.**

2. **Oblong Baking Pan,** 2½" deep, 11⅞" wide, 18¼" long, gray large mottled with applied handles, seamless body. Good plus, **$75.00.**

3. **Covered Kettle,** 6½" tall, 9" diameter, gray large mottled, seamless body. Good plus, **$110.00.**

Row 2:

1. **Berlin-Style Covered Kettle,** 9" tall, 11" diameter, light gray medium mottled, cobalt blue trim & handles, seamless body. Near mint, **$125.00. Note:** I believe this is a product of the Federal Enameling & Stamping Company, of Pittsburgh, PA.

2. **Side Snipe Ladle,** 14⅝" long, ladle 1⅝" deep, 4½" diameter not including the side pouring lip. Lip measures 1½" long. Gray large mottled with rivetted handle, eyelet for hanging. Good plus, rare shape & size, **$175.00.**

3. **Pitcher & Bowl,** pitcher measures 10⅜" tall, 7¼" diameter, gray medium mottled. Marked "L & G Mfg. Co." in an oval. This is the mark of the Lalance & Grosjean Manufacturing Company. Good plus. Bowl measures 3¾" deep, 14½" diameter, gray large mottled, eyelet for hanging. Good plus, both pieces **$155.00. Note:** Even though these two pieces don't go together I put them together so you could compare the big difference in the grays.

Row 3:

1. **Coal-Hod,** 15" tall, 10½" diameter, 18" long, solid bluish gray inside & out. Seamed body. Embossed "GM." Good plus, rare shape, **$195.00.**

2. **Oval Foot Tub,** 8¾" deep, 12⅞" wide, 18¾" top length not including the handles, dark gray medium mottled, seamed body. Good plus, **$120.00.**

Row 1:
1. **Miner's Dinner Bucket,** round, 10½" tall, 6¾" diameter, gray large mottled. Tin cup fits down inside the neck on the cover. Tin cup measures 1½" deep, 3" diameter. Cover fits over lunch bucket. Food tray is missing. Good plus, rare shape, **$275.00. Note:** The wooden bail handle has indentations that lock the cover down while carrying.
2. **Lady Finger Pan,** ½" deep, 11½" long, 6" wide, gray large mottled. Marked "Agate. Nickel-Steel-Ware L & G Mfg. Co." Near mint, rare shape, **$395.00. Note:** This is a larger size lady finger pan.
3. **Oval Three-Piece Lunch Bucket,** 7¾" tall, 6½" wide, 9" long, gray large mottled. The three pieces include bottom section. Cup fits over the neck of the coffee flask, and flask fits into the top part of the lunch bucket. Good plus, rare shape, **$325.00.**

Row 2:
1. **Strainer,** eight-sided, 3¾" high, 8" diameter, gray large mottled, with three spatula feet. Near mint, **$165.00.**
2. **Thumb Scoop,** 5½" long including handle, 2⅝" wide, gray large mottled. Near mint, rare shape & size **$175.00.**
3. **Oval Vegetable Dish,** 5" tall, 8¼" wide, 11" long not including handles, gray large mottled. Marked "Granite-Iron-Ware. Pat. May 30, 76." Rivetted handles with black wooden inserts, seamless body. Near mint, extremely rare shape, **$495.00.**
4. **Soup Ladle,** 7¾" long, ladle part ⅞" deep, 3⅛" top diameter, gray small mottled, rivetted handle. Good plus, **$75.00. Note:** At first glance, this piece looks like a sauce ladle. Usually sauce ladles have a pouring spout, whereas soup ladles do not. This is the smallest soup ladle I have seen.
5. **Strainer with Side Handle,** eight-sided, drain pan connected by three spatula feet, 4⅜" high, 8" diameter, gray large mottled. Near mint, rare shape, **$295.00. Note:** The side handle for carrying. The bottom drain pan serves as a tray to catch the remaining water when vegetables are washed.

Row 3:
1. **Footed Mold,** 2⅜" deep, 5¼" wide, 6½" long, gray medium mottled, rolled top edge. It is not meant to have a cover. The mold rests on 4 rivetted feet on the bottom of the melon shaped mold. Good plus, rare shape, **$175.00. Note:** This is the smallest size I have seen. The maker's name has been blotted out.
2. **Sugar Bowl,** squatty shape, 5⅛" tall, 4⅝" diameter, gray medium mottled. Good plus, **$295.00.**
3. **Milk Pitcher,** squatty shape, 4⅞" tall, 4⅞" diameter, gray large mottled. Good plus, rare size, **$185.00.**
4. **Melon Mold,** 3¼" deep, 5" wide, 6½" long, gray large mottled. Near mint, rare shape & size, **$155.00. Note:** This mold is unusual because it has an applied metal band on the edge that the cover fits over. The name "melon mold" refers to the shape, not to its use.

Row 4:
1. **Toddy Strainer,** 6" long, 2⅞" wide, gray medium mottled, perforated shell shaped, rivetted handle. Advertised in the 1800's "Agate Cook Book" as "Agate Toddy Strainer. No. 10. Each 15¢." Good plus, extremely rare shape, **$525.00.**
2. **Fish Tool,** 13" long, 3" wide, solid gray, perforated in a diamond pattern, rolled tubular hook handle. Good plus, rare color & shape, **$155.00. Note:** This tool was used for scaling & serving fish.
3. **Tea Strainer,** 4" diameter, ⅞" deep, gray medium mottled, perforated bottom. Near mint, **$85.00. Note:** Tea strainers were placed over cups or glasses to strain different liquids such as tea or lemonade.

155

Row 1:

1. **Clabber Cup,** 2⅜" deep, 3⅞" diameter, gray medium mottled, seamed body, rivetted handle & feet, perforated side & bottom. Good plus, rare shape, **$200.00. Note:** I have been told this is a clabber cup. I have found no reference to this piece otherwise. It is used to drain clabber from cheese. Clabber is a thick sour or curdled milk separated out in the cheesemaking process.

2. **Coffee Biggin,** 6½" tall including the biggin, 3½" diameter, gray large mottled. 5 pieces including coffee pot, tin biggin, 2 spreaders, & cover. Good plus, rare shape, **$255.00. Note:** Notice the unusual shape of the handle, flat instead of the common curved handle.

3. **Round Griddle with handle,** ⅝" deep, 11" diameter, gray large mottled, handle has eyelet for hanging & is embossed "National." Near mint, **$125.00. Note:** A faint marking is visible on the underside flat surface of the griddle, reading "Royal Granite, Nesco."

4. **Lightning Egg Beater**, bottom section, 5¼" deep, 3⅞" diameter, gray large mottled, seamed body. Inside on the bottom edge is a rivetted loop that held the top cover section secure while beating the eggs. The cover & beater is missing. Near mint, rare shape, **$95.00. Note:** This is shown in the late 1800's "Agate" cookbook.

5. **Teapot,** squatty shape, 4¼" tall, 3⅜" diameter, gray medium mottled, seamless body. Good plus, rare shape & size, **$170.00.**

Row 2:

1. **Boston Cream Can,** (Milk Kettle), 5½" tall, 3⅜" diameter, gray large mottled, rivetted strap handle, seamed body. Labeled "Graystone Enameled Steelware. National Enameling & Stamping Co. Baltimore. Md. U.S.A. patented Oct 9, 1884, July 1, 1896, Sept 29, 1896, July 19, 1898, Sept 12, 1899, No. 81. Milk Kettle Perfectly Pure, Absolute Safety in Use." Good plus, **$150.00.**

2. **Covered Cuspidor,** 5½" tall, 4¾" diameter, gray large mottled, rivetted handle & seamed bottom. Marked "Agate Ware L & G Mfg. Co." Near mint, extremely rare shape, **$225.00.**

3. **Pie Plate,** 1" deep, 8¾" diameter gray medium mottled. Embossed "Ideal Wonder Plate." Good plus, rare shape, **$195.00.**

4. **Tea Steeper,** with matching granite cover, 5¼" tall, 3⅞" diameter, medium mottled gray, seamless body. Good plus, **$125.00. Note:** The cover is hinged on the top part of the strap handle.

5. **Teakettle,** 3⅞" tall, 5¾" diameter, gray large mottled. Black wooden bail handle & cover knob, seamed bottom & spout. Partial label reads "Patented 1894, & July 18, 1896." Good plus, rare size, **$200.00**

Row 3:

1. **Round Griddle,** ⅝" deep, 16¼" diameter, gray medium mottled, looped wire bail handle, rivetted ears. The "Agate Cookbook 1889 Agate Patent" advertised this as the "Beauty Griddle." Good plus, rare shape, **$125.00.**

2. **Tart Pan,** ⅞" deep, 6" diameter, gray large mottled. Good plus, **$45.00.**

Row 4:

1. **Griddle,** oblong shape with handles, ¾" deep, 10" wide, 21" long, gray medium mottled, rivetted handles. marked "Granite Iron Ware. Pat Oct 9, 84 & July 21, 96." Good plus, rare shape, **$135.00.**

2. **Oval Clothes Boiler,** 14½" deep, 12¾" wide, 18½" long not including the handles, medium mottled gray. Partial label reads "Sterling Enameled Nickeled Steelware No. Newark, N.Y., Buffalo, Chicago, Made in U.S.A." Good plus, rare shape, **$140.00.**

Row 1:
1. **Steam Coffeepot Insert,** 8½" tall, 4⅝" diameter. The top nickel-plated cover on the coffeepot extends ⅜" over the pot so it can fit securely into the nickel-plated holder. The spout of the pot is covered. Good plus, extremely rare shape, **$485.00. Note:** The 1892 Manning, Bowman & Co. catalogue refers to this pot as "The International Pot, Pearl Agate Reservoir." The bag or pack holds the ground coffee & thus keeps the liquid extract or beverage perfectly clear & pure.
2. **Steam Coffee Pot Holder,** 8½" deep, 5⅜" diameter, nickel-plated, goes with Item No. 1 on Row 1. Holds the hot water to keep beverages hot while serving or for a period of time. Marked "Patent." Good plus, **$485.00.** 2 pieces including No. 1 & 2 on this row.
3. **Coffee Biggin,** 9¾" tall including tin biggin, 5⅜" diameter, gray large mottled, seamed body. Near mint, rare shape, **$495.00. Note:** The 1892 Manning, Bowman catalog advertises this pot as "'Good Morning' Coffee Percolator, with combination Textile Fabric Filter, Planished Extension Top & White Metal Spout Patented September 30, 1884." This is the first gray pot I have seen with a wooden handle.

Row 2:
1. **Agate Patent "Windsor" Saucepan with Ring,** 3¼" deep 7" diameter, 7⅞" diameter where ring is attached. The ring is attached to the saucepan with four rivets, rivetted handle, gray large mottled. Good plus, rare shape **$185.00. Note:** This saucepan is shown in the 1800's Agate cook Book. It states comes with a tin cover for $1.20 each or with an agate cover for $1.35 each. The ring on the pan allows it to sit down in the open burner of the cook stove closer to the heat.
2. **Deep Sauce Pan,** 7¾" tall, 6" top diameter, 4⅝" bottom diameter, dark gray medium mottled, seamed body, rivetted handle. Good plus, rare shape, **$135.00. Note:** I believe this sauce pan could be an insert for a bain marie. A bain marie is a vessel that holds hot water and has other vessels of food placed inside the hot water. Also note the rim around the center of the sauce pan. This holds the saucepan partially out of the hot water.
3. **Bucket,** shape, 5" deep, 4¾" diameter, gray medium mottled, seamed body, rivetted ears, wire bail. Near mint, **$95.00. Note:** I believe this shape bucket was designed to fit into something because there is an extended rim three quarters of the way up the bucket. Possibly it could have fit into a bain marie, lunch bucket, or a teakettle.

Row 3:
1. **Washboard,** overall measurements, 23½" long, 11¾" wide, granite surface 12" long, 10⅝" wide, American gray medium mottled. Good plus, extremely rare color, rare shape, **$265.00. Note:** This is the first one of these I have seen with this type of scrubbing surface.
2. **Dipper,** Agate, Extra Strong, half oval handle, dark gray medium mottled, rivetted handle. Good plus, rare size, **$110.00. Note:** This is advertised in the 1800's "Agate" Cook Book as No. 12, 5¼" x 3¼" each .55.

Row 4:
1. **Candlestick,** "Save-All." 2" high to top of the candleholder, 6⅜" diameter, gray medium mottled, rivetted finger ring. Good plus, rare shape, **$275.00. Note:** This is called a Save-All candlestick because the four center prongs are designed to hold the candle securely so it can burn down to the very end.
2. **Spit Cup,** 3" tall, 4" diameter, gray medium mottled, seamless body, rivetted handle & thumb lift. Good plus, rare shape, **$195.00. Note:** These were carried & used by both men & women who chewed tobacco or used snuff.
3. **Water Carrier,** 15¾" tall, 10" diameter, gray medium mottled, seamed body, rivetted handles, covered spout, ears & support piece on the handle. Near mint, extremely rare color, shape & size, **$950.00. Note:** Advertised in the 1800's "Agate" Cook Book as the water carrier in the three-piece Agate "King" toilet sets & also in the Agate "Prince" toilet sets. Water carrier priced at $3.00 each. The other two pieces were a slop jar with a bail, $4.00 each & an oval foot tub with foot $2.50 each. Complete set $9.50.

SECTION 7
RED AND WHITE

Row 1:

1. **Coffeepot,** 9½" tall, 5⅞" diameter, old red and white medium swirl with white interior and cobalt blue trim, seamless body, rivetted handle. Good plus, extremely rare color, shape and size, **$1,650.00.**
2. **Teakettle,** 6" tall, 6¼" diameter, old red and white large swirl, solid red interior, seamless spout and body. Notched ears designed to keep the wire bail handle in an upright position, which keeps the handle cool for carrying. Good plus, extremely rare color, shape and size, **$1,800.00.**
3. **Coffeepot,** 8½" tall, 5⅜" diameter, old red and white medium swirl with white interior, cobalt blue trim, seamless body, rivetted handle. Good, extremely rare color, shape and size, **$1,550.00.**

Row 2:

1. **Milk Can,** 9¼" tall, 4⅞" diameter, old red and white large swirl with white interior and dark blue trim, rivetted ears, seamless body and wire bail. Good plus, extremely rare color, shape and size, **$2,700.00. Note:** The design of the ears. They seem to be applied in two sections and rivetted to the body.
2. **Cup and Saucer,** Cup 2⅛" deep, 4¼" diameter, old red and white large swirl with white interior, dark blue trim and handle. Near mint. Saucer, 1" deep, 6" diameter, old red and white swirl inside and out with dark blue trim. Mint, extremely rare color, shape and size, 2 pieces, **$1,050.00.**
3. **Teapot,** 9½" tall, 5¾" diameter, old red and white swirl with white interior, dark blue trim, rivetted solid red handle. Good plus, extremely rare color, shape and size, **$2,000.00.**

Row 3:

1. **Milk Pan,** 2" deep, 8⅜" diameter, old red and white medium swirl with white interior and dark blue trim. Good plus, extremely rare color, shape and size, **$400.00.**
2. **Chamber Pot,** 5" deep, 9" diameter, old red and white medium swirl with white interior, and dark blue trim, rivetted strap handle, seamless body. Mint, extremely rare color, shape and size, **$2,650.00. Note:** This piece is mint. To find a piece of old red and white swirl in mint condition is almost impossible. This is the reasoning for the price.

Row 4:

1. **Wash Basin,** 3½" deep, 12¼" diameter, old red and white large swirl with white interior and dark blue trim, eyelet for hanging. Near mint, extremely rare color, shape and size, **$750.00.**

160

Row 1:

1. **Canisters** (3), #1- 5" tall, 3⅜" diameter, old red & white large swirl, white interior with tiny blue specks, red trim with black lettering reading "Epices." #2- 6¾" tall, 4½" diameter. Marked "Cafe." #3- 5¾" tall, 3¾" diameter. Marked "Thé." All near mint, extremely rare color, shape & size, **$1,350.00.**

2. **Oblong Baking Pan,** with molded handles, 2⅛" deep, 10⅜" wide, 15¼" long not including the handles, old red & white large swirl with white interior, cobalt blue trim, eyelet for hanging. Good plus, extremely rare color, shape & size, **$1,675.00.**

3. **Pudding Pan,** 3" deep, 8½" diameter, old red & white large swirl with white interior, cobalt blue trim. Good plus, extremely rare color, shape & size, **$400.00.**

Row 2:

1. **Water Pitcher,** 9⅛" tall, 6" diameter, old red & white large swirl inside & out. Good plus, extremely rare color, shape & size, **$2,300.00**

2. **Tea Strainer,** 1" deep, 3¾" diameter, old red & white large swirl inside & out. Good plus, extremely rare color, shape & size, **$1,250.00.**

3. **Mush Mug,** 5" deep, 6¼" diameter, old red & white large swirl, white interior, cobalt blue trim. Good plus, extremely rare color, shape & size, **$985.00.**

4. **Pie Plate,** ⅞" deep, 9¾" diameter, old red & white large swirl with white interior, cobalt blue trim. Near mint, extremely rare color, shape & size, **$400.00.**

Row 3:

1. **Cuspidor** (2 pieces), 5⅛" tall, 10⅞" diameter. Top cover section is the old red & white large swirl inside & out. The bottom section is solid dark blue with white interior & cobalt blue trim. Good plus, extremely rare color, shape & size, **$1,250.00. Note:** No, this is not something I put together, this is the way I got it. I believe it was originally purchased this way because the tops & bottoms of cuspidors could be purchased separately, or perhaps the original bottom was thrown away & this color bottom was purchased.

2. **Soup Ladle,** 15½" long, 1½" deep, 3¾" diameter, old red & white large swirl inside & out, cobalt blue trim & handle. Near mint, extremely rare color, shape & size, **$550.00.**

3. **Coffee Boiler,** 13¼" tall, 10¾" diameter, old red & white large swirl with white interior, cobalt blue trim & handle, seamed body, rivetted spout, ears, & handle. Good plus, extremely rare color, shape & size, **$2,100.00.**

Special Note: Sometimes it is necessary to show a few pieces from Book 1, in order to complete a full page of a certain color that is extremely rare & hard to find. Also it's nice to be able to show & compare pieces that have been found since my first book.

Row 1:
1. **Mug,** 3⅛" deep, 3¼" diameter, old red & white large swirl, white interior, cobalt blue trim, rivetted handle, seamless body. Near mint, extremely rare color, shape & size, **$525.00.**
2. **Soup Ladle,** 13¾" long, 1⅝" deep, 3½" diameter, old red & white large swirl inside & out, black handle. Near mint, extremely rare color, shape & size, **$550.00.**
3. **Water Pitcher,** 9⅛" tall, 6⅛" diameter, old red & white large swirl, white interior, dark blue trim, seamless body. Near mint, extremely rare color, shape & size, **$2,850.00.**
4. **Cup,** 2" deep, 2⅞" diameter, old red & white large swirl with white interior, red trim & handle. Near mint, extremely rare color, shape & size, **$525.00.**
5. **Funnel,** 6⅛" tall, 5⅞" diameter, old red & white swirl inside & out, black trim & handle. Near mint, extremely rare color, shape & size, **$1,675.00.**

Row 2:
1. **Coffeepot,** 8⅝" tall, 5¼" diameter, old red & white medium swirl, white interior with cobalt blue trim, rivetted handle & cover, seamless body. Good plus, extremely rare color, shape & size, **$1,550.00.**
2. **Teakettle,** 7" tall, 9¼" bottom diameter, old red & white large swirl, white interior with wooden bail, seamed body & spout. Near mint, extremely rare color, shape & size, **$2,100.00.**
3. **Teapot,** 8¼" tall, 4½" diameter, old red & white large swirl, white interior with black trim & handle, seamless body. Near mint, extremely rare color, shape & size, **$2,875.00.**

Row 3:
1. **Coffee Boiler,** 12" tall, 9⅜" diameter, old red & white large swirl, white interior with dark cobalt blue trim & handle, seamed body, rivetted spout, ears, & handle. Near mint, extremely rare color, shape & size, **$2,450.00.**
2. **Cup,** 2" deep, 2⅞" diameter, old red & white large swirl, white interior with red trim. Near mint, extremely rare color, shape & size, **$525.00. Note:** The handle on this cup is the red & white swirl while the cup in Row 1 has a solid red handle.
3. **Pie Plate,** ⅞" deep, 9¾" diameter, old red & white large mottled, white interior, with cobalt blue trim. Near mint, extremely rare color, shape & size, **$400.00.**
4. **Water Pail,** 8½" deep, 11⅝" diameter, old red & white large swirl, white interior with cobalt blue trim & ears, wooden bail, rivetted ears. Near mint, extremely rare color, shape & size, **$2,000.00.**

Note: Most of the pieces shown on this page have black streaked through the dark red color. Some of the pieces also have black streaked through the white on the outside. All of the pieces shown are heavy and the enamel on the old red and white is very thick. I believe that most of the pieces are triple coated. The red coloring is quite dark, as you can see. The color of the trim also varies.

Many people get circa 1950 red & white confused with the old red & white. You can easily compare the difference in this book. The circa 1950 red & white is lighter in weight, the construction is quite different, also the red coloring is not as dark as the old red. One reason collectors confuse the two is that there is very little old red & white to be found for comparison.

The extreme rarity of the old red & white mottled or swirled pieces is based on the depth of the red coloring as well as the shape, size, & condition. It could be a common shape or size in another color. Example, a medium size coffee or teapot in gray is fairly common compared to an old red & white mottled or swirled medium size coffee or teapot.

Row 1:
1. **Coffee Biggin,** 4 pieces, including the biggin, spreader, cover & pot. 9¼" tall including the biggin, 5¼" diameter, red & white medium mottled with white interior & red trim, seamless body. Near mint, extremely rare color & shape, **$595.00.**
2. **Lavabo & Basin,** lavabo measures 12" tall not including the dolphin-shaped spigot. 5¾" wide, 9⅝" long, red & white large mottled, white interior & red trim. Basin is 9⅞" high, 3¼" deep, 13¾" long, red & white large mottled inside & out with red trim. Good plus, extremely rare color & size, **$595.00.**
3. **Berlin Style Kettle,** 4½" deep, 6½" diameter, red & white large mottled, white interior, red trim, rivetted ears, wooden bail handle, seamless body. Marked "Elite Austria Reg'd 6-16." Snow on the Mountain. Good plus, extremely rare color & rare shape, **$285.00.**

Row 2:
1. **Teapot,** 8¾" tall, 5¼" diameter, red & white large mottled with white interior, red trim, seamed body. Near mint, extremely rare color & shape, **$675.00. Special Note:** This teapot is a very rare example of "Snow on the Mountain" because the color is reversed. The red is the overall lumpy effect instead of the overall lumpy white effect that you usually see on "Snow on the Mountain."
2. **Coffee Carrier,** 8½" tall, 5¼" diameter, red & white large mottled with white interior, red trim, seamed body with wire bail. Good plus, extremely rare color & rare shape, **$550.00. Note:** I believe "Coffee Carrier" is the generic name given to this piece by today's collectors, because in the old trade catalogues they are referred to as utility kettles for milk, beer or oysters. The tapered body helps to keep them from tipping over.
3. **Coffee Biggin,** 4 pieces, including the biggin, spreader, cover & pot. 9½" tall, including the biggin. 4¾" diameter, red & white large mottled with white interior, red handle & trim, seamed body. Near mint, extremely rare color & shape, **$595.00.**

Row 3:
1. **Two-handled Egg Plate or Pan.** 1⅜" deep, 5¾" diameter not including the handles, red & white large mottled with white interior, red trim. Marked "Saint-Servais Belgique." Good plus, extremely rare color, **$225.00.**
2. **Funnel,** 5¼" tall, 4⅛" diameter, red & white large mottled inside & out, red trim. "Snow on the Mountain." Near mint, extremely rare color, **$235.00. Note:** This funnel has the usual lumpy white enamel over the red in comparison to #1 on Row 2 of this page. I believe "Snow on the Mountain" is a generic term used for the lumpy type finish by today's collectors, because I have found no reference to this name in any of the old trade catalogues or ads. Most people have a tendency to call anything with a white finish over the color "Snow on the Mountain."
3. **Tea Strainer,** 1" deep, 4" diameter, red & white large mottled with white interior, fancy perforated bottom. Good, extremely rare color & shape, **$165.00. Note:** This is an extremely rare shape & color for a tea strainer.

Note: I believe that all the pieces on this page are of foreign origin.

Row 1:

1. **Utensil Rack,** (tools not original). 19¼" back height, 12" wide. Drip tray 1⅜" deep, 4¼" wide, 14" long, red & white large mottled front & back. Has a heavy gauge metal bar that holds the utensils. Tools: Soup ladle 1½" deep, 3⅛" diameter, 11¾" long. Handled skimmer with perforated bottom ¾" deep, 4¾" diameter, 13¾" long. Tasting spoon ¾" deep, 2½" diameter, 12¾" long. Good plus, extremely rare color, rare shape. Utensil rack and three utensils near mint, **$525.00.**

Row 2:

1. **Handled Gravy or Soup Strainer,** with screen bottom, 2¼" deep, 6¼" diameter, red & white medium mottled with white interior, red trim. "Snow on the Mountain." This piece has an illegible mark. Good plus, rare color, **$115.00.**

2. **Coffee Biggin,** (3 pieces) including pot, biggin, & cover. 9⅝" tall including the biggin, 4¾" diameter, red & off-white large mottled with white interior & red trim. Near mint, extremely rare color & shape, **$595.00. Note:** The white in this piece has a mixture of light gray in it. The biggin has a perforated metal bottom with spring action rim that holds the biggin in place.

Row 3:

1. **Slop Bucket,** with matching cover, 11¾" tall, 9⅝" diameter, red & white large mottled with white interior, red trim, rivetted wire ears, seamed bottom, with wooden bail handle. Near mint, extremely rare color, **$495.00.**

2. **Water Pitcher,** 9" tall, 6⅜" diameter, red & white large mottled with white interior, rivetted handle & seamless body. "Snow on the Mountain." Extremely rare color & shape, **$325.00. Note:** This piece has a very lumpy effect of white enamel that has been applied over the red, this piece is also very heavy. The red & white "Snow on the Mountain" is much harder to find than the green or blue.

Row 1:
1. **Coffeepot,** 9½" tall, 5½" diameter, red & white, large swirl, black trim, white interior, seamed body. Good plus, rare color, **$200.00. Note:** The handle is red & white swirl. Circa 1950.
2. **Oval Platter,** 1¼" deep, 13" wide, 17½" long, red & white, large swirl, black trim, circa 1950. Mint, rare color, shape & size, **$175.00.**
3. **Covered Two-Handled Pan,** 4⅝" tall, 8⅛" diameter, red & white, large swirl, white interior, black trim, circa 1950. Mint, **$110.00.**

Row 2:
1. **Straight-Sided Kettle**, 6¾" tall, 8¾" diameter, red & white, large swirl, black trim, white interior, seamless body. Mint, **$225.00. Note:** The handles are solid with no openings, circa 1930.
2. **Handled Sauce Pan,** 2⅜" tall, 5⅜" diameter, red & white, large swirl, black trim & handle, white interior, seamless body, circa 1930. Mint, **$95.00.**
3. **Coffeepot,** 8" tall, 5½" diameter, red & white large swirl, black trim & handle, white interior, seamless body. Mint, rare color, **$250.00. Note:** This coffeepot has an aluminum coffee basket, circa 1930.

Row 3:
1. **Teakettle,** 5" tall, 5½" diameter, red & white, large swirl, white interior, black trim & ears, black wooden handle, Bakelite knob, seamless body, circa 1950. Near mint, rare color, shape & size, **$265.00.**
2. **Coffeepot,** 8¾" tall, 5½" diameter, red & white, large swirl, black trim, white interior, Bakelite knob, seamless body, circa 1950. Near mint, rare color, **$235.00.**
3. **Mugs,** 3" deep, 3½" diameter, red & white large swirl, white interior, black trim & handle, seamless, circa 1950. Mint, ea. **$45.00. Note:** The coffeepot & 6 mugs were bought as a set.

Row 4:
Stack Refrigerator Containers, red & white, large swirl inside & out, seamless, circa 1950. Near mint, 4 piece set, **$550.00.** Pieces are listed in order from bottom piece to top piece.
1. 2¾" deep including cover, 6⅞" wide, 10⅛" long.
2. 2¾" deep, 6⅜" wide, 9⅝" long.
3. 2½" deep, 6¾" wide, 8⅝" long.
4. 2⅜" deep, 5⅛" wide, 7¾" long.
5. **Coffeepot,** 8½" tall, 5½" diameter, red & white large swirl, black trim, Bakelite knob, white interior, seamless body, aluminum coffee basket, circa 1950. Mint, rare color, **$265.00.**

Row 1:
1. **Teapot,** 7¾" tall, 4¾" diameter, deep red & white large swirl with white interior, black trim, seamed body, circa 1950. Near mint, rare color, **$145.00.**
2. **Teapot,** 8" tall, 4⅞" diameter, red & white large swirl with white interior, dark blue trim, seamed body, circa 1960. Mint, rare color, **$115.00.**
3. **Teapot,** 8" tall, 4⅞" diameter, red & white large swirl with white interior, dark blue trim, seamed body, circa 1960. Mint, rare color, **$115.00. Note:** Teapot #1 is smaller, has black trim & is also deeper red than the others in this row. I believe this is circa 1950. Also I chose these 3 pots so you could compare color as well as the difference types of swirling. Basically, all 3 of these teapots are lightweight, although #1 is slightly heavier.

Row 2:
1. **Mug,** 3½" deep, 3¾" diameter, deep red & white large swirl with white interior, black trim, circa 1950. Good plus, **$55.00.**
2. **Mug,** 3½" deep, 3¾" diameter, deep red & white large swirl with white interior, black trim, circa 1950. Near mint, **$45.00.**
3. **Oblong Pudding Pan or Vegetable Dish,** 2" deep, 6½" top width, 8½" top length, deep red & white large swirl inside & out, black trim, circa 1950. Near mint, rare color & shape, **$150.00.**
4. **Oblong Pudding Pan or Vegetable Dish,** 2" deep, 6½" top width, 8½" top length, deep red & white large swirl inside & out, black trim, circa 1950. Near mint, rare color & shape, **$165.00. Note:** This piece has a lot of red swirling whereas #3 has more of the white.

Row 3:
1. **Teakettle,** 7¼" tall, 7" diameter, red & white large swirl with white interior, black trim, ears & handles, seamless body, circa 1930. Good plus, rare color & shape, **$195.00. Note:** Even though this is earlier than circa 1950, I felt it necessary to show these 2 teakettles because there is confusion as to when these were made. Some people refer to this as reproduction, but this type of granite ware was made prior to reproduction pieces & is heavier.
2. **Fry Pan,** ⅞" deep, 6⅜" diameter, red & white large swirl inside out, black handle trim. Handle is applied with a screw & washer. Circa 1970. Mint, rare color, **$135.00.**
3. **Fry Pan,** 1¼" deep, 7⅞" diameter, red & white large swirl inside & out, black trim & handle. Mint, rare color, **$135.00.**
4. **Fry Pan,** 1" deep, 7⅛" diameter, red & white large swirl inside & out, black trim & handle. Mint, rare color, **$135.00. Note:** The 3 fry pans in this row are a set.
5. **Teakettle,** 7¼" tall, 7" diameter, red & white large swirl with white interior, black trim, ears & handle, seamless body, circa 1930. Good plus, rare color & shape, **$195.00.**

Row 1:

1. **Teapot,** 8" tall, 5" diameter, red & white, large swirl, white interior, bright blue trim, seamed body. Circa 1960. Mint, rare color, **$115.00. Note:** This teapot is lightweight.

2. **Nest of Bowls,** All are red & white, large swirl, white interior, black trim, circa 1950. Near mint, rare color,
    1. 3½" deep, 9" diameter, **$65.00.** (Bottom bowl)
    2. 3¼" deep, 8¼" diameter, **$55.00.**
    3. 3" deep, 7½" diameter, **$45.00.**
    4. 2¾" deep, 6½" diameter, **$45.00.**
    5. 2¼" deep, 5¾" diameter, **$45.00.**

3. **Stack Dinner Carrier,** bottom section 2⅝" deep, 5⅞" diameter. Middle section 2⅛" deep, 5¼" diameter where cover fits into the top section. Red & white swirl, white interior, cobalt blue trim. Overall height 6½" not including the carrying handle. Circa 1960. Mint, rare color & shape, **$325.00.**

Row 2:

1. **Creamer,** squatty shape, 3¼" deep, 4" middle diameter, red & white large mottled inside & out, black trim, circa 1980. Mint, rare color & shape, **$65.00.**

2. **Sugar Bowl,** squatty shape, 4½" tall, 4" middle diameter, red & white, large mottled inside & out, black trim, circa 1980. Mint, rare color & shape, **$65.00.**

3. **Set of Six Cups & Saucers,** in the original box. Cup, 1⅞" deep, 2¾" diameter. Saucer, ½" deep, 4¾" diameter. Red & white large mottled inside & out, black trim. Labeled, "Fine Enamel Ware," Dishwasher safe, made exclusively for CGS International Inc., Miami, Florida. Made in China, circa 1980. Mint, rare color, shape & size, complete **$135.00.**

4. **Butter Melter,** 2½" deep, 2⅝" diameter, red & white, large mottled inside & out , circa 1980. Near mint, rare color & shape, **$65.00.**

5. **Pedestal Sugar or Sherbert,** 2½" high, 4¼" diameter, red & white, large mottled inside & out, dark blue trim, circa 1960. Near mint, rare color & shape, **$65.00. Note:** I have also seen this shape with a cover.

Row 3:

1. **Mug,** 3" deep, 3⅜" diameter, red & white large mottled, white interior, black trim, circa 1960. Near mint, rare color, **$40.00.**

2. **Plate,** ⅞" deep, 10¼" diameter, red & white swirl inside and out, black trim, circa 1950. Near mint, rare color, **$45.00.**

3. **Mug,** 3" deep, 3⅜" diameter, red & white large mottled, white interior, black trim, circa 1960. Near mint, rare color, **$40.00.**

4. **Teakettle,** 6¼" high, 7⅛" diameter, red & white, large swirl, white interior, black trim & handle, circa 1960. Mint, rare color, **$165.00.**

5. **Covered Kettle,** 4" high including cover, 8¼" top diameter not including handles. Red & white large swirl inside & out, black trim. Circa 1950. Near mint, rare color, **$45.00. Note:** Cover has a recessed handle.

Row 4:

1. **Handled Sauce Pan,** 3" deep, 4⅝" top diameter. Red & white large mottled inside & out, seamless body, wooden handle. Circa 1960. Near mint, rare color, **$75.00.**

2. **Partial Salad Set,** small bowl, 1¾" deep, 6⅜" top diameter. Large bowl, 3¼" deep, 11½" top diameter. All bowls are red & white large swirl inside & out, black trim. Circa 1960. Near mint, rare color, 6 pieces **$195.00. Note:** There should be six small bowls.

SECTION 8
SOLID WHITE AND WHITE WITH COLORED TRIM

Row 1:
1. **Covered Jar,** 3¼" high, 3" diameter. Mint, **$40.00. Note:** This jar was used for cotton balls or pins.
2. **Scoop** 2¾" deep, 2⅜" wide, 9¼" long, solid white, seamless body. Good plus, **$135.00.**
3. **Candlestick or Chamberstick** with carrying handle, 2" high, 5" square base, solid white. Near mint, rare shape, **$150.00.**
4. **Crank Wall Phone,** 22" long, 7½" deep, 8" wide, solid white, mouthpiece and receiver is like a black Bakelite material, mouthpiece collar and bells are solid brass. Good plus, extremely rare color and shape, **$1,550.00.**
5. **Candlestick or Chamberstick,** scalloped style with carrying handle, 2" high, 6" diameter, solid white. Good plus, **$110.00.**
6. **Slotted Cake Spoon,** 11⅞" long, spoon 2¼" wide, solid white. Near mint, rare shape, **$45.00. Note:** One of the uses of this slotted spoon was mixing batters.
7. **Covered Mug,** 4⅛" high, 3½" diameter, solid white. Marked "Germany." Mint, rare shape, **$85.00. Note:** This covered mug was used to keep coffee and soups hot.

Row 2:
1. **Tea Strainer,** scalloped shape, 6⅛" long, 1" deep, 4" diameter, fancy perforated bottom, solid white. Good plus, rare shape, **$75.00.**
2. **Handled Griddle,** 21" long, 7½" wide, solid white. Griddle is on a cast iron base that has three molded feet. The front near the handle is slightly tapered down toward the cup on the handle to catch the fat or juices from the meats. The wooden handle is applied by a brass band. Griddle is marked on the back "J & J Siddons 8 Bars." Good plus, extremely rare shape, **$185.00.**
3. **Tea Strainer,** triangular shape, 4" triangle, 1" deep, fancy perforated bottom, solid white. Near mint, rare shape and size, **$95.00.**

Row 3:
1. **Colander,** handled, 2½" high, 7½" top diameter not including handles, solid white. Good plus, **$60.00. Note:** This type could be also placed over the top of a kettle for straining because of the length of the handles.
2. **Coffee Flask,** 4½" high, 3½" diameter, solid white. Marked "Iron Clad Enameled Ware. I Best Quality." Mint, extremely rare color and shape, **$435.00.**
3. **Tea Strainer,** screen bottom, ¾" deep, 3¾" top diameter not including handle, solid white. Screen bottom is held in by three metal prongs that clamp on the outside edge of the tea strainer. Marked "Germany." Mint, **$55.00.**
4. **Wash Basin,** with eyelet for hanging, 2¾" deep, 10½" diameter, solid white. Mint, **$35.00.**

Row 4:
1. **Trivet,** round, ¾" high, 7¾" diameter, solid white, fancy cutout designs, four molded feet. Mint, rare shape, **$110.00.**
2. **Cat Spoon Rest,** ⅝" deep, 3¾" diameter, solid white on cast iron. Marked "59." Good plus, extremely rare shape, **$175.00.**
3. **General Electric Toaster,** 7½" high, 6⅝" wide, 11¼" long including handles, white with dark brown Bakelite handles and base. Marked "General Electric Co., Bridgeport, Conn., Made In U.S.A. Ontario, Calif. volts 115 Cat. No. 129T77 Watts 1150." Near mint, extremely rare color, rare shape, **$225.00.**
4. **Oyster Patty,** 1½" deep, 5¼" long including handle, solid white, underside has three attached shell-shaped feet. Good plus, rare color and shape, **$160.00. Note:** These were used for baking oysters.
5. **Lion Mold,** 4½" high, 5⅛" wide, 7" long bottom edge, solid white. Good plus, extremely rare shape, rare color, **$250.00.**

Row 1:

1. - 3. **Canisters,** 7½" high, 5" diameter, solid white, dark blue trim & lettering. Mint, each $85.00.

4. **Covered Jar,** 1¾" high, 2¾" diameter, solid white with black trim. Mint, **$40.00. Note:** This was used for pins.

5. **Boiler Insert & Boiler,** insert: 10" long, 6½" wide, perforated bottom, solid white, black handles. Boiler: 7½" high to top of cover knob, 7⅜" wide, 10¾" long not including handles, solid white with black trim & handles. Mint, 2 pieces, **$95.00.**

Row 2:

1. **Molasses Pitcher,** 5½" high, 3½" diameter, solid white, dark blue handle & trim. Mint, rare shape, **$155.00. Note:** The small pouring lip.

2. **Creamer,** squatty shape, 3¾" high, 4" diameter, solid white, cobalt blue trim. Mint, rare shape, **$95.00.**

3. **Spoon,** 11¾" long, solid white with solid red trim 7" down on the handle. Good plus, **$25.00.**

4. **Coffeepot,** 8" high to top of the glass insert, 5" bottom diameter, solid white, red trim & handle, dark blue granite coffee basket. Near mint, **$65.00.**

5. **Spoon,** 13¼" long, solid white with solid red trim on the handle. Good plus, **$25.00. Note:** The difference in how the red trim varies on the two spoons on this row.

6. **Coffeepot,** squatty shape, 2¾" high to top of the cover handle, 4¾" bottom diameter, black trim. Mint, extremely rare shape, **$165.00.**

7. **Covered Creamer,** 4¾" high, 3¼" bottom diameter, solid white, black trim. Mint, rare shape, **$95.00. Note:** Later ads from the 1930's & 1940's advertised this shape as a covered creamer.

Row 3:

1. **Custard Cup,** 1⅞" deep, 3¼" top diameter, white with green trim & lettering. Marked "Savory Ware." Mint, rare shape, **$55.00. Note:** One of the other uses for these cups were to test the muffin or cake mixture to see if the oven was too hot and would burn the muffins or cake. Also referred to as individual muffin cups.

2. **Handled Skimmer,** 15¼" long, 4½" diameter, flat perforated bottom, white with green trim & handle. Marked "Savory Ware." Near mint, **$35.00.**

3. **Custard Cup,** 2⅜" deep, 4" diameter, white with green trim. Marked "Savory Ware." Mint, rare shape, **$55.00.**

4. **Milk Can,** 6¼" tall, 5" diameter, white with green trim & handle, wooden bail. Marked "Savory Ware." Near mint, **$75.00.**

5. **Sugar Shaker,** handled, 5" high, 2½" top diameter, white with green trim. Marked $\frac{B}{W}$. Near mint, extremely rare shape, rare color, **$195.00.**

6. **Soup Ladle,** 14" long, 3⅞" ladle diameter, white with green trim & handle. Marked "Savory Ware." Mint, **$30.00.**

7. **Egg Cup,** 2" deep, 2" diameter, white with green trim. Mint, rare shape, **$95.00.**

8. **Milk Pitcher,** 7¼" tall, 5¼" diameter, white with green trim & handle. Near mint, **$65.00.**

9. **Ant Cup,** 1" deep, 3⅞" top diameter, white with green trim. Mint, extremely rare shape, **$155.00. Note:** One of these was placed under each leg of a piece of furniture that held food. The leg rested on the inner raised section of the ant cup. Water was placed in outer inside rim. This kept ants from crawling up the legs of the furniture.

10. **Handled Skimmer,** 15" long, 4⅜" diameter, rounded perforated bottom, white with green trim & handle. Marked "Savory Ware." Mint, **$35.00.**

Row 4:

1. **Corner Candle Box,** 11" back height, 5¼" diameter, white trimmed in cobalt blue. Good plus, extremely rare shape & size, **$195.00. Note:** This was used for holding homemade candles.

2. **Hatchery Thermometer,** 2⅞" high, 4⅜" long, white with black base. Marked "Amer. Ther. Co. St. Louis, Made In U.S.A." Mint, rare shape, **$65.00. Note:** This thermometer was used to make sure the temperature was controlled for hatching baby chicks.

3. **Teakettle,** 8" high, 8" diameter, white with black trim & knob, wooden bail. Near mint, **$70.00.**

4. **Oyster Measure,** 4⅛" deep, 3½" diameter, white with cobalt blue trim. Marked "L. & G. Mfg. Co." Near mint, extremely rare shape, **$150.00.**

5. **Sauce Ladle,** 9" long, 2½" diameter, white with black trim & handle. Mint, rare shape, **$40.00.**

6. **Cuspidor,** 2 piece, 2⅜" high, 8" diameter, white with cobalt blue trim. Marked "Sweden." Near Mint, **$95.00.**

Row 1:

1. **Hanging Scale,** with enameled tray. Tray ½" deep, 11" diameter, white with dark blue trim. The metal bail handle that holds the enamel tray is designed to be pushed in on each side, dropping the tray down so it can be stored flat when not in use. Good plus, **$195.00.**

Row 2:

1. **Four Tumblers** in leather carrying case. Tumbler 3" deep, 2⅞" diameter, white with cobalt blue trim. Marked "K.E.R. Sweden," also shows what appears to be a bell shape with a flag in the center. Leather carrying case 5" deep, 3½" diameter. Near mint, complete **$110.00. Note:** I'm sure these tumblers had many versatile uses, for example; picnics or when traveling.

2. **Nasal Irrigator,** 4¼" deep, 3½" diameter, white trimmed in black. Labeled "Hospital Quality Enameled Ware, The Asepticon Co. New York. Trade Mark." with a star in the center. "Made In The U.S.A." Mint, **$55.00. Note:** This type was shown in their catalogue with or without a front handle.

3. **Nasal Irrigator,** 4¼" deep, 3½" diameter, white with navy trim. **Note:** This one may look like #2 on this row but it is lighter in weight & has a navy trim instead of black. This looks older. Mint, **$45.00.**

Row 3:

1. **Oblong Vegetable Dish,** 1½" deep, 4⅝" wide, 6¼" long, white trimmed in cobalt blue. Mint.

2. **Oblong Vegetable Dish,** 2⅛" deep, 7" wide, 9½" long, white trimmed in cobalt blue. Mint.

3. **Oblong Vegetable Dish,** 1⅞" deep, 6" wide, 7⅛" long, white trimmed in cobalt blue. Mint.
No. 1, 2 & 3 are a set. Price for 3 pieces **$100.00.**

Row 4:

1. **Bowl,** 2½" deep, 7" top diameter, white trimmed in cobalt blue. Labeled "Tru-Blu Quality Enamelware. Sanitary. Durable." Has eyelet for hanging. Mint, **$45.00.**

2. **Pitcher & Wash Basin.** Pitcher measures 8" to top of the lip, 5¾" diameter. White with black handle & trim, seamless body. Near mint. Basin measures 2¼" deep, 8⅝" top diameter. White with black trim. Good plus. 2 pieces, **$95.00.**

3. **Straight-Sided Kettle,** 3¼" deep, 7" diameter, white with cobalt blue trim & small side handle. Eyelet for hanging. Labeled the same as No. 1 on this row. Mint, **$50.00.**

Row 5:

1. **Egg Plate or Pan,** 1" deep, 6⅜" diameter, white with black handles & trim. Good plus, **$40.00.**

2. **Sauce Pan,** 2¼" deep, 6⅜" diameter, white with cobalt handle & trim. Labeled the same as No. 1 on Row 4. Mint, **$40.00.**

3. **Pudding Pan,** 1½" deep, 7" diameter, white trimmed in cobalt blue. Labeled the same as No. 1 on Row 4. Eyelet for hanging. Mint, **$35.00.**

Row 1:

1. **Butter Dish,** 4¾" tall, 8⅞" diameter, white with cobalt blue trim, seamless body & spun knob. Marked "L & G Mfg. Co." Mint, rare color & shape, **$185.00.**

2. **Teapot,** tall squatty shape with metal pedestal & ribbed body, 10" to top of the opalescent glass insert in the cover, 6" body diameter at the widest point, 3¾" metal pedestal diameter, white with black handle. Circa 1920. Mint, rare shape, **$185.00.**

3. **Stack Dinner Carrier,** with 3 food containers. The top 2 containers each measure 2⅞" deep not including the cover, 5¼" diameter. Bottom container 2½" deep, 5¼" diameter. The cover serves as a plate when turned upright. White with cobalt blue trim. Metal handle holds containers together as well as being used as a carrying handle. Marked "KER Sweden 14 C.M." Mint, **$85.00.**

Row 2:

1. **Coffee Biggin,** squatty shape, pictured with spreader. Including pot, biggin, spreader, & cover. 8" to top of the cover knob including the biggin, 4¾" diameter, white with cobalt blue trim. Near mint, **$145.00.**

2. **Oval, Fluted Melon Mold,** 3¼" deep, 7⅝" wide, 11¼" long, solid white with metal ring for hanging. Good plus, rare shape & size, **$110.00.**

3. **Teapot,** squatty shape, 4½" tall, 3¾" wide, white with cobalt trim, handle, & knob. Good plus, **$95.00.**

4. **Mug** with electric heating element, 5¼" high, 3" bottom diameter, white with cobalt blue trim. The 3 feet have attached porcelain knobs. Marked "Gen. Elec. Co. Type L-30 Volts 110 Amp 1.4 U.S.A." Near mint, **$95.00. Note:** This mug could have been used for warming beverages or to heat water for shaving.

Row 3:

1. **Countertop Scale,** "Hobart," 10¼" high, 5½" wide, 13½" long, white with metal trim. Metal plate reads "Manufactured by Dayton Scale Division, The Hobart Manufacturing Co. Troy Ohio. U.S.A." Near mint, **$115.00. Note:** The metal pan is missing.

2. **Thermometer,** used for candy & deep frying, 11" long, 1½" wide, solid white with black & red lettering. Marked "Amer. Ther. Co. St. Louis, MO U.S.A." Mint, **$85.00.**

3. **Funnel,** squatty shape, 4¾" long, 7½" diameter, white with black trim & handle. Good plus, **$45.00.**

4. **Spit Cup,** 2⅝" deep, 4⅝" diameter, solid white, hinged cover with thumb rest. Thumb rest is also hinged to the handle. Seamless body. Marked "Czecho-slovakia." Good plus, rare shape, **$75.00.**

5. **Oval Butter Kettle or Carrier,** 7" tall, 6½" wide, 8¾" long, white with cobalt blue trim, metal carrying handle with extra metal center piece to strengthen the handle for carrying. Good plus, **$135.00.**

Row 4:

1. **Ladle,** with fancy perforated bottom, 13¼" long, 1¼" deep, 2¾" diameter, white with black trim & handle. Good plus, **$45.00.**

2. **Side Snipe Ladle,** 14½" long, 1¾" deep, 4½" diameter, not including the spout, solid white, rivetted handle. Near mint, rare shape & size, **$135.00. Note:** Side snipe ladles have a side lip, making it easier to pour liquids.

3. **Strainer,** with kettle handle, 1⅜" deep, 5½" diameter, white with cobalt blue trim, rivetted handles, fancy perforated sides & bottom. Good plus, **$65.00.**

183

SECTION 9
SOLID COLORS AND SOLID COLORS ON CAST IRON

Row 1:
1. **Coffee Biggin,** tall squatty shape, 10½" high including biggin & cover, 4¼" bottom diameter, solid red inside & out, black trim & handle. Five pieces including coffee biggin, cover, pot & 2 solid red spreaders. Near mint, rare shape, **$110.00.**
2. **Teapot,** squatty shape, 3¾" high, 2¼" diameter, solid red, black trim. There is an embossed emblem on the teapot that displays three sail ships & one large boat. There is also an attached embossed emblem displaying an anchor & the word "Ludwigshafen." Near mint, rare shape & size, **$85.00. Note:** This could possibly have been a souvenir.
3. **4 piece Soup Tureen Set.** Soup tureen 8¾" high including cover, 8" diameter, solid red outside, white interior, black trim & handles. Ladle, 12½" long, black handle, solid red ladle. Round tray, ⅝" deep, 11¼" diameter, solid red, black trim. Near mint, rare color & shape, **$375.00.**
4. **Handled Scoop,** flat bottom, 5¾" long including handle, 1¾" wide, solid red. Marked "Portugal." Near mint, extremely rare color, shape & size, **$135.00.**
5. **Coffee Biggin,** 9½" high including biggin & cover, 4½" diameter, solid red, white interior, black trim. Four pieces including pot, biggin, cover, & spreader. Near mint, rare shape, **$95.00.**

Row 2:
1. **Teakettle,** 5¾" high, 6¼" diameter, solid red, white interior, black trim & handle. Marked on bottom , "Poland L. G." & pictures a teakettle. Near mint, **$75.00.**
2. **Egg Poacher,** 3 pieces, cover, insert & handled pan, 3¼" high, 4¼" diameter, solid red. Insert 1" high, 3¾" diameter. Good plus, **$95.00. Note:** The insert has four holes on the top of the rim for steam to escape onto the egg for poaching. Handles have holes for hanging.
3. **Coffee Biggin,** squatty shape, 10⅝" high including biggin & cover, 6¼" diameter. Five pieces including cover, biggin, two white spreaders & coffeepot. Near mint, rare shape, **$125.00.**
4. **Teapot or Creamer,** 4" high, 3¼" diameter, solid red. The hinge on the cover is made so the cover can be taken off for cleaning. Near mint, **$75.00. Note:** This shape is advertised as being used as an individual teapot or creamer.
5. **Oblong Pudding or Vegetable Dish,** 1⅞" deep, 8⅝" long, 6½" wide, solid red, black trim. Near mint, **$50.00.**

Row 3:
1. **Sugar Bowl,** 5" high, 3⅜" diameter, solid red, black trim. Circa 1970. Good plus, **$30.00.**
2. **Grater,** flat handle, 10" long, 3⅝" wide, solid red. Good plus, **$95.00.**
3. **Creamer,** 3½" deep, 3⅜" diameter, solid red, black trim. Circa 1970. Good plus, **$30.00.**
4. **Double Boiler,** 7½" high, 6" diameter, solid red, white interior. Near mint, **$65.00.**
5. **Pie Plate,** shallow, 1" deep, 8" diameter, solid red. Good plus, **$25.00.**
6. **Creamer,** squatty shape, 4½" deep, 4⅛" diameter, solid red, white interior, black trim & handle. Good plus, **$65.00.**

Row 4:
1. **Hanging Soap Dish,** 5¾" back height, 5¼" long, 3" wide, solid red with fancy embossed back. Good plus, **$75.00.**
2. **Ice Box or Refrigerator Dish,** 3¼" high, 8" long, 5" wide, solid red, black trim. Cover is solid red. Near mint, **$25.00. Note:** These were used for storing food in ice boxes or refrigerators. They usually came in sets of 3, 4, or 5.
3. **Partial Tea Set,** (two cups), cup, 2¼" deep, 3¼" diameter, solid red, white interior, gold trim. Marked "Made in Germany 446." Oval Tray, ½" deep, 14" wide, 17½" long, solid red, gold trim. Marked "Vewag 446." Creamer, 5¼" deep, 3½" diameter, solid red, white interior, gold trim. Marked "Vewag, Dec, 446." Sugar Bowl, 4¼" high, 4¾" diameter, solid red, white interior. Marked "Vewag 446." All good plus, 5 pieces **$295.00. Note:** I believe a teapot goes with this set.
4. **Dust Pan,** 13⅜" long, 10½" wide, solid red. Near mint, extremely rare shape, rare color, **$245.00.**

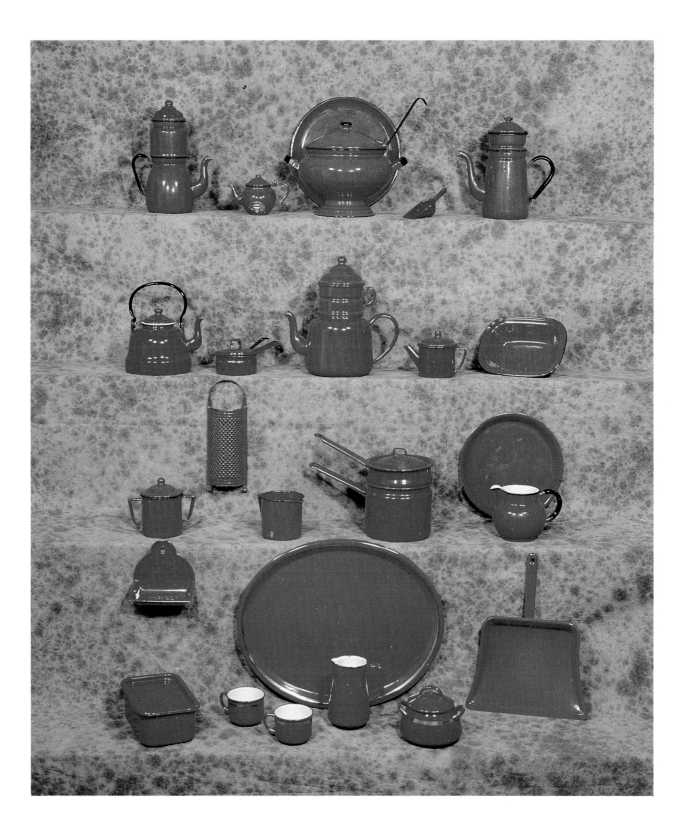

Row 1:

  1. **Coffeepot,** 9" high, 5¼" diameter, red inside & out, black trim & handles, tall bulbous shape. Near mint, **$65.00.**
  2. **Handled Bread Pan,** 12" x 12" width not including the handle, solid red outside, white lettering & decoration, black exterior. Recipe showing how to make San Francisco Sourdough Pan Bread & Sheet Bread. Recipe is taken from Sourdough Jack's Cookery. Marked "The Bettinger Corporation." Near mint, rare color & shape, **$110.00. Note:** This could have been a promotional giveaway.
  3. **Teakettle,** gooseneck, 7½" high, 8¾" diameter, solid red, white interior, black trim. Mint, **$95.00.**

Row 2:

  1. **Tea Strainer,** 1" deep, 3¾" top diameter not including handle, solid red inside & out, fancy perforated bottom. Near mint, rare color & shape, **$95.00. Note:** Perforated means that the holes are made for draining off liquids. Fancy perforated means that the perforations are made in a fancy design.
  2. **Spice Scoop,** 1¾" deep including the covered back section of the scoop, 4¼" long including the handle, solid red decorated with gold bands & trim, white interior, seamless body. Near mint, extremely rare color, shape & size, **$135.00.**

Row 3:

  1. **Canisters** (6), 6⅜" high, 4" diameter, solid red decorated with gold bands, white lettering, white interior, covers & cover bands are nickel plated over brass. Rice, Currants, Peas, Sugar, Coffee, Tea. Good plus, rare color, shape, 5 at each **$110.00,** Tea, **$65.00.**
  2. **Teakettle,** 7¼" high, 9¼" diameter, solid red inside & out, black trim, metal cover with wooden knob, wooden carrying handle applied to an extra metal piece added to the body, rare shape, **$100.00.**

Row 4:

  1. **Spoon** 13¼" long, solid red inside & out, black handle. Near mint, **$35.00.**
  2. **Pudding Pan,** 2⅞" deep, 9⅞" diameter, solid red, white interior, black trim, with wide rim & hole for hanging. Near mint, **$30.00.**
  3. **Coffeepot,** 6⅞" high, 3½" diameter, solid red, black inside, metal cover with wooden knob, wooden handle. Near mint, rare shape, **$95.00.**
  4. **Pudding Pan,** 2¾" deep, 9¾" top diameter, solid red, white interior, black trim, narrow rim. Near mint, **$30.00.**
  5. **Handled Skimmer,** 14½" long, solid red inside & out, black handle. Marked, "Made in Poland." Good plus, **$25.00.**

Row 1:
 1. **Handled Egg Pan,** 7 eyes, 1⅛" deep, 9⅞" diameter. Each eye measures ⅜" deep, 2⅝" diameter. Solid red inside & out. Mint, **$110.00.**

Row 2:
 1. **Teapot,** squatty shape, 6" tall, 6" diameter, solid red with black trim & knob, white interior, seamless body. Near mint, **$65.00.**
 2. **Funnel,** 6¼" long, 5" diameter, applied handle & spout, solid red with white interior. Near mint, **$40.00.**
 3. **Coffeepot,** 9" high to top of the glass insert, 5¾" diameter, solid red with white interior, aluminum coffee basket. Circa 1930. Near mint, **$55.00.**

Row 3:
 1. **Hanging Soap Dish,** with perforated insert, & attached wire sponge & toothbrush holder, 7½" back height, ⅞" deep, 3⅞" wide, 5¼" long, solid red. Good plus, rare shape & size, **$95.00.**
 2. **Salesman's Sample Wash Basin,** 1⅛" deep, 4½" diameter, solid red inside & out with black trim, eyelet for hanging. Mint, rare shape, **$65.00.**
 3. **Snail Baking Pan,** ⅝" deep, 6¼" diameter, 8" long, solid red with loop for hanging. Mint, extremely rare shape & size, **$185.00.**
 4. **Salt Box,** 7⅞" tall, 4½" to top of the wooden cover, 3¾" wide, 5¾" long, solid red. Labeled. "Genuine Swedish K.E.R. Enameled Ware. Guaranteed Pure & Of Higher Quality." Also marked on bottom "Kockums K.E.R. Sweden 15C/M." Mint, rare shape, **$225.00.**

Row 4:
 1. **Oval Roaster,** with wire insert, 8½" tall, 9" wide, 14¼" long not including the handles, solid red inside & out with blue trim & handles. Wire insert: ⅜" high, 8" wide, 11⅝" long. Near mint, **$110.00.**
 2. **Candlestick,** shell-shaped with finger ring, 1½" tall, 5¾" diameter, solid red with black trim. Near mint, rare color & shape, **$195.00.**

Row 1:

1. **Handled Flat Grater,** 1" high, 4½" wide, 6½" long, cream with green handle. Near mint, rare color, **$135.00.**
2. **Flour canister,** 9" tall, 7¼" diameter, cream with green trim, lettering, & handles. The cover handle has a brass plate embossed "Judge Brand 18 c/m." Canister is marked "Foreign." Good plus, rare color & shape, **$135.00.**
3. **Cracker Jar or Beer Growler,** 6¼" high, 5⅝" diameter, cream with green trim & handles, seamless body. Good plus, rare shape & size, **$125.00. Note:** I'm not sure that this is a cracker jar. It could be a beer growler. This is not the original cover. I don't believe it had a cover.

Row 2:

1. **Oblong Pudding or Vegetable Dish,** 2" deep, 6½" top width, 8½" top length. Advertised as "Apple Green" outside & "Tangerine" inside. "Harmonizing colors, Vollrath Ware," Sheboygan, Wisconsin. Marked "Vollrath U.S.A." Good plus, **$30.00.**
2. **Custard Cup,** 2¼" deep, 3⅝" top diameter, green with cream interior. Mint, rare color & shape, **$55.00.**
3. **Teapot,** 4½" tall, 5" diameter. Apple green outside & tangerine inside. "Harmonizing Colors, Vollrath Ware." Mint, rare color, shape & size, **$140.00.**
4. **Custard Cup,** 2⅝" deep, 4½" diameter, apple green outside with tangerine inside. "Harmonizing Colors, Vollrath Ware." Marked "Vollrath U.S.A." Mint, rare color & shape, **$55.00.**
5. **Bowl,** 2½" deep, 5¾" diameter, apple green outside with tangerine inside. "Harmonizing Colors, Vollrath Ware." Marked "Vollrath U.S.A." Near Mint, **$25.00.**

Row 3:

1. **Mixing Bowl,** 4" deep, 7" diameter, apple green outside with tangerine inside. "Harmonizing colors, Vollrath Ware." Near mint, **$25.00.**
2. **Oval Roaster,** 8" tall, 10⅝" wide, 17" long not including the handles, cream & green inside & out. Roaster embossed "Savory." Good plus, **$85.00.**
3. **Mixing Bowl,** 4½" deep, 8¾" diameter, apple green outside with tangerine inside. "Harmonizing Colors, Vollrath Ware." Near mint, **$25.00.**

Row 1:

1. **Covered Kettle,** ribbed, 6" high, 7⅜" diameter, cream trimmed in green. Near mint, **$40.00. Note:** Kettle is encircled by 16 ribs.

2. **Coffeepot,** 7¾" high, 5½" diameter, cream with green trim, weld handle, seamed body. Near mint, **$55.00. Note:** This handle is welded to the body of the pot, not rivetted. Also, note the cover knob is welded.

3. **Pie Plate,** 1½" deep, 10" diameter, cream with green trim. Good plus, **$25.00.**

4. **Teapot,** 5¾" high, 3½" diameter, cream with green trim. **Note:** Spun knob refers to a round molded knob applied to the cover or sometimes molded with the cover. Near mint, rare size, **$145.00.**

5. **Milk Can,** matching lock cover, 9" high, 4¾" diameter, cream with green trim, green wooden bail handle. Near mint, rare color, shape & size, **$155.00. Note:** The grooves around the rim of the cover fit down into the neck of the milk can. When the cover is turned, the indentations on the neck lock the cover securely to the milk can.

6. **Coffee Biggin,** 5¼" high, 4¾" diameter, cream with aqua green trim. The top edge of the spout is trimmed in black. The handle is like a Bakelite material. Marked "Kockums, 1 1IT." In a circle there is a bell with the marks "KER Sweden." Near mint, **$110.00. Note:** The trim is more aqua green than the usual green we see. I believe this is the foreign version of the cream with the green trim.

Row 2:

1. **Cracker Jar, or Beer Growler,** 6½" high, 6⅜" diameter not including the weld handles, cream with green trim & handles. Good plus, rare shape & size, **$135.00.**

2. **Berry Bucket,** 5" high, 3½" diameter, cream with green trim, wire bail, seamless body. Good plus, rare size, **$85.00.**

3. **Double Boiler,** "Belle" shape, 6½" high, 5½" diameter, cream with green trim & handles, seamless body. Near mint, rare shape, **$75.00.**

4. **Ice Box or Refrigerator Dish,** 2¾" high, 4¼" wide, 7⅞" long, cream with green trim. Marked in a circle "U.S. Certified Stainless Ware." Good plus, **$25.00.**

5. **Teakettle,** 5" high, 5¾" diameter, cream with light green trim & handle. Near mint, **$65.00.**

Row 3:

1. **Colander,** footed & handled, 4" high, 8¾" diameter not including handles, light cream with green trim. Good plus, **$75.00.**

2. **Convex Kettle,** 8½" high, 10¼" diameter. Mint, **$35.00. Note:** Advertisement for this kettle shown in Lisk's 50th anniversary catalogue 1889 to 1939 reads "Convex Kettle-Non-Boil-Over." Enameled cover set down inside upper rim. When contents boil up, cover raises, steam escapes & cover settles back into place. "Flintstone Ivory Enameled Ware," green trim. Called cream & green by today's collectors. Mint, **$35.00.**

3. **Custard Cup,** 2¼" deep, 3⅜" diameter, cream with green trim. Near mint, rare color & shape, **$55.00.**

4. **Oval Roaster,** 4¼" high, 7¾" wide, 8¾" long not including handles, cream with green trim. Near mint, rare shape & size, **$145.00. Note:** This was designed so the top could also be used as a separate baking or serving pan.

Row 1:
1. **Ribbed Style Tube Mold,** 2⅞" deep, 8¼" diameter, solid cobalt blue with white interior. Good plus, **$95.00.**
2. **Round Miner's Dinner Bucket** 8¾" tall, 7 diameter, solid cobalt blue with white interior, seamed body. Includes bucket, cover, food insert & dessert tray. Good plus, rare shape, **$175.00. Note:** The long bail handle was designed to secure the cover when raised for carrying. No 2-3 4pieces complete.
3. **Dessert Tray & Food Insert** for the 4 piece Round Miner's Dinner Bucket. Dessert tray ⅞" deep, 6¾" diameter. Food insert 4" deep, 6¾" diameter. Both are solid cobalt blue with white interiors. Both Good plus. **Note:** If you did not recognize this as a dessert tray it's because it has been mistaken for a small pie plate by others as well.

Row 2:
1. **Handled Sauce Pan,** 2⅞" deep, 5" diameter, solid cobalt blue with white interior, seamless body. Good plus, **$30.00.**
2. **Ice Container,** 2⅞" deep, 6⅞" diameter, solid cobalt blue with white interior. Container has a ½" hole in the bottom for drainage. The top part of the container has a metal rim around it with 2 fancy ring handles. Fancy embossed metal holder is 3¾" deep, 7" diameter. Metal container is marked "Meriden Silver Plate Co. Quadruple Plate." Good plus, extremely rare shape & size, **$195.00.**
3. **Stove Pan,** 2⅞" deep, 9⅜" wide, 11" long, solid cobalt blue with white interior. The 4 feet are rivetted, this could have possibly been used for cooking meats, so the fat could be drained away from the meat, or it could have been used for draining or washing foods. Good plus, **$65.00. Note:** This piece is enameled over cast iron.
4. **Measure,** 4¾" tall, 3½" diameter, solid cobalt blue with white interior, rivetted lip & strap handle, seamed body. Good plus, rare shape, **$95.00.**

Row 3:
1. **Pie Plate,** ⅞" deep, 9" diameter, solid cobalt blue with white interior. Good, **$25.00.**
2. **Soap Saver,** 3½" deep, 3¾" diameter, solid cobalt blue with white interior, fancy perforations with rivetted hinged & latch, metal ring with attached chain & wooden bail. Good plus, extremely rare shape, **$165.00. Note:** Leftover soap scraps were placed in the soap saver, then submerged in the hot water to be used for washing clothes.
3. **Handled Pan,** 2¼" deep, 4⅝" diameter, solid cobalt blue with white interior, seamless body. Good plus, rare size, **$55.00.**
4. **Egg Fry Pan,** 7 eyes, 1⅞" deep, 10¼" diameter solid cobalt blue with white interior, rivetted handle. Good, **$40.00.**

Row 1:

1. **Turk's Head Tube Mold,** turban style, 3¾" deep, 9" diameter, solid cobalt blue with white interior. Good plus, rare shape, **$95.00.**

2. **Muffin Pan,** 11 cups, each cup 1⅝" deep, 2½" diameter. Overall size 7⅝" wide, 11⅛" long. Solid cobalt blue with traces of very fine white flecks inside & out. Mint, rare shape & size, **$125.00. Note:** This piece is enameled over cast iron.

3. **Mush Mug,** 6" deep, 7" diameter, solid cobalt blue with white interior, rivetted handle, seamless body. Climax bottom. Good, **$75.00. Note:** Climax bottom refers to the copper band around the bottom edge. The copper band was constructed to protect the bottom edge of the pot from chipping and burning.

Row 2:

1. **Chick Feeder,** 2¼" tall, 8¾" diameter, solid cobalt blue with white interior. Cover embossed "Hoeft & Co. Inc. N. Chicago, U.S.A. Moe's Line. Pat. Aug 18, 1914." Good plus, extremely rare shape & size. **$155.00. Note:** The feeder is filled with chick feed, then the cover, which has 12 holes, 1 for each chick's head, is placed back on the feeder. The cover keeps the chicks from scratching the feed out, which prevents waste.

2. **Coffee Carrier,** 6½" tall including the handled cup, 4¾" diameter, solid cobalt blue with white interior, wire ears, wire bail, seamed body. Good plus, rare shape, **$95.00. Note:** When the cover is removed it is used as a handled cup for drinking.

3. **Percolator Funnel,** 8¾" deep, 4¼" diameter, solid cobalt blue with white funnel & interior, rivetted handle, seamed body. Good plus, rare color & shape, **$110.00.**

4. **Melon Mold,** 3¾" deep including tin cover, 5½" wide, 7¼" long, solid cobalt blue with white interior, handled tin cover. Marked "10." Mint, rare color, **$95.00.**

Row 3:

1. **Fish Kettle or Poacher;** Kettle 6" deep, 11¼" wide, 20" long, solid cobalt blue with white interior, rivetted handles, seamed body, tin cover. Perforated insert measures 10" wide, 19" long, with 5" high handles & is solid white. Good plus, **$95.00.**

Row 1:
1. **Ring Mold,** 2¼" deep, 8⅛" diameter, solid yellow with white interior. Good plus, **$65.00.**

Row 2:
1. **Coffee Biggin,** includes pot, biggin, 2 spreaders & the cover. 9" tall, 5⅜" solid yellow with white interior & spreaders, seamless body. Good plus, rare shape, **$90.00.**
2. **Ring Mold,** 2¾" deep, 10" diameter, solid yellow with light cream interior & black trim. Marked "Cream City Ware. Milwaukee" with a star in the middle of a circle. Good plus, **$95.00.**
3. **Teakettle,** 6¼" tall, 7" diameter, solid yellow with white interior, black handle & trim, seamless body with seamed spout. Marked "Made In Poland-18." Piece also has a picture of a teakettle on the bottom. A chain is attached to the cover & the ear of the teakettle. Good plus, **$50.00.**

Row 3:
1. **Soup or Cereal Bowl,** 2⅝" deep, 6" diameter, solid yellow with white interior, & black trim. Near mint, **$25.00.**
2. **Covered Sugar,** 4⅞" tall, 3¾" diameter, solid yellow inside & out with black trim. Circa 1970. Good plus, **$30.00.**
3. **Creamer,** 3½" deep, 3¾" diameter, solid yellow inside & out with black trim. Circa 1970. Good plus, **$30.00.**
4. **Teapot,** 5½" tall, 4⅞" diameter, solid yellow with white interior, black trim & handle, seamed body & spout. Marked "12 C/M." Good plus, **$45.00.**

Row 4:
1. **Hand Skimmer,** 8⅜" long, 4½" wide, perforated, solid yellow with hole for hanging. Good plus, rare shape, **$125.00.**
2. **Footed Colander,** 4½" high, 10¼" diameter, solid yellow with white interior, perforated sides & bottom. Good plus, **$45.00.**

Row 5:
1. **Triangular Sink Strainer,** 3½" high, 10¾" long, 8⅜" wide, solid yellow with white interior, cobalt blue trim, perforated sides & bottom, 3 ring-shaped feet. Good plus, **$40.00.**
2. **Candlestick,** 1¾" deep, 5¾" diameter, solid yellow inside & out with black ring handle, trim & neck. Good, **$65.00.**
3. **Water Pail,** 9⅜" deep, 10½" diameter, solid yellow with white interior, black ears & trim, wooden bail handle. Good plus, **$55.00.**

Row 6:
1. **Handled Strainer,** 4" deep, 7¼" diameter, solid yellow, black trim & handles, fancy perforated round bottom. Good, **$35.00. Note:** The tipping handle is on the opposite end. Marked "Made In Poland. 46." Shows a picture of a teakettle with the letter "S" on the side.
2. **Footed Colander,** 5" high, 10⅛" diameter, solid yellow with dark blue trim, black handles, perforated bottom & sides. Marked "Japan." Circa 1970. Good plus, **$30.00. Note:** One of the things I have noticed is that most of the older colanders have smaller perforations than the later ones.

Special Note: This photograph of the solid yellow color shows how the shade of a color can vary. This is one of the reasons there is so much confusion about colors. It is very difficult to say you have a specific color. Color variations can be changed by conditions such as the environment were the piece was made, and/or chemical balance or mixture.

Section 9: Solid colors and Solid Colors on Cast Iron

Row 1:

1. **Bean Pot,** 7¾" tall, 5¾" top diameter not including handles, 3¾" bottom diameter, solid blue, white interior, fancy perforated cover, rivetted handles, seamless body. Near mint, **$125.00. Note:** I am not sure this is a bean pot. It has been termed a bean pot by some collectors but I still have reservations as I have not found any information on this particular piece.

2. **Measure,** 4½" tall, 3½" diameter, solid blue, white interior, dark blue trim, seamless body. Mint, rare color, **$165.00. Note:** All the solid blue colors have been termed robin egg blue by some collectors. As you can see by the overall view of this page, there are many shades of solid blue & several companies made the color. The La Lance & Grosjean Mfg. Co. was one company that did make and label their solid blue "Robin Egg Blue."

3. **Oblong Strainer with Kettle Hook,** 7½" long, 4⅞" top diameter tapering to 1" diameter on top & 3" bottom diameter tapering to ¾" diameter, solid blue, white interior, perforated bottom, seamed body, wire hanger. Near mint, rare shape, **$140.00. Note:** This is the solid blue that is closest in color to robin egg blue.

4. **Rose Bowl,** 2¾" deep, 5" diameter, solid blue, white interior, seamless body. Near mint, rare shape & size, **$145.00. Note:** I believe this bowl was used to dry flower petals from the garden as I have seen many rose bowls shaped like this in glass.

5. **Cream Can,** 6" tall, 3" diameter, solid blue, white interior, dark blue trim & ears, wire bail. Mint, rare color, shape & size, **$195.00. Note:** The unusual shape of the round ears holding the wire bail.

6. **Heat Minder,** ½" deep, 8½" diameter, solid blue with black band, black exterior, solid wood handle. Near mint, **$35.00. Note:** I believe this was placed under a cooking kettle on the gas or electric stove to help spread the heat evenly on the bottom of the kettle thus preventing scorching. I believe it was also used as a trivet for hot items.

Row 2:

1. **Tea Steeper,** 4½" high, 4¼" diameter, solid light blue, seamless body, rivetted spout & handle. Marked "Elite Austria. 9 Reg'd – 6." Good plus, **$65.00.**

2. **Scoop,** 2⅜" diameter, 5¼" long, solid blue, white interior. Near mint, rare shape, **$135.00. Note:** This is the larger version than shown in Book I.

3. **Egg Cup,** 2¾" high, 2" diameter, solid light blue, white interior. Good plus, rare shape, **$40.00.**

4. **Baby Food Warmer & Three-in-One Combination Stove,** Baby Food Warmer with pit bottom, 5" high to top of cover knob, 3¾" top diameter, solid blue. Labeled "For Baby." Milk Warmer, remove cover, fill cup ¼" full of water, insert bottle. Both Good plus, rare shape & size, set **$140.00. Note:** Pit bottom refers to the ⅜" recessed bottom on the warmer that fits down into the top of the stove. Combination Stove, 4" high, 6¼" diameter, solid blue granite ware top, tin sides & bottom painted solid blue. Labeled "Sterno 3 in 1 Combination 1. Milk warmer, 2. Cooker, 3. Stove, Reg. U.S. Pat. Off." This warmer is heated by "Sterno Canned Heat For Instant Heat." Also comes with a sterno extinguisher & can opener.

5. **Oblong Strainer with Kettle Hook,** 8½" long, 4" diameter tapering to 1¼" diameter at the top, 3¼" bottom diameter tapering to ¾", solid blue, white interior, screened bottom, hole for hanging. Near mint, rare shape, **$140.00.**

6. **Butter Dish,** 3" high, 3⅞" top diameter, 7" bottom diameter including collar base, solid blue, white interior. Marked "Robvr Rhenania, Germany." Pictures a head of a lion between what resembles two smoke stacks. Good plus, rare color, shape & size, **$155.00.**

7. **Sauce Pan,** 3" deep, 4⅞" top diameter not including pour spout, solid light blue, white interior. Marked on the handle "Stransky," handle has a brass eyelet for hanging. Good plus, rare shape & size, **$75.00. Note:** The two pour spouts—one large rivetted spout on the right, one small spout without rivets on the left.

Row 3:

1. **Stein,** 11¾" tall, 3¾" top diameter, 4¼" bottom diameter, solid blue, white interior. The cover has what appears to be a pewter band with a thumb lift that hinges & attaches to another hinged pewter band on the handle. Marked with a lion standing with his front paws on a coffee boiler. Good plus, extremely rare shape & size, **$225.00.**

2. **Cup Measure,** 2¼" deep, 2" diameter, solid blue, white lettering, white interior. Marked "G. M." in a circle. Embossed on the side in white "0.11." Good, **$30.00.**

3. **Footed Bread Raiser,** 11" high, 17½" including handles, 12½" bottom diameter, solid light blue, white interior, cobalt blue trim & handles, vented tin cover. Good plus, **$145.00.**

4. **Lobster Mold,** 3¾" deep, 7" wide, 10" long not including the handle, solid blue, white interior with lobster imprint, handle for hanging. Mold is enameled on a cast iron base. Good plus, rare shape & size, **$135.00.**

5. **Melon Mold,** 3⅝" deep, 5¾" wide, 7¾" long, solid blue, white interior, tin cover embossed "no. 50." Near mint, rare shape, **$155.00.**

Row 1:

1. **Coffeepot,** 9" tall, 5½" diameter. solid aqua, white interior, black trim & handle, black stemmed coffee basket. Glass insert is embossed "Pyrex, Made In U.S.A." Circa 1930. Near mint, **$65.00.**

2. **Mug,** 3" deep, 3⅝" diameter, medium blue with white interior, black trim & handle. Marked "Made in Poland 8." Also marked with a picture of a teakettle. Good plus, **$20.00.**

3. **Water Pitcher,** 9¼" tall, 6¼" diameter, mauve rose with white interior, black trim, seamless body. Near mint, **$85.00.**

4. **Teapot,** squatty-shaped, 4¼" tall, 3⅞" diameter, aquamarine with white interior, black trim, seamless body. Good plus, **$30.00.**

5. **Coffeepot,** 9" tall, 5½" diameter, light green inside & out, dark green trim & handle, seamless body. Glass insert is embossed "Bend Clip End Outward Under Perk. Lid, Break No More. Cardella Mfg. Co. Cleveland, Ohio." Good plus, **$50.00.**

Row 2:

1. **Covered Straight-Sided Kettle,** 6½" tall, 6½" diameter, dark green with white interior, & cobalt blue trim. Cover embossed "16." Near mint, **$30.00.**

2. **Covered Straight-Sided Kettle,** 9" tall, 10¼" diameter, solid cobalt blue inside & out. Cover & the two handles are embossed "Savory." Near mint, **$35.00.**

3. **Teakettle,** 7½" tall, 8" diameter, red with black interior, bottom, trim & handle, seamless body. Handle is embossed "Memco." Near mint, rare shape, **$100.00.**

Row 3:

1. **Coffeepot,** 5⅛" tall, 3¾" diameter, including the coffee basket insert, light blue inside & out with black trim, handle, & coffee basket. Good plus, **$95.00. Note:** This piece had versatile uses. It was advertised & used as a percolator with the coffee basket, but when the coffee basket was removed the piece could be used as a covered sauce pan that holds 1⅛" pints for general cooking.

2. **Coffee Biggin,** tall, includes coffeepot, perforated biggin & cover. 10" tall, including the biggin, 5¼" diameter, solid red inside & out, black trim & handles, seamless body. Good plus, **$75.00.**

3. **Coffee Biggin,** tall, includes coffeepot, perforated biggin & metal plated cover. 10¼" tall, 5" diameter, solid green inside & out, black perforated biggin, handles & trim, seamless body. Good plus, **$75.00.**

4. **Cuspidor,** 4¼" tall, 7½" diameter, blue inside & out with black trim. Good plus, **$85.00.**

Row 4:

1. **Round Covered Roaster,** 6¼" tall, 8½" diameter not including the handles. Delft blue cover, & black bottom, seamless body. Good plus, **$65.00. Note:** The cover is designed so the steam can collect on the ridges, thus basting whatever is being cooked.

2. **Oval Covered Roaster,** 7⅜" tall, 11¼" wide, 16½" long not including the handles, solid green inside & out with dark blue trim. Cover embossed "Lisk." Metal steam vent on the cover is embossed "Pat May 2, 1911." Good plus, **$50.00.**

3. **Round Covered Roaster,** 6½" tall, 9½" diameter not including the handles, solid red cover has top ridges; black bottom, seamless body. Good plus, **$65.00.**

Row 1:

1. **Sauce Pan,** 2¾" deep, 6" diameter, reddish orange, white interior, black trim & handle. Circa 1960. Good plus, **$20.00.**

2. **Stack Dinner Carrier,** 15¼" tall including the four food containers & cover, 5" diameter, orange, white interior, black trim. Marked on the bottom "Made In Poland. 12." Shows a picture of a teakettle with the ⨆ marking in the middle of the teakettle. Circa 1960. Near mint, **$95.00.**

3. **Double Boiler,** 7" tall to top of the cover knob including the insert, 5¾" bottom diameter, orange, white interior, black trim, handles & knob. Circa 1960. Good plus, **$30.00.**

Row 2:

1. **Fry Pan,** 1⅝" deep, 9⅜" diameter, yellow, white interior, black trim & handle. Circa 1960. Good plus, **$30.00.**

2. **Turtle Trivet,** ¾" high, 5⅞" diameter, orange top & bottom, fancy cut-out center. Circa 1960. Good plus, **$40.00.**

3. **Sauce Pan,** 2¾" deep, 6" diameter, yellow, white interior, black trim & handle. Circa 1960. Good plus, **$20.00.**

Row 3:

1. **Mug,** 3½" deep, 3¾" diameter, red, white interior, black trim. Circa 1960. Good plus, **$10.00.**

2. **Sectioned Plate,** 1" deep, 11" diameter, red inside & out, black trim. Circa 1960. Mint, **$20.00.**

3. **Water Pitcher,** 10¼" tall, 5⅞" diameter, olive green, white interior, black trim & handle. Marked "Made In Poland, 15." Shows a picture of a teakettle with the ⌇ marking in the middle of the teakettle. Circa 1960. Good plus, **$30.00.**

4. **Sectioned Plate,** 1" deep, 11" diameter, aqua green inside & out, black trim. Circa 1960. Mint, **$20.00.**

5. **Mug,** 3½" deep, 3¾" diameter, aqua green, white interior, black trim. Circa 1960. Good plus, **$20.00.**

Row 4:

1. **Corn Pot,** 9½" tall, 11¼" diameter, yellow inside & out, brown trim, handles & cover. Labeled "Ceramic On Steel. 11½" Qt. Corn Pot Sunshine Yellow General Housewares Corp. 1988." Mint, **$20.00.**

2. **Oval Two-Handled Pan,** 1½" deep, 5⅞" wide, 7⅞" long, green inside, black exterior & handles. Circa 1970. Good plus, **$15.00.**

3. **Oval Two-Handled Pan,** 1¼" deep, 4⅜" wide, 6¼" long not including the handle, blue inside, black exterior & handles. Circa 1970. Good plus, **$15.00.**

4. **Oval Two-Handled Pan,** 1½" deep, 7¼" wide, 9⅜" long not including the handles, orange inside, black exterior & handles. Circa 1970. Good plus, **$15.00. Note:** Nos. 2, 3, & 4 on this row are all part of a three-piece set.

5. **Covered Two-Handled Pan,** 6" tall, 7⅜" diameter, reddish orange, white interior, black cover knob. Circa 1980. Mint, **$20.00. Note:** The metal protection bands on the outer edge of the pan & cover.

SECTION 9: SOLID COLORS AND SOLID COLORS ON CAST IRON

Row 1:
1. **Muffin Pan,** 11-cup, 1½" deep, 7⅝" wide, 11⅛" long. Each cup measures 1⅜" deep, 2½" diameter, solid red with cream interior. Cast iron base marked "Griswold Erie PA. U.S.A. 949C." Circa 1940. Near mint, rare color, shape & size, **$145.00.**

Row 2:
1. **Hatchet,** 11¼" long. Hatchet head measures 3¼" wide, 4½" high from the bottom of the hatchet head. Lavender blue with white handle on a cast iron base. Hatchet has embossed cutout of what appears to be George Washington's head. Hatchet head & handle have holes for hanging. Good plus, extremely rare color, shape & size, **$295.00. Note:** This may have been a souvenir or a premium that was given away to commemorate a special event.
2. **Handled Skillet,** ⅞" deep, 4⅝" wide, black with light gray medium mottled, cast iron base. Near mint, **$35.00. Note:** Notice how the handle is molded on the corner of the pan instead of on the side.
3. **Advertising Paperweight,** 1⅛" high, 2⅛" wide, 2⅝" long, red with black body. Cast iron base is embossed on the back: "Ferro Enamels S.U.P.P. By 33 Cleveland. O. Buy From Bob." Mint, extremely rare shape & size, **$125.00.**
4. **Footed Trivet,** ¾" high, 5" wide, 8⅞" long, solid green, fancy pattern on the top, cast iron base. Good plus, **$55.00.**

Row 3:
1. **Handled Cast Iron Skillet,** 1" deep, 4⅜" diameter, solid red with cream interior, pouring spout on each side. Embossed on the bottom "Cast Iron Skillet, O. Griswold, Erie PA. U.S.A. 562." Circa 1940. Mint, extremely rare color, shape & size, **$140.00. Note:** This could be a salesman's sample to show the construction, durability, & beauty of their wares.
2. **Handled Cast Iron Skillet,** black with green medium mottling, ⅞" deep, 3¾" diameter with a lip on each side for pouring. Marked on the bottom "Wagner" in an oval. Good plus, extremely rare color, shape & size, **$110.00. Note:** This piece also could have been a salesman's sample.
3. **Cow-Shaped Serving Tray,** ½" deep, 6¼" wide, 12⅜" long, solid aqua-green, cast iron base. Circa 1940. Near mint, extremely rare color, shape & size, **$135.00. Note:** I believe this was used in a restaurant to serve steak. I have seen another one of these that was not enameled. It has two lifters that fit in the top & bottom grooves for carrying. Marked "Iron Art."
4. **Flat Iron,** 4¼" tall, 3⅜" wide, 6¼" long, charcoal & light gray large mottled. "Snow on the Mountain." Embossed on the handle "Rosieres." Near mint, extremely rare color, shape & size, **$155.00. Note:** This type iron was placed on the stove to heat for ironing clothes.
5. **Flat Iron,** 4" high, 3¾" wide, 6½" long, gray & light gray medium mottled. Top embossing appears to be "Narcounioes," is not clearly visible because of the thick enamelling. Good plus, extremely rare color, shape & size, **$120.00.**

Row 4:
1. **Horse Spoon Rest,** 1⅜" deep, 7" wide from bottom of the neck to top of the ears, 9" long from the nose to the end of the mane, dark brown with black mane. Good plus, **$165.00.**
2. **Muffin Pan,** 11-cup, 1" deep, 8⅝" wide, 12¾" long. Each cup measures ¾" deep by 3⅛" diameter, light gray medium mottled. Cups & strap handles welded together. Strap handles marked "3.W. & L. Mfg. Co." Near mint, extremely rare shape & size, **$250.00.**

Row 5:
1. **Lamb Cake Mold,** wooden base not original. Back section measures 8½" to top of the lamb's head. 2⅛" wide across the bottom, 11¼" long not including the handles. Front section 8" to top of the lamb's head. 2⅛" wide across the bottom, 10¾" long not including the handle. Solid black on cast iron. Good plus, extremely rare color, shape & size, **$295.00. Note:** As you can see the back section is larger than the front. The reason for this is that the cake batter is poured into the back section, then the front section is placed over the back section. Then the cake is baked.
2. **Handled Cast Iron Skillet,** with a lip on each side for pouring. Black with red medium mottling, ⅞" deep, 3¾" diameter, marked on the bottom "Wagner" in an oval. Good plus, extremely rare color, shape & size, **$110.00. Note:** This piece also could be a salesman's sample.
3. **Flat Iron Trivet,** ⅞" deep, 6" long, 3⅞" wide, charcoal & light gray medium mottled, fancy cutout top. Near mint, rare color & shape, **$110.00. Note:** This trivet was used to rest a flat iron.
4. **Dutch Boy,** 16" high, base measures 6⅞" wide, 8" long, brick red with iridescence. Marked "Dutch C-S-1." Near mint, extremely rare color, shape & size, **$295.00. Note:** I believe this is meant to be a doorstop.

Row 6:
1. **Fish Mold,** 2⅛" deep, 8¼" wide, 7¼" from the top fin to the tail fin, solid cobalt blue with white interior. Good plus, rare shape & size, **$135.00.**

206

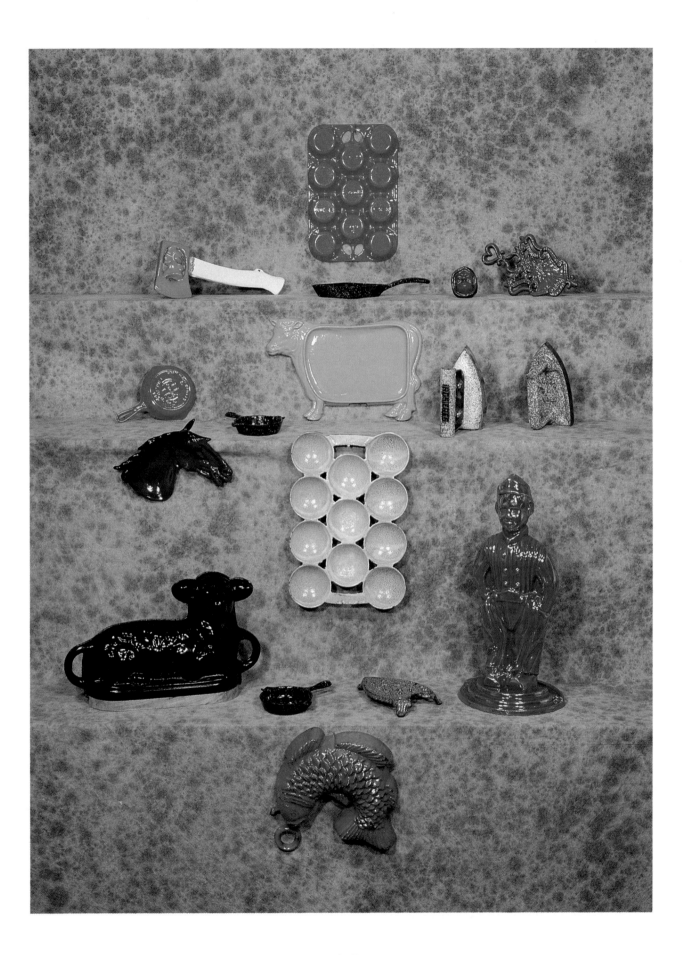

SECTION 10
BROWN AND WHITE

Row 1:
   1. **Oval Pudding or Vegetable Dish,** 1½" deep, 7½" wide, 9½" long, brown & white large swirl with white interior. Near mint, rare color & shape, **$245.00.**

Row 2:
   1. **Milk Can,** 9½" tall, 4¾" diameter, brown & white large swirl, white interior, black trim, seamless body with flat ears & wire bail. Near mint, rare color & shape, **$675.00.**
   2. **Teakettle,** 7" tall, 7⅜" diameter, brown & white large swirl, white interior, seamed spout & bottom, wire bail with Alaska handle, rivetted ears that are shaped to lock the handle in an upright position to keep the handle cool. Good plus, extremely rare color, shape & size, **$895.00.**
   3. **Water Pitcher,** 8¾" tall, 6¼" diameter, brown & white large swirl, white interior, black trim, rivetted handle & seamless body. Near mint, rare color & shape, **$475.00.**

Row 3:
   1. **Coffee Biggin,** including the pot, biggin, cover & spreader. 7¼" tall, 3½" diameter, brown & white large swirl, white interior, rivetted handle with seamed spout & bottom. Height of pot not including the biggin is 3¾". Holds exactly 1½ measuring cups to top of pot. Near mint, extremely rare color, shape & size, **$2,650.00.**
   2. **Funnel,** squatty shaped. 5½" long spout, 6" diameter, brown & white large swirl, white interior, black trim & handle, seamed spout & rivetted handle. Good plus. extremely rare color, rare size, **$260.00.**
   3. **Measure,** 6¼" tall, 4" diameter, brown & white large swirl with white interior, black trim, rivetted strap handle & seamed body. Good plus, rare color & shape, **$450.00.**
   4. **Covered Bucket,** 4" tall, 3⅝" diameter, brown & white large swirl, white interior, black trim, wire bail, rivetted ears, seamless body, & tin cover with wooden knob. Near mint, extremely rare color, shape & size, **$495.00.**

Row 4:
   1. **Double Boiler,** 8½" tall, 8" diameter, brown & white large swirl, white interior, dark brown trim & handles, seamed bottom & rivetted handles. Good plus, rare color, **$375.00.**
   2. **Teapot,** 11" tall, 7" diameter, brown & white large swirl, white interior, black trim, rivetted handle & seamed spout. Near mint, rare color & size, **$550.00.**
   3. **Round 2-piece Roaster,** 8½" tall, 12" diameter, brown & white large swirl inside & out, black trim & handles, metal sliding steam vent on the cover, rivetted handle. The two wire cover locks lock the cover in position. The bottom section has 3 molded indentations that serve as feet & also hold liquid in the bottom of the roaster. Near mint, rare color & shape, **$325.00. Note:** Most round roasters I have seen did not have inserts.

Row 1:

1. **Mug, Camp or Mush,** 4⅝" deep, 6⅛" diameter, brown & white large swirl, white interior, cobalt blue trim, rivetted handle, seamless body. Good plus, rare color, shape & size, **$265.00. Note:** These mugs were also used for cooking mush over campfires, thus, the name camp or mush mug.
2. **Mug,** 3⅛" deep, 4" diameter, brown & white large swirl, white interior, cobalt blue trim, rivetted handle, seamless body. Good plus, rare color, **$135.00.**
3. **Colander,** footed, deep, 4⅛" high, 10⅛" top diameter not including handles, brown & white large swirl, white interior, brown handles & trim, rivetted foot & handles. Near mint, rare color, **$325.00.**
4. **Tumbler,** 3½" deep, 3¼" diameter, brown & white large swirl, white interior, brown trim. Near mint, extremely rare color & shape, **$325.00.**
5. **Colander,** footed, deep, 3¾" high, 9½" top diameter not including handles, brown & white large swirl, white interior, cobalt blue trim & handles. Near mint, rare color, **$325.00. Note:** I chose to picture these two colanders to show you the two different sizes. The first one has brown trim & handles while the second one has cobalt blue trim & handles.

Row 2:

1. **Creamer,** squatty shape, 4⅞" tall, 3⅝" diameter, brown & white large swirl, white interior, black trim, rivetted handle. Near mint, extremely rare color & shape, **$1,000.00.**
2. **Sugar Bowl,** squatty shape, 6" tall, 4⅜" diameter, brown & white large swirl, white interior, black trim & wooden knob, rivetted handles. Near mint, extremely rare color & size, **$1,100.00.**
3. **Spooner,** 5" high, 4¼" diameter, brown & white large swirl, white interior, black trim. Near mint, extremely rare color & shape, **$1,225.00.**

Row 3:

1. **Oval Foot Tub,** 6⅞" deep, 14" wide, 17¾" long not including handles, brown & white large swirl, white interior, cobalt blue trim, rivetted handles, seamless body. Good plus, rare color, shape & size, **$325.00.**
2. **Jelly Roll Pan,** (or mountain cake pan) 1¼" deep, 10" diameter, brown & white large swirl, white interior, cobalt blue trim. Good plus, **$135.00. Note:** Jelly roll pans have straight sides, whereas pie plates have angled sides. These are used to make jelly rolls or mountain cakes.

Row 4:

1. **Fry Pan,** 2" deep, 10⅜" top diameter not including handle, brown & white large swirl, white interior. Near mint, rare color & shape, **$325.00. Note:** This fry pan is on heavy cast iron. Also note the rolled handle for extra support.
2. **Spoon,** 13⅜" long, 2¼" spoon width, brown & white large swirl, handle is brown & white large swirl inside & out. Interior of the spoon's bowl is white. Near mint, rare color, **$135.00.**
3. **Fry Pan,** 2" deep, 12¼" diameter, brown & white large swirl, white interior, brown rivetted handle with eyelet for hanging. Near mint, rare color & shape, **$325.00.**

Row 1:

1. **Tumbler,** 4¾" deep, 3½" diameter, reddish brown and white large swirl, white interior, cobalt blue trim. Near mint, rare color, shape and size, **$230.00.**

2. **Coffee Biggin,** 10½" tall, including the covered biggin, 5½" diameter, reddish brown and white large swirl, white interior, cobalt blue trim. Good plus, rare color, shape and size, **$525.00. Note:** These two pieces are the only ones I have seen in this color. I believe they are foreign.

3. **Coffeepot,** 9¾" tall, 6½" diameter, dark brown and white medium mottled, white interior, black wooden handle and knob, brass plated cover and protection bands, seamed body. Mint, rare color and shape **$395.00.**

Row 2:

1. **Cream Can,** 8" tall, 4¼" diameter, brown and white fine mottled inside and out, seamed body, wooden bail. Near mint, **$140.00.**

2. **Biscuit Sheet,** 12 cups, ⅜" deep, 8½" wide, 11" long. Each biscuit cup ¹⁄₁₆" deep, 2¼" diameter, brown and white medium mottled inside and out, "Onyx Ware." Near mint, extremely rare color, shape and size, **$1,100.00.**

3. **Biscuit Cutter,** 1¾" tall, 1" deep, 2¼" diameter, brown and white medium mottled inside and out, black strap handle that is applied through a slit on each side of the hole in the top of the cutter then each end of the handle is bent over to hold the handle on the biscuit cutter. "Onyx Ware." Near mint, extremely rare color and shape, **$795.00. Note:** Both the biscuit sheet and biscuit cutter are products of the Columbian Enameling and Stamping Co.

4. **Saucer,** ¾" deep, 6⅛" diameter, brown and white medium mottled inside and out. Labeled "Columbian Enameling and Stamping Company, Terre Haute, Indiana Reg. U.S. Pat. Office Triple Coated 'Onyx' 6⅛" Saucer. The World's Best Enamel Ware. Onyx Ware Certificate. We Warrant This Piece of Ware Absolutely Satisfactory or Your Money Back." Mint, **$65.00.**

Row 3:

1. **Coffee Boiler,** 12" tall, 9½" diameter, brown and bluish gray large swirl inside and out, seamed body, rivetted handle, ears and spout, wire bail. Near mint, **$495.00.**

2. **Majestic Ad,** shows a set of Majestic kitchen wares that were given free when you attended one of their demonstrations and purchased their Majestic cooking range. Good plus, **$25.00. Note:** This ad shows a variety of wares including granite ware, copper and tin.

3. **Drainer Pan,** insert, 3¼" deep, 11" diameter, brown and white large marbelized inside and out. Near mint, **$40.00. Note:** I believe this is "Majestic Ware." Near mint.

4. **Combination Cooker,** 6⅜" deep, 10¼" diameter, brown and white large marbelized inside and out, rivetted spout, ears & back metal handle, wooden bail, seamless body. Near mint, **$55.00. Note:** Tin cover is missing. Also, note the metal handle tips up to hold the tin cover secure while pouring. Both No 3 & 4 on this row go together.

Row 1:
1. **Biscuit sheet,** 24 cups, ⅜" deep, 11¼" wide, 16¼" long. Each cup measures ¹⁄₁₆" deep, 2¼" diameter. Brown & white medium mottled inside & out. "Onyx Enamel Ware," Columbian Enameling & Stamping Co. Good plus, extremely rare color, shape & size, **$950.00.**

Row 2:
1. **Coffee Flask,** 4⅜" tall, 3½" diameter, brown & white fine mottled inside & out, seamless body. Near mint, extremely rare shape, **$495.00.**
2. **Milk Can,** 9" tall, 5¼" diameter, brown & white medium mottled inside & out with black trim, seamed body, wooden bail. "Onyx Enamel Ware." Good plus, **$110.00.**
3. **Pudding Pan,** 2⅛" deep, 7¼" diameter, brown & white medium mottled inside & out with black trim. "Onyx Enamel Ware." Good plus, **$20.00.**

Row 3:
1. **Teapot,** 6¼" tall, 4⅛" diameter, dark brown & white fine mottled inside & out, black trim, seamless body, black wooden bail handle. Near mint, **$75.00.**
2. **Covered Bucket,** with matching granite lid, 6" tall, 6⅞" diameter, dark brown & white fine mottled inside & out, black trim, seamless body, black wooden bail handle. Near mint, **$75.00.**
3. **Graduated Measuring Cup,** 4⅛" deep, 4⅝" diameter, each ring equals a 1 cup measurement, dark brown & white fine mottled inside & out, black strap handle & trim. Good plus, **$85.00. Note:** Notice how much darker the brown is on several of the pieces on this page, once again showing how the colors can vary.

Row 4:
1. **Pie Plate,** 1" deep, 9½" diameter, dark brown & white medium mottled inside & out with black trim. Good plus, **$15.00.**
2. **Pie Plate,** shallow, ¾" deep, 8⅞" diameter, dark brown & white medium mottled inside & out with black trim. Good plus, **$20.00.**
3. **Pie Plate,** deep, 1¼" deep, 9⅝" diameter, brown & white medium mottled inside & out with black trim. Good plus, **$15.00. Note:** The bottom of this pie plate has a raised center area 1¼" from the edge. I chose to show these pie plates together so you can see the variations of the sizes, & shapes, as well as color.

Row 1:
1. **Fry Pan,** 1⅛" deep, 7¼" diameter, dark brown & white medium mottled inside & out, black handle & trim. "Onyx Ware." Good plus, **$95.00.**

Row 2:
1. **Scoop,** body of scoop measures 2" deep, 2¾" wide, 5¼" long not including the handle. Overall length with handle is 9½". Reddish brown with white specks, fine mottled, white interior, seamed back, rivetted seamed handle. Marked "Elite Austria Reg'd." Good plus, rare shape & size, **$225.00.**
2. **Mug,** 3" deep, 3" diameter, dark brown & white medium mottled inside & out, black rolled handle & trim, seamed body. "Onyx Ware." Mint, rare shape, **$115.00.**
3. **Teakettle,** 5¼" tall, 6½" diameter, brown with white specks, fine mottled, white interior, seamed bottom & spout, rivetted ears, wire bail. The wooden handle for the bail is missing. Marked on the bottom "D.R.G.M." & also shows a picture of a lion standing with his front paws on a coffeepot. Good plus, **$195.00.**

Row 3:
1. **Turk's Head Scalloped Turban Mold,** 1⅝" deep, 3⅞" diameter, reddish brown with white specks, fine mottled, white interior. Marked "Elite." Mint, rare shape & size, **$140.00.**
2. **Milk Pitcher,** 5½" tall, 4½" diameter, brown & white medium mottled inside & out, black rivetted weld handle, seamless body. "Onyx Ware." Good plus, rare shape, **$135.00.**
3. **Mug,** 2" deep, 3⅜" diameter, brown with white specks, fine mottled, white interior, black trim, seamless body, rivetted strap handle. Near mint, **$65.00.**

Row 4:
1. **Coffeepot,** 10¼" tall, 6⅛" diameter, reddish brown with white specks, fine mottled, white interior, rivetted spout & handle, seamless body. Good plus, **$155.00.**
2. **Milk Can,** 12" tall, 7⅛" diameter, brown & white medium mottled inside & out, black trim & ears, seamed body, black wooden bail handle. "Onyx Ware." Good plus, **$195.00.**
3. **Milk Pitcher,** 8½" tall, 5⅜" diameter, brown with white specks, fine mottled, white interior, seamless body, rivetted hollow handle. Marked on the bottom "D.R.G.M." also pictures a lion standing with his front paws on a coffeepot. Near mint, rare shape, **$185.00.**

SECTION 11
RECREATIONAL AND HOUSEHOLD ITEMS

Row 1:

1. **Picture Frame,** 10⅞" high, 6⅛" wide, decorated with a picture of a bridge, pink flowers & birds that appear to be peacocks. The overall blue lacy design is on a white background of the frame. Near mint, extremely rare shape, **$495.00.**

2. **Checkerboard,** overall measurements 18½" x 18½", red & black decorated with a white border. Near mint, extremely rare color & shape, **$2,000.00.**

3. **Tobacco Humidor,** 6¾" high, 5⅛" diameter, light brown fine mottled, black trim & lettering. Label is fired on the piece. Labeled "Marque De Commerce L'Islet. Poeles. Et. Fournaises Qualite Garantie. La Fonderie. D. L'islet. L'tee L'islet Station. P.O." Mint, rare shape, **$240.00. Note:** This is supposed to represent a furnace from the L'islet Foundry. The cover top is shaped like a floor heat grate. Inside the three piece cover is a metal plate with a screw so the plate can be removed & a sponge can be placed between the metal plate & the cover. This sponge keeps the tobacco moist.

Row 2:

1. **Checkerboard,** overall measurements 18" x 18," cream decorated with brown. Mint, extremely rare color & shape, **$2,000.00.**

2. **Checkerboard,** overall measurements 19" by 20½", green decorated with cream. Marked "Marietta Hollow-Ware Enameling Co., Marietta, Pennsylvania Patented, No. 885707." Near mint, extremely rare color & shape, **$2,000.00.**

218

Row 1:

1. **Clock,** 9⅝" tall, 9⅝" wide, white decorated with black trim, numbers & fancy outer border, inner border light blue, light pink & light green. Mint, extremely rare color & shape, **$325.00. Note:** This inner border is referred to as a "Pearlized" finish because it appears to have an iridescent effect. Marked "8 Day Germany."

2. **Clock,** school house style, 9½" long, 6⅝" wide, yellow decorated with a light orange & dark orange design, beveled glass window covering the pendulum. Marked "8 Day Germany." Mint, extremely rare color & shape, **$425.00.**

Row 2:

1. **Clock,** 11¾" long, 9⅝" wide, white decorated with 14 different scenes in a blue Delft style with a light gray border. Mint, extremely rare color and shape, **$450.00.**

Row 3:

1. **Clock,** 10⅝" diameter, white decorated with a blue Delft style scene. Marked "8 Day Germany." Mint, extremely rare color & shape, **$375.00.**

2. **Clock,** 8¾" top to bottom, 9½" wide, decorated with 8 different nursery rhyme characters. Marked "8 Day Germany." Mint, extremely rare color & shape, **$595.00.**

Note: All the clocks pictured are in perfect working order & priced accordingly.

Row 1:

1. **Doorstop,** 5⅜" tall, 1¾" wide, 10¾" long, light brown shading to a darker brown. Good plus, extremely rare color, shape & size, **$295.00. Note:** This pearlized piece is on a heavy metal base with iridescent finish.

2. **Plaque,** 10¼" x 9", white decorated with a cobalt blue windmill scene & cobalt blue border, brass eyelets on each side for hanging. Near mint, extremely rare color & shape, **$185.00. Note:** This plaque came from a dairy farm in Wisconsin.

3. **Electric Toaster,** with retractable overhead wire warming rack. 9" tall, 4½" wide, 8" long, black granite base over heavy metal, black wooden carrying handle & knobs, toaster body is chrome plated, base embossed "Simplex Quality. T211 V110. A 4.5.S482261. patent applied for 1909." Mint, extremely rare shape, **$325.00.**

Row 2:

1. **"Dog" Nutcracker,** on cast iron, 6" to top of the dog's head, 13" long from the dog's nose to the tip of the tail, base 3⅜" wide, 9⅝" long, dark gray shading to a lighter gray. Good plus, extremely rare shape, rare color, **$375.00. Note:** The nut is cracked by raising dog's tail & placing nut in the dog's mouth, then pressing down on the tail.

2. **Inhaler** (2 piece), 9" to top of the lip including the base, 5" diameter, dark lavender blue & white medium mottled, dark blue trim. Embossed with a man holding the inhaler up to his nose & mouth. Marked in black letters in a circle "Innalateur Nicolav. Mo?ele Depose." Near mint, extremely rare color, shape & size, **$235.00. Note:** The 3 sections of two holes around the bottom rim of the inhaler for steam to escape.

3. **"Dog" Nutcracker,** on cast iron, 6¼" to top of the dog's head, 10¾" long from the dog's nose to the tip of the tail. Base, 3¾" wide, 5¾" long, brown dog, white base. Near mint, extremely rare color, **$350.00. Note:** Most of these dog nutcrackers bodies are in three sections that include each side & the tail. They are held together by a large screw that goes through the center of the dog's body.

Row 3:

1. **Washboard,** 23¾" long, 12½" wide, solid cobalt blue, metal soap saver. Embossed "Patent Pending. Trade Ⓦ Mark O-Joy. Wayne Mfg. Co. St. Louis, Mo." The wooden part of the washboard on the back side is marked "No. 10 O-Joy Enamel. Patent Pending. Wayne Manufacturing Company, St. Louis, Mo. U.S.A." Good plus, rare shape, **$135.00.**

2. **Fruit Press,** metal part 21¾" high to top of the handle, 8½" wide from foot to foot, 10¾" long from foot to foot, granite ware insert, 4⅜" deep, 6⅜" diameter, spout 2" long, bluish gray, white interior, seamless body, insert on a heavy metal base. Good plus, extremely rare shape, **$265.00.**

Top Left:
1. **Oil Lamp,** cylinder-style, 9" to top of the oil fount, 5½" diameter, 21½" to top of the glass chimney, brown & white relish pattern medium mottled, oil fount & protection bands are brass, with metal footed base. This lamp has been electrified. Good plus, extremely rare color shape, **$1,750.00. Note:** I believe this is a product of the Manning Bowman Co. In their 1892 catalog they show lamps that are very similar in style.

Top Right:
1. **Hoosier Cabinet,** maple, 5' 10" overall height. Bottom section measures 18" wide, 22" long. Enamel work top is 24" long & pulls out to create a 19" deep work area, cream with green trim. Mint, rare color, shape & size, **$895.00. Note:** Hoosier cabinets come in different sizes, with a variety of colored enamel work surfaces. Some examples I have seen have an overall white work surface with either blue & white, green & white, or even orange & white, medium mottled trim. They also have variations of the woods used, such as all oak or maple, or a combination of oak & maple.

Bottom:
1. **Enamel Picture,** 17½" wide, 20½" long not including the frame. I believe this is of English origin because of the style of the house. I have seen similar pictures displayed on calendars. These were entitled "Chandler's Cottage." The workmanship is superb and it certainly would be an added attraction to anyone's collection. If anyone should have verified information about this picture I would appreciate hearing from them. Mint, extremely rare color, shape and size, **$950.00.**

Section 12
Metal Trimmed Pieces, White Metal, Nickel Plate, Pewter, Quadruple Silver Plate, Etc.

Row 1:

1. **Coffeepot,** with metal mountings & protection bands, 8½" tall, 5¾" diameter, light lavender & white large mottled, white interior. Good plus, rare color & shape, **$395.00.**
2. **Teakettle or Table Kettle,** squatty shape with metal mountings & protection bands, 8½" tall, to top of the cover finial, 6¾" diameter, white decorated with a leaf design & brown bands, hinged cover. Mint, extremely rare color & shape, **$795.00.**
3. **Creamer,** squatty shape with metal mountings & protection bands, 4¾" tall, 4½" diameter, white decorated with a leaf design & brown bands. Mint, rare shape, **$350.00.**

Row 2:

1. **Teapot,** squatty shape with metal mountings & protection bands, 7¼" tall, 6" diameter, white decorated with a blue & white scroll & flower band & decorated pink bands. Good plus, **$225.00.**
2. **Glass Holder** with metal handle & protection bands, 2" high without the glass, 3" top diameter, decorated with penguins with blue, gold & white background. Embossed on the bottom "WOIV." This could be the mark of the artist who decorated the piece. Mint, extremely rare color, shape & size, **$195.00. Note:** In the 1892 Manning Bowman catalog, they advertise this item as a soda & mineral water glass holder. It states these holders are made for tumblers of standard size, but may be changed to order in lots of not less than one dozen of a kind.
3. **Napkin Ring** with metal protection bands, 1½" high, 2⅛" diameter, pink decorated with three black & white birds, rivetted seam. Near mint, extremely rare color, shape & size, **$225.00.**
4. **Teapot** with metal mountings & protection bands, 5¾" high, 3⅝" diameter, white decorated with the Statue of Liberty. Mint, extremely rare color, shape & size, **$850.00. Note:** I believe this teapot was decorated to commemorate the unveiling of the Statue of Liberty October 28, 1886.
5. **Teapot,** squatty or melon shaped with metal mountings & protection bands, 7½" tall, 6¾" diameter, shaded blue background decorated with a white & gold colored floral & leaf design. Mint, rare color & shape, **$495.00. Note:** In the 1892 Manning Bowman catalog, this shaped teapot was advertised as a "Little Brown Jug" teapot.

Row 3:

1. **Sugar Bowl,** with metal mountings & protection bands, 7¾" tall, 4⅞" diameter, white decorated with a castle scene. Mint, rare shape, **$395.00.**
2. **Teapot,** with metal mountings & protection bands, 11" tall, 5½" diameter, white decorated with a castle scene. Mint, **$325.00.**
3. **Creamer** with metal mountings & protection bands, 5⅞" tall, 3⅞" diameter, white decorated with a castle scene. Mint, rare shape, **$350.00.**
4. **Waste Bowl,** with metal mountings & protection bands, 3¾" tall to top of the scalloped edge, 5" diameter, white decorated with a castle scene. Mint, extremely rare shape, **$425.00. Note:** Waste bowls were used at the table for social dinners. The left-over coffee or tea was poured from the cups into the waste bowl.

Row 1:
1. **Butter Dish,** 7" high, 5" middle diameter not including scalloped edge, gray large mottled, metal mounted cover, bands, handles & scalloped edge. Butter tray insert ¾" deep, 4¾" diameter, gray large mottled, pewter trimmed. Butter knife, embossed "Standard Pat. 25." Near mint, extremely rare color & shape, **$725.00.**
2. **Teapot,** 6¼" high, 3⅞" diameter, gray medium mottled, metal mounts, scalloped top edge, cover, handle, spout & protection bands. Mint, extremely rare color, shape & size, **$595.00.**
3. **Castor Set,** 14" high to top of the handle, 5¾" base diameter. Castor holder, 7½" diameter, 1⅝" deep. Each hole that holds a castor is 1⅞" diameter. Gray large mottled, metal mounts, handle & protection bands. Holds five glass castors. Mint, extremely rare color, shape & size, **$2,950.00.**
4. **Butter Tray Insert,** for butter dish (No. 5 of this row) ⅝" deep, 4⅝" diameter, gray medium mottled, metal mounts. Mint, No. 4 & 5, 3 pieces, **$795.00. Note:** The finger hole in the center of the insert. This is used to lift the insert out of the butter dish base. I believe it would also serve to help circulate the cold air around the butter.
5. **Butter Dish,** 6¾" high, 5⅜" middle diameter, gray medium mottled, metal trimmed cover, protection bands & handle. **Note:** Butter knife is missing.

Row 2:
1. **Sugar Bowl,** squatty shape, 6¾" high, 5⅝" middle diameter, gray large mottled, metal mounts, cover & handles. Mint, rare shape, **$525.00.**
2. **Teapot,** squatty shape, 8½" high, 7⅛" middle diameter, gray large mottled, metal mounts, cover & handle. Mint, rare shape, **$410.00.**
3. **Syrup Pitcher** squatty shape, 6" tall, 4¼" middle diameter, gray large mottled, hinged cover. Mint, extremely rare shape, **$975.00. Note:** This is pictured in the 1892 Manning, Bowman & Co. catalog. It's called a syrup pitcher & comes with 2 types of metal trims, white metal or nickel plate. The nickel plate were each $3.00.

Row 3:
1. **Teapot,** 10" high, 5⅝" diameter, gray medium mottled, metal mounts, cover & handle. Mint, **$250.00.**
2. **Goblet,** 7⅜" high, 3¾" top diameter, 3¼" base diameter, gray large mottled, quadruple silver plate trim. Near mint, extremely rare color, shape & size, **$795.00. Note:** The fancy embossed band around the top & bottom edge. Marked "Manning Bowman & Co. 300." This is part of a five piece water set, shown in the 1892 Manning, Bowman & Co. catalog. "Patent Perfection Granite Ironware" The set is advertised as "No 250 water set with double ice pitcher. 4 pints, pair goblets, a slop bowl & a 16" waiter, all quadruple silver plate trim. Complete $26.00." A waiter is a tray, either oval or round. This set's waiter is oval with gray large mottling trimmed in quadruple silver plate.
3. **Teapot,** 11½" high, 6" diameter, gray medium mottled, metal mounts, cover & handle. Good plus, **$200.00.**

Row 4:
1. **Creamer,** 6" high, 3¾" wide, gray large mottled, with metal mounts, scalloped top edge, pewter spout & handle. Mint, rare shape, **$350.00.**
2. **Teapot,** 11" high, 5⅝" diameter, gray large mottled, metal mounts, scalloped top edge, pewter handle, spout & cover. Mint, **$275.00.**
3. **Sugar Bowl,** 8½" tall, 5⅛" diameter, with gray large mottled, metal mounts, scalloped top edge, cover, & handles. Mint, rare shape, **$495.00.**

Row 1:

1. **Creamer,** with metal trim & mountings 4½" tall, 3¼" diameter, white decorated with a floral design of calla lilies, roses, violets, leaves, & ferns. Mint, rare shape, **$350.00. Note:** The 1892 Manning Bowman Co. catalogue refers to pieces that are similar to this design & decoration as "Patent Decorated Pearl Agateware with White Metal Mountings & Protection Bands. Patented June 5, 1883, Registered January 13, 1885." Pieces like these were made in series & also numbered. The decorations were referred to by letter. For example, No. 9450 series, decoration O with white porcelain inside. White metal mountings were $22.00/dozen. Nickel plated mountings were $2.50 for each pot. As you can see white metal mountings were cheaper than the nickel plated versions. It is also important to note that these metal trims have been generically labeled as pewter trim & mountings. In actuality they are either white metal, nickel plated, or another type of Britannia. I personally have not seen literature referring to this type of agateware trimmed in pewter. I refer to some pieces as metal trim & mountings. This is the way the catalogue advertises these pieces. In some instances where there is no reference to the metals or coatings used, I use the generic name used by collectors today, such as pewter trimmed.

2. **Teapot,** with metal trim, & mountings 9⅞" tall, 5" diameter, white decorated with floral design of calla lilies, roses, violets, leaves & ferns, Mint, **$295.00.**

3. **Covered Sugar,** with metal trim & mountings, 7½" tall, 4" diameter, white decorated with floral design calla lilies, roses, violets, leaves & ferns. Mint, rare shape, **$350.00.**

Row 2:

1. **Teapot,** with metal trim & mountings, 9¾" tall, 5⅝" diameter, white decorated with a floral design of pink roses & violets. Mint, **$295.00.**

2. **Castor Set or Dinner Castor,** 16¼" to top of the handle, 5¼" base diameter. Castor holder 7½" diameter, 2½" deep, white metal mountings & protection bands, quadruple silver plate, white decorated with a floral design of pink roses with five castor bottles. Mint, extremely rare color, shape & size, **$3,500.00. Note:** Similar set is shown in the 1892 Manning, Bowman catalogue. These castor sets could be purchased with different handles. The plain handle such as this one was 25¢ less. One of the statements made was that, when the acids from mustards & vinegars came in contact with the granite enamel it would not be affected. "From these handsome designs it will be seen that the goods are therefore more desirable than those made entirely of metal." In comparison of price, the nickel plated sets were each $5.00 whereas the silverplate was $5.75. Different bottles were also available.

3. **Teapot,** with metal trim & mountings, 11" tall, 5¼" diameter, white decorated with lily of the valley, roses, violets, & ferns. Mint, **$295.00.**

Row 3:

1. **Footed Creamer** with white metal mountings, 5⅜" tall, 3⅛" diameter, white decorated with pink & blue fuchsias. Near mint, extremely rare shape, **$425.00. Note:** The handles on these footed pieces are white decorated with another type of yellow & pink flowers.

2. **Footed Teapot,** with white metal mountings, 11" tall, 5" diameter, white decorated with pink & blue fuchsias. Near mint, extremely rare shape, **$425.00.**

3. **Footed Sugar Bowl,** with white metal mountings, 5⅝" deep, 4¼" wide, white decorated with pink & blue fuchsias. Near mint, extremely rare shape, **$425.00. Note:** The white metal mountings are marked "Manning, Bowman & Co. No. 9500" on all three pieces on this row.

Special Note: The matching numbers etched into the metal mounting on the bottom of each piece on this row indicate this is a matched 3 piece set. Each piece has a variation in the design; one of the reasons for this is that they are sometimes decorated by different artists at the factory.

SECTION 13
SHADED

Row 1:

1. **Advertising Cardboard Sign,** 8¾" wide, 13" long, advertising "Ask for Shamrock Enameled Ware, Shapleigh Hardware Co." also advertising their "Diamond Edge" trademark in a diamond. Good plus, rare shape & size, **$150.00. Note:** I believe this sign was given to dealers & jobbers to display along with their "Shamrock" Enamel Ware.

Row 2:

1. **Coffeepot,** 9" tall, 5¼" diameter, deep sea green shading to a moss green, white interior, seamless body. Near mint, rare color, **$325.00.**
2. **Mug,** 2½" deep, 3⅜" diameter, deep sea green shading to a moss green, white interior, rivetted handle. Mint, rare color, **$65.00.**
3. **Mustard Pot,** 3⅞" high, 2⅞" wide, deep sea green shading to a moss green, white interior, seamless body. Near mint, extremely rare color, shape & size, **$395.00. Note:** The cover has a hole on the outer edge for the spoon handle to fit into. I know these were advertised as mustard or horseradish pots but I believe they also were used for jams & jellies as many of the granite ware items had versatile uses.
4. **Double Boiler,** 7¼" high, 5½" diameter, deep sea green shading to a moss green, white interior, seamless body, rivetted handles. Good plus, rare color, **$185.00.**

Row 3:

1. **Measure,** 4½" tall, 3½" diameter, deep sea green shading to a moss green, white interior, rivetted handle, seamless body. Good plus, rare color, shape & size, **$235.00.**
2. **Cream Can,** 7⅝" high, 4" diameter, deep sea green shading to a moss green, white interior, rivetted wire-shaped ears, seamless body. Near mint, rare color, **$265.00.**
3. **Covered Berlin-Style Kettle,** 6¼" high, 7¾" wide, deep sea green shading to a moss green, white interior, rivetted wire ears, wire bail with Alaska handle, seamless body. Good plus, rare color & shape, **$140.00.**
4. **Molasses Pitcher,** 6" high, 3⅜" diameter, deep sea green shading to a moss green, white interior, seamless body. Near mint, rare color & shape, **$295.00. Note:** On the molasses pitcher, the cover covers the spout. Also, the spout does not have a strainer on the inside like the coffee or teapot spouts.

Row 4:

1. **Milk Can,** 11½" high, 6" diameter, deep sea green shading to a moss green, white interior, rivetted handles, wire bail, seamless body. Near mint, rare color, **$235.00.**
2. **Pie Plate,** shallow, ¾" deep, 9" diameter, deep sea green shading to a moss green, white interior. Mint, rare color, **$45.00.**
3. **Windsor Dipper,** 13" long, dipper 2¾" deep, 4⅝" diameter, deep sea green shading to a moss green, white interior, rivetted hollow seamed handle with eyelet for hanging. Good plus, rare color, **$95.00.**
4. **Teakettle,** 8" to top of the cover handle, 10" bottom diameter, deep sea green shading to a moss green, white interior, semi-seamless body, wire bail with Alaska handle. Good plus, rare color & shape, **$265.00.**

Note: I believe all these items pictured on this page are "Shamrock Ware" because of the similarity of the color on each piece. These wares are also referred to as "shaded," blended or banded.

233

Row 1:

1. **Milk Can,** 9¼" high, 5" diameter, deep sea green shading to a moss green, white interior, rivetted wire ears & handle, wooden bail, seamless body. "Shamrock Ware." Good plus, rare color, **$210.00.**

2. **Milk Can,** 10¾" high, 5⅝" diameter, deep sea green shading to a moss green, white interior, rivetted handle & ears, wire bail, seamless body. "Shamrock Ware." Good plus, rare color, **$210.00. Note:** No. 1 on this row has wire ears whereas this milk can has flat, two pieced ears.

3. **Coffeepot,** 8" high, 4⅞" diameter, deep sea green shading to a moss green, white interior, rivetted handle & spout. "Shamrock Ware." Near mint, rare color, **$325.00.**

Row 2:

1. **Creamer,** 5⅝" tall, 3¾" diameter, deep sea green shading to a moss green, white interior, rivetted handle. "Shamrock Ware." Good plus, rare color & shape, **$195.00.**

2. **Covered Bucket,** 7¼" high, 6½" diameter, deep sea green shading to a moss green, white interior, rivetted wire ears, wooden bail, seamless body. "Shamrock Ware." Good plus, rare color, **$185.00.**

3. **Serving Bowl,** 3⅝" deep, 8⅜" diameter, deep sea green shading to a moss green, white interior, black trim. "Shamrock Ware." Good plus, rare color, **$55.00.**

Row 3:

1. **Teapot,** squatty shape, 7¼" high, 7" diameter, deep sea green shading to a light moss green, white interior, rivetted handle. Good plus, rare shape, **$295.00.**

2. **Syrup,** squatty shape, 7" high, 4¼" diameter, sea green shading to a light moss green, white interior, rivetted handle, seamed body, nickel-plated copper cover with thumb rest. Good plus, extremely rare color & shape, **$550.00. Note:** I believe this color is "Everglade" from The Strong Manufacturing Co. Bellaire, Ohio.

3. **Sugar Bowl,** 6" high, 3¾" diameter, deep sea green shading to a light moss green, white interior, rivetted handles, seamless body. Good plus, rare color & shape, **$265.00.**

4. **Teapot,** 9" tall, 5⅜" diameter, sea green shading to a light moss green, white interior, rivetted handle, seamless body. Good plus, rare color, **$265.00. Note:** This color has the same deep sea green color as the other pieces on this row but it shades to a lighter moss green. I believe this color is "Everglade" also from The Strong Manufacturing Co. Bellaire, Ohio.

Row 4:

1. **Oval Foot Tub,** handled, 7⅜" high, 15" wide, 16¾" long, deep sea green shading to a moss green, white interior, seamless body. Good plus, rare color & shape, **$215.00.**

2. **Oval Roaster,** two piece, 8¼" high, 11½" wide, 15⅝" long not including handles, deep sea green shading to a moss green, white interior. Embossed "Jersey." Good plus, rare color, **$195.00. Note:** This is the only shape in "Shamrock Ware" I have seen embossed. I'm not sure what Jersey stands for. It could be the name of the company who made the roaster before it was enameled or it could just be where it was made.

Row 1:
1. **Coffeepot,** 9¼" tall, 6" diameter, brilliant blue shading to a lighter blue, white interior, black trim & handle, seamless body. Good plus, rare color, **$295.00. Note:** The unusual ring handle on the cover.
2. **Colander,** footed, deep, 4½" high, 11" diameter, brilliant deep blue shading to a lighter blue, white interior, black trim & handles. Good plus, rare color, **$165.00. Note:** Some colanders are deep & some are shallow. In referring to colanders, "deep" does not mean a measurement.
3. **Teapot,** 8¼" high, 5" diameter, brilliant deep blue shading to a lighter blue, white interior, black trim & handle, seamless body. Good plus, rare color, **$295.00.**

Row 2:
1. **Candlestick,** 2" top diameter not including candle holder section, 5½" diameter, brilliant deep blue shading to a lighter blue, white exterior, round finger ring. Good plus, rare color & shape, **$195.00. Note:** The exceptionally wide rim on the neck of the candle holder.
2. **Oval Roaster,** two-piece, 8¼" high, 11¾" wide, 17¼" long not including the handles, brilliant deep blue shading to a lighter blue inside & out. Bottom section of the roaster has a deep recessed bottom that curves up on the inside of the roaster. This prevents burning the food and allows juices to run off. Good plus, rare color, **$255.00. Note:** The cover is embossed with scroll work & lettering. "H.S.B. & Co. Revonoc." H.S.B. & Co. stands for Hibbard, Spencer, Bartlett, & Company. They were jobbers that were located in Chicago, Illinois & sold Revonoc Wares.
3. **Measure,** 4⅜" tall, 3¾" diameter, brilliant blue shading to a lighter blue, white interior, black trim & handle, rivetted handle & spout, seamed body. Good plus, rare color & shape, **$185.00.**

Row 3:
1. **Coffee Boiler,** 11⅝" high, 9½" diameter, brilliant blue shading to a lighter blue, white interior, black trim & handle, seamed body, wooden bail. Good plus, rare color, **$245.00. Note:** The wire ears are applied to the body in two sections.
2. **Water Pitcher,** 9⅞" tall, 6⅜" diameter, brilliant deep blue shading to a lighter blue, white interior, black trim & handle, seamless body. Mint, rare color, **$295.00.**

Note: The close resemblance of the color shading. These pieces could all be from Hibbard, Spencer, Bartlett, & Company. "Revonoc."

Row 1:

1. **Teapot,** 10" tall, 5⅝" diameter, deep violet shading to a lighter violet, white interior, seamed body. Good plus, rare color, **$295.00. Note:** I believe this to be "Thistle Ware" distributed by Norvell-Shapleigh Hardware Co., St. Louis.
2. **Pie Plate,** deep, 1¼" deep, 9" diameter, deep violet shading to a lighter violet, white interior. "Thistle Ware." Near mint, **$65.00.**
3. **Measure,** 8¼" tall, 6¾" diameter, deep violet shading to a lighter violet, white interior, rivetted handle, seamless body, "Thistle Ware." Mint, rare color, shape & size, **$325.00.**

Row 2:

1. **Creamer,** 5⅜" tall, 3⅜" diameter, deep violet shading to a lighter violet, white interior, rivetted handle, seamless body. Near mint, rare color & shape, **$195.00.**
2. **Cream Can,** 7¾" tall, 4" diameter, brown shading to a lighter brown, white interior, wooden bail, seamless body. Near mint, rare color & shape, **$185.00.**
3. **Coffeepot,** 10¾" tall, 6" diameter, brown shading to gold, white interior. Labeled "Enamel Art Ware" Norvell-Shapleigh Hardware Co., St. Louis. Near mint, rare color, **$325.00.**
4. **Creamer,** 5½" tall, 3¾" diameter, brown shading to a lighter brown, white interior, seamless body. Near mint, rare color & shape, **$195.00.**
5. **Boston Cream Can,** 7½" tall, 4" diameter, deep violet shading to a lighter violet, white interior, rolled handles on the matching cover & body, seamless body. Near mint, rare color, shape & size, **$225.00.**

Row 3:

1. **Boston Milk Can,** 11¼" tall, 6" diameter, light brown shading to a lighter brown, white interior, matching lock lid, seamless body. Near mint, rare color, shape & size, **$165.00. Note:** Boston milk or cream cans are called this because they also have a side handle. They sometimes have a bail handle as well.
2. **Shell Mold,** 1½" deep, 3" wide, 3¼" long, brown shading to tan, white interior, has a ring for hanging. Mint, rare color, shape & size, **$155.00.**
3. **Round Miner's Dinner Bucket,** 9½" tall, including food insert, 7¼" diameter. Food insert, 6¼" deep, 6¾" diameter "Thistle Ware." Deep violet shading to a lighter violet, white interior, seamless body, wire ears, wooden bail. Near mint, rare color, **$325.00. Note:** The food insert can be used as a separate section for warming foods.
4. **Cup,** 2⅛" deep, 4¼" diameter, deep violet shading to a lighter violet, white interior. Near mint, **$45.00.**
5. **Coffeepot,** 11½" tall, 6⅛" diameter, light blue shading to a lighter blue, white interior, black trim & handle, seamless body, glass insert on cover marked "Pyrex" Made in U.S.A., aluminum coffee basket. Mint, **$125.00. Note:** This is a lighter blue than "Bluebelle Ware."

Row 4:

1. **Creamer,** 5" tall, 3¼" diameter, brown shading to a lighter brown, white interior, seamless body, rivetted handle. Near mint, rare color & shape, **$195.00. Note:** The two different sizes of the brown shaded creamers on this page as well as the depth of color variations. I believe they are both from the same makers.
2. **Oblong Baking Pan,** 2 handled, 2" deep, 8⅝" wide, 14½" long not including handles, deep sea green shading to a moss green, white interior, rivetted handles. "Shamrock Ware." Good plus, rare color, **$125.00.**
3. **Molasses Pitcher,** 6" tall, 3½" diameter, brown shading to a lighter brown, white interior, rivetted handle & spout, seamless body. Good plus, rare color & shape, **$295.00. Note:** The spout is covered.

Row 1:

1. **Coffeepot,** 9½" tall, 6" diameter, shading from green to ivory, white interior, black trim & handle, seamless body, rivetted handle. Good plus, **$225.00. Note:** This coffeepot was advertised as "Old Ivory" Genuine Triple Coated Blended Enameled Ware manufactured by Banner Stamping Works, U.S.A.

2. **Water Pitcher,** 9¾" tall, 7¼" diameter, brown shading to gold, white interior, brown handle & trim, seamless body, rivetted handle. Good plus, rare color, **$155.00.**

3. **Teapot,** 9½" tall, 6" diameter, same color & manufacturer as No. 1 on Row 1 on this page, seamless body, rivetted handle. Near mint, **$250.00.**

Row 2:

1. **Teapot,** 9" tall, 5¼" diameter, brown shading to a lighter brown, white interior, seamless body, rivetted handle. Near mint, rare color, **$225.00.**

2. **Teakettle,** 7½" tall, 8" diameter, deep violet shading to a lighter violet, white interior, seamed body, wooden bail. Good plus, rare color & shape, **$250.00. Note:** I believe this is "Thistle Ware."

3. **Mustard or Horseradish Pot,** with ladle, Mustard Pot, 3½" tall, 2⅜" diameter, light blue shading to white decorated with gold leaf bands, white interior, seamless body. Numbered 448-21. Ladle, 4¾" long, ladle diameter 1⅛", white decorated with gold leaf. Near mint, rare color & shape, **$195.00.**

4. **Coffeepot,** 8⅜" tall, 5¼" diameter, blue shading to white, white interior, black trim & handle, seamed body. Near mint, **$225.00.**

Row 3:

1. **Butter Churn,** floor model dasher type, 17½" high without the wooden cover, 10½" diameter, bluish green shading to off white, white interior, black trim & handles, seamed body. Good plus, extremely rare color, **$795.00.**

2. **Fry Pan,** 2⅛" deep, 11⅜" diameter, green shading to ivory, white interior, black handle, cast iron base. "Old Ivory Ware." Near mint, rare color, **$180.00.**

3. **Cream Can,** 6¾" tall, 4" diameter, bluish green shading to off white, white interior, black trim & ears, wire bail & ears, seamless body. Good plus, rare color, **$155.00.**

4. **Vase,** 14⅛" high, 6" diameter, shading from red to black, red interior. Marked "Germany." Near mint, extremely rare shape & rare color, **$285.00.**

5. **Teapot,** 8" tall, 4⅝" diameter, bluish green shading to off white, white interior, black trim, seamed body. Near mint, **$225.00.**

Row 1:
1. **Covered Bucket,** matching cover, 5¼" high, 4¾" diameter, blue shading to lighter blue back to blue, white interior, black trim & ears, enameled rivetted wire ears, wooden bail, seamless body. Good, rare color & size, **$195.00.**
2. **Covered Bucket,** matching cover, 7½" high, 7⅜" diameter, blue shading to lighter blue back to blue, white interior, black trim & ears, enameled rivetted wire ears, wooden bail, seamless body. Mint, rare color, **$165.00.**
3. **Covered Bucket,** matching cover, 6⅜" high, 6⅛" diameter, blue shading to lighter blue back to blue, white interior, black trim & ears, enameled rivetted wire ears, wooden bail. Good plus, rare color, **$165.00.**

Row 2:
1. **Convex Sauce Pan,** lipped, 2½" deep, 4⅝" diameter, blue shading to lighter blue back to blue, white interior, black trim & tubular handle with eyelet. Near mint, rare size, **$65.00.**
2. **Convex Sauce Pan,** lipped, 4⅜" deep, 8½" diameter, blue shading to lighter blue back to blue, white interior, black trim & tubular handle with eyelet. Good plus, **$40.00.**
3. **Coffeepot,** 9" high, 4½" diameter, blue shading to lighter blue back to blue, white interior, black trim & handle, seamed body. Mint, **$225.00.**
4. **Custard Cup,** 2½" deep, 3⅞" diameter, blue shading to lighter blue back to blue. "Bluebelle Ware." Good plus, rare color & shape, **$55.00.**

Row 3:
1. **Maslin-Style Kettle,** with matching granite lid, 10" high, 10½" diameter, blue shading to lighter blue back to blue, white interior, black trim & handle, seamless body, with sidetipping handle, wire bail. Good plus, **$135.00.**
2. **Plate,** ¾" deep, 9¾" diameter, blue shading to lighter blue back to blue, white interior. "Bluebelle Ware." Near mint, rare shape, **$65.00.**
3. **Farmers Mug,** 4" deep, 5" diameter, blue shading to lighter blue back to blue, white interior, rivetted handle, seamless body. "Bluebelle Ware." Good plus, **$55.00.**
4. **Round Roaster,** 7¼" high, 12¼" diameter not including handles, blue shading to lighter blue back to blue, white interior, black trim & handles, seamless body. Good plus, rare color, **$165.00.**

Row 4:
1. **Cuspidor,** medium size, 4" high, 9⅜" diameter, blue shading to lighter blue back to blue, white interior, black trim, seamless body. Good plus, **$125.00.**
2. **Advertising Coaster,** ⅜" deep, 4" diameter, blue shading to lighter blue, white interior. Marked in a double circle, "Norvell-Shapleigh Hdw. Co. St. Louis Distributors Bluebelle Ware." Good plus, extremely rare shape, **$165.00. Note:** This coaster does not have the black trim.
3. **Cuspidor,** large size, 5⅛" high, 10¾" diameter, blue shading to lighter blue back to blue, white interior, black trim. Near mint, **$125.00.**
4. **Cuspidor** (or Lady's Spittoon), 4" high, 7¼" top diameter, blue shading to lighter blue back to blue, white interior, "Bluebelle Ware." Good plus, rare shape & size, **$195.00.**

Row 1:

1. **Colander,** footed, deep, 5⅛" high, 8¾" diameter not including handles, blue shading to light blue back to blue, white interior, fancy perforations. "Bluebelle Ware," distributed by Norvell-Shapleigh Hardware Co., St. Louis, Mo. Mint, rare color, **$165.00. Note:** Other enameling companies also made the blue shaded.

2. **Milk Can,** matching cover, 10⅛" tall, 5½" diameter, blue shading to lighter blue, back to blue, white interior, black trim, rivetted enamel wire ears, wooden bail, seamless body. Good plus, rare color, **$175.00.**

3. **Teapot,** squatty shape, 6¾" high, 3¾" diameter, blue shading to lighter blue back to blue, white interior, black trim & handle, seamless body. Near mint, rare shape & size, **$265.00. Note:** This seems to be a darker blue. I'm not sure this is "Bluebelle Ware" although we must remember that pieces do vary in color according to environment and the enamel mixture.

Row 2:

1. **Molasses Pitcher,** 6" high, 3½" diameter, blue shading to light blue back to blue, white interior, seamless body, rivetted covered spout & handle. Good plus, rare color & shape, **$265.00. Note:** This molasses pitcher does not have the black trim & handle.

2. **Teapot,** 8⅜" high, 4¼" diameter, blue shading to lighter blue back to blue, white interior, rivetted spout, seamless body. Near mint, rare color, **$235.00.**

3. **Oval Roaster,** 8" high, 11½" wide, 15½" long not including handles, blue shading to lighter blue back to blue, white interior, black trim & handles, seamless body & cover. Embossed "Jersey." Good plus, rare color, **$120.00.**

Row 3:

1. **Covered Berlin-Style Kettle,** with matching cover, 9" high, 10⅝" diameter, blue shading to lighter blue back to blue, white interior, seamless body, enameled wire rivetted ears, wire bail with Alaska handle. Good plus, rare color, **$135.00.**

2. **Shallow Pie Plate,** ⅜" deep, 9" diameter, blue shading to lighter blue back to blue, white interior, black trim. Good plus, rare color, **$25.00.**

3. **Handled Custard Cup** (or individual muffin cup), 1⅞" deep, 3½" diameter not including handles, blue shading to lighter blue back to blue, black trim & handles. Good plus, rare color & shape, **$75.00. Note:** The handled custard cups are harder to find.

4. **Milk Can,** matching cover, 9" high, 4¾" diameter, blue shading to lighter blue back to blue, white interior, rivetted enamel wire ears, black wooden bail, seamless body. Near mint, rare color, **$195.00.**

Row 4:

1. **Pitcher & Bowl,** Pitcher 10" tall, 5¾" diameter not including lip & handle, blue shading to lighter blue back to blue, white interior, seamless body, rivetted handle. Bowl 4" deep, 14½" diameter, blue shading to lighter blue back to blue, white interior, eyelet for hanging. "Bluebelle Ware." Good plus, rare color, shape & size, 2 pieces, **$225.00. Note:** I believe these 2 pieces are part of a wash set.

2. **Chamber Pail,** matching cover, 10¼" high 9½" diameter, blue shading to lighter blue back to blue, white interior, black trim, enameled wire ears, wooden bail, seamless body. Good plus, rare color & shape, **$155.00.**

Row 1:
1. **Cocoa Dipper,** 14½" long, bowl measures 2¾" deep, 4" top diameter, deep sea green shading to a moss green with white interior & black wooden handle. "Shamrock Ware." Near mint, extremely rare color & shape, **$325.00.**

Row 2:
1. **Advertising Pitcher,** 6" tall, 4¾" diameter, blue shading to white & back to blue, white interior, decorated with gold bands, seamless body. Advertising C.G. Hibbert & Co's Blue Label Bass, Est. 1767. Marked in the bottom in an oval is "Eastwood & Doherty Sydenham S.E." Near mint, extremely rare shape, rare color, **$195.00. Note:** I believe this is a bar pitcher that was given to businesses to promote this product.
2. **Water Pitcher,** 9¼" tall, 6" diameter, blue shaded to white & back to blue, white interior, gold trim, decorated with birds, fruit & leaf design, seamless body. Good plus, rare color, **$155.00.**

Row 3:
1. **Measure,** 7⅝" tall, 5¼" diameter, deep sea green shading to a moss green with white interior, seamless body. "Shamrock Ware," distributed by Norvell-Shapleigh Hardware Co. St. Louis. This company was the sole distributor of this ware. Good plus, rare color & shape, **$235.00.**
2. **Candlestick,** with finger ring, 2⅛" tall, 5⅞" diameter, green shading to cream. Marked on bottom in a double circle, "Made In England, O.J.E.Co." Good plus, rare shape & size, **$110.00.**
3. **Pudding Pan,** 3¼" deep, 9⅜" diameter, brilliant lavender blue shading to a light blue & back to lavender, white interior with black trim. Near mint, rare color, **$75.00.**

Row 4:
1. **Milk Can,** with matching granite lock cover, 9¼" tall, 5" diameter, tan shading to brown, white interior, black wooden bail, seamless body with rivetted ears, cover handle. Near mint, rare color & shape, **$195.00.**
2. **Biscuit Cutter,** 1¾" tall, 2¼" diameter, light gray shading to green, inside & out, black strap handle. Good plus, extremely rare color & shape, **$595.00. Note:** The applied strap handle fits through slots in the top of the cutter. Cutter has one large air hole in the center of the top. This is the only shaded biscuit cutter I have seen. I consider this extremely rare.
3. **Milk Can,** with matching lock cover, 13" tall, 10" diameter, white shading to light blue with white interior, applied wire ears & strap cover handle, wooden bail, with seamless body. Good plus, rare color, shape & size, **$250.00. Note:** This is the largest milk can I have seen in this color.

SECTION 14
RELISH PATTERN

Row 1:

1. **Convex Pitcher,** 6⅜" high tall, 5⅛" diameter, brown & white medium mottled, relish pattern, white interior, cobalt blue trim, rivetted handle, seamless body. Good plus, rare color, **$160.00. Note:** This pattern is generally termed "relish" by collectors because it looks like pickle relish. The 1892 Manning, Bowman & Company catalogue advertises this color as a handsomely mottled color, the variety of contrasting tint making a most attractive exhibit & greatly aiding in selling the ware. This color is advertised as "Chocolate with white porcelain inside." Patented June 5, 1883, Registered January 13, 1885.

2. **Water Pitcher & Wash Basin.** Pitcher 8⅜" high, 6⅛" diameter, brown & white medium mottled, relish pattern, white interior, cobalt blue trim, rivetted handle, seamless body, wash basin 2½" deep, 10" diameter, brown & white medium mottled, relish pattern, white interior, cobalt blue trim. Both pieces good plus, rare color, 2 pieces, **$225.00.**

3. **Water Pitcher,** 7½" high, 5⅜" diameter, brown & white medium mottled, relish pattern, white interior, cobalt blue trim, seamless body. Good plus, rare color, **$160.00.**

Row 2:

1. **Boston Cream Can,** 6" tall, 3½" diameter, brown & white medium mottled, relish pattern, white interior, cobalt blue trim, rivetted strap side handle, seamed body. Good plus, rare color & size, **$260.00.**

2. **Coffeepot,** 5½" tall, 3½" diameter, light brown & white medium mottled, relish pattern, white interior, cobalt blue trim, rivetted handle & hinged cover with seamed body. Good plus, extremely rare color & size, **$275.00. Note:** This light relish pattern has a pink shade to it. This coffeepot holds exactly 1½ cups of liquid.

3. **Syrup Pitcher,** 6½" high, 3½" diameter, brown & white medium mottled, relish pattern, white interior, seamed body. Cover is embossed on the inside "Pat. Jul, 16, 72." Good plus, extremely rare color & shape, **$695.00. Note:** The 1892 Manning, Bowman & Company catalogue advertises this as a "Syrup Pitcher with central spout & cut-off. Air-tight & ant-proof. No drippings outside. Assorted tints. White metal. Per dozen $16.00. Nickel plate each $1.60."

4. **Tea Steeper,** 4⅞" tall, 4" diameter, brown & white medium mottled, relish pattern, white interior, cobalt blue trim & rivetted handle, seamless body. Good plus, rare color, **$165.00.**

Row 3:

1. **Coffee Boiler,** 11" high, 8¾" diameter, brown & white medium mottled, relish pattern, white interior, cobalt blue trim, rivetted strap handle, wire bail, seamed body. Near mint, rare color, **$225.00.**

2. **Measure,** 6½" tall, 4¼" diameter, brown & white medium mottled, relish pattern, white interior, cobalt blue trim, rivetted strap handle, seamed body. Good, rare color & shape, **$170.00.**

3. **Covered Stove Pot,** 8½" tall, 8" diameter, light brown & white medium mottled, relish pattern, white interior, cobalt blue trim, rivetted flat ears, wire bail, seamless body. Good plus, rare color & shape, **$195.00. Note:** This pot also has the pink shade to it like the 1½ cup coffeepot on this page.

Row 1:

1. **Milk Can,** 8⅞" tall, 5¼" diameter, dark blue & white medium mottled relish pattern, white interior, dark blue trim, black wooden bail, seamed body, rivetted ears. Near mint, rare color, **$225.00.**

2. **Batter Jug,** 10¼" tall, 8⅜" diameter, dark blue & white medium mottled relish pattern, white interior, dark blue trim, wooden bail, seamed body & spout, rivetted ears & bottom strap handle, tin spout cover. Near mint, extremely rare color, rare shape, **$550.00. Note:** Batter jugs were used for storing batter in a warm place such as warming ovens on top of the woodburning stove. The batter would then always be ready for cooking. The tin spout cover was used to keep dirt & insects out of the batter.

3. **Boston Milk Can,** 9" tall, 5¾" bottom diameter, dark blue & white medium mottled relish pattern, white interior, dark blue trim, rivetted side strap handle, seamed body. Good plus, rare color & shape, **$200.00.**

Row 2:

1. **Seamless Bottom** with protection bands for coffee or teapots, 2¼" deep, 4⅞" top diameter, dark blue & white medium mottled relish pattern, white interior. Mint, rare color & shape, **$185.00. Note:** This piece was shown in Book I, Section 2, on page 77. It was referred to as a cereal bowl. Since then, I have acquired an 1892 Manning, Bowman & Co. catalogue. It advertises this piece as a seamless bottom with protection bands for coffee or teapots. The upper sections of the coffee or teapots were made of extra fine polished metal with Britannia mountings and were to be applied to this type of bottom. The company felt that since the granite bottom did not contain poisonous chemicals, it was safer than the different type metal bottoms. They advertised these bottoms as pure as "china."

2. **Teapot,** 5⅛" tall, 3½" diameter, dark blue & white medium mottled relish pattern, white interior, black wooden handle & knob, seamed body. Good plus, rare color, shape & size, **$345.00.**

3. **Individual Muffin Cup,** 1⅛" deep, 2⅞" diameter, dark blue & white medium mottled relish pattern, white interior, dark blue trim. Mint, rare shape, **$70.00. Note:** This muffin cup was used to test a sample of cake mixture for the texture & also the heat degree of the oven.

4. **Coffeepot,** 5⅛" tall, 3½" diameter, dark blue & white medium mottled relish pattern, white interior, wooden handle, seamed body. Good plus, rare color, shape & size, **$325.00. Note:** This pot has a metal protection band around the top edge. The cover is brass & the bottom of the pot has an attached copper protection bottom that is embossed "Patent Pending."

5. **Creamer,** 4½" tall, 3⅝" diameter, dark blue & white medium mottled relish pattern, white interior, dark blue trim, rivetted handle, seamless body. Near mint, rare color & shape, **$225.00.**

Row 3:

1. **Coffee Boiler,** 11" tall, 8⅝" diameter, dark blue & white medium mottled relish pattern, white interior, dark blue trim, rivetted ears & side handle, seamed body. Good plus, rare color, **$275.00.**

2. **Cup,** 2⅜" deep, 4" diameter, dark blue & white medium mottled relish pattern, white interior, dark blue trim, rivetted handle. Good plus, rare color, **$55.00.**

3. **Teapot,** 10¼" tall, 6¾" diameter, dark blue & white medium mottled relish pattern, white interior, dark blue trim, rivetted handle, seamless body, applied metal top protection band, metal thumb rest on handle. The bottom of the pot has an applied brass protection bottom. Embossed "L & G Mfg. Co." in an oval. Trademark for The La Lance & Grosjean Manufacturing Co. Good plus, rare color, **$325.00.**

Row 1:

1. **Teakettle,** 10" high, 6½" diameter, green & white relish pattern, white interior, nickel-plated trim, black wooden bail. The Manning, Bowman & Co. 1892 catalogue advertises this teakettle as a "KIOTO" Mottled Table Kettle. Patented June 5, 1883 registered January 13, 1885. Mint, extremely rare color, shape & size, **$695.00. Note:** This type of kettle could also be purchased with a nickel-plated stand and spirit lamp.

2. **Pie Plate,** 1½" deep, 9½" diameter, green & white relish pattern, white interior, cobalt blue trim. Good plus, rare color, **$25.00.**

3. **Melon Mold,** 4¾" deep, 6⅝" wide, 9⅛" long, green & white relish pattern, white interior, tin cover with wire handle. Embossed "NO 80." Mint, extremely rare color, **$235.00. Note:** The bottom edge of the mold has an applied tin band which the tin cover fits over securely.

4. **Water Pitcher,** 7¾" tall, 5¾" diameter, green & white relish pattern, white interior, cobalt blue trim, seamless body, rivetted handle. Good plus, rare color, **$150.00**

Row 2:

1. **Milk Pitcher,** 6⅛" tall, 4½" diameter, green & white relish pattern, white interior, cobalt blue trim, seamless body, rivetted handle. Good plus, rare color & size, **$175.00.**

2. **Coffeepot,** 6½" tall, 3⅞" diameter, green & white relish pattern, white interior, cobalt blue trim, seamed body, rivetted handle. Good plus, rare color & size, **$195.00.**

3. **Teakettle,** 6¼" tall, 6¾" diameter, green & white relish pattern, white interior, wire bail wrapped in a cane-like material, seamless body, rivetted ears. Good plus, rare color, shape & size, **$255.00.**

4. **Creamer,** 4½" tall, 3¾" diameter, green & white relish pattern, white interior, cobalt blue trim, seamless body, rivetted handle. Good plus, rare color & shape, **$195.00.**

5. **Boston Cream Can,** 7¼" tall, 4⅜" diameter, green & white relish pattern, white interior, cobalt blue trim, seamed body, rivetted side-strap handle. Near mint, rare color & shape, **$210.00.**

Row 3:

1. **Coffee Boiler,** 11¼" tall, 8⅝" diameter, green & white relish pattern, white interior, cobalt blue trim, seamed body, rivetted ears & handle, wire bail. Good plus, rare color, **$195.00.**

2. **Boston Milk Can,** 10½" tall, 6⅞" diameter, green & white relish pattern, white interior, cobalt blue trim, seamed body, rivetted side-strap handle. Good plus, rare color & shape, **$195.00.**

3. **Coffeepot,** 11" tall, 7½" diameter, green & white relish pattern, white interior, seamed body, black wooden handle & knob, copper applied bottom. Embossed "Patent Pending." Fancy embossed metal cover. Mint, rare color, **$265.00. Note:** The 1892 Manning Bowman & Co. catalogue refers to this particular color as "Tinted Mottled Series with White Porcelain Inside."

SECTION 15
CHRYSOLITE

Row 1:
    1. **Teakettle,** 7¼" high, 7⅞" diameter, dark green & white medium swirl, white interior. Good plus, extremely rare color, shape & size, **$895.00.**
    2. **Cuspidor,** 4¼" deep, 7½" diameter, dark green & white large swirl, white interior. Near mint, rare color, **$425.00.**
    3. **Stove Kettle,** with matching granite cover, 6¾" high, 8½" diameter, dark green & white large swirl, white interior. Labeled "Chrysolite, No. 470 Stove Kettle. The Hibbard Spencer Bartlett & Co. Chicago." This company was the distributor for Chrysolite. Near mint, rare color, **$395.00.**

Row 2:
    1. **Oblong Baking Pan or Stove Pan,** 2" deep, 8⅛" wide, 9⅝" long not including handles, dark green & white large swirl, white interior, molded handles. "Chrysolite." Near mint, rare color, **$225.00.**

Row 3:
    1. **Butter Churn,** 17¾" high, 9" diameter, floor model, dasher type, dark green & white large swirl, white interior, black rivetted handles, wooden dasher & cover. "Chrysolite." Good plus, extremely rare color & size, **$1,985.00. Note:** This churn also has a granite storage cover to keep the butter clean after churning.
    2. **Gas Heater,** 26¾" high, 21½" long, 5½" wide, dark green & white large mottled, black trim. Marked "Manufactured by The Enamel Steel Tile Co., Bellaire, Ohio, T111." Mint, extremely rare color, shape & size, **$1,200.00.**
    3. **Tile Stove Board,** 32½" long, 20½" wide, dark green & white with white tile inlay, oak backboard & border. Marked on underside "Tile stove board Pat. Dec. 18, 1902. Manufactured by The Enamel Steel Tile Co., Bellaire, Ohio." Good plus, extremely rare color, shape & size, **$795.00.**

Special Note: The gas heater & tile stove board in the dark green & white are the only pieces I have seen marked by the manufacturer. No 3 on Row 1 on this page has a label with the jobber's name that was the distributor for Chrysolite. This label also states that this piece is "Chrysolite." I believe all these pieces are "Chrysolite," even though they are not all marked. Chrysolite is the darkest of all the green & white swirls or mottled.

Row 1:

1. **Miner's or Farmer's Mug,** 3⅞" deep, 5" diameter, dark green & white large mottled with white interior, black rivetted handles & trim, seamless body. Mint, rare color & size, **$145.00. Note:** A miner's or farmer's mug is smaller than a mush or camp mug.

2. **Teapot,** 9¼" tall, 5¾" diameter, dark green & white large mottled with white interior, black, trim & rivetted handle, seamed body. Near mint, rare color, **$425.00.**

3. **Syrup,** 7⅝" tall, 3½" diameter, dark green & white large mottled with white interior, rivetted handle, seamed body, nickel plated copper cover with thumb lift. "Chrysolite." Mint, extremely rare color & shape, **$1,495.00. Note:** Most pieces of granite ware have the seams covered with enameling. However, on these syrups where the bottom section is applied to the upper section the seam is not enameled over.

Row 2:

1. **Advertising Railroad Mug,** 2¾" deep, 2⅞" diameter, dark green & white large mottled with white interior, dark blue rivetted handle & trim, seamless body. Embossed on the side with white letters, "Rock Island Lines." Good plus, rare color & shape, **$140.00.**

2. **Advertising Railroad Mug,** 2¾" deep, 3⅜" diameter, dark green & white medium mottled with white interior, dark blue rivetted handle & trim, seamless body. Embossed on the side in white letters, "Illinois Central Railroad." Good plus, rare color & shape, **$150.00.**

3. **Complimentary Advertising Mug,** 2¾" deep, 3⅜" diameter, dark green & white medium mottled with white interior, dark blue rivetted handle & trim, seamless body. Embossed on the side in white letters, "Compliments of Hibbard, Spencer, Bartlett & Co." Good plus, rare color & shape, **$695.00. Note:** These were jobbers that sold "Chrysolite."

4. **Advertising Railroad Mug,** 2¾" deep, 2⅞" diameter, dark green & white medium mottled with white interior, dark blue rivetted handle & trim, seamless body. Embossed on the side in white letters, "C St.P M & O Ry.", abbreviations for Chicago, St. Paul, Minneapolis, & Omaha Railways. Good, rare color & shape, **$120.00. Note:** It is no wonder that few of these mugs survived over the years with the rough travel & use they endured.

Row 3:

1. **Cream Can,** 7¾" tall, 4" diameter, dark green & white large swirl with white interior, black trim, rivetted ears, seamless body, & wire bail handle. Good plus, rare color & size, **$650.00.**

2. **Milk Can,** 9½" tall, 4⅞" diameter, dark green & white large mottled with white interior, black trim, rivetted ears, seamless body, & wire bail handle. Good plus, rare color, **$550.00.**

3. **Cream Can,** 7" tall, 4⅜" diameter, dark green & white large mottled with white interior, black trim, rivetted neck & ears, seamed body & wire bail handle. Near mint, extremely rare color, shape & size, **$850.00.**

Row 4:

1. **Milk Can,** 11½" tall, 6⅛" diameter, dark green & white medium mottled with white interior, black trim, rivetted wire ears, & seamless body. Near mint, rare color & size, **$595.00. Note:** Notice the variations of the shapes of the ears on the cream & milk cans. Also note some pieces have more white in them which gives them a lighter appearance.

Row 1:
1. **Tea Steeper,** with matching granite cover, 4⅞" tall, 4¼" diameter, dark green & white large mottled with white interior, dark blue handle & trim, rivetted spout & handle, seamless body. Near mint, extremely rare color & shape, **$425.00.**
2. **Fry Pan,** 1¾" deep, 9¼" diameter, dark green & white large mottled with white interior, dark blue rivetted handle & trim. "Chrysolite." Good plus, rare color, **$275.00.**
3. **Covered Bucket,** 5¼" tall, 4⅝" diameter, dark green & white large swirl with white interior, dark blue trim, rivetted ears & seamless body, black wooden bail handle. Near mint, extremely rare color & shape, **$425.00.**

Row 2:
1. **Covered Bucket,** 5¾" tall, 6" diameter, dark green & white large mottled with white interior, black trim, seamless body, wooden bail handle. Good plus, rare color, **$325.00.**
2. **Teakettle,** 8¼" tall, 9¾" diameter, dark green & white large swirl with white interior, dark blue trim, rivetted ears, seamed body & spout, wooden bail handle. Near mint, extremely rare color & shape, **$895.00.**
3. **Covered Bucket,** 5¾" tall, 5¾" diameter, dark green & white large mottled, white interior, dark blue trim, rivetted ears, seamless body, black wooden bail. Near mint, rare color, **$375.00.**

Row 3:
1. **Pitcher & Wash Basin,** Pitcher, 10¾" tall, 7⅝" diameter, dark green & white large mottled with white interior, dark blue trim, rivetted handle. Wash basin, 3⅛" deep, 11⅜" diameter, dark green & white large mottled with white interior, dark blue trim. Both good plus, rare color & size, two pieces, **$595.00.**
2. **Oval Foot Tub,** 4½" deep, 14¾" wide, 18½" long not including the handles, dark green & white large mottled with white interior, black rivetted handles & trim, seamless body. Good plus, rare color, shape & size, **$325.00.**

259

Row 1:
1. **Mush Mug,** 5⅛" deep, 6" diameter, dark green & white large mottled, white interior, dark blue trim & rivetted handle, seamless body. "Chrysolite." Good, rare color & size, **$95.00.**
2. **Mug,** 3½" deep, 4" diameter, dark green & white large mottled, white interior, dark blue trim & rivetted handle, seamless body. "Chrysolite." Good plus, rare color, **$110.00.**
3. **Mug,** 2⅞" deep, 3⅜" diameter, dark green & white large mottled, white interior, dark blue trim, rivetted handle, seamless body. "Chrysolite." Good plus, rare color, **$115.00.**
4. **Mug,** 2¾" deep, 2¾" diameter, dark green & white large mottled, white interior, dark blue trim & rivetted handle, seamless body. "Chrysolite." Good plus, rare color, **$120.00.**

Row 2:
1. **Plate,** ¾" deep, 9" diameter, dark green & white large swirl, white interior, dark blue trim. Near mint, rare color & shape, **$155.00.**
2. **Cup,** 2⅛" deep, 4¼" diameter, dark green & white large swirl, white interior, dark blue trim & rivetted handle, seamless body. Mint, rare color, **$130.00.**
3. **Teapot,** 8½" high, 5¼" diameter, dark green & white large mottled, white interior, dark blue trim, rivetted handle, seamed body. "Chrysolite." Near mint, extremely rare color, shape & size, **$595.00.**
4. **Colander,** footed, deep, 4⅝" high, 10⅝" diameter not including handles, dark green & white large mottled, white interior, dark blue trim. "Chrysolite." Near mint, extremely rare color & shape, **$450.00.**

Row 3:
1. **Berlin-Style Covered Kettle,** 5⅝" high, 7⅝" diameter not including ears, dark green & white large swirl, white interior, dark blue trim, wire bail, seamless body. "Chrysolite." Mint, rare color, **$265.00.**
2. **Spoon,** 9½" long, bowl of spoon 2", dark green & white large mottled, white interior on the bowl of the spoon. Good plus, rare color & size, **$115.00.**
3. **Trivet,** four molded feet, ⅝" high, 5" wide, 6" long, lighter green & white large swirl. Near mint, extremely rare color, shape & size, **$495.00. Note:** The green is not as dark as on the other pieces in this photo. It appears that more white is flowing into the green, giving it a lighter effect.
4. **Pie Plate,** 1" deep, 8¾" diameter, dark green & white large mottled, white interior, dark blue trim. Near mint, rare color, **$110.00.**
5. **Custard Cup,** 2" deep, 3¾" diameter, dark green & white large mottled, white interior, dark blue trim. Near mint, rare color & shape, **$125.00.**
6. **Coffeepot,** 7⅞" high, 4½" diameter, dark green & white large swirl, white interior, dark blue trim, seamless body. "Chrysolite." Good plus, rare color, **$425.00.**

Row 4:
1. **Water pitcher,** 8" high, 4⅛" diameter, dark green & white large swirl, white interior, dark blue trim & handle. Good plus, rare color, **$325.00.**
2. **Double Boiler,** flared bottom, 8" high, 6⅝" top diameter, 9⅝" bottom diameter, dark green & white large mottled, white interior, dark blue trim & handles, top section seamless, bottom section seamed, rivetted handles. "Chrysolite." Mint, rare color, **$425.00.**
3. **Pudding Pan,** 2" deep, 8½" diameter, dark green & white large mottled, white interior, dark blue trim. Good plus, rare color, **$155.00.**
4. **Spoon,** 15" long, bowl of spoon 2⅜", dark green & white large mottled, white interior on the bowl of the spoon. Good plus, rare color & size, **$115.00.**

SECTION 16
CHICKEN WIRE PATTERN AND SNOW ON THE MOUNTAIN

Special Note: Not all the chicken wire patterns in this section are Snow On The Mountain. As you can see some of the chicken wire pattern does not have the lumpy white Snow On The Mountain finish. This section with the Snow On The Mountain pieces was best suited for the chicken wire pattern because of the similarities in the pattern to Snow On The Mountain.

Row 1:
1. **Handled Strainer,** 5" deep, 4⅞" diameter, white with light blue veins, chicken wire pattern, dark blue trim, white interior, perforated sides & bottom, rivetted handles, seamed body. Good plus, **$95.00.**
2. **Egg Plate or Pan,** 1¾" deep, 9⅜" diameter not including the handles, white with light blue veins, chicken wire pattern, dark blue trim, white interior. Near mint, **$75.00.**
3. **Egg Cup,** 1½" high, 1⅞" top diameter, 1⅝" bottom diameter, white with blue large mottling, white interior with dark blue trim. Near mint, rare shape, **$135.00. Note:** The top diameter where the egg sits is larger than the bottom diameter.
4. **Canister,** 8⅛" deep, 5¾" diameter barrel shaped, white with light blue veins, chicken wire pattern, white interior with dark blue trim. Near mint, rare shape, **$125.00. Note:** There is faint lettering of the word "Sukker" on the side of the canister. (Cover not original.)

Row 2
1. **Farmer's or Miner's Mug,** 4½" deep, 5" diameter, white with light blue veins, chicken wire pattern with Snow on the Mountain finish. Near mint, **$55.00. Note:** Notice how sharp & well defined the pattern is on this mug compared to some of the other pieces on this page. I have noticed by photographing pieces together that they range greatly in pattern & depth of color. This piece has a very lumpy feel to the finish.
2. **Covered Convex-shaped Kettle,** 6½" tall, 9" diameter, white with light blue veins, chicken wire pattern, white interior with dark blue trim. Marked "S.E.L." & shows a picture of two swords crossed. Near mint, **$65.00.**
3. **Sugar Bowl,** or 2-handled soup, 3⅛" deep, 4⅞" diameter, white with light blue veins, chicken wire pattern, white interior with dark blue trim. (Cover is missing.) Near mint, rare shape, **$85.00.**

Row 3:
1. **Syrup or Molasses Pitcher,** 11" tall, 5⅞" diameter, white with light blue veins, chicken wire pattern, white interior, rivetted handle & cover, seamed body. Good plus, rare shape & size, **$165.00.**
2. **Teakettle,** 7½" tall, 8⅝" diameter, white with light blue veins, chicken wire pattern, white interior. Numbered "12-22-25." This could be the date it was made. Good plus, **$110.00.**

Row 1:

1. **Teapot,** 9" high, 5½" diameter, white & light blue large swirl inside & out, black handle & trim, seamless body. Good plus, **$255.00.**
2. **Cup,** 2" deep, 4⅜" diameter, white & light blue large swirl inside & out, black handle & trim. Near mint, **$65.00.**
3. **Spatula,** 15" long, 3½" wide white & light blue medium mottled front & back, chicken wire pattern, Snow on the Mountain. Flat hook handle, fancy oblong perforations. Good plus, rare color & shape, **$145.00.**
4. **Candlestick or Chamberstick,** 2¼" high, 5¼" diameter, white & light blue medium mottled inside & out, light blue trim, rivetted thumb rest. Near mint, rare color & shape, **$395.00.**
5. **Coffeepot,** 9" tall, 5½" diameter, white & light blue large swirl inside & out, black handle & trim, seamless body. Near mint, **$235.00.**

Row 2:

1. **Coffee Biggin,** including cover, spreader, biggin & pot. 7½" tall including biggin, 4⅛" bottom diameter, white & light blue medium mottled, white interior, seamless body. Marked "B.B. 4" Near mint, rare color & shape, **$325.00.**
2. **Covered Bucket,** with matching granite cover, 5¾" tall, 6" diameter, white & light blue large mottled inside & out, black trim, wooden bail handle rich black handle & trim. Advertised as "Azure Marble Enamel, White Azure Blue Marbleized Figure." Near mint, rare color, **$275.00.**
3. **Coffeepot,** 6¾" tall, 3⅜" diameter, white with blue veins & white interior, rivetted handle & spout, chicken wire pattern. The bottom of the pot is marked with a lion standing with his front paws on a coffeepot, also marked with the letter "B." Good plus, rare size, **$265.00.**
4. **Creamer,** squatty shape, 5" tall, 3⅜" diameter, white with blue veins, white interior, chicken wire pattern, rivetted handle. This piece is marked the same as #3 in this row. Good plus, rare color & shape, **$165.00.**

Row 3:

1. **Covered Berlin Style Kettle,** 7¼" tall, 7⅜" diameter, blue & white large mottled inside & out, black trim, wooden bail. Seamless body. Good plus, **$135.00.**
2. **Coffee Carrier,** 11½" tall, 6⅛" diameter, white & light blue large mottled with white interior, chicken wire pattern, seamed body with wire bail. Near mint, rare shape & size, **$285.00.**
3. **Chamber Pail,** 11¼" tall, 10½" diameter, white & light blue large mottled inside & out, black trim, wooden bail handle, seamless body. Near mint, **$200.00.**

265

Row 1:

1. **Boston Milk Can,** 8¼" high, 3¾" diameter, green veins of large mottling with a white overall lumpy effect, white interior & green trim. Marked "Elite Austria." Near mint, rare color & shape, **$225.00. Note:** Snow on the Mountain comes in several colors. It is called Snow on the Mountain because of the lumpy overall effect of the white.

2. **Boston Milk Can,** 8½" high, 3⅞" diameter, green veins of large mottling with an overall white lumpy effect, white interior, green trim. Marked "Elite Austria." Good plus, rare color & shape, **$185.00. Note:** I chose to show these two Boston milk cans together because at first glance, you would say they are the same. Note how the handle is recessed on the cover on No. 1. On this one the handle goes almost to the edge of the cover & is much wider. The side handle on No. 1 is rounded, whereas this one has a flat strap side handle. These are called Boston milk cans because of the side handle.

3. **Tea Strainer,** 1" deep, 4" diameter not including handle, green veins of large mottling with an overall white lumpy effect, white inside, fancy perforated bottom. Near mint, rare color & shape, **$165.00. Note:** This piece is not marked.

4. **Oblong Deep Stove Pan,** handled, 2" deep, 6¾" wide, 11¾" long not including handles, green veins of large mottling with an overall white lumpy effect, white interior, green trim. Marked "Elite Austria." Good plus, **$75.00. Note:** Stove pans were used either on top of the stove for cooking or in the oven for baking.

5. **Individual Muffin Cup,** 1¾" deep, 2⅞" top diameter, green veins of large mottling with an overall white lumpy effect, white interior, green trim. Marked "Elite Austria." Near mint, rare shape, **$65.00.**

6. **Salt Box,** 10½" back height, box 5¾" high, 5¼" wide, 7" long, green veins of large mottling with an overall white lumpy effect, white interior & back section, green trim. Good plus, extremely rare color & shape, **$425.00. Note:** Cover is mottled on both sides, seamed body. Marked "Elite Austria."

Row 2:

1. **Teapot,** 6" high, 6¼" diameter, green veins of large mottling with an overall white lumpy effect, white interior, green trim. Marked "Elite Austria." Good plus, rare shape, **$165.00.**

2. **Covered Berlin-Style Sauce Pan,** 5½" high, 7⅜" diameter, green veins of large mottling with an overall white lumpy effect, white interior, green trim. Marked "Elite Austria." Good plus, **$115.00. Note:** It is very unusual that this pan is marked "Elite Austria" four times–three times on the handle & once on the bottom.

3. **Molasses Pitcher,** 6⅛" high, 3¾" diameter, green veins of large mottling with an overall white lumpy effect, white interior, green trim, seamless body. Marked "Elite Austria." Good plus, rare color & shape, **$235.00. Note:** The cover has an applied thumb lift and also covers the spout of the molasses pitcher.

4. **Molasses Pitcher,** 5" high, 3⅜" diameter, green veins of large mottling with a white overall lumpy effect, white interior, green trim, seamless body. Marked "Elite Austria." Good plus, rare color, shape & size, **$265.00.**

Row 3:

1. **Covered Bucket,** with matching granite cover, 10" high, 8¼" diameter, green veins of large mottling with a white overall lumpy effect, white interior, green trim, seamless body, wooden bail. Marked "Elite Austria." Good plus, rare color, **$225.00.**

2. **Deep Pie Plate,** 1⅝" deep, 11" diameter, green veins of large mottling with a white overall lumpy effect, white interior, green trim. Marked "Elite Austria." Near mint, **$45.00.**

3. **Candlestick or Chamberstick,** scalloped style, deep, 1½" deep, 5¾" diameter, with finger ring & thumb rest, green veins of large mottling with a white overall lumpy effect. Good plus, rare color & shape, **$325.00. Note:** This piece is not marked. I noticed pieces that don't have the green trim are not marked.

4. **Double Boiler,** 8½" high including the insert, 7" diameter. Green veins of large mottling with a white overall lumpy effect, green trim. Marked, "Elite Austria." Near mint, rare color & shape, **$265.00.**

Row 1:

1. **Colander,** footed, deep, 5½" high, 11¾" diameter not including handles, green veins of large mottling with a white overall lumpy effect, white interior, green trim, with fancy bottom & side perforations. Near mint, rare color, **$135.00.**

2. **Oblong Tray,** ¾" deep, 13⅜" wide, 17⅝" long, green veins of large mottling with a white overall lumpy effect, white interior, green trim. Marked "Elite Austria." Good plus, rare shape, **$95.00.**

3. **Canister,** 8½" high, 6¼" diameter, green veins of large mottling with white overall lumpy effect, white interior, green trim. Marked "Elite." Good plus, **$75.00.**

Row 2:

1. **Measure,** 6½" tall, 3¾" diameter, green veins of large mottling with a white overall lumpy effect, white interior, green trim, seamless body & lip. Marked "Elite Austria." Good plus, rare color & shape, **$135.00.**

2. **Tea Steeper,** 4¼" high, 3¾" diameter, green veins of large mottling with a white overall lumpy effect, white interior, green trim. Marked "Elite Austria." Near mint, rare color, shape & size, **$225.00.**

3. **Coffeepot,** 9¾" high, 5" diameter, green veins of large mottling with a white overall lumpy effect, white interior, green trim, seamless body. Marked "Elite Austria." Good plus, **$210.00.**

4. **Creamer,** 4⅞" high, 3¾" diameter, green veins of large mottling with a white overall lumpy effect, white interior, green trim, seamless body. Marked "Elite Austria." Near mint, rare color & shape, **$190.00.**

5. **Coffeepot,** 6¾" high, 3½" diameter, green veins of large mottling with a white overall lumpy effect, white interior, green trim, seamless body. Marked "Elite Austria." Good plus, rare size, **$265.00.**

Row 3:

1. **Fish Kettle or Poacher** with white handled perforated insert. Insert, ⅜" deep, 6" wide, 17⅛" long. Fish Kettle, 6" high, 7¼" wide, 18½" long not including handles, green veins of large mottling with a white overall lumpy effect, white interior, green trim, seamless body, rivetted handles. Marked "Elite Austria." Good plus, rare color, 2 pieces, **$135.00. Note:** This kettle was used for poaching foods. The handled insert made it easy to lift foods out of the liquid in the poacher.

2. **Covered Bucket,** 7¼" high, 5" diameter, green veins of large mottling with white overall lumpy effect, white interior, green trim, seamless body, wooden bail. Marked "Elite Austria." Good plus, extremely rare color, shape & size, **$265.00.**

3. **Teakettle,** 7½" high, 9½" diameter, green veins of large mottling with white overall lumpy effect, white interior, green trim, seamless body. Marked "Elite Austria." Good, **$110.00. Note:** Wooden bail is missing.

SECTION 17
END OF DAY

Row 1:
1. **Teapot,** squatty shape, 7" tall, 6⅞" diameter, light blue, medium blue, dark blue, cobalt blue & pink large mottled with white interior, black trim, handle & knob, seamless body. Near mint, extremely rare color, shape & size, **$895.00.**
2. **Cover,** 7⅝" diameter, lavender, white, yellow, green & brown medium mottled with white interior, rivetted handle. Good plus, extremely rare color, **$65.00.**
3. **Pudding Pan,** 3⅜" deep, 10⅛" diameter, lavender, white yellow, green & burnt orange medium mottled with white interior. Marked "Purity Ware P.S.B. 16." Near mint, extremely rare color, **$285.00.**
4. **Teapot,** 8¼" tall, 5⅝" diameter, green, pink & white large mottled with white interior, green handle & trim, seamed body & rivetted handle. Good plus, extremely rare color & shape, **$795.00.**

Row 2:
1. **Teapot,** squatty shape, 5¼" tall, 5¾" diameter, yellow, cobalt blue, medium blue, burnt orange, black, brown & green large swirl, white interior, black handle, spout, cover knob & trim, seamless body. Near mint, extremely rare color & shape, **$495.00.**
2. **Coffeepot,** 7" tall, 4½" diameter, burnt orange, cobalt blue, red, green, yellow & brown large swirl, white interior, black handle, trim, & cover knob, seamless body. Near mint, extremely rare color & size, **$495.00.**
3. **Teapot,** squatty shape, 4½" tall, 4¾" diameter, medium blue, burnt orange, yellow, cobalt blue, black, brown, green, & dark blue large swirl, white interior, black handle, spout, cover knob & trim, seamless body. Near mint, extremely rare color, shape & size, **$595.00.**

Row 3:
1. **Teapot,** squatty shape, 4" tall, 4½" diameter, yellow, red, cobalt blue, green, burnt orange, medium blue, brown & light blue large swirl with tangerine interior, seamless body. Marked "Vollrath." Near mint, extremely rare color, shape & size, **$695.00. Note:** The Vollrath Company, Sheboygan, Wisconsin, made a line of harmonizing colors with tangerine interior. Circa 1920. This ware was meant to compliment the kitchen. Because this teapot has the tangerine interior instead of the white interior, I believe this "End of Day" ware was made circa 1920.
2. **Oval Platter,** 1" deep, 8⅝" wide, 13¾" long, red, cobalt blue, yellow, green, light blue & white large swirl. Good plus, extremely rare color & rare shape, **$975.00.**
3. **Teapot,** squatty shape, 5¾" tall, 5½" diameter, orange, yellow, green & black large swirl with white interior, black handle & trim, seamless body & rivetted handle. Good plus, extremely rare color & shape, **$625.00.**

Row 1:
1. **Water Pitcher,** 10½" tall, 6½" diameter, unusual brown, white & cobalt blue large swirl, gray interior with fine blue flecks, cobalt blue trim, rivetted handle, seamless body. Good plus, extremely rare color & shape, **$475.00.**
2. **Oblong Tray,** ¾" deep, 11⅜" wide, 13⅜" long, green, white, dark blue, burgundy & gold large swirl, gray exterior & trim. Near mint, extremely rare color & rare shape, **$595.00.**
3. **Holder For Bottled Beverage & Ice,** 8" tall, 7¼" diameter, cobalt blue, white & light blue large mottled, cobalt blue trim, white interior, wooden handles. Good plus, extremely rare color, shape & size, **$975.00.**

Row 2:
1. **Ash Tray,** ⅞" deep, 6¾" diameter, white, cobalt blue, yellow, burgundy, green, red & orange large swirl, green exterior. Near mint, extremely rare color, **$175.00.**
2. **Teapot,** squatty shape, 5¼" tall, 5" diameter, blue, red, yellow & green, large swirl, white interior, red trim, seamless body. Good plus, extremely rare color, shape & size, **$595.00. Note:** This teapot is exceptionally heavy. I believe it is triple coated.
3. **Ash Tray,** ¾" deep, 6" diameter, black, red, dark green & dark blue large swirl top & bottom. Mint, extremely rare color, **$295.00. Note:** It is believed that this ash tray was a product of the Columbian Enameling & Stamping Company, Terre Haute, Indiana.

Row 3:
1. **Teakettle,** 6½" tall, 7" diameter, orange, dark blue & yellow large mottled, orange interior, black trim, wooden bail & cover, seamless body. Circa 1940. Mint, extremely rare color & shape, **$325.00.**
2. **Cup,** 1¾" deep, 4½" diameter, cobalt blue, white & green large mottled, white interior, black rivetted handle & trim, extremely rare color & rare shape, **$125.00. Note:** This coloring of "End of Day" does not show the green to its advantage because the cobalt is so prominent.
3. **Teapot,** squatty shape, 4⅜" tall, 3⅞" diameter, green, burgundy, dark blue, white, yellow, brown & orange large swirl, white interior, seamed body. Good plus, extremely rare color, shape & size, **$595.00.**
4. **Coffeepot,** 10" tall, 7" diameter, cobalt blue, white & green large mottled, white interior, black trim & handle, seamed body, rivetted handle. Near mint, extremely rare color, **$425.00.**

Row 4:
1. **Spoon,** 16" long, bowl of spoon 2½" wide, cobalt blue, white & green large mottled, white interior, black handle. Good plus, extremely rare color, shape & size, **$195.00.**
2. **Wash Basin,** 3½" deep, 12¾" diameter, cobalt blue, white & green large mottled, white interior, black trim, eyelet for hanging. Near mint, extremely rare color & rare size, **$250.00.**
3. **Handled Skimmer,** 18" long, skimmer diameter 6", cobalt blue, white & green large mottled front & back, black handle. Near mint, extremely rare, color shape & size, **$295.00.**

Row 1:
1. **Teapot,** 8½" tall, 5⅝" diameter, pink white, green, blue & dark blue large mottled, pink interior, black trim & handle. Good plus, extremely rare color & shape, **$450.00.**
2. **Funnel,** 4¼" high, 3⅝" diameter, light green, white, yellow, pink & dark blue, white interior. Good plus, extremely rare color, shape & size, **$275.00.**
3. **Fry Pan,** 1⅝" deep, 9¾" diameter, white, light green, blue & brown large swirl, white interior, black trim & handle. Good plus, extremely rare color & shape, **$485.00.**
4. **Ashtray,** squatty shape, 2⅞" high, 3⅛" diameter, gray, reddish brown, blue, black, yellow & green, gray interior. Near mint, extremely rare color, rare shape & size, **$145.00. Note:** This ashtray has a screw hole in the bottom where it was fastened to something.
5. **Coffee Carrier,** 10¼" tall, 5⅞" diameter, pink, white & green large swirl, white interior, rivetted wire ears, wire bail, seamed body. Good plus, extremely rare color, shape & size, **$795.00.**

Row 2:
1. **Combination Cigarette,** Match Holder & Ashtray, white, black, blue, brown & green large swirl inside & out. Embossed on the side of the match holder is "1832." Good plus, extremely rare color, shape & size, **$425.00. Note:** Articles such as this are becoming quite collectible as smoking becomes less popular.
2. **Wash Basin,** 3¾" deep, 13¼" diameter, white, pink & green large mottled, white interior, cobalt blue trim. Good plus, extremely rare color & rare size, **$375.00.**
3. **Teapot,** squatty shape, 4¾" tall, 4½" diameter, white, orange & black feathered, gray bands, handle & spout, gray interior, dark blue trim, metal cover. Good plus, extremely rare color, shape & size, **$265.00. Note:** Cover is not original.

Row 3:
1. **Teakettle,** 7" tall, 8" diameter, light blue, white, yellow, pink & cobalt blue medium mottled, white interior. Marked "Purity Ware, P.S.B. Reg'd. 20." Good plus, extremely rare color, shape & size, **$550.00.**
2. **Candlestick,** 2¼" tall, 5⅛" diameter, blue, white & black large mottled inside & out. Good plus, extremely rare color, shape & size, **$450.00.**
3. **Oblong Tray,** with molded handles, ¾" deep, 11⅝" wide, 14¾" long not including the handles, blue, yellow, gray, orange & red large swirl, white exterior, black trim. Embossed on the top of the tray with a cream color lion. Good plus, extremely rare color, rare size, **$895.00.**

Row 1:
1. **Teapot,** 8" high, 5⅛" diameter, light blue lumpy cobblestone effect decorated with white & brown with slight traces of darker blue, chicken wire pattern, white interior, black trim, black wooden handle & knob, seamed body, rivetted handle. Good plus, extremely rare color, **$495.00.**
2. **Coffeepot,** 10½" high, 7¼" diameter, light blue lumpy cobblestone effect, decorated with white & brown with slight traces of darker blue, chicken wire pattern, white interior, black trim, black wooden handle & knob, seamed body, rivetted handle. Good plus, extremely rare color, **$495.00.**
3. **Teapot,** 8½" high, 5⅝" diameter, light blue lumpy cobblestone effect, decorated with white & brown with slight traces of darker blue, chicken wire pattern, white interior, black trim, black wooden handle & knob, seamed body, rivetted handle. Good plus, extremely rare color, **$495.00.**

Row 2:
1. **Oblong Baking Pan,** 2⅛" deep, 10⅜" wide, 14½" top length including molded handles, light blue lumpy cobblestone effect, decorated with white & brown with slight traces of darker blue, chicken wire pattern, white interior, black trim, molded handles, seamless body. Good plus, extremely rare color, shape & size, **$475.00.**
2. **Coffeepot,** 7½" high, 4⅝" diameter, light blue lumpy cobblestone effect, decorated with white & brown with slight traces of darker blue, chicken wire pattern, white interior, black trim, black wooden handle & knob, seamed body, rivetted handle. Good plus, extremely rare color, shape & size, **$495.00.**
3. **Maslin-Style Covered Sauce Pan,** 7" high, 9" diameter, light blue lumpy cobblestone effect, decorated with white & brown with slight traces of darker blue, chicken wire pattern, white interior, black trim & handle, black wooden knob, seamless body. Near mint, extremely rare color, **$325.00.**

Row 3:
1. **Teapot,** 10½" high, 6¾" diameter, light blue lumpy cobblestone effect, decorated with white & brown with slight traces of darker blue, chicken wire pattern, white interior, black trim, seamless body, rivetted handle. Good, extremely rare color, **$265.00. Note:** This teapot handle has the same pattern as the coffee boiler on Row 4 No. 1 has. Also, note, this teapot has a seamless body. All the other pots on this page have wooden handles & seamed bodies. These are some of the reasons I chose to show you the different coffee & teapots along with the number of sizes, pattern, and color variations they came in.
2. **Lipped Handled Sauce Pan,** 3¼" deep, 6" diameter, light blue lumpy cobblestone effect, decorated with white & brown with slight traces of darker blue, chicken wire pattern, white interior, black trim, & handle, seamless. Good plus, extremely rare color, **$165.00.**
3. **Teakettle,** shallow pit bottom, 9" tall, 11" diameter, light blue lumpy cobblestone effect, decorated with white & brown with slight traces of darker blue, chicken wire pattern white interior, black trim, rivetted ears, black wooden bail, seamed body. Good plus, extremely rare color, shape & size, **$795.00.**

Row 4:
1. **Coffee Boiler,** shallow pit bottom, 11" tall, 9½" diameter, light blue lumpy cobblestone effect, decorated with white & brown with slight traces of darker blue, chicken wire pattern white interior, black trim & rivetted ears, wire bail, seamed body. Good plus, extremely rare color & shape, **$450.00.**
2. **Pie Plate,** shallow, ¾" deep, 9" diameter, light blue lumpy cobblestone effect, decorated with white & brown with slight traces of a darker blue, chicken wire pattern, white interior, black trim. Good, **$55.00.**

Special Note: This particular color pattern is achieved by using a color transfer pattern for the veins of brown & white with the slight traces of darker blue. The Jacob Vollrath Mfg. Co. of Sheboygan, Wisconsin produced Duchess Ware as one of their lines. Suzanne Berger was kind enough to copy a black & white insert that was inside a catalogue that also had a handwritten date of 1890. From what she could gather it looked as though the Jacob Vollrath Co. had plans for different combinations in the Duchess line, such as Duchess dark blue with white interior, & even Duchess pink with white interior. The copy also substantiates the name "Duchess." The only consumer catalogue I have seen offering this line was Vollrath's 1903 catalogue which only had a coffeepot illustrated.

Technically, because of the numerous colors on this ware, & because it is hard to place some of the categories of wares in a specific field, I felt Duchess Ware was best suited in the End of Day section of this book.

Row 1:
1. **Water Pitcher,** convex style, 8⅜" deep, 6¾" diameter, deep burgundy with veins of white, yellow, dark blue, green & pink, chicken wire pattern, white interior. Marked on the bottom "Elite Austria." Near mint, extremely rare color, shape & size, **$895.00.**
2. **Handled Sauce Pan,** 3⅞" deep, 8⅞" diameter, brown with veins of white, dark blue, yellow, pink & green, chicken wire pattern, white interior, black trim. Good plus, extremely rare color, **$195.00. Note:** This is the only piece of this color I have seen. I believe this piece is also "Elite."
3. **Berlin-Style Kettle,** 7½" tall, 8⅞" wide, not including the handles, red with veins of white, green & blue, chicken wire pattern, white interior. "Elite." Good plus, extremely rare color & shape, **$350.00.**

Row 2:
1. **Teapot,** squatty shape, 6¼" tall, 4¾" diameter, green with veins of white, pink yellow & maroon, chicken wire pattern, white interior. Marked "Elite Austria, Reg'd." Near mint, extremely rare color, shape & size, **$495.00.**
2. **Kettle,** deep pit bottom, 5½" deep, 9¾" diameter, green with veins of white, pink, yellow & maroon, chicken wire pattern, white interior. Marked "Elite Austria, Reg'd." Near mint, extremely rare color & shape, **$295.00.**
3. **Creamer,** 5" tall, 3¾" diameter, green with veins of white, pink, yellow & maroon, chicken wire pattern, white interior. Marked "Elite Austria." Near mint, extremely rare color, shape & size, **$465.00.**

Row 3:
1. **Teakettle,** 5" tall, 5½" diameter, deep burgundy with veins of white, yellow, dark blue, green & pink, chicken wire pattern, white interior, rivetted ears, seamless body, black wooden bail. Marked "Elite Austria." Near mint, extremely rare color, shape & size, **$895.00.**
2. **Coffee Biggin,** 10½" tall, including the biggin, 5⅜" diameter, deep burgundy with veins of white, yellow, dark blue, green & pink, chicken wire pattern, white interior, rivetted handles, seamless body. Marked "Elite Austria. Reg.d. 1½." Near mint, extremely rare color, shape & size, **$1,195.00.**
3. **Milk Pitcher,** convex style, 6¾" deep, 4⅞" diameter, deep burgundy with veins of white, yellow, dark blue, green & pink, chicken wire pattern, white interior, rivetted handle, seamless body. Marked "Elite Austria Reg'd. 5." Good plus, extremely rare color, shape & size, **$550.00.**

Row 1:
1. **Cuspidor,** salesman's sample, 2" high, 3⅜" diameter, white, green & cobalt blue large swirl, inside & out, heavy cast iron seamless body. Good plus, extremely rare color, shape & size, **$900.00**
2. **Cuspidor,** 5¾" high, 8¼" diameter, brown, green, beige, orange, black & yellow large swirl, white interior, orange trim, & bottom. Good plus, extremely rare color & shape, **$1,000.00.**
3. **Cuspidor,** salesman's sample, 2" high, 3⅜" diameter, white, red, light blue, dark blue, & maroon inside & out, heavy cast iron seamless body. Mint, extremely rare color, shape & size, **$1,150.00**

Row 2:
1. **Teapot,** 5" tall, 5½" diameter, brown, cobalt blue, medium blue, yellow, burnt orange & green large swirl with white interior, black handle, spout & trim. Near mint, extremely rare color & shape, **$495.00. Note:** I find it interesting that I could show you these particular pots with so many color variations as well as the different sizes & shapes. No two seem to be alike in color. One may have a soft subdued look while another may have a very brilliant look.
2. **Covered Bucket,** 8" tall, 7" diameter, wooden bail handle, light brown, white, yellow, cobalt blue & pink large mottled with white interior. Marked "Purity Ware B & B Reg'd." Good plus, extremely rare color, **$450.00.**
3. **Cover,** 7½" diameter, burnt orange, green, medium blue, brown & dark blue inside & out. The cover handle has a brass plate embossed "Judge Brand 10 C/M." Good plus, extremely rare color, **$75.00.**
4. **Butterdish,** with attached bottom tray, 4" tall, 5¾" bottom tray diameter white, blue, & brown large mottled with white interior & black trim. Good plus, extremely rare color, shape & size, **$495.00.**

Row 3:
1. **Water or Milk Pitcher,** 9" tall, 6¼" diameter, white, light blue, orange, black & gray large swirl, white interior, seamless body. Good plus, extremely rare color & shape, **$825.00.**
2. **Cover,** 9" diameter, white, pink green, medium blue & cobalt blue large mottled on both sides. Good plus, extremely rare color, **$65.00.**
3. **Ashtray,** shell shaped, 1" tall, 3¾" wide, green, red, dark blue & yellow. This ashtray is on a heavy metal base & is only enameled on the upper side. Embossed "Verona, Pat Pend. 554." Extremely rare color, rare shape, **$165.00.**
4. **Cake Safe,** 5½" tall, 12¼" top diameter, 10⅜" bottom diameter. White, red, green & yellow large mottled with white interior & red trim. Good plus, extremely rare color, shape & size, **$550.00. Note:** I have taken both the top & bottom dimensions of this piece to show you how much it tapers off toward the bottom. The wider sides at the top leave room for your hands when lifting cake or pastries from the cake safe.

Row 1:
1. **Coffeepot,** 8" tall, 5" diameter, light blue cobblestone effect, decorated with white, brown, & cobalt blue chicken wire pattern. White interior with black wooden handle, knob & trim, seamed body, & rivetted handle. Duchess Ware. Good plus, extremely rare color, **$495.00.**
2. **Coffeepot,** 10" tall, 5¾" diameter, red with veins of white, green, yellow & blue. Chicken wire pattern. White interior. End of Day. Rivetted handle & spout, seamless body. Good plus, extremely rare color, **$895.00. Note:** This piece is not marked. I believe this piece is "Elite" because #3 Row 3 on this page is marked "Elite."
3. **Hanging Soap Dish,** 4½" back height, 1" deep, 4½" wide, 5¼" long, chicken wire pattern, deep burgundy with veins of white, yellow, dark blue, green, & pink, white interior. Marked "Elite, Austria Reg'd." Near mint, extremely rare color & shape, **$365.00.**

Row 2:
1. **Teapot,** small squatty shape, 4¼" tall, 3⅞" diameter, white with red, yellow, blue, & green large swirl. Marked "Elite, Austria." Good plus, extremely rare color, shape & size, **$425.00.**
2. **Bowl,** 3¼" deep, 5¾" diameter, light blue with veins of white, yellow, dark blue & pink, chicken wire pattern, white interior. Good, extremely rare color, **$140.00.**
3. **Handled Basket,** 7" tall, 6¼" diameter, white, light blue, light green, & light orange large swirl inside & out. Good plus, extremely rare color, shape & size, **$410.00.**
4. **Mug,** 4⅜" deep, 3¾" diameter, very light gray, green, & pink with faint veins of light blue, medium mottled with white interior & dark blue trim. Good plus, extremely rare color, **$195.00.**
5. **Individual Pudding or Tart Pan,** 1½" deep, 4⅝" diameter, interior is white, green, blue, brown & gray large mottled. Exterior is charcoal gray & white medium mottled. Good plus, extremely rare color, **$125.00.**

Row 3:
1. **Trivet,** 4 molded feet, ¾" high, 6" diameter, cream, cobalt blue, red, green, gray & black large mottled. Trivet is on a heavy metal base. Good plus, extremely rare color, shape & size, **$395.00.**
2. **Oblong Tray,** 1" deep, 9¾" wide, 14¾" long. Red, yellow & green large swirl top & bottom. Near mint, extremely rare color, shape & size, **$650.00.**
3. **Teakettle,** 6½" tall, 7⅛" diameter, "old" red, white, dark blue, yellow & green veins, chicken wire pattern, white interior, rivetted ears, seamless body, wooden bail handle. Marked "Elite." Near mint, extremely rare color, shape & size, **$975.00.**

Row 1:

1. **Turk's Head Tube-Style Turban Mold,** 4¾" deep, 10" diameter, blue, cobalt blue & white, white interior, cobalt blue trim, medium mottled. Near mint, extremely rare, **$575.00.**
2. **Teapot,** 9" high, 5¾" diameter, blue, cobalt blue & white, white interior, cobalt blue trim & handle, large mottled, seamed body, tin cover & thumb rest on the handle. Good plus, extremely rare color, **$425.00.**
3. **Cup,** 2⅜" deep, 3⅜" diameter, blue, cobalt blue & white, white interior, cobalt blue trim, large mottled. Good plus, extremely rare color, **$125.00.**
4. **Turk's Head Tube-Style Turban Mold,** 4" deep, 8" diameter, blue, cobalt blue & white, white interior, cobalt blue trim, medium mottled. Good plus, extremely rare color, **$425.00.**

Row 2:

1. **Milk Pitcher,** 6" tall, 4" diameter, light blue, cobalt blue & white, white interior, cobalt blue trim & handle, medium mottled, rivetted handle, seamless body. Good plus, extremely rare color & shape, **$225.00.**
2. **Bread Pan,** 2¾" deep, 6" wide, 11" long, blue, cobalt blue & white, white interior, cobalt blue trim, large mottled, envelope ends. Good plus, extremely rare color & shape, **$295.00. Note:** Envelope ends refer to the seamed ends of the bread pan that are shaped like envelope flaps.
3. **Covered Bucket,** 4¾" tall, 6¼" diameter, blue, cobalt blue & white, white interior, cobalt blue trim, large mottled, seamed body, wire bail. Near mint, extremely rare color, **$450.00.**

Row 3:

1. **Coffeepot,** 7¼" high, 4½" diameter, blue, cobalt blue & white, white interior, cobalt blue trim & handle, large mottled, rivetted handle, seamed body. Good plus, extremely rare color, **$395.00.**
2. **Fruit Jar Filler,** 2½" high including neck, 4⅜" top diameter, 2¼" neck diameter, blue, cobalt blue & white, white interior, cobalt blue trim & handle, large mottled, rivetted handle & neck. Good plus, extremely rare color, **$225.00.**
3. **Turk's Head Turban-Style Mold,** 2¼" deep, 6¼" diameter, blue, cobalt blue & white, white interior, cobalt blue trim, large mottled. Mint, extremely rare color, **$425.00.**
4. **Soup Ladle,** 11½" long, to top of the handle. Ladle 1⅝" deep, 3¾" top diameter, blue, cobalt blue & white inside & out, cobalt blue trim, & handle, large mottled, rivetted handle, eyelet for hanging. Good plus, extremely rare color, **$135.00.**
5. **Oblong Pudding or Vegetable Dish,** 1½" deep, 7" wide, 9⅞" long, light blue, cobalt blue & white, white interior, cobalt blue trim. Good plus, extremely rare color, **$255.00.**

Note: I believe these are all "Royal Granite Steel Ware" products from Crown Industries, Binghamton, New York, even though the density of the pattern & color vary. Different environments such as weather, workers & such make a difference in the finished product.

Row 1:
  1. **Teapot,** squatty-shaped, 6¼" tall, 5½" diameter, deep burgundy with veins of white, yellow, dark blue, green & pink, chicken wire pattern, white interior, rivetted handle, seamed spout & bottom. Marked "Austria." Near mint, extremely rare color, shape & size, **$575.00. Note:** The little ear on the top edge of the pot, which holds the cover secure while pouring.
  2. **Round Tray,** ¾" deep, 10¾" diameter, white, pink dark green, light & dark blue large swirl, exterior is black & white medium mottled with black trim. Near mint, extremely rare color, rare shape, **$595.00.**
  3. **Teapot,** squatty shape, 5¼" tall, 4⅞" diameter, yellow, pink, blue, green & white with white interior, seamless body. Marked "Elite Austria, 1." Good plus, extremely rare color & shape, **$525.00.**

Row 2:
  1. **Toothbrush Holder,** 5⅛" deep, 3½" diameter, white, light brown, dark brown, orange, burnt orange & red, white interior with dark brown trim. Good plus, extremely rare color & shape, **$225.00.**
  2. **Teapot,** 8½" tall, 4⅞" diameter, deep burgundy with veins of white, yellow, dark blue, green & pink, white interior, rivetted handle, seamed spout, chicken wire pattern. Marked "Elite Austria 1½". Good plus, extremely rare color, **$495.00.**
  3. **Covered Container,** 6⅜" tall, 5¼" diameter, white, dark green, & black large swirl, dark green interior, seamless body. Good plus, extremely rare color, **$275.00. Note:** The container has a recessed strap handle on the cover.

Row 3:
  1. **Cup,** 2½" deep, 3⅝" diameter, white, red, green, light & dark gray large mottled, white interior with red trim & handle, seamless body. Near mint, extremely rare color, **$215.00. Note:** The open end of the handle was designed so that the cups could be stacked inside of each other for easier storage.
  2. **Salad or Mixing Bowl,** 4⅛" deep, 9⅞" diameter, white, red, & cobalt blue large swirl, with white interior & cobalt blue trim. Near mint, extremely rare color, shape & size, **$650.00.**
  3. **Creamer,** 5½" tall, 3⅛" diameter, white, red, cobalt blue & green, large swirl, white interior with red trim, & handle, seamless body. Mint, extremely rare color, shape & size, **$495.00.**
  4. **Oval Tray,** ⅞" deep, 13¼" wide, 17½" long, red with veins of white, dark blue, yellow & green, white interior, chicken wire pattern. Marked "Elite Austria." Good plus, extremely rare color, shape & size, **$975.00.**

SECTION 18
EMERALD WARE

Row 1:

1. **Covered Berlin-Style Kettle,** 7½" high, 9" diameter, green & white large swirl, white interior, cobalt blue trim, rivetted wire shaped ears, wire bail, seamless body, matching cover with spun knob. Near mint, rare color, **$325.00.**

2. **Funnel,** squatty shape, 4" high, 5¾" diameter, green & white large swirl, white interior, cobalt blue trim, rivetted handle. Near mint, extremely rare color & shape, **$450.00.**

3. **Spoon,** 13" long, to top of the handle, spoon 2¼" at the widest point, green & white large swirl, interior of the spoon is white. Good plus, extremely rare color & shape, **$115.00.**

4. **Funnel,** squatty shape, 5" high, 7¼" diameter, green & white large swirl, white interior, cobalt blue trim, rivetted handle. Good plus, extremely rare color & shape, **$395.00.**

5. **Teakettle,** 7½" high, 9" diameter, green & white large swirl, white interior, wire bail with Alaska handle, seamed body & spout. Good plus, extremely rare color, shape & size, **$650.00. Note:** "Alaska handle" refers to the coil-shaped wire handle. Wooden handles often got too hot on the stove & burned. The Alaska handle was believed to remain cooler.

Row 2:

1. **Round Miner's Dinner Bucket,** 10" high, including the insert, 7⅛" diameter. Insert, 6½" high, 6⅞" diameter, green & white large swirl, white interior, cobalt blue trim, wooden bail, seamless body. Near mint, extremely rare color, shape & size, **$1,150.00.**

2. **Lipped Preserving Kettle,** 3⅞" deep, 9" diameter, green & white large swirl, white interior, cobalt blue handle & trim, top-tipping handle, wire bail, seamless body. Near mint, rare color, **$265.00.**

3. **Jelly Roll Pan,** deep, 1¼" deep, 9" diameter, green & white large swirl, white interior, cobalt blue trim, Good plus, rare color & shape, **$135.00.**

Row 3:

1. **Pitcher & Basin,** Pitcher 8⅞" high, 6¼" diameter, green & white large swirl, white interior, cobalt blue handle & trim, rivetted handle, seamless body. Wash Basin, 3" deep, 11" diameter, green & white large swirl, white interior, cobalt blue trim, eyelet for hanging. Both good plus, rare color & shape, 2 pieces, **$695.00.**

2. **Chamber Pail,** 10¾" deep, not including the cover, 10½" diameter, green & white large swirl, white interior, cobalt blue trim, wooden bail. I did not include the cover measurement on this piece because it is not the original one. Good plus, extremely rare color & shape, **$375.00.**

Row 1:
1. **Large Flared Dipper,** 15¾" long, 3½" deep, 6½" diameter, green & white large swirl with white interior, black handle & trim. Mint, extremely rare color, shape & size, **$495.00.**
2. **Fry Pan,** 1⅞" deep, 9⅞" diameter, green & white large swirl with white interior, dark blue trim, rivetted handle. Good plus, extremely rare color & shape, **$375.00.**
3. **Salad or Mixing Bowl,** 5½" deep, 11¼" diameter, green & white large swirl with white interior, dark blue trim & rivetted handle. Good plus, extremely rare color, shape & size, **$325.00.**

Row 2:
1. **Tea Steeper,** 6⅛" tall, 4⅜" diameter, green & white large swirl with white interior, dark blue trim & handle. Rivetted spout & handle. Good plus, extremely rare color & shape, **$425.00.**
2. **Double boiler,** 9" tall including the insert, 6⅜" diameter, green & white large swirl with white interior, dark blue trim & rivetted handles. Near mint, extremely rare color, **$525.00.**
3. **Coaster,** ½" deep, 4" diameter, underside is green & white large swirl, white interior, dark blue trim, rivetted handle. Near mint, extremely rare color & shape, **$225.00.**
4. **Soup Ladle,** 12" long, 1½" deep, 3¾" diameter, green & white large swirl with white interior, dark blue trim, rivetted handle. Near mint, extremely rare color, shape & size, **$235.00.**

Row 3:
1. **Oblong Baking Pan,** 2⅛" deep, 10⅜" wide, 14¾" long not including the molded handles, green & white large swirl with white interior. Near mint, extremely rare color & shape, **$495.00.**

Row 4:
1. **Wash Basin,** 3" deep, 10⅞" diameter, green & white large swirl with white interior, dark blue trim, eyelet for hanging. Good plus, extremely rare color, **$145.00.**
2. **Oblong Baking Pan,** 2⅛" deep, 8½" wide, 14¼" long, green & white large swirl with white interior, dark blue trim & rivetted handles, seamless body. Near mint, extremely rare color & shape, **$495.00.**

Row 1:

1. **Covered Bucket,** matching granite cover with spun knob. 5¼" tall, 4½" diameter, green and white large swirl with white interior, dark blue trim and ears, seamless body and wire bail, rivetted wire ears. Mint, extremely rare color and size, **$525.00.**

2. **Covered Bucket,** matching granite cover with spun knob, 6½" tall 5¾" diameter, green and white large swirl, white interior, dark blue trim and ears, seamless body. Good plus, extremely rare color, **$395.00.** **Note:** Bucket #1 on this row has the rivetted wire ears and wire bail handle. This bucket, #2, has the flat rivetted ears and wooden bail handle. Also note the depth of the color variation of all the pieces on this page. This is why it is important to show a grouping of the same colors and shapes for comparison.

3. **Water Pitcher,** 8¾" tall, 6¼" diameter, green and white large swirl, white interior, dark blue trim and handle, seamless body, rivetted handle. Good plus, rare color and size, **$550.00.**

4. **Mug,** 2⅞" deep, 2⅞" diameter, green and white large swirl, white interior, dark blue trim & handle, seamless body, rivetted handle. Good plus, rare color and size, **$150.00.**

5. **Mug,** 2¾" deep, 2¾" diameter, green and white large swirl, white interior, dark blue trim, seamless body, rivetted handle. Good plus, rare color and size, **$150.00.**

6. **Water Pitcher,** 7½" tall, 5¼" diameter, green and white large swirl with white interior, dark blue trim and handle, seamless body and rivetted handle. Good plus, rare color and shape, **$550.00.** **Note:** Compare the depth of color on this piece to #3 on this row.

Row 2:

1. **Coffeepot,** 9⅛" tall, 5½" diameter, green and white large swirl, white interior, dark blue trim and handle, seamless body and rivetted handle. Mint, rare color and shape, **$550.00.** **Note:** By seeing all these coffeepots together once again you can compare the shades of color along with the size and shape variations.

2. **Coffeepot,** 10¼" tall, 5¾" diameter, green and white large swirl, white interior, dark blue trim and handle seamless body, rivetted spout and handle. Near mint, rare color & shape, **$550.00**

3. **Coffeepot,** 10⅛" tall, 5¾" diameter, green and white large swirl, white interior, dark blue trim, seamless body, rivetted handle. Near mint, rare color & shape, **$550.00.**

4. **Coffeepot,** 8¾" tall, 4⅝" diameter, green and white large swirl, seamed body, rivetted spout and handle. Near mint, rare color, shape & size, **$595.00.** **Note:** This coffee pot and #2 on this row both have rivetted spouts, whereas the others do not.

Row 3:

1. **Coffee Boiler,** 11¾" tall, 8⅝" diameter, green and white large swirl, white interior, dark blue trim & handle, seamed body, enameled wire shaped ears, wire bail handle. Mint, extremely rare color, **$595.00.**

2. **Pie Plate,** 1¼" deep, 8⅞" diameter, green and white large swirl, white interior, dark blue trim. Good plus, extremely rare color, **$95.00.**

3. **Pie Plate,** 1¼" deep, 9" top diameter, green and white large swirl with white interior, dark blue trim. Good plus, extremely rare color, **$75.00.**

4. **Coffee Boiler,** 11¾" tall, 9¼" diameter, green and white large swirl, white interior, dark blue trim and handle, seamed body and rivetted handle, flat shaped ears. Wire bail handle. Near mint, extremely rare color, rare shape, **$525.00.** **Note:** Both coffee boilers pictured have different shaped ears and covers. Also note the depth of color variation as well as the size difference.

Special Note: I felt it very necessary to photograph these pieces together to show the differences in colors & shapes. Note how the greens vary as well as the shape. Teapots #1 & #5 on Row #2 have seamless bodies & the handles are green & white swirl whereas #3 on Row #1 has a seamed body & the handle is dark blue. All three teapots, as you can see, are different sizes. It is believed that teapots & other items were purchased by the enameling companies from other manufacturers. A reason for this could have been that it was less expensive for the enameling companies to buy their blanks than manufacture the pots themselves. I do believe that all of the pieces shown here are "Emerald Ware" from The Strong Manufacturing Co. of Sebring, Ohio.

Row 1:
1. **Teapot,** 9⅛" tall, 4¾" diameter, green & white large swirl, white interior, dark blue trim, rivetted handle & seamless body. "Emerald Ware" from The Strong Manufacturing Co. Sebring, Ohio. Near mint, extremely rare color & shape, **$675.00.**
2. **Measure,** 6" tall, 4¼" diameter, green & white large swirl, white interior, dark blue trim & handle. Rivetted handle, seamless body. Near mint, extremely rare color, shape & size, **$750.00.**
3. **Teapot,** 9⅝" tall, 5¼" diameter, green & white large swirl, white interior, dark blue trim & handle, seamed body. Near mint, extremely rare color & shape, **$675.00.**
4. **Measure,** 5" tall, 3½" diameter, green & white large swirl, white interior, dark blue trim & handle, seamless body, rivetted handle. Near mint, extremely rare color, shape & size, **$750.00.**
5. **Teapot,** 8⅝" tall, 4¼" diameter, green & white large swirl, white interior, & dark blue trim, seamless body, rivetted handle. Near mint, extremely rare color, shape & size, **$675.00.**

Row 2:
1. **Covered Berlin-Style Kettle,** matching cover with spun knob, 5½" to top of the cover knob. 6" diameter, green & white large swirl with white interior & dark blue trim. Seamless body with rivetted two piece flat ears & wire bail handle. Near mint, rare color, shape & size, **$395.00.**
2. **Covered Berlin-Style Kettle,** matching cover with spun knob, 7½" tall, 9" diameter, green & white large swirl, white interior, dark blue trim, seamless body, enameled wire ears, wire bail handle. Near mint, rare color, **$325.00. Note:** Compare the shape of the ears on this pot & #3 to #1 on this row. Also note how the swirling as well as how the sizes & coloring of the kettles vary.
3. **Covered Berlin-Style Kettle,** matching cover with spun knob, 7" tall, 8¼" diameter, green & white large swirl, white interior, dark blue trim, seamless body, enameled wire ears, wire bail handle. Near mint, rare color, **$325.00.**

Row 3:
1. **Milk Can,** with matching granite cover, 9" tall, 5" diameter, green & white large swirl, white interior, dark blue trim, enameled wire ears, seamless body & wooden bail. Near mint, extremely rare color, shape & size, **$950.00.**
2. **Milk Can,** with matching granite cover. 11¾" tall, 6" diameter, green & white large swirl, white interior, dark blue trim, enameled wire ears, seamless body & wooden bail handle. Near mint, extremely rare color, shape & size, **$950.00.**
3. **Cream Can,** with matching granite cover. 7¾" tall, 4" diameter, green & white large swirl, white interior, dark blue trim, rivetted 2-piece flat ears, seamless body & wooden bail handle. Near mint, extremely rare color, shape & size, **$1,075.00.**
4. **Milk Can,** with matching granite cover. 11½" tall, 6⅛" diameter, green & white large swirl, white interior, dark blue trim, enameled wire ears, wooden bail & seamless body. Good plus, extremely rare color, shape & size, **$850.00.**
5. **Milk Can,** with matching granite cover. 9" tall, 4¾" diameter, green & white large swirl, white interior, dark blue trim, rivetted 2-piece flat ears, seamless body & wooden bail handle. Good plus, extremely rare color, shape & size, **$850.00. Note:** This milk can and #3, the cream can, have the rivetted 2-piece flat ears whereas the other milk cans have the wire ears. Milk can #1 on this row has a rivetted cover handle; all the others have molded handles.

SECTION 19
DECORATED

Special Note: A large variety of decorated granite ware exists. The age of the pieces in this section varies from the early 1900's till the present. All the pieces pictured on this page are from the early 1900's.

Row 1:
1. **Coffee Biggin,** including the cover, biggin, spreader and pot. 10½" high including biggin, 5⅝" diameter, white decorated with a blue checkered pattern, white interior, dark blue trim, seamless body. Marked "10 B.B 17213 Depose 12." Near mint, rare color and shape, **$395.00.**
2. **Coffee Biggin,** including the pot, biggin, and cover. 8½" high including biggin, 4½" diameter, white decorated with a blue checkered pattern, white interior with dark blue trim, seamless body. Marked "10 B.B 17213 Depose 6." Near mint, rare color and shape, **$395.00.**
3. **Oval Handled Pan,** 1¼" deep, 7⅜" wide, 12⅛" long, not including handles, white decorated with a blue checkered pattern, white interior with dark blue trim, Marked "2 B.B." Good plus, rare color and shape, **$115.00.**
4. **Hanging Matchbox,** 6¼" back height, 2¾" to top of the cover, 2⅞" wide, 4¾" long, white decorated with a blue checkered pattern, white interior with dark blue trim. Has a scratch pad on the cover. Marked "Allumettes B.B. 2 17213 Depose." Good plus, rare color and shape, **$210.00.**
5. **Coffee Carrier,** 10½" tall, 6⅛" diameter, white decorated with a blue checkered pattern, white interior with dark blue trim, wire bail, seamless body. Marked "B.B. 5 17213 Depose." Good plus, rare color and shape, **$265.00.**

Row 2:
1. **Hanging Utility Rack,** with 3 cups. Marked "Cristaux, Savonnoir; Savon Mineral." Utility Rack 3¾" back height, 5¼" wide, 14¼" long. Each cup 3½" deep, 4⅛" diameter, white decorated with a blue checkered pattern, white interior with dark blue trim. Good plus, rare color and shape, **$295.00. Note:** Each cup's bottom fits down in the utility rack ½". Each cup is marked "B.B. 2 17218," rack is not marked.
2. **Canisters,** (4) #1. 7" high, 5" diameter, marked "Sucre." #2 6½" high, 4" diameter marked "Cafe." #3 6" high, 3" diameter, marked "Pates." #4. 5½" high, 3½" diameter, marked "Chicoree." All white decorated with a blue checkered pattern, white interior with dark blue trim. Marked "B.B. 10-17213." Good plus, rare color, set of 4, **$295.00.**

Row 3:
1. **Upcooker,** with cover, 5¾" high, 6⅛" diameter, cover 5⅝" diameter, turned up outer edge is ¼" deep. White decorated with a blue checkered pattern, white interior with dark blue trim. Good plus, rare color and shape, **$225.00. Note:** Cover has a finger ring for lifting. Also, the cover is perforated so the boiling liquids can run back through the holes. This prevents the liquids from boiling over on the stove. The center perforation holds a funnel so more liquid can be added when necessary. Marked "10 B.B. 17213 Depose."
2. **Handled Cover,** ¼" high, 5¼" diameter, white decorated with blue checkered type pattern, white interior with dark blue trim. Near mint, rare color, shape and size, **$95.00. Note:** The centers of these covers are raised. Also note how the size of the checkered patterns on this page varies.
3. **Handled Straight Sided Pan,** with matching cover, 8" tall, 10⅞" diameter, white decorated with a blue checkered pattern, white interior and dark blue trim. Marked "B.B. 17213 Depose." Near mint, rare color, **$165.00.**
4. **Handled Cover,** ¼" high, 6⅞" diameter, white decorated with blue checkered pattern, white interior with dark blue trim. Near mint, rare color and shape, **$85.00. Note:** These covers are not marked.
5. **Salt Box,** 8⅝" back height. Box 4¼" deep, 3⅝" wide, 5⅞" long, white decorated with blue checkered pattern, white interior with dark blue trim. Marked "Sel B.B. 17213 Depose." Good, rare color and shape, **$145.00.**

Row 1:
1. **Hanging Match Box,** 6¼" back height. Box 2¾" tall, 2⅞" wide, 4¾" long, white decorated with a red & gray checkered pattern with white interior, black trim & lettering. Scratch pad on cover. Marked "Allumetttes 11 B. B. 12560K." Near mint, extremely rare color, rare shape, **$395.00.**
2. **Coffee Carrier,** 8¾" tall, 4½" diameter, white decorated with a blue checkered pattern, white interior with dark blue trim, wire bail. Marked "B.B. 3 18195 Depose." Near mint, rare color & shape, **$295.00.**
3. **Coffee Biggin,** including the pot, biggin, spreader & cover. 10¼" tall, 5⅛" diameter, cobalt blue large checkered pattern, white interior & red trim. Good plus, **$395.00. Note:** The spreader has perforations & is placed in the upper part of the biggin. When the water is poured over the spreader it "spreads" the water evenly through the coffee in the bottom of the biggin.
4. **Teapot,** 6-sided, 5¾" tall, 4⅞" diameter, white decorated with a blue checkered pattern, white interior with dark blue trim. Marked "Elite, Czecho-Slovakia, Reg'd 18203." Near mint, rare color & shape, **$165.00.**
5. **Teapot,** squatty shape. 4½" tall, 3⅞" diameter, white decorated with a red checkered pattern, white interior, red trim. Marked "B.B. 18186 Depose." Near mint, extremely rare color, rare shape, **$185.00.**

Row 2:
1. **Coffee Carrier,** 7" tall, 4" diameter, white decorated with orange checkered pattern, white interior with red trim & ears, wire bail, seamed body. Near mint, rare color & shape, **$295.00.**
2. **Canisters,** #1- 6½" tall, 4" diameter, marked "Cafe." Good plus. #2- 7" tall, 4¼" diameter, marked "Farine." Good plus. #3- 6" tall, 3½" diameter, marked "Pates." Good plus, rare color, set of 3, **$295.00.**
3. **Molasses Pitcher,** 5¼" tall, 5" diameter, white decorated with blue checkered pattern, white interior with dark blue trim. Marked "6 B. 1820S Depose." Good plus, rare color & shape, **$265.00.**

Row 3:
1. **Coffee Carrier,** 9¾" tall, 5⅝" diameter, white decorated with light blue checkered pattern, white interior with red trim, seamed body, wire bail. Good plus, rare color & shape, **$265.00. Note:** Tin cover not original.
2. **Coffee Biggin,** 12¾" tall, including the biggin, 5½" diameter, white decorated with red checkered pattern, white interior with red trim, handles & spout, seamed body. Good plus, rare color & shape, **$350.00.**
3. **Coffee Biggin,** 13¾" tall, including biggin, 5½" diameter, white decorated with red checkered pattern, white interior with red trim, handles & spout, seamed body. Good plus, extremely rare color & shape, **$595.00.**
4. **Coffee Biggin,** 9¼" tall, 4¾" diameter, white decorated with red checkered pattern, white interior with red trim & handle. Good plus, extremely rare color & shape, **$595.00. Note:** Number 4 has the checkered pattern on the spout also whereas the larger one has a solid red spout.

Note: All the pieces pictured are from the early 1900's.

Row 1:

1. **Teapot,** 8" high, 4¾" diameter, white decorated with a scalloped blue design, white interior. Marked in a diamond "Made in U.S.A. Pat. Nesco 10-13-25 'Bonny Blue'." Near mint, rare color, **$195.00.**

2. **Mixing Bowl,** 5" deep, 11" diameter, white decorated with a scalloped blue design, white interior. Marked in a diamond "Made in U.S.A. Pat. Nesco 10-13-25 'Bonny Blue'." Good plus, rare color & size, **$125.00.**

3. **Teapot,** 7¼" high, 4¼" diameter, white decorated with a scalloped blue design, white interior. Marked in a diamond "Made in U.S.A. Pat. Nesco 5-13-26." Good plus, rare color, **$145.00.**

Row 2:

1. **Colander,** footed, 3½" high, 11" diameter not including handles, white decorated with a blue scalloped design, blue handles, white interior. Marked in a double circle "Design Reg'd. 1924." Near mint, rare color, **$135.00.**

2. **Sugar Bowl,** 4" high, 3⅛" diameter, white decorated with a blue scalloped design, blue handles, white interior. Marked in a circle "McClary's Canada Design Registered 1924." Good plus, rare color & shape, **$150.00. Note:** Cover knob has been replaced.

3. **Creamer,** 3" tall, 3⅛" diameter, white decorated with a blue scalloped design, blue handle, white interior. Marked the same as the sugar bowl on this row. Good plus, rare color & shape, **$150.00.**

4. **Pudding Pan,** 3" deep, 10½" diameter, white decorated with a blue scalloped design, white interior. Marked in a diamond "Made In U.S.A. Nesco." Mint, rare color, **$120.00.**

Row 3:

1. **Trivet,** ⅜" high, 6¾" diameter, white decorated with a blue scalloped design. Good, rare color & shape, **$140.00. Note:** This piece is not marked.

2. **Teakettle,** 7½" tall, 10⅛" diameter, white decorated with a blue scalloped design, white interior. Marked in a diamond "Made In U.S.A. Nesco." Good plus, rare color, shape & size, **$410.00.**

3. **Milk Pitcher,** 6½" tall, 4¾" diameter, white decorated with a blue scalloped design, blue handle, white interior. Marked in a diamond "Made In U.S.A. Pat. Nesco 5-13-26. Bonny Blue." Mint, rare color & shape, **$175.00.**

Row 4:

1. **Water Pail,** 9½" deep, 11⅜" diameter, white decorated with a blue scalloped design, white interior, wooden bail. Marked in a diamond "Made In U.S.A. Pat. Nesco 10-12-25. Bonny Blue." Good, rare color, **$110.00.**

2. **Two Piece Oval Roaster,** 7½" high, 10" wide, 15¼" long not including handles, white decorated with a blue scalloped design, blue handles, white interior, has four protruding molded feet. Embossed under the cover handle "McClary's" McClary's is made in Canada. Mint, rare color, **$195.00.**

    Note: At first glance of this page you have probably said "that's Bonny Blue Ware," but as you see after looking & reading the descriptions of this ware, it is not all Bonny Blue Ware & it is not all made in one particular year nor was it all made in the U.S.A. by one manufacturer. This is one good example why it's very hard to attribute a piece to a single manufacturer or a single year. Unless a piece is marked, embossed, or labeled, we cannot be sure of its origin. Some companies have certain characteristics such as the way the enamel is applied, handles, seams, spouts, colors & so on. Sometimes this helps us to identify the manufacturer & the year it was made.

Row 1:

1. **Cup & Saucer.** Cup 2" deep, 3⅞" diameter, white with black trim, decorated with pink roses & blue violets. Also decorated with gold bands & the name "Mabel." Saucer, ⅞" deep, 5¾" diameter, white with black trim, decorated with gold bands, circa 1900. Good plus, 2 pieces, **$95.00.**
2. **Coffeepot,** 8½" tall, 5¼" diameter, cream decorated with pink roses & reddish brown trim, seamed body & spout. Numbered "878," circa 1900. Good plus, rare color, **$155.00.**
3. **Measure,** 5⅞" tall, 3⅝" diameter, shaded pink & green, decorated with pink roses & gold bands, black trim with white interior, rivetted handle & seamed body, circa 1900. Good plus, rare color, **$110.00.**

Row 2:

1. **Teapot,** 5½" tall, 4¾" diameter, white decorated with a floral design. Marked "Reservoir, Made In China, -107P-02-12cm." Circa 1980. Mint, **$70.00.**
2. **Soup Plate,** 1¼" deep, 9" diameter, white decorated with fruit, flowers & leaf design, dark blue trim. Circa 1980. Mint, **$30.00.**
3. **Measure,** 7½" tall, 3⅞" diameter, decorated with a floral design. Circa 1900. Good plus, rare color, **$85.00.**
4. **Soup Plate,** same as #2 on this row. Circa 1980. Mint, **$30.00.**
5. **Cream Can,** 7¾" tall, 4" diameter, white decorated with pansies & leaf design, embossed with the name "Florence," light blue trim, rivetted handle & ears, wooden bail & seamless body. Circa 1900. Good plus, rare color, shape & size, **$395.00.**

Row 3:

1. **Matching Pitcher & Bowl,** Pitcher 9" tall, 5½" diameter, white decorated with a pansy & leaf design with brown trim, rivetted handle & seamless body. Bowl, 3¼" deep, 11½" diameter. Both marked "813." Circa 1900. Good plus, rare shape, set **$425.00. Note:** I chose to show the bowl separately because the bowl shows the complete design that is on both sides of the pitcher as well.

Row 1:

1. **Coffee Carrier,** 8½" high, 5" diameter, white decorated with a dark blue feathered pattern, solid light blue bands, darker blue trim, white interior, wire ears, wire bail. Good plus, rare color & shape, **$240.00. Note:** Coffee carriers usually do not have a neck like the milk & cream cans do, instead, the bodies are completely tapered.

2. **Bell,** 5¼" high, 2⅜" diameter, white decorated with pink & yellow roses with lavender & black bands, white interior, brass handle & clapper. Good plus, extremely rare shape, **$295.00.**

3. **Crumb Tray,** 9¼" high, 10¼" wide, light blue decorated with lavender violets, green & blue leaves with a shrub-like border, brown trim. Good plus, extremely rare shape, **$395.00. Note:** This was used to hold crumbs that were brushed from the table. There usually is a crumb brush that goes with the crumb tray.

4. **Teapot,** tall squatty shape, 8½" high, 6" diameter, white decorated with pink, darker pink & gold bands, brown trim & middle band, seamed body, rivetted handle. Good plus, rare shape, **$150.00.**

Row 2:

1. **Toothbrush Holder,** 5½" deep, 3½" diameter, black trimmed with a pink rose, black interior. Near mint, rare color & shape, **$165.00. Note:** This is part of a wash set.

2. **Coffeepot,** 8" high, 4¼" diameter, orange decorated with black & white checkered design, black spout, handle, knob & trim, white inside. Marked "Elite. Czecho-Slovakia. Reg'd." Rare color, **$195.00.**

3. **Teapot,** 5¾" tall, 4¼" diameter, white with orange & green shading, decorated with light & dark green design, green handle & spout, white interior, shaded, decorated. Circa 1980. Mint, **$45.00.**

4. **Teapot,** 6½" tall, 5¼" diameter, white decorated with red poppy, green floral design & band on cover. marked "Reservoir. Made In China 807p-101. 14CM." Circa 1980. Mint, rare color, **$50.00.**

Row 3:

1. **Partial Salad Set,** large bowl, 3" deep, 10¼" diameter, four plates, ⅝" deep, 7⅛" diameter, white decorated with a fruit pattern trimmed in brown. The large bowl is decorated inside and outside. The small plates are decorated on just the outside. This ware is "Corona Enamelware, manufactured by Enterprise Enamel Co., Bellaire, Ohio." Mint, for 5 pieces, **$245.00.**

Row 4:

1. **Chocolate or Coffeepot,** 11¼" tall, 6½" diameter, white decorated with a blue & purple floral design, trimmed with gold color bands, side-hinged cover, attached wooden side handle. Marked on the bottom with two lions holding a shield with the letter "U" in the shield & the No. 101. Good plus, rare shape & size, **$250.00.**

2. **Oval 3-Piece Dinner Bucket,** 7⅜" high, including the insert, 6½" wide, 9" long, white shading to a light blue to white then back to light blue, decorated on front & back with yellow & pink flowers, black trim & handle. Marked "Stewart, Moundsville, W. Va." Near mint, rare color & shape, **$575.00.**

3. **Teapot,** 9½" tall, 5⅝" diameter, white decorated with a blue floral & leaf design, dark blue trim. Extremely rare shape, **$250.00. Note:** The unusual shaped handle resembles an old sleigh runner. Also, note the unusual ruffled top edge on the teapot & the domed cover with the unique handle.

SECTION 19: DECORATED

Definitions

Reproduction is something made by, copying, close imitation, duplication of a previously existing item.

New means never existing before, produced for the first time.

So you see, it is very difficult to categorize this section. For example, the mugs & milk can on Row 1 of this section were produced in these shapes prior to their being reproduced in close imitation circa 1980 but the decorated design & finish of the old has not been duplicated. Therefore, I hesitate to call any of the later granite ware a reproduction. The shape could be a close imitation of the old with the new finish or decoration being a whole new concept.

Row 1:

1. **Mug,** 2⅞" deep, 3⅝" diameter, white decorated with a blue & white cow & flower scene on front & back, white interior, cobalt blue trim & handle. Marked "happy holland design." Embossed on the bottom "Made in Poland 8." Also, shows a picture of a squatty tea kettle. Circa 1980. Mint, **$20.00.**
2. **Mug,** 2⅞" deep, 3⅝" diameter, white decorated with a blue & white cow & flower scene on front & back, white interior, cobalt blue trim & handle. Marked "happy holland design." Embossed on the bottom "Made In Poland 8." Also, shows a picture of a squatty tea kettle. Circa 1980. Mint, **$20.00.**
3. **Milk Can,** 8½" tall, 4½" diameter, white decorated with a blue & white cow & flower scene on front & back, white interior, cobalt blue trim & handle, wooden bail, seamed body, Marked "happy holland design." Embossed on the bottom "Made In Poland lltr." Also, shows a picture of a squatty teakettle. Circa 1980. Mint, **$60.00.**
4. **Mug,** 3" deep, 3½" diameter, white decorated with a red checked pattern, white interior, black trim. Circa 1980. Mint, **$20.00. Note:** I was told these were connected with the Big Boy Restaurants. I don't know for sure if they were given as a gift or if you could just buy them.
5. **Handled Sauce Pan,** 2⅞" deep, 6¼" diameter, light gray & white, dark blue flecks inside & out, decorated with ducks. This is a product of General Housewares Corp., Terre Haute, Indiana. Made circa 1990. Labeled "Ceramic on Steel Lifetime Warranty. Cooktop To Tabletop To Refrigerator." Mint, **$25.00.**

Row 2:

1. **Serving bowl,** 2⅞" deep, 7⅛" diameter, white decorated with yellow striped panels. The bottom outside section of the bowl is also yellow, white interior. Near mint, **$35.00. Note:** Where the yellow striped panels end on top of the bowl, black shows through. Circa 1960.
2. **Cup,** 2⅛" deep, 4" diameter, light blue decorated with bears, balloons & a tree, white interior, dark blue trim & handle. Marked "TrEs Marca Reg. Monterrey, Mexico." Circa 1980. Mint, **$25.00.**
3. **Teakettle,** chicken, white decorated with black dot design made to represent the body & head of a chicken, red head, cone & handle, yellow beak. Top part of the teakettle has a metal protection band. Also, the inside of the cover has a metal band & bottom attached. The red handle is a hard plastic. Marked on the bottom "Good Morning! National Housewares. Designed by Edger Weekium T.M." I'm not sure this is the right spelling for the designer because it's hard to make out. Also marked "Made In Taiwan." Circa 1990. Mint, rare shape, **$65.00.**
4. **Individual Bowls,** 1¾" deep, 4" diameter, white decorated with bright cobalt blue striped panels. The bottom outside section of the bowl is bright cobalt blue, white interior. Circa 1960. Near mint, each **$35.00.**

Row 3:

1. **Mug,** 3⅛" deep, 3½" diameter, brown shading to a light beige, decorated with western scenes, cowboy on a horse, covered wagon & a coffeepot over a campfire. Circa 1970. Mint, **$35.00.**
2. **Sectioned Plate,** 1¼" deep, 11" diameter, brown shading to a light beige, decorated with western scenes, cowboy on a horse, covered wagon & a coffeepot over a campfire. Circa 1970. Mint, **$35.00.**
3. **Coffeepot,** 9¼" tall, 6½" diameter, yellow decorated with a cowboy hat & a rope on one side. The other side has a chuck wagon & a cook preparing a meal on a campfire. Brown trim, cover & handle, seamed body. Circa 1970. Good plus, **$70.00.**
4. **Mug,** 3" deep, 3⅜" diameter, white decorated with a yellow checked pattern, white interior, black trim. Circa 1980. Near mint, **$20.00.**

Row 1:

1. **Round Tray,** 1⅜" deep, 13¾" diameter, white decorated with red & blue flowers, green leaves, shaded yellow background in the center of the tray, orange lacy effect border. Labeled "Tiger. Special Enamel Trademark, Kansai Horo (other part of this word is missing on the label). Made in Japan." Circa 1980. Mint, **$45.00.**

2. **Salad or Fruit Bowl,** 3⅛" deep, 11⅞" diameter, white decorated inside & out with orange flowers that resemble oriental poppies with green, brown & yellow leaves, yellow border, black trim. Circa 1980. Mint, **$45.00.**

Row 2:

1. **Covered Sugar,** 5¼" tall, 4¾" diameter, white decorated with pink, blue & gold flowers, green leaves, blue trim & handles. Circa 1980. Mint, **$40.00.**

2. **Soup Plate,** 1¼" deep, 8¾" diameter, white decorated with fruits & green leaves, blue decorated border. Circa 1980. Mint, **$30.00.**

3. **Covered Sugar,** 5" tall, 3½" diameter, white decorated with light & dark cobalt blue flower pattern & leaves, cobalt blue trim. Circa 1980. Mint, **$40.00.**

4. **Creamer,** 3½" high, 3⅞" diameter, same decoration & trim as No. 3 on this row. Circa 1980. Mint, **$40.00.**

Row 3:

1. **Covered Casserole,** 4¾" tall, 8½" diameter not including the molded handles, white decorated with fruits & leaves, black trim. Good plus, **$55.00. Note:** This covered casserole looks like the decoration is the same as the other pieces on this row but it does not have the green shaded background & there is a variation in the decoration. Circa 1970.

2. **Mug,** 3" deep, 3½" diameter, green shading to white decorated with fruits & leaves, white interior, cobalt blue trim. Circa 1970. Good plus, **$25.00.**

3. **Round Tray,** 1⅛" deep, 11⅞" diameter, green shading to white decorated with fruits & leaves, black trim. Circa 1970. Good plus, **$55.00.**

4. **Mug,** 3" deep, 3½" diameter, green shading to white decorated with fruits & leaves, white interior, cobalt blue trim. Circa 1970. Good plus, **$25.00.**

5. **Teapot,** 7¾" tall, 4¾" diameter, green shading to white decorated with fruits & leaves, white interior, cobalt blue trim, seamed body. Circa 1970. Good plus, **$65.00. Note:** All the pieces on this page are lightweight.

Section 20
Child's Items, Miniatures and Salesman's Samples

Row 1:

1. **Child's Starter Plate,** ⅜" deep, 8¾" diameter, white decorated with blue horse & trim. Marked "Kockums," on the bottom is pictured a bell with a flag & the letters "KER Sweden" in circle. Below the circle is marked "20 CM." Near mint, **$50.00.**

2. **Child's Starter Mug,** 2¾" deep, 3" diameter, white trimmed in brown decorated with a Dutch girl & boy kissing. Good plus. **$35.00.**

3. **Child's Feeding Dish,** 1⅞" deep, 8" diameter not including handles or spout, pink decorated with Dutch girl & boy. Girl appears to be knitting. Marked "W Germany." Mint, extremely rare shape, rare color, **$135.00. Note:** The warming compartment is made of a brass base with a highly polished nickel finish. This base was filled with warm water to keep food warm.

4. **Teapot,** 4" high, 2½" top diameter, 2⅞" bottom diameter, medium mottled American gray, tin cover with wooden acorn-shaped knob. Near mint, extremely rare color, shape & size, **$525.00. Note:** This is sometimes referred to by today's collectors as a miniature batter jug. I have also seen the larger pots with this straight spout referred to as water carriers.

5. **Child's Starter Plate,** ¾" deep, 7⅞" diameter, white decorated with Indians, brown trim. Mint, **$60.00.**

Row 2:

1. **Handled Strainer,** 6¾" long including both handles, 2¾" top diameter, fancy perforated rounded bottom, solid cobalt blue with white interior. Good plus, rare shape, **$65.00. Note:** This is smaller than the one shown in Book 1.

2. **Mixing Bowl,** 1⅝" deep, 4" top diameter, solid cobalt blue. Near mint, **$45.00. Note:** The mixing bowl, handled sauce pan, fry pan & the kettle with the wire bail handle are all part of the domestic science set.

3. **Handled Sauce Pan,** 1⅞" deep, 4½" diameter, solid cobalt blue. Near mint, **$50.00.**

4. **High Chair Tray,** 8¾" wide, 16⅞" long, white decorated in blue with a girl & boy catching butterflies. Good plus, rare shape, **$65.00. Note:** This tray was made to fit into the wooden tray on a high chair. It could then be removed for easy cleaning.

5. **Fry Pan,** ⅞" deep, 5⅛" diameter, solid cobalt blue. Near mint, **$65.00.**

6. **Handled Skimmer,** 8" long, 1⅜" diameter, solid cobalt blue, white interior. Mint, **$75.00.**

7. **Kettle,** 1⅞" deep, 4" top diameter, solid cobalt blue, wire bail. Good plus, **$50.00.**

8. **Handled Soup Ladle,** 7¾" long, 2" ladle diameter, solid cobalt blue, white interior. Mint, rare shape, **$65.00.**

Row 3:

1. **Rack with Matching Utensil,** utensil rack 7¾" high, 5¼" wide, solid red. Matching handled skimmer, 6" long, 2" diameter, solid red handle & back, skimmer is large mottled. Red & white on the front. Good plus, extremely rare color, shape & size, 2 pieces, **$695.00.**

2. **Handled Soup Ladle,** 5½" long, 1¼" ladle diameter, medium dark blue. Mint, rare shape, **$65.00.**

3. **Turks Head Mold,** 1" deep, 1⅞" diameter, solid light blue, white inside. Mint, extremely rare shape & size **$235.00.**

4. **Rack with Matching Utensil.** Utensil rack, 6¾" high, 4⅝" wide, solid light blue. Matching handled skimmer, 5⅝" long, 1⅜" diameter. Near mint, extremely rare color, shape & size, **$695.00.**

5. **Fish Mold,** 3" long, solid light blue, white interior. Mint, extremely rare shape & size, **$265.00.**

Row 4:

1. **Lionel Electric Stove,** 32½" to top of oven, 11½" wide, 26" long, cream & green around the oven door with black trim. Rest of the stove is cream with black trim. Backplate over the two electric burners pictures a little chef winking & carrying a tray. Metal name plate is marked "The Lionel Corporation, New York No. 455, 1250-Watts-110-115 Volts." Good plus, extremely rare color, shape & size, working condition **$1,975.00.**

Row 1:
1. **Child's Hoosier Kitchen Cabinet,** oak with enamel slide-out work top. 39" overall height, bottom section is 14" wide and 22" long. Enamel work top measures 9" wide and 22¾" long. White with black trim. Mint, extremely rare color, shape and size, **$1,150.00. Note:** Items shown on cabinet are described in this section of the book.

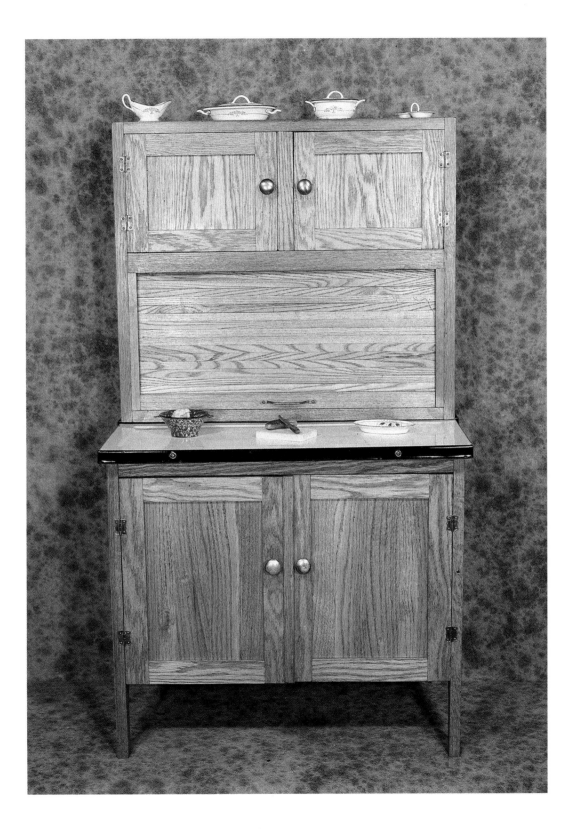

Row 1:

1. **Child's Plate,** ¼" deep, 6" diameter, white decorated with a nursery rhyme scene, trimmed in cobalt blue. Nursery rhyme reads "Dickory Dickory Dock The Mouse Ran Up The Clock." Good plus. **$40.00.**

2. **Child's Plate,** ¼" deep, 6" diameter, white decorated with a nursery rhyme scene, trimmed in cobalt blue. Nursery rhyme reads "The Clock Struck One The Mouse Ran Down Dickory Dickory Dock." Good plus, **$40.00.**

3. **Child's Plate,** ¼" deep, 6" diameter, white decorated with a nursery rhyme scene, trimmed in cobalt blue. Nursery rhyme reads "Ding Dong Bell, Pussy's In The Well. Who Put Her In? Little Tommy Green." Good plus, **$40.00.**

Row 2:

1. **Miniature Clock,** 2⅝" diameter, white decorated with a floral design. Marked "Germany." Mint, extremely rare color, shape & size, working order, **$325.00.**

2. **Coverless Roaster,** salesman's sample, 1⅛" deep, 4¼" wide, 6⅛" long not including handles. The inside raised well is ⅝" deep, reddish brown & white medium mottled inside & out, rivetted wire handles, seamless body. "Cream City Ware." Garnet, Milwaukee, Geuder, Paeschke & Frey Co. Good plus, extremely rare color, shape & size, **$425.00. Note:** This sample could have been given as a premium for a promotional advertisement or just as a gift to a child when the mother of the house purchased a certain amount of granite ware. This was also a way for the salesman who carried these samples to show the construction, durability, colors & uses of the items they were selling.

3. **Wood-Burning Stove,** salesman's sample, 20⅞" high, 8¾" deep, 13" long, solid blue nickel-plated trim. Embossed "Qualified Range Co. Ft. Recovery O." Near mint, extremely rare color, shape & size, **$3,600.00. Note:** The grates in this stove actually can be shaken to release the ashes from wood or coal, whichever is used.

4. **Wash Basin,** salesman's sample, 1¼" deep, 4" top diameter, light blue & white large mottled, white interior, black trim. Near mint, rare color, shape & size, **$85.00.**

5. **Fry Pan,** ⅜" deep, 2⅝" diameter, light blue & white large mottled inside & out, black handle. Good plus, rare color, shape & size, **$195.00.**

314

Row 1:

1. **Teapot,** squatty shape, 2⅛" high, cover missing, 3¼" middle diameter, white, light blue, green, brown, dark blue, pink, End of Day, "Confetti," seamed body, rivetted handle. Good plus, extremely rare color, shape and size, **$185.00. Note:** The many variations of the colors and patterns in the pieces on this page in the "Confetti" pattern.

2. **Handled Sauce Pan,** 1⅝" deep, 3" top diameter not including handle, white, light blue, green, brown, dark blue, pink, pastel yellow, white interior, End of Day, "Confetti" pattern, rivetted handle, seamless body. Mint, extremely rare color, **$170.00.**

3. **Footed Slop Bucket,** 3⅝" deep, 3¾" diameter, white, light blue, green, brown, dark blue, pink and pastel yellow, white interior, wire bail, rivetted ears. End of Day, "Confetti" pattern. Good plus, extremely rare color and shape, **$225.00. Note:** I believe this slop bucket should have a cover with an odorless valve because the top part of the bucket has a ridge where a cover will fit.

4. **Oblong Roasting Pan,** 1" deep, 2¾" wide, 4⅞" long, white, light blue, green, brown, dark blue, pink, pastel yellow white interior, End of Day, confetti pattern. Mint, extremely rare color and shape, **$235.00.**

5. **Tumbler,** 2⅛" deep, 2" diameter, white, light blue, green, brown, dark blue, pink and pastel yellow, white interior, End of Day, confetti pattern. Good plus, extremely rare color, shape and size, **$250.00.**

Row 2:

1. **Open Sugar,** 1⅝" deep, 2⅞" diameter, white, light blue, green, brown, dark blue, pink and pastel yellow End of Day, confetti pattern. Good plus, **$235.00.**

2. **Teapot,** 3½" tall, 2½" diameter, white, light blue, green, brown, dark blue, pink and pastel yellow, white interior, rivetted spout and handle, seamless body, End of Day, confetti pattern. Near mint, extremely rare color, shape and size, **$295.00.**

3. **Creamer,** 2⅜" deep, 1¾" diameter not including spout, white, light blue, green, brown, dark blue, pink and pastel yellow, white interior, rivetted handle and spout, seamless body, End of Day, "Confetti" pattern. Near mint, extremely rare color, shape and size, **$295.00.**

4. **Handled Divided Vegetable Dish,** ¼" deep not including handle, 1⅝" diameter each rounded section, 3½" overall length, white, light blue, green, dark blue, pink and pastel yellow on both sides, End of Day, Confetti pattern. Near mint, extremely rare color, shape and size, **$295.00.**

Row 3:

1. **Sugar,** cover missing, 1⅝" deep, 1⅞" diameter, light gray and white medium mottled, rivetted handles, seamless body. Good, rare shape, **$30.00.**

2. **Oblong Roasting Pan,** ⅜" deep, 2¼" wide, 3⅞" long not including handle, light gray and white medium mottled. Near mint, **$110.00.**

3. **Fry Pan,** ½" deep, 2⅛" diameter, light gray and white medium mottled. Good plus, **$120.00.**

4. **Teakettle,** 3⅜" tall, 3½" diameter, light gray and white medium mottled, rivetted handle and spout. Good plus, extremely rare color, shape and size, **$495.00.**

5. **Handled Sauce Pan,** ⅞" deep, 2⅛" diameter, light gray and white medium mottled. Good plus, **$80.00.**

6. **Wash Basin,** 1" deep, 3⅝" top diameter, light gray and white medium mottled, ring for hanging. Good plus, **$65.00.**

7. **Funnel,** 2⅛" to top of the spout, 1¾" diameter, light gray and white medium mottled, rivetted handle. Near mint, rare size, **$115.00.**

Row 4:

1. **Salesman's Sample Wash Basin,** 1⅛" deep, 4⅛" diameter. Good plus, extremely rare color and shape, **$195.00. Note:** Left side black, middle section solid light gray, right side white, black trim. This salesman's sample shows how one company achieved the number of enamel applications on their wares. The black was applied first, secondly, the off-white enamel, third the blue enamel, making the black the single all over undercoat. The off-white is the double coat and the blue is the triple coating.

2. **Water Pail,** 3⅜" deep, 3¾" diameter, green and dark green swirl effect, red trim, white interior, applied ears, seamless body, wire bail. Good plus, extremely rare color and shape, **$185.00.**

3. **Cuspidor,** Salesman's Sample, 2" deep, 3⅜" diameter, white, green and cobalt blue inside and out, large swirl, seamless body, enameled over cast iron, End of Day. Good plus, extremely rare color, shape and size, **$900.00.**

Row 1:

1. **Roaster,** 3" tall, 5" diameter, dark blue with white specks inside & out, speckled pattern. Centennial souvenir. Mint, extremely rare shape & size, **$195.00. Note:** This roaster was given away as a promotional souvenir to celebrate the Columbian Enameling & Stamping Company's first 100 years. This is an advertising cross collectible because of its desirability to both advertising & enamel ware collectors. Label reads "1871 Columbian 100 Years 1971."

2. **Roaster,** 3" tall, 5" top diameter, a shade of darker blue than No. 1 on this row, white specks inside & out, speckled pattern. Marked & fired onto the enamel "The high tech, low care, faster cookware." Also, GHC. This is General Housewares Co. logo. Mint, extremely rare color & shape, **$135.00. Note:** This roaster was given away in the circa 1980 filled with jelly beans as a promotion for their "Ceramic on Steel" wares.

3. **Roaster,** 3" tall, 5" diameter, black with white specks, speckled pattern. Mint, extremely rare shape & size, **$135.00. Note:** Roaster No. 1 on this row was shown in Book 1, but I chose to show it with these other two to show you the difference in the colors & also the paper label in comparison to the fired-on markings.

Row 2:

1. **Wash Basin,** salesman's sample, 1⅛" deep, 3¾" diameter, light blue on both sides, black trim. Marked "Republic Ware." Mint, rare color, shape & size, **$150.00. Note:** Salesman's samples can advertise a company's name, location, color & their particular line of wares that they made along with the shapes. They can also be identified with paper labels. With different designs & colors some labels represent the quality of the wares as well.

2. **Wash Basin,** Salesman's Sample 1⅛" deep, 3¾" diameter, light cream on both sides, black trim. Marked "Republic Ware." Mint, rare color, shape & size, **$150.00. Note:** Both Nos. 1 & 2 on this row are advertising the company's wares. The advertising is fired into the enameling.

Row 3:

1. **Wash Basin,** salesman's sample, ⅞" deep, 3⅜" diameter, solid orange on both sides. Marked "Lisk." Mint, rare color, shape & size, **$150.00. Note:** This basin is advertising the company name.

2. **Wash Basin,** salesman's sample,⅞" deep, 3⅜" diameter, charcoal gray & white, fine mottled on both sides. Mint, rare color, shape & size, **$125.00. Note:** This label represents their top quality line.

3. **Wash Basin,** salesman's sample, ⅞" deep, 3¼" diameter, black with white specks on both sides, speckled pattern. Paper label "Lisk." Mint, rare color, shape & size, **$125.00. Note:** This label represents their next best line.

4. **Wash Basin,** salesman's sample, ¾" deep, 3⅜" diameter, light gray inside, blue & white medium mottled outside. Marked "The Cleveland Stamping & Tool Co., Cleveland, O., Manufacturers of Lava & Volcanic Enameled Ware." Near mint, extremely rare color, shape & size, **$165.00. Note:** This basin advertises the company & location plus two lines of their wares.

Row 4:

1. **Wash Basin,** salesman's sample, ¾" deep, 3⅝" diameter, white inside, shaded dark blue to lighter blue. Marked "Sample from The Strong Mfg. Co., Sebring, Ohio." Near mint, extremely rare color, shape & size, **$185.00. Note:** This basin is marked "sample." Most are not marked "Sample" even though we know they are salesman's samples. These salesman's sample wash basins also vary in size.

2. **Wash Basin,** salesman's sample, ⅞" deep, 3⅜" diameter, solid green on both sides. Marked "Lisk." Near mint, rare color, shape & size, **$150.00.**

3. **Wash Basin,** salesman's sample, ⅞" deep, 3½" outside diameter, white inside, dark cobalt & white large mottled. Marked "Enterprise Enamel Company, Bellaire, O., Azurelite." Good plus, **$165.00. Note:** This basin advertises the company name plus their line of ware.

4. **Wash Basin,** salesman's sample, ⅞" deep, 3⅜" diameter, solid red on both sides. Marked "Lisk." Mint, rare color, shape & size, **$150.00.**

319

Section 20: Child's Items, Miniatures and Salesman's Samples

Row 1:

1. **Wash Basin,** salesman's sample, 1¼" deep, 4⅝" top diameter, blue & white medium mottled, white inside, black trim. Mint, rare color & shape, **$85.00.**
2. **Wash Basin,** salesman's sample, 1¼" deep, 4¾" top diameter, American gray medium mottled on both sides. Near mint, rare color & shape, **$75.00.**
3. **Wash Basin,** salesman's sample, 1¼" deep, 5⅛" top diameter, green & white fine mottled on both sides, black trim. Mint, rare color & shape, **$85.00.**
4. **Wash Basin,** salesman's sample, 1¼" deep, 4⅞" top diameter, American gray large mottled on both sides. Mint, rare color & shape, **$75.00.**
5. **Wash Basin,** salesman's sample, 1¼" deep, 4¼" top diameter, blue & white large mottled, white insides, light blue trim. Mint, rare color & shape, **$85.00.**

Row 2:

1. **Wash Basin,** salesman's sample, ⅞" deep, 3⅜" top diameter, light gray on both sides, blue trim. Mint, rare color & shape, **$65.00. Note:** This is referred to as pearl gray.
2. **Wash Basin,** salesman's sample. Near mint. **Note:** This is the reverse side of the basin shown on page 319, Row 3, No. 4. Marked "The Cleveland Stamping & Tool Co., Cleveland, O. Manufacturers of Lava & Volcanic Enameled Ware." Near mint, extremely rare color, shape and size, **$165.00**
3. **Wash Basin,** salesman's sample. Good plus. **Note:** This is the reverse side of the basin shown on page 319, Row 4, No. 3. Marked "Enterprise Enamel Company, Bellaire, O, Azurelite." Good plus, **$165.00.**
4. **Wash Basin,** salesman's sample, ⅞" deep, 3¼" top diameter, white with black, speckled on both sides, black trim. Mint. **Note:** This color was advertised as "salt & pepper." Near mint, rare color & shape, **$55.00.**

Row 3:

1. **Wash Basin,** salesman's sample, ⅞" deep, 3⅜" top diameter, light blue & white medium mottled, white inside, & dark blue trim. Mint, rare color & shape, **$85.00.**
2. **Wash Basin,** salesman's sample, 1¼" deep, 4⅝" top diameter, white, blue, rust, brown, & black, large mottled on both sides with black trim, End of Day. Mint, extremely rare color & shape, **$285.00.**
3. **Wash Basin,** salesman's sample, 1¼" deep, 4⅝" top diameter, American gray large mottled on both sides. Mint, rare color & shape, **$75.00.**
4. **Wash Basin,** salesman's sample, ⅞" deep, 3⅜" top diameter, white, light blue, cobalt blue, black, & rust brown, large swirl on both sides, End of Day. Mint, rare color & shape, **$285.00.**
5. **Wash Basin,** salesman's sample, 1¼" deep, 4⅞" top diameter, light brown shading to a darker brown, with white inside, shaded. Near mint, rare color & shape, **$75.00.**

Row 4:

1. **Wash Basin,** salesman's sample, 1⅛" deep, 4¼" top diameter, cobalt blue & white large mottled, with white interior & black trim. Mint, rare color & shape, **$130.00.**
2. **Wash Basin,** salesman's sample, Mint. **Note:** This is the reverse side of the basin shown on page 319, Row 4, No. 1. Marked "Sample from The Strong Mfg. Co., Sebring, Ohio." Near mint, rare color & shape, **$185.00.**
3. **Wash Basin,** salesman's sample, 1⅛" deep, 4⅛" top diameter. Left side: blue & white fine mottled. Middle section: solid off white. Right side; solid black. Reverse side—left side: black. Middle section: solid light gray. Right side: white. Good plus. **Note:** This salesman's sample shows the number of enamel applications. The black was applied first, the off white, then the blue, making the black the single all over undercoat. You can actually feel the raised ridge where the extra coats of enamel were applied. This is the reverse side of the basin shown on page 317 Row 4, No. 1. Good plus, rare color & shape, **$195.00.**
4. **Wash Basin,** salesman's sample, ¾" deep, 3⅝" top diameter, dark green shading to a lighter green, white inside, shaded. Shamrock Ware, distributed by Norvell-Shapleigh Hardware Co., St. Louis, Missouri. Mint, rare color, shape & size, **$85.00. Note:** This one is not marked inside.
5. **Wash Basin,** salesman's sample, 1¼" deep, 4⅛" top diameter, blue & white large mottled, white inside, black trim. Mint, rare color, shape & size, **$130.00.**

Row 5:

1. **Wash Basin,** salesman's sample, 1⅛" deep, 4⅛" top diameter. Left side black, right side white with blue medium mottling, black trim. Mint, extremely rare color, shape & size, **$225.00. Note:** This basin is triple coated: black, white and blue.
2. **Wash Basin,** salesman's sample, 1⅛" deep, 4¼" top diameter, solid light green on both sides, dark green trim. Mint, rare color, shape & size, **$55.00.**
3. **Wash Basin,** salesman's sample, 1¼" deep, 4½" top diameter, solid yellow on both sides, black trim. Good plus, rare color, shape & size, **$55.00. Note:** The rim looks like someone took a bite out of it. These may have been made from the company's scrap metal.
4. **Wash Basin,** 1¼" deep, 4⅝" top diameter, lavender blue & white large mottled, white inside, black trim. Mint, rare color, shape & size, **$95.00.**

Row 1:
1. **Wash Basin,** salesman's sample, 1⅛" deep, 4⅝" top diameter, light green, dark green, red, yellow, cobalt blue, orange, white interior. "End of Day." Near mint, extremely rare color, shape & size, **$155.00.**

Row 2:
1. **Pie Plate,** 1" deep, 4¾" top diameter, yellow, white interior, cobalt blue trim. Good plus, rare shape, **$30.00.**
2. **Pitcher & Bowl.** Pitcher, 4" to top of the lip, 3¼" diameter. Bowl, 1½" deep, 6¼" top diameter. Pitcher white, cobalt blue, light blue, pink, yellow & green, white inside. Bowl same coloring as pitcher except it has the coloring on both inside & out. "Confetti" pattern, End of Day. Good plus, extremely rare color, shape & size, 2 piece set, **$425.00.**
3. **Pie Plate,** ¾" deep, 5½" top diameter, cobalt blue & white medium mottled, white interior, black trim. Good plus, extremely rare color, shape & size, **$140.00.**

Row 3:
1. **Wash Basin,** salesman's sample, 1¼" deep, 4⅞" top diameter, cobalt blue & white large swirl, white interior, black trim. Good plus, rare color, shape & size, **$85.00.**
2. **Tea Set,** eight pieces, in the original box. Teapot, 3" tall, 2⅜" diameter, all pieces are solid light blue inside & out. Marked "Germany." Creamer, 1⅜" deep, 1⅜" top diameter. Cups, 1" deep, 1½" top diameter, Saucers, ⅜" deep, 2½" top diameter. Open sugar, ⅞" deep, 1¾" top diameter. Box pictures the globe of the world with markings "J.M. Pag Nurnberg. Around The World Rundum Die Welt. Tee-Service, Tea-Set. Service De The, Servicio De Té, No 2/900/2 Made In Germany." Mint, rare color, shape & size, **$895.00.** **Note:** Sets in the original box are rare, because the boxes usually get thrown away. Also the box may advertise the place where the set was made as well as who manufactured it like the one pictured here.
3. **Two-handled Covered Kettle,** 2⅝" tall, 3½" top diameter, brown shading to orange, gray interior. Labeled "Saint-Trond, Belgique." Mint, rare color, shape & size, **$175.00. Note:** This piece is on a heavy metal base.

Row 4:
1. **Wash Basin,** salesman's sample, 1¼" deep, 4⅜" top diameter, green & white large mottled, white interior, black trim. Near mint, rare color, shape & size, **$85.00.**

Row 5:
1. **Wash Basin,** salesman's sample, ¾" deep, 3⅜" top diameter, mauve pink inside & out, black trim. Near mint, rare color, shape & size, **$60.00.**
2. **Wash Basin,** advertising salesman's sample, ¾" deep, 3⅝" top diameter, deep sea green shading to a moss green, white interior. Marked "Sample From The Strong Mfg. Co., Sebring, Ohio." Mint, extremely rare color, shape & size, **$185.00.**
3. **Wash Basin,** salesman's sample, ¾" deep, 3⅝" top diameter, deep sea green shading to a moss green, white interior. Mint, extremely rare color, shape & size, **$185.00. Note:** This wash basin shows the reverse side of the sample of No. 2 on this row so you can see what the color of Shamrock Ware looks like. The Norvell-Shapleigh Hardware Co., St. Louis, was the sole distributor of this ware.

Row 1:

1. **Bathtub,** salesman's sample, 1⅝" deep, 4½" long, white inside, beige outside. Enameled over cast iron. Embossed "Kalypso." Good plus, rare shape and size, **$185.00.**

2. **Teapot,** 5½" high, 3½" bottom diameter, solid cobalt, white inside. Good plus, rare shape and size, **$160.00.**

3. **Tub,** salesman's sample, 3⅛" deep, 4¼" long, white, enameled over cast iron. Embossed "Iron City." Near mint, rare shape and size, **$185.00.**

4. **Teapot,** 4¾" high, 2⅝" bottom diameter, solid blue, cobalt blue trim, white inside. Marked "Western Due Leoni Qualita Superiore Bassano." Also, pictured on the bottom are 2 lions standing on a kettle. Inside kettle is marked "S.V." Mint, rare shape and size, **$185.00.**

5. **Bathtub,** salesman's sample, 2⅛" deep, 6⅜" long, white,. enameled over cast iron. Embossed "L. Wolff Mf'g Co." Mint, rare shape and size, **$185.00.**

Row 2:

1. **Child's Cup and Saucer,** cup 1¾" deep, 2½" top diameter, yellow outside decorated with multi-colored flowers, white inside. Saucer, ¾" deep, 4" diameter, yellow decorated with multi-colored flowers. Good plus, 2 pieces **$45.00.**

2. **Domestic Science Set, Nos. 1–5.**
   1. **Baking Pan,** ⅞" deep, 4½" long, cream, red trim. Good plus, **$55.00.**
   2. **Pudding Pan,** 1¾" deep, 5" top diameter, cream, red trim. Good plus, **$45.00.**
   3. **Handled Kettle,** 1⅞" deep, 4⅛" top diameter not including handles, cream, red trim. Good plus, **$55.00.**
   4. **Pie Plate,** ½" deep, 4¾" top diameter, cream, red trim. Mint, **$55.00.**
   5. **Pan,** 1⅞" deep, 4⅛" top diameter, cream, red trim. Good plus, **$45.00. Note:** This is the same size as No. 3 in the set except it does not have the handles.

Row 3:

1. **Teapot,** 4⅜" high, 3⅛" diameter, white, cobalt blue trim. Good plus, rare shape and size, **$120.00.**

2. **Toy Stove,** electric, 7" high, 7" top length, 5" bottom length, 4⅝" wide, solid gray stove top on a white stove. Oven door opens. Embossed "Baby Baudin" on the top of the stove. Near mint, extremely rare color, shape and size, **$750.00.**

3. **Fish Mold,** 3⅞" long, 1¼" widest part of the body, green and white, medium mottled. Mint, rare color, shape and size, **$225.00.**

4. **Miniature Electric Rage,** 14¾" high, 15" long, 6½" wide, blue enamel panels. Marked "Empire" under warming shelf. Ad states "The only Practical Miniature Electric Range is the Empire. Empire furnishes two models of miniature electric ranges. The larger model has two side ovens. The smaller one has a large single oven. Both are as efficient for all cooking and baking as any large range. These toys are instructive. They teach girls to cook and bake in a practical way. The ovens are large enough for small cakes, pies, potatoes and other dishes. The cooking top is roomy too. The legs, door frames, cooking top and shelf are heavily nickel-plated and sturdily constructed. Body is Black Japanned finish. The heating element is designed to give economical operation and even temperatures to both ovens. It operates on standard electric light socket. Made by Metal Ware Corporation, Chicago, Ill., Two Rivers, Wis." Cross collectible. Good plus, extremely rare color, shape and size, **$985.00. Note** the difference in this stove from the one photographed for Book 1. There are no off and on knobs on this stove. Also, the maker's metal plate is on the left side. Metal plate reads "Metal Ware Corp., Two Rivers, Wis., volts 110, watts 600, Cat. No. B27."

Row 1:
1. **Teakettle,** bell shaped, 3½" tall, 4" bottom diameter, dark charcoal gray & white large mottled, gray interior, rivetted spout & ears, seamed bottom. Mint, extremely rare color, shape & size, **$625.00.**
2. **Teakettle,** 3¼" to top of the cover knob, 3½" bottom diameter, solid blue, white interior, seamed bottom. Near mint, extremely rare color, shape & size, **$595.00.**
3. **Teakettle,** 3¼" tall, 3½" bottom diameter, light gray & white medium mottled, darker gray mottled interior, rivetted ears & spout, seamed bottom. Good plus, extremely rare color, shape & size, **$550.00.**

Row 2:
1. **Tea Set,** eight piece, in the original box. Coffee pot, 3⅞" tall, 2¼" lower section diameter. Open Pedestal Sugar, 1¼" high, 1¾" top diameter. Creamer, 1⅝" deep, 1½" diameter. Cup, 1½" deep, 1⅝" top diameter. Saucer, ½" deep, 3⅛" top diameter. White decorated with a black & light blue design, dark blue trim. Original box has part of the label. Marked "B.W. 385" only part of the numbers are there. I believe this is a product of the Bing Toy Co., Germany. Mint, extremely rare color, shape & size, complete with box, **$1,000.00. Note:** Scribbled on the inside of the box "5 years old." This could have been the age of the child when she received the set as a gift.

Row 3:
1. **Partial Tea Set,** 11 pieces. Teapot, 3¼" tall, 3" diameter. Covered Sugar, 2⅛" tall, 1¾" diameter. Creamer 1¾" high, 1⅜" diameter. Cup, 1" deep, 2" top diameter. Saucer, ⅜" deep, 3⅛" top diameter. Light blue inside & out, decorated with red & blue flowers with yellow centers & green foliage. Good plus, rare color & shape, **$340.00. Note:** The cover on the teapot is not original, also, one cup & saucer is missing.

Row 1:

1. **Bathtub,** salesman's sample, 1½" deep, 2⅞" wide, 5" long, light green. Embossed "Richmond." Good plus, rare shape & size, **$125.00.**

2. **Teapot,** 6" tall, 2⅞" bottom diameter, blue & white fine mottled, light gray interior, seamless body. Good plus, rare color, shape & size, **$195.00.**

3. **Child's Wash Basin,** 1¾" deep, 7⅛" top diameter, cobalt blue & white large mottled, white interior, cobalt blue trim. Good plus, extremely rare color, shape & size, **$165.00.**

4. **Miniature Potty,** 1¾" deep, 3⅜" diameter, white, cobalt blue, pink, green, blue, pastel yellow, dark maroon, white interior, rivetted handle, seamless body, "Confetti" pattern, End of Day. Mint, extremely rare color, shape & size, **$595.00.**

5. **Coffeepot,** 5⅜" tall, 3⅜" bottom diameter, white with red trim, black interior, seamed body. Near mint, rare shape & size, **$140.00.**

6. **Wash Basin,** salesman's sample, 1¼" deep, 3⅜" top diameter, blue & white large mottled, white interior, blue trim. Embossed in a shield "SMP." Good plus, extremely rare color, shape & size, **$175.00.**

Row 2:

1. **Child's Tea Set,** in original box, 17 pieces including the covers. Teapot, 3½" tall, 2½" diameter. Covered Sugar 2" tall, 2½" diameter. Creamer, 2⅛" tall, 2" diameter. Saucer, ⅝" deep, 3⅞" diameter. Cup, 1¾" deep, 2⅜" top diameter. Cobalt blue decorated with gold leaf. Near mint, extremely rare color, shape & size, complete with box, **$1,495.00. Note:** Baumann of Amberg & Bing of Nuremberg made doll dishes & utensils at the end of the last century so it is possible this set was one that was made there. The inside of the box cover has the G.B.N. label. The side of the box also has G.B.N. 11283/6 with a price sticker from Gimbels: $4.50. Another sticker states "Royal Blue Dishes Belonged to Mother as a Child."

Special Note: Sets in original boxes are rare & hard to find & usually demand a higher price.

Row 1:

1. **Oval Vegetable Tureen,** with matching cover, 1⅝" high, 3½" wide, 4¾" long not including handles, white decorated with a blue design & blue bands, gold leaf trim, rivetted handles, seamless body. Near mint, extremely rare shape & size, **$225.00. Note:** This could have been used for vegetables as there is no hole in the cover for a ladle.

2. **Gravy or Sauce Boat,** 1⅜" tall, 1¼" wide, 3" long not including the handle, white decorated with a blue design & blue bands, gold leaf trim, rivetted handle & foot. Near mint, rare shape, **$195.00.**

3. **Oval Platter,** ½" deep, 4" wide, 6" long, white decorated with a blue design & blue bands, gold leaf trim. Mint, **$75.00. Note:** This could also be an under plate for the oval tureen, No. 1 on this row.

4. **Oval Deep Soup Tureen,** 1¾" high, 2¼" wide, 3" long not including handles, white decorated with a blue design & blue bands, gold leaf trim. Near mint, extremely rare shape & size, **$225.00. Note:** The cover has a hole for the ladle to fit in the tureen. Ladle is missing.

5. **Plate,** ⅜" deep, 3⅝" diameter, white decorated with blue design & blue bands, gold leaf trim. Note: There are ten of these plates in this set. Mint, **$25.00.**

6. **Handled Divided Vegetable Dish,** ⅜" deep not including center handle, 2" wide, 2⅝" long, white decorated with blue design & blue bands, gold leaf trim. Near mint, rare shape, **$195.00.**

Row 2:

1. **Wash Basin,** ⅞" deep, 3⅜" top diameter, solid blue. Near mint, **$45.00.**

2. **Two-Handled Roasting Pan,** ⅜" deep, 1⅞" wide, 3⅞" long not including handles, solid light blue. Good plus, **$35.00.**

3. **Two-Handled Sauce Pan,** ⅞" deep not including handles, 2⅜" top diameter, solid blue. Near mint, rare shape, **$65.00. Note:** The rounded bottom on this pan & the turned-up handles.

4. **Fry Pan,** ½" deep, 2⅜" diameter not including the handle, solid blue. Good plus, **$50.00.**

5. **Two-Handled Egg Plate,** ½" deep not including handles, 2⅝" top diameter, solid blue. Good plus, **$55.00.**

6. **Oval Two-Handled Roasting Pan,** ⅜" deep, 2" wide, 3⅛" long not including handles, solid blue. Mint, extremely rare shape & size, **$120.00. Note:** This is the first time I have seen an oval roasting pan. Usually they are oblong.

7. **Handled Sauce Pan,** ⅞" deep, 2" diameter, solid blue. Mint, **$60.00.**

Row 3:

1. **Funnel,** 2⅛" to top of the spout, 1⅞" diameter, white with light blue trim. Good plus, **$55.00.**

2. **Cuspidor,** salesman's sample, 2-piece, 1½" deep including cover, 3½" bottom diameter, white. Mint, extremely rare shape & size, **$265.00.**

3. **Plate,** ⅜" deep, 3" diameter, white decorated & trimmed with gold leaf floral design. Mint, **$25.00.**

4. **Gravy or Sauce Boat,** 1⅜" to top of the lip, 1¼" wide, 3" long not including the handle, white decorated & trimmed with a gold leaf floral design. Near mint, rare shape, **$195.00.**

5. **Oval Platter,** ½" deep, 2⅝" wide, 4⅛" long, white decorated & trimmed with a gold leaf floral design. Near mint, **$75.00.**

6. **Handled Divided Vegetable Dish,** ⅜" deep not including center handle, 2" wide, 2⅝" long, white decorated & trimmed with a gold leaf floral design. Near mint, rare shape, **$195.00.**

Row 4:

1. **Tumbler,** 2¼" deep, 2¼" top diameter, reverse cobalt blue & white large mottled, triple coated. White interior, cobalt blue trim. Near mint, extremely rare color, shape & size, **$155.00. Note:** I refer to this color as reverse cobalt blue & white because it appears the cobalt blue was applied first with white over it.

2. **Fry Pan,** 1" deep, 4¼" top diameter not including the handle, reverse cobalt blue & white large mottled, white interior, cobalt blue trim, rivetted handle. Good plus, **$135.00.**

3. **Handled Griddle,** footed, 1½" high tapering down to the back top edge to 1¼" high. 2⅜" wide, 4½" long not including handle, reverse cobalt blue & white large mottled, white interior, cobalt blue handle, rivetted feet handle & griddle sections. Near mint, extremely rare color, shape & size, **$235.00. Note:** The reason for the tapered top edge & the grooved griddle sections is so the juice from the meat can drip into the grooved back edge & then be poured off.

4. **Handled Sauce Pan,** ⅞" deep, 3⅛" diameter not including handle, reverse cobalt blue & white large mottled, white interior, cobalt blue trim & handle. Good plus, **$110.00.**

5. **Bean Pot,** 4⅛" tall, 3⅜" middle diameter, reverse cobalt blue & white large mottled, white interior, cobalt blue trim, seamed body, rivetted ears, wire bail. Near mint, extremely rare color, shape & size, **$195.00. Note:** All the pieces on this row are part of a set.

Row 1:
1. **Soup Plate,** ¼" deep, 1½" diameter, charcoal gray, white large mottled. Good, **$20.00.**
2. **Miniature Potty,** ⅜" deep, 1½" top diameter, white with cobalt blue trim, rivetted handle, seamless body. Marked "Go Way Back___." Good plus, extremely rare color, shape, **$140.00. Note:** This is the smallest potty I have seen.
3. **Oblong Roasting Pan,** 2⅝" long, 1" wide, charcoal gray & white large mottled. Good plus, **$65.00.**
4. **Grater,** 3¾" high including handle, 1½" wide, solid blue. Mint, rare shape & size, **$185.00. Note:** This is the smallest grater I have seen.
5. **Fluted Mold,** ⅜" deep, 2⅛" top diameter, charcoal gray & white large mottled. Near mint, rare shape, **$115.00.**
6. **Grater,** 4½" high including handle, 1⅝" wide, solid light blue. Mint, rare shape, **$155.00.**
7. **Two-Handled Saucepan** with matching cover, 1⅛" deep, 1⅝" diameter not including handles, charcoal gray, white large mottled. Near mint, **$75.00.**
8. **Mug,** 1" deep, 1⅛" diameter, brown & white large swirl, white interior, rivetted handle. Good, extremely rare color, shape & size, **$465.00.**
9. **Soup Plate,** ¼" deep, 1½" diameter, charcoal gray & white large mottled. Mint, **$20.00. Note:** All the charcoal gray & white large mottled pieces on this row are part of a set.

Row 2:
1. **Candlestick or Chamberstick,** ¾" deep, 2⅞" top diameter, light blue, white interior, rivetted handle. The neck of the candlestick is also rivetted to the base. Near mint, extremely rare color, shape & size, **$395.00.**
2. **Crumb Tray,** 2½" high including handle, 2⅝" diameter, dark blue & white medium mottled. Mint, extremely rare color, shape & size, **$185.00.**
3. **Fluted Mold,** ¾" deep, 2" top diameter, dark blue & white medium mottled. Mint, rare color & shape, **$155.00.**
4. **Two-Handled Saucepan** with matching cover, 1⅜" deep, 2⅛" top diameter not including handles, tan shading to reddish brown, white interior, brown trim, shaded. Mint, rare color, **$75.00.**
5. **Two-Handled Saucepan,** ¾" deep, 2" diameter, dark blue & white medium mottled. Near mint, rare color, **$75.00.**
6. **Colander,** footed, 1¾" high, 3¾" top diameter not including handles, reddish brown shading to tan, white interior, brown trim, rivetted handles & foot, ring for hanging, fancy design perforations. Good plus, rare color, shape & size, **$325.00. Note:** Even though the two-handled saucepan in this row is part of this set, note how they have adapted the shading to a better advantage. The shading on the sauce pan starts with the lighter shading on top whereas the colander starts with the dark shading on top.

Row 3:
1. **Wash Basin,** ¾" deep, 2¾" diameter, charcoal gray & white large mottled. Good plus, **$45.00.**
2. **Pail,** 2" deep, 1⅞" diameter, charcoal gray & white large mottled, wire bail. Good plus, rare shape, **$165.00.**
3. **Fry Pan,** ⅜" deep, 2⅝" diameter not including handle, charcoal gray & white large mottled. Good plus, **$95.00.**
4. **Mush Mug,** 1⅝" deep, 1⅞" top diameter, charcoal gray & white large mottled, seamed body, rivetted handle. Good plus, rare shape & size, **$65.00.**
5. **Fluted Mold,** ⅝" deep, 2⅝" top diameter, charcoal gray & white large mottled. Good, rare shape, **$75.00. Note:** All the pieces on this row in the charcoal gray & white large mottled are part of a set. Also note, the pieces on Row 1 on this page in the charcoal gray & white large mottled are a much smaller scale than this set. I believe the smaller pieces are from a doll's set.

Row 4:
1. **Two-Handled Saucepan,** with matching cover, 1¾" deep, 2⅛" diameter, reddish dark brown & white large mottled, rivetted handles, seamed body. Mint, extremely rare color, rare shape & size, **$175.00.**
2. **Two-Handled Saucepan,** with matching cover, 1¾" high, 2⅛" diameter, green & white medium mottled, seamed body, rivetted handles. Near mint, rare color, shape & size, **$140.00. Note:** The different shapes of the handles on the saucepans on this row.
3. **Fry Pan,** ⅜" deep, 1⅞" top diameter not including the handle, cobalt blue, white interior, rivetted handle. Near mint, rare color, shape & size, **$125.00.**
4. **Colander,** footed, 1¾" high, 3⅜" top diameter not including handle, reddish brown & white fine mottled, rivetted handle. Mint, extremely rare color, shape & size, **$285.00. Note:** This colander was made with only one handle, which is very unique.

Row 1:
1. **Tea Set,** 12 pieces. Cup measures 1½" deep, 1⅞" top diameter, rivetted handles. Saucer measures ¾" deep, 3" top diameter. Open sugar, 1⅝" high, 2⅛" top diameter. Coffeepot, 4¾" tall, 2½" bottom diameter, rivetted spout & handle with seamless body. Creamer, 2⅛" tall, 1¾" bottom diameter, rivetted handle. All pieces are solid light blue with white interior. Near mint, extremely rare shape & size, **$595.00.**

Row 2:
1. **Colander,** handled & footed. 1¼" high, 3⅛" top diameter not including the handles, red & white medium mottled inside & out with black trim, seamless body. Good plus, extremely rare color, rare shape & size, **$525.00.**
2. **Elephant,** 2½" to top of the trunk, 1⅛" wide, 3" long, cast iron base, solid gray. Mint, rare color, shape & size, **$155.00. Note:** I was told this was part of a set of four toy circus elephants.
3. **Bread Raiser,** footed, 2⅞" high, 3⅜" top diameter not including the handles, 2⅛" bottom diameter, solid blue with white interior, vented tin dome cover with black wooden knob. Good plus, extremely rare shape & size, **$495.00. Note:** This is the smaller version of the two pictured in this section.
4. **Coffeepot,** 3⅜" tall, 2⅛" bottom diameter, gray & white large mottled inside & out, rivetted handle, seamed body. Good plus, extremely rare color, shape & size, **$395.00.**
5. **Potty,** 1¾" deep, 2¾" top diameter, blue & white large swirl, white interior, black, trim & handle, seamless body. Good plus, extremely rare color, shape & size, **$595.00.**

Row 3:
1. **Pail,** 2" deep, 2⅛" top diameter, solid light lavender blue inside & out, wire bail, seamless body. Good plus, rare color & shape, **$175.00.**
2. **Fry Pan,** ½" deep, 2⅝" top diameter, solid light lavender blue inside & out, rivetted handle. Good plus, rare color, **$125.00.**
3. **Fluted Turban Style Mold,** 1⅛" deep, 3½" top diameter, solid light lavender blue inside & out, rivetted loop with wire hanger. Good plus, rare shape, **$155.00.**
4. **Grater,** 4⅛" tall, 1½" wide, solid light lavender blue inside & out. Near mint, rare color & shape, **$165.00.**
5. **4-eyed Egg Pan,** ⅜" deep, 2⅞" top diameter, solid light lavender blue inside & out, rivetted handle. Good plus, rare color, **$145.00.**
6. **Handled Bean Pot,** with matching cover, 1¾" deep, 2⅝" top diameter, solid light lavender blue inside & out, rivetted handles, seamless body. Near mint, rare color, shape & size, **$135.00.**

Row 4:
1. **Oblong Roasting Pan** with handle & pouring spout, ⅝" deep, 2⅜" wide, 4½" long, solid light lavender blue inside & out. Near mint, rare color, **$120.00.**
2. **Fish Mold,** ½" deep, 1½" wide, 3⅞" long, solid light lavender blue inside & out. Mint, rare color, shape & size, **$195.00.**
3. **Fry Pan,** ⅞" deep, 5" top diameter, white with black trim. Mint, **$55.00.**

Row 5:
1. **Bathtub with Insert,** salesman's sample. Insert, 2" deep, 2" wide. Bottom tapering to 5" long. Bathtub base, 2½" to top including feet, 2⅞" wide, 6⅜" long. White on cast iron base. Marked "FO 12 PAT JUN 8" & what appears to be "1908" – the date is not very clear. "Standard Ideal Co. Limited Port Hope." Good plus, rare color, shape & size, **$185.00. Note:** This salesman's sample with insert shows customers the inner construction of the bathtub.
2. **Pitcher,** 1⅝" tall, ¾" diameter, solid green with black handle, seamless body. Near mint, extremely rare shape & size, **$165.00. Note:** This is the smallest pitcher I have seen. Also notice on the front of the pitcher is some form of black lettering, which is not legible.
3. **Colander,** footed & handled, 1⅞" high, 4⅜" top diameter, brown with light gray interior, rivetted handles. Good plus, rare color, shape & size, **$285.00. Note:** I believe this is the "Domestic Science" size.
4. **Miniature Electric Range,** with yellow enameled panel, black body, 10⅝" tall, 7½" wide, 15" long. One side oven with rack. Nickel plated legs & door hinges. Good plus, rare color, shape & size, **$495.00.**
5. **Child's Potty,** 3¼" deep, 5¾" top diameter, white with light blue trim & handle. Near mint, **$35.00.**

Row 1:

1. **Mush Mug,** 2" deep, 2⅜" diameter, white with fine blue flecks inside & out, seamless body, rivetted handle. Near mint, **$75.00. Note:** All the pieces on Row 1 & 2 are part of a set.
2. **Oblong Roasting Pan,** ⅝" deep, 4½" long including handle & spout, 2¼" wide, white with fine blue flecks on both sides, seamless body, rivetted handle. Mint, **$95.00.**
3. **Oval Platter,** ½" deep, 2⅝" wide, white with fine blue flecks on both sides. Near mint, **$60.00.**
4. **Dust Pan,** 5½" including handle, 3¼" wide, white with fine blue flecks on both sides. Good plus, rare shape, **$135.00.**
5. **Fluted Mold,** 1" deep, 3¼" top diameter, white with fine blue flecks inside & out. With rivetted loop for hanging. Good plus, rare shape, **$95.00.**
6. **Gravy or Sauce Boat,** 1⅜" tall, 3" top length, rivetted handle & foot, white with fine blue flecks inside & out. Good plus, rare shape, **$175.00.**

Row 2:

1. **Sauce Pan,** 1¼" deep, 2⅜" diameter, white with fine blue flecks inside & out, rivetted handle. Near mint, **$55.00.**
2. **Spatula or Turner,** 5" long, 1⅜" wide, white with fine blue flecks inside & out, rivetted hook handle. Good plus, rare shape, **$110.00.**
3. **Funnel,** 2¼" long, 1¾" top diameter, white with fine blue flecks inside & out, rivetted handle. Mint, **$55.00.**
4. **Grater,** 4⅝" long including handle, 1¾" wide, white with fine blue flecks inside & out. Mint, rare shape, **$165.00.**
5. **Handled Strainer,** 1⅛" deep, 5" long including handle, white with fine blue flecks inside & out, rivetted handle & kettle hook. Good plus, rare shape, **$95.00. Note:** The kettle hook is the hook opposite the handle that holds the strainer up on the kettle when straining.
6. **Ladle,** 4¼" long, ladle diameter 1⅛", molded handle, white with fine blue flecks inside & out. Good, rare shape, **$45.00. Note:** A molded handle is molded as part of the piece rather than applied by rivets.
7. **Wash Basin,** 1⅛" deep, 3¾" top diameter, with ring for hanging, white with fine blue flecks inside & out. Mint, **$45.00.**

Row 3:

1. **Mug,** 2" deep, 2¼" diameter, white with black trim & handle, rivetted handle. Near mint, **$20.00. Note:** A rivetted handle has been applied to the piece with rivets.
2. **Molasses Pitcher,** 4" deep, 2⅞" diameter, reddish brown, light green & gray mottled inside, seamless body, rivetted handle. Good, rare color, shape & size, **$95.00.**
3. **Cuspidor,** salesman's sample, 2⅛" high, 2¾" top diameter, enameled over cast iron, white enamel interior. The outside is not enameled. Good plus, rare shape & size, **$215.00.**

Row 4:

1. **Sauce Pan,** 2⅛" deep, 3½" top diameter, solid yellow, white interior. Good plus, **$40.00**
2. **Teapot,** 5½" to top of cover handle, 3½" bottom diameter, white with black trim, handles, seamed body. Near mint, **$85.00.**
3. **Teapot,** squatty shape, 4" high, 4⅛" middle diameter, solid blue, white interior, black trim. Good plus, **$75.00.**

Row 1:
1. **Oblong Baking Pan,** 1" deep, 4⅜" wide, 7⅜" long, cobalt blue, white interior, rivetted ear that holds the wire ring for hanging. Good plus, **$50.00.**

Row 2:
1. **Covered Saucepan,** 2¼" tall, 3½" diameter, cobalt blue, white interior, rivetted handles. Good plus, **$60.00.**
2. **Handled Saucepan,** 2" deep, 2½" diameter not including handles, cobalt blue, white interior, rivetted handles. Good plus, **$55.00.**
3. **Handled Kettle,** 1¼" deep, 3¼" top diameter not including handles, cobalt blue, white interior, rivetted handles. Good plus, rare shape, **$65.00.**
4. **Handled Strainer,** 1⅝" deep, 3" top diameter, cobalt blue, white interior, rivetted handles, tipping handle on opposite end, perforated bottom & side. Good plus, rare shape, **$85.00.**
5. **Handled Kettle,** 1¾" deep, 3⅜" top diameter not including handles, cobalt blue, white interior, rivetted handles. Good plus, **$55.00.**

Row 3:
1. **Plate,** ⅝" deep, 3⅞" top diameter, cobalt blue, white interior. Good plus, **$25.00.**
2. **Soup Ladle,** 7½" long ladle, 1½" deep, 2⅜" top diameter, cobalt blue, white interior, rivetted handle. Good plus, **$40.00.**
3. **Handled Skimmer,** 7" long, skimmer 2⅜" diameter, cobalt blue, white interior, rivetted handle. Good plus, **$65.00.**
4. **Plate,** ⅝" deep, 3⅞" top diameter, cobalt blue, white interior. Good plus, **$25.00.**

Row 4:
1. **Syrup,** 4" high, 2¾" diameter, cobalt blue, white interior, seamed body, rivetted handle. Good plus, rare color, shape & size, **$165.00.**
2. **Two-Handled Egg Plate,** ⅞" deep, 4" top diameter, cobalt blue, white interior, rivetted ears, wire bail, seamed body. Good plus, **$60.00.**
3. **Water Pail,** 3¾" deep, 3¾" top diameter, cobalt blue, white interior, rivetted ears, wire bail, seamed body. Good plus, rare color, shape & size, **$155.00.**
4. **Plate,** ⅝" deep, 3⅞" top diameter, cobalt blue, white interior. Good plus, **$25.00.**
5. **Handled Kettle,** 1¾" deep, 4¼" top diameter, cobalt blue, white interior, rivetted handle. Good plus, **$55.00.**

Row 5:
1. **Straight-Sided Saucepan,** 1⅜" deep, 3" diameter, cobalt blue, white interior, rivetted handle. Good plus, **$55.00.**
2. **Covered Bucket,** 4¼" tall, 4¼" diameter, cobalt blue, white interior, rivetted handle. Good plus, **$75.00.** **Note:** The cover has a metal rim that fits down inside the bucket and holds the cover tight.
3. **Pitcher,** 4⅛" tall, 3⅝" diameter, dark cobalt blue, white interior, seamed body, rivetted handle. Good plus, rare color, shape & size, **$135.00.**
4. **Pedestal Bowl,** two handles, 2⅜" deep, 4⅝" top diameter, cobalt blue, white interior, rivetted handles & pedestal. Good plus, **$135.00. Note:** This could be an open sugar.
5. **Lipped Saucepan,** 1⅝" deep, 3⅜" top diameter, cobalt blue, white interior, rivetted handle. Good plus, **$55.00.**

Row 1:

1. **Three Piece Roaster,** salesman's sample. Roaster 2½" to top of cover, 4" wide, 5¾" long not including handles, blue and white fine mottled inside and out, black trim, rivetted handles. The top of the cover is embossed REED and has two metal steam vents. Mint. Handled insert, ¼" deep not including handles. 3⅜" wide, 5⅜" long, blue and white fine mottled outside, white interior, rivetted handles, black trim. Mint, extremely rare color, shape and size, 3 pieces **$1,295.00. Note:** This roaster is a replica of the original "Reed" roaster from the Reed Manufacturing Company, Newark, New York. They were famous for their Reed Sanitary Self-Basting roaster embossed "Reed." The salesman's sample "LISK" roaster was featured in Book 1.

Row 2:

1. **Partial Tea Set,** cup, 1½" deep, 2" diameter. Saucer, ⅜" deep, 3" diameter. Teapot, 4" high, 3½" diameter. Light blue, green, pink, black, yellow and white large mottled. These pieces have white interiors, except for the saucers which have the colored interiors, End of Day. Good plus, extremely rare color, shape and size, **$475.00. Note:** Cover is not original.

Row 3:

1. **Saucepan,** 1⅞" deep, 2⅜" diameter, American gray medium mottled, seamless body, handle has eyelet for hanging. Good plus, rare color, shape and size, **$110.00.**
2. **Dust Pan,** 5½" including the handle, 3¼" wide, dark bluish gray and white medium mottled on both sides. Near mint, rare color and shape, **$175.00.**
3. **Colander,** footed, 1¾" high, 3¾" top diameter not including the handles, rivetted handles, American gray large mottled. Mint, extremely rare color, shape and size, **$575.00.**
4. **Grater,** 4¼" high including handle, 1⅝" wide, gray and white medium mottled on both sides. Mint, rare color, shape and size, **$165.00.**
5. **Child's Mug,** 2¼" deep, 2⅝" diameter, seamless, American gray medium mottled. Good plus, rare color, shape and size, **$95.00.**

Row 4:

1. **Tea Set,** cup, 1⅜" deep, 2" top diameter. Saucer, ⅜" deep, 3" diameter. Sugar Bowl, 2½" high 1¾" middle diameter. Teapot, 5⅜" tall, 2¾" diameter. Creamer, 2" tall, 1½" diameter. All pieces are solid light blue, white interiors, rivetted handles, seamless bodies. Near mint, rare color, shape and size, the complete set, **$495.00.**

Row 1:
    1. **Miniature Delft-Style Clock,** face measures 2¼" wide, 3⅛" long, white decorated with blue Delft-style scene. Marked "Made In Germany." Mint, extremely rare color, shape & size, **$495.00.**

Row 2:
    1. **Oval Clothes Boiler,** 1⅝" deep, 2¼" wide, 3⅛" long not including the handles, blue & white medium mottled inside & out, seamed body. Near mint, extremely rare color, shape & size, **$495.00.**

    2. **Tub,** advertising salesman's sample, tub size not including the standard, 1⅝" deep, 3⅛" wide, 6" long. Tub is enameled pink over a cast iron base. The standard is embossed "Contour Bath, By American Standard." Good plus, rare color, shape & size, **$165.00.**

    3. **Sauce or Gravy Boat,** with attached drip tray, 2¼" tall. Boat section measures 1" deep, 4" long, 2" wide. Attached drip tray measures 2¾" wide, 4⅜" long. White, light blue, green, cobalt blue, dark maroon, pink & yellow, inside & out, "Confetti" pattern, End of Day. Near mint, extremely rare color, shape & size, **$325.00. Note:** Liquids can be poured from either end.

Row 3:
    1. **Tea Set,** 13 pieces including teapot & cover, creamer, covered sugar, 4 cups & saucers. Teapot 4½" tall, 3" diameter, tubular handles & seamless body. Creamer measures 2" tall, 1⅞" diameter, rivetted handle. Covered sugar 2½" tall, 1¾" diameter. Cup, 1⅜" deep, 1⅞" top diameter, rivetted handles. Saucers ⅝" deep, 3" diameter. Reddish-pink shading to a lighter pink, with gold trim & decorations. Shaded. Complete set near mint, extremely rare color, **$625.00.**

Row 4:
    1. **Serving Set,** 11 pieces including 4 soup plates, oval platter, gravy boat, oval vegetable tureen with matching cover, covered butter dish, oval bread tray. Soup plate ½" deep, 3⅝" top diameter. Oval platter ½" deep, 3⅜" wide, 5⅜" long. Gravy boat, 1⅜" high, 1¼" wide, 3" long. Oval vegetable tureen 1¾" tall, 3½" wide, 4¾" long. Covered butter dish 1⅝" tall, 3¼" base diameter. Oval bread tray with fancy side perforations & perforated handles ¾" deep, 2⅛" wide, 4" long. All pieces are white with a light green decorated border. Near mint, extremely rare shape & size, **$1,150.00. Special Note:** This is the only set I have seen with the covered butter dish. I have never seen a miniature butter dish before this one.

Row 5:
    1. **Miniature Electric Range,** 10⅝" to the top of the oven, 6⅞" wide, 14¼" long, green painted body with white enameled oven door. Oven door has a heat indicator that actually works. Heat indicator reads: "Warm/Hot/Very Hot/Little Lady Ranges, Kokomo Indiana. U.S.A." The front lower section is labeled "Alliance." The metal trim & legs are nickel plated. Good plus, extremely rare color, shape & size, **$985.00.**

342

Row 1:
1. **Partial Tea Set,** 9 pieces. Cup, 1" deep, 1½" diameter. Saucer, ⅜" deep, 2½" diameter. Creamer, 1¼" high, 1¼" bottom diameter. Teapot, 3⅛" tall, 2⅜". Covered sugar, 1⅞" tall, 1⅞" top diameter. White decorated with a blue & yellow floral design, blue trim. Marked "Germany." Good plus, **$495.00. Note:** There should be two more cups & saucers to this set.

Row 2:
1. **Partial Tea Set,** 15 pieces. Cup, 1" deep, 1½" top diameter. Saucer, ⅜" deep, 2½" top diameter. Plate, ⅜" deep, 3¼" top diameter. Creamer, 2" tall, 1⅛". Teapot, 3¼" tall, 2⅜". White trimmed with green bands of what looks similar to a shamrock pattern. Good plus, **$525.00. Note:** The sugar bowl is missing.

Row 3:
1. **Water Pail,** 3" deep, 3¼" top diameter, light blue, white interior, rivetted ears, seamless body, wooden bail. Near mint, rare shape, **$185.00.**
2. **Pitcher & Bowl.** Pitcher, 3⅝" tall, 2⅞". Bowl, 1⅜" deep, 4¾" top diameter. White with light blue & dark blue flecks inside & out. Good plus, 2 pieces, **$195.00.**
3. **Slop Bucket,** 2¾" deep including the cover, 3¼" top diameter, white with light blue & dark blue flecks inside & out, rivetted ears, wooden bail, reed wrapped handle, seamless body. Good plus, **$85.00. Note:** The cover of the slop bucket has a tapered down hole in the center. When the refuse is poured into the bucket, this tapered hole prevents the refuse from slopping over the cover's edge.

Row 4:
1. **Handled Saucepan,** 2" deep, 2⅞" diameter, light blue, white interior, rivetted handle, seamless body. Good plus, **$55.00.**
2. **Turk's Head Mold,** ⅞" deep, 2¼" diameter, light blue, white interior, seamless body. Mint, extremely rare shape & size, **$235.00.**
3. **Salt Box,** 3⅞" back height, 1⅝" deep, 2¼" long, light blue inside & out, wooden cover, seamed body. Mint, extremely rare color, shape & size, **$725.00.**
4. **Fish Mold,** 2½" high, 3" long, light blue, white interior, ring for hanging. Mint, extremely rare shape & size, **$265.00.**
5. **Handled Strainer,** 1⅛" deep, 3" top diameter, light blue, white interior, rivetted handle & kettle hook. Near mint, rare shape & size, **$165.00. Note:** This strainer fits over the top of a kettle or bowl. The kettle hook on the opposite end keeps the strainer from slipping down in the kettle.

Row 1:

1. **Tool Rack,** 5" high from top of tool bar, 2¾" wide, white decorated with dark & light blue design, dark blue trim. Mint, extremely rare color, shape & size, **$595.00. Note:** This should have three tools, usually, a handled flat skimmer, round-bottom skimmer & soup ladle.

2. **Two-Handled Saucepan,** with matching cover, 2¾" high, 3" diameter not including handle, white decorated with dark & light blue design, dark blue trim. Mint, **$85.00.**

3. **Miniature Clock,** decorated with a floral pattern that resembles pansies. Labeled "Uhrenfachgeschatz-Schmuch Herman Siegl. A 5020 Salzburg Griesgasse 7." Mint, extremely rare color, shape & size, working order, **$325.00.**

4. **Two-Handled Saucepan,** with matching cover, 2" high, 2⅞" diameter not including handles, white decorated with dark & light blue design, dark blue trim. Mint, **$85.00.**

5. **Colander,** 1⅝" high, 3⅜" top diameter not including handles, 2⅛" bottom diameter, white decorated with dark & light blue designs, dark blue trim. Mint, extremely rare color, shape & size, **$435.00.**

Row 2:

1. **Two-Handled Saucepan,** with matching cover, 2½" high, 3" diameter, solid light green inside & out, black trim & knob. Marked "Pama Trademark" in a circle, also labeled "Made By Pama Super Quality Enamelled Ware." Near mint, extremely rare color, **$145.00.**

2. **Teakettle,** 2¾" tall, 2⅞" diameter, solid light green inside & out, black trim & knob. Marked the same as the above. Near mint, extremely rare color, shape & size, **$435.00.**

3. **Oval Covered Casserole,** matching cover, 2½" high, 4" long including handles, 2½" wide, solid light yellow with black trim on handle, white interior. Enameled over cast iron. Marked "Made in Sweden Husqvarna." Good plus, extremely rare shape & size, **$165.00.**

Row 3:

1. **Two-Handled Bean Pot,** matching cover, 1¾" tall, 2½" top diameter not including handles, solid blue. Good plus, rare shape & size, **$155.00.**

2. **Two-Handled Bean Pot,** matching cover, 2¾" high, 3" top diameter, solid blue, white interior. Good plus, rare shape & size, **$165.00. Note:** I chose to show these two bean pots side by side so you could see the different shapes of the handles & bodies.

3. **Footed Bread Raiser,** 2¾" high, 4" top diameter not including handles, 3" bottom diameter, solid blue, white interior, vented tin domed cover with black wooden knob. Near mint, extremely rare shape & size, **$550.00. Note:** The tin cover has perforations that vent the bread when it rises.

4. **Open Sugar,** 1⅝" high, 2⅜" top diameter, 1½" bottom diameter, solid blue, white interior. Near mint, rare shape & size, **$140.00.**

Row 4:

1. **Child's Teapot,** 3½" high, 3" diameter, beige decorated on one side with a toy rooster, a girl sitting on a bench holding a present & a boy with a stick. The backside is decorated with a roly poly, doll & a toy pull rabbit. Marked "Made In Germany." Good plus, rare shape & size, **$135.00.**

2. **Plate,** salesman's sample, ⅝" deep, 4¾" diameter, yellow & white on both sides, large swirl, black trim. Circa 1950. Near mint, **$95.00. Note:** I believe these pieces were used by salesmen or jobbers to show customers and to get their reactions on how well a particular item might sell for color, shape & durability.

3. **Two Handled Round Wash Tub,** 2½" deep, 4½" top diameter, American gray large mottled, seamed body. Good plus, extremely rare color, shape & size, **$325.00.**

Row 1:
1. **Saucer,** ⅝" deep, 3½" top diameter, solid blue with white interior. Good plus, **$30.00.**
2. **Cup & Saucer.** Cup measures 1⅞" deep, 1⅞" top diameter, solid blue with white interior. Near mint. 2 pieces, **$65.00. Note:** The tubular handle is applied with rivets, & the top of the handle is rivetted on the left side. The bottom is rivetted on the right side. Near mint. Saucer is the same as No. 1 on this row. Good plus.
3. **Oblong Serving Tray,** ½" deep, 5⅝" wide, 7⅞" long, solid blue with white interior. Good plus, **$65.00.**
4. **Cup,** same as No. 2 on this row. Near mint, **$35.00.**
5. **Teapot,** 5½" tall, 2⅞" diameter, tubular rivetted, seamed handles, seamless body, solid blue with white interior. Near mint. **$225.00. Note:** All the pieces in this set on this row display perfectly on the serving tray (No. 3 on this row).

Row 2:
Special Note: Even though some of these colanders are shown elsewhere in this section I thought it would be interesting to show you how they can vary in shape & size, as well as design. Some of the colanders are in one piece with a footed bottom that is molded whereas others may have a rivetted or applied foot for a bottom. The handles are also rivetted or applied & some are in a flat or up position. The perforations vary: some colanders have perforations in the bottom only whereas others have their sides as well as their bottoms perforated. Some of the perforations are fancy in design.
1. **Colander,** footed & handled, 1¾" deep, 3¾" top diameter not including the rivetted handles, rivetted foot, fancy perforated design, metal ring for hanging, reddish brown shading to tan, white interior with brown trim. Good plus, rare color, shape & size, **$325.00.**
2. **Colander,** handled & footed, 1¼" deep, 3⅛" top diameter not including the handles, red & white medium mottled inside & out with black trim, seamless body with molded foot, perforated bottom. Good plus, extremely rare color, rare shape & size, **$525.00.**

Row 3:
1. **Colander,** handled & footed, 1¼" deep, 2⅝" top diameter not including the handles, blue & white medium mottled inside & out, seamless body with molded perforated bottom. Good plus, rare color, shape & size, **$425.00.**
2. **Colander,** handled & footed, 1¾" deep, 4¼" top diameter not including the handles, blue & white medium mottled inside & out, seamless body with molded, perforated bottom. Good plus, extremely rare color, rare shape & size, **$450.00.**
3. **Colander,** handled & footed, 1¾" deep, 3¾" top diameter not including the rivetted handles, applied foot, perforated bottom. American gray large mottled inside & out. Mint, extremely rare color, shape & size, **$465.00.**

Row 4:
1. **Teakettle,** 4¼" tall, 3⅜" diameter, solid blue inside & out, seamed body & spout, rivetted ears, metal bail. Good plus, rare color, shape & size, **$425.00.**
2. **Water Pail,** with reed handle, 3¼" deep, 3⅞" top diameter, solid light blue inside & out, decorated with white & cobalt blue squares, with gold leaf design & bands. Rare shape, **$135.00.**

Row 5:
Special Note: Once again I have chosen to show you the variations in these graters, such as the different shapes. Some are molded all in one piece to include the handle & feet; some have an added wire that forms the handle, feet, with a back support wire. On the latter type edges are rolled over to hold the wire, then it is enameled along with the piece. Some graters are flatter than others, & the perforations vary in the size of the holes as well as design. Last but not least there are variations in sizes & colors.
1. **Grater,** 3¾" tall including the feet, 1½" wide, solid blue front & back, small perforations, wire handle, feet, & wire back support. This is the smallest grater I have seen. Mint, rare shape & size, **$185.00.**
2. **Grater,** 4½" tall including the feet, 1⅝" wide, blue & white fine mottled front & back, small perforations, wire handle, feet, & back support. Near mint, rare shape, **$165.00.**
3. **Grater,** 4¼" tall including the feet, 1⅝" wide, bluish green & white medium mottled front & back, large perforations, flat molded handle & feet. Mint, rare color, shape & size, **$175.00.**
4. **Grater,** 4¼" tall, including the feet, 1⅝" wide, bluish green & white medium mottled front & back, large perforations, flat molded handle & feet. Mint, rare color, shape & size, **$175.00.**
5. **Grater,** 4¼" tall including the feet, 1⅝" wide, gray & white medium mottled, wire handle, feet, & back support, small perforations. Mint, rare color, shape & size, **$175.00.**
6. **Grater,** 4⅜" tall including the feet, 1¾" wide, grayish blue & white medium mottled front & back, large perforations, flat molded handle & feet. Mint, rare color, shape & size, **$175.00.**

SECTION 21
THE HUNT GOES ON!

Special Note: This section was set aside for last minute finds by other people as well as myself. It contains an assortment of colors & shapes as well as age variations from the late 1800's til the present. Even though some of the items are newer, they should be shown so people will be versed on the time of production, as well as who manufactured & who distributed the items.

Row 1:
1. **Clock,** 7" x 7", white decorated with a blue Delft-style scene of a windmill & people. 8-day. Marked "Germany." Mint, extremely rare color, shape & size, **$395.00.**

Row 2:
1. **Coffeepot,** 6½" tall, 4" bottom diameter solid yellow with black trim & white interior, seamed body. Circa 1980. Good plus, **$45.00.**
2. **Waste Bowl,** 4⅛" deep, 5⅛" diameter, white metal handles, trim, & protection band. White decorated with lilies of the valley, pink rose buds & ferns. Mint, extremely rare shape, **$425.00.**
3. **Milk Pitcher,** 6¼" tall, 5¼" diameter, solid yellow decorated around the neck with a black & white design, white interior with black handle & trim. Good plus, **$55.00.**

Row 3:
1. **Hot Plate,** ¼" high, 6" square, light beige, decorated with two ladies playing tennis. Good plus, **$70.00.** **Note:** This could have been given to commemorate a tennis match.
2. **Lady Finger Pan,** overall measurements ½" deep, 4⅞" wide, 11⅞" long. Each finger is ¼" deep, 1" wide, 3⅝" long. Solid blue outside with white interior. Near mint, extremely rare color & shape, **$325.00.**
3. **Frigidaire Hot Plate,** ⅛" high, 4½" square, light green decorated with a black rooster & design. Advertising on back reads, "The Pot Rooster. Porcelain, the finish that stays new looking forever! Heat resistant "Roost" for hot pots & pans. Useful spoon rest. Colorful wall decoration. Rust Proof! Acid Proof! Heat Proof! Resists Stains! Scratch Proof! Cleans in a Jiffy! Only Frigidaire has refrigerators, ranges, food freezers, washers & dryers, finished in lifetime Porcelain. See your Frigidaire Dealer. Veos Tile Co. Rehoboth, Mass." Good plus, **$75.00.**

Row 4:
1. **Commemorative Plate,** ¾" deep, 9" diameter, dark green decorated with two American Flags & an American emblem. Border is decorated with a floral pattern that resembles poppies. A man's name etched in white: Joseph H. Ebright. Near mint, extremely rare color, shape & size, **$215.00. Note:** I believe this plate was given to commemorate a veteran's service or event. Notice that there are only 9 stars on the flag & emblem.
2. **Measure,** 6¼" tall, 4¼" bottom diameter, deep sea green shading to a moss green, white interior, seamless body & lip, rivetted handle. Distributed by Norvell-Shapleigh Hardware Co. of St. Louis. They were the sole distributors of the "Shamrock Ware." Good plus, rare color, **$245.00.**
3. **Teakettle,** 7¾" tall, 9⅝" bottom diameter, labeled "Old Ivory Enameled Ware, Sole Manufacturers, Republic Stamping & Enameling Co. Canton, Ohio, U.S.A. Pat Applied For." Label is also stamped "5¾." Also pictures a lady in a circle. Bottom label reads "The beautiful hand decorations on this ware are burned into the enamel & will not wash off." Mint, rare color, **$295.00.**

Row 5:
1. **Oval Platter,** 1⅛" deep, 13" wide, 16" long, white decorated with fruits, brown trim, "Corona" Enamelware. Mint, **$95.00.**

Row 1:
1. **Cuspidor,** 4¾" high, 8¼" diameter, one-piece seamless, light blue & white large mottled, triple coated, very heavy. White interior with black trim. Good plus, rare color & shape, **$365.00.**
2. **Coffeepot,** 9½" tall, 5½" diameter, cobalt blue & white medium mottled w/gray interior, seamless body, rivetted handle. Good plus, **$195.00.**
3. **Camp or Mush Mug,** 5¼" deep, 7⅛" diameter, light blue & white large mottled, white interior, dark blue trim & rivetted handle, seamless body. Near mint, **$175.00.**

Row 2:
1. **Handled Sauce Pan,** with matching granite lid, 6½" tall, 7½" diameter, light aqua green & white large swirl, white interior with black handles & trim, seamless body. Circa 1930. Near mint, **$135.00.**
2. **Funnel,** squatty shaped, 4" tall, 5⅝" diameter, blue & white large swirl with white interior, cobalt blue rivetted handle & trim. "Blue Diamond Ware." Near mint, rare color & size, **$235.00.**
3. **Coffeepot,** straight-sided with aluminum coffee basket, 8⅜" tall, 5⅜" bottom diameter, light aqua green & white large swirl with white interior, black handle & trim. Circa 1930. Near mint, **$195.00.**

Row 3:
1. **Two-piece Oval Roaster,** 8" tall, 10½" wide, 14½" long not including the handles, black with red medium mottling inside & out. Cover has self-basting indentations. The bottom section of the roaster has ridges to keep foods from sticking while cooking. Good plus, rare color, **$125.00.**
2. **Slop Bucket,** 10" tall, 10¼" diameter, blue & white medium mottled, white interior, black wooden handle, ears & trim, seamless body. Near mint, rare shape, **$225.00.**

Row 4:
1. **Oval Perforated Fish Poacher Insert,** with wire handles, 11" wide, 18⅞" long, American gray large mottled. Near mint, **$95.00. Note:** This piece has 10 round, molded feet that protrude down to keep the insert from sitting flat on the bottom of the fish poacher.

Row 1:

1. **Pedestal Bowl,** 3½" deep, 6⅝" top diameter, green & white large mottled inside & out, black trim. Circa 1950. Good plus, rare shape, **$65.00.**
2. **Soup Plate,** 1⅜" deep, 10¼" top diameter, green & white large mottled inside & out, black trim. Circa 1960. Good plus, **$25.00.**
3. **Teakettle,** 6½" to tall, 7¼" bottom diameter, green & white large mottled, white interior, black trim & handle, seamed body. Circa 1960. Good plus, **$125.00.**
4. **Soup Plate,** 1⅜" deep, 10¼" top diameter, green & white large mottled inside & out, black trim. Circa 1960. Good plus, **$25.00.**
5. **Mug,** 3½" deep, 3⅞" top diameter, green & white large mottled inside & out, black trim. Circa 1950. Good plus, **$30.00.**

Row 2:

1. **Saucepan,** 3" deep, 6¼" top diameter, black & white speckled inside & out. Labeled "Ceramic on Steel 1qt. Saucepan Graniteware II. General Housewares Corp., Terre Haute, Indiana." 1989. Mint, **$25.00.**
2. **Sauce pan,** small, 3" deep, 6¼" top diameter. Saucepan, large, 3⅜" deep, 7⅛" top diameter. Light gray with white & blue flecks inside & out, blue handle & trim. Labeled "Sassy Pans General Housewares Corp." 1989. Mint, each **$25.00.**
3. **Saucepan,** 3½" deep, 7⅝" top diameter, light gray with white & blue flecks inside & out, light gray handle & trim. Labeled "Sassy Pans." 1989. Mint, **$25.00.**

Row 3:

1. **Mug,** 3½" deep, 3¾" top diameter, yellow & white large mottled inside & out, black trim. Circa 1970. Good plus, **$30.00.**
2. **Plate,** ¾" deep, 10⅛" top diameter, yellow & white large mottled inside & out, dark blue trim. Circa 1970. Near mint, **$25.00.**
3. **Pail,** 6¼" deep, 7¾" top diameter, white, pink, brown, light green large mottled, white interior, black trim & ears, wire bail, seamless body. Circa 1980. Mint, **$165.00. Note:** This type of coloring looks like it was meant to resemble the old "End of Day." The quality of the finish & construction is very good. The weight is fairly heavy compared to other later pieces.
4. **Spoon,** 12⅛" long, spoon 2½" wide, brown with white flecks on both sides. 1990. Mint, **$5.00.**
5. **Two-Handled Covered Pan,** 3" tall, 5¼" top diameter not including the handle, brown with white flecks inside & out. 1990. Mint, **$10.00.**

Row 4:

1. **Covered Sugar,** 4½" tall, 4" diameter not including handles, blue & white large mottled inside & out, black trim. 1989 Mint, **$55.00.**
2. **Coffeepot,** 8" tall, 4⅞" bottom diameter, blue & white large mottled inside & out, black trim. Labeled "CGS International Inc., Miami, Florida." 1989. Mint, **$30.00.**
3. **Creamer,** 3¼" deep, 4" diameter, blue & white large mottled inside & out, black trim. 1989. Mint, **$55.00.**

Section 21: The Hunt Goes On!

Row 1:

1. **Teapot,** squatty, 5" tall, 4⅝" diameter, gray & light gray relish mottling inside & out. Made in Romania between 1989 & 1991. Mint, **$25.00.**

2. **Mug,** 3" deep, 3⅜" diameter, yellow & green large mottling, yellow interior, black trim. Circa 1980. Good plus, **$20.00.**

3. **Stack Dinner Carrier,** 16" to top of the carrying handle including the four food containers & cover, 5¾" diameter, gray & light gray relish type mottling inside & out. Near mint, **$75.00. Note:** The four food containers are held together while carrying by a metal carrier with a Bakelite-type handle. This resembles the Romanian ware, but there is quite a difference in the texture of the finish. The Romanian ware is rough to the touch, whereas this piece is smooth & lighter in color. I believe it could possibly be circa 1950.

4. **Bowl,** 1¾" deep, 6½" top diameter, yellow & green large mottled inside & out, black trim. Circa 1980. Good plus, **$15.00.**

5. **Pail,** 5" deep, 6" top diameter, gray & light gray relish type mottling inside & out, seamed body, wooden bail. Labeled "E.R.O. Made in Romania." Red & silver label has what looks like a squatty teapot. Made between 1989 & 1991. Mint, **$30.00. Note:** This ware is fairly heavy & well constructed. Some people have bought this ware as old.

Row 2:

1. **Teapot,** 8" tall, 5" bottom diameter, dark aqua green & white large swirl, white interior, black trim, seamed body. Circa 1970. Good plus, **$45.00.**

2. **Mug,** 3⅛" deep, 3¼" diameter, dark aqua green & white large swirl, white interior, black trim. Circa 1970. Good plus, **$25.00.**

3. **Colander,** footed, 4⅜" deep, 9⅜" top diameter, light blue & white large mottled inside & out, black handles & trim, fancy perforated bottom & sides. Circa 1980. Mint, **$25.00.**

4. **Butter Melter,** 2⅝" deep, 2⅝" bottom diameter, light blue & white large mottled inside & out. Circa 1980. Mint, **$25.00.**

5. **Napkin Rings,** 1¼" wide, 1⅝" diameter, red & white large mottled inside & out, black trim. Circa 1980. Mint, extremely rare color, shape & size, each **$45.00.**

6. **Milk Pitcher,** 5¾" tall, 4¾" bottom diameter, white, orange red, light bluish green, yellow & black inside & out. 1989-1990. Mint, **$70.00. Note:** This piece is fairly heavy. The finish is extremely lumpy. I have heard that this piece & others like it came from Mexico. Also, this piece looks like it was meant to resemble old "End of Day."

Row 3:

1. **Bowl,** 1¾" deep, 6⅜" top diameter, yellow & red large mottled inside & out, black trim. Circa 1970. Good plus, **$20.00.**

2. **Sectioned Plate,** ¾" deep, 11¾" top diameter, yellow & red large mottled inside & out, black trim. Circa 1970. Mint, **$25.00.**

3. **Mug,** 3" deep, 3⅜" diameter, yellow & red, yellow interior, black trim. Circa 1970. Good plus, **$25.00.**

4. **Covered Berlin-Style Kettle,** 7" tall, 7½" diameter, yellow & red large mottled, yellow interior, black trim, wire bail, seamless body. Circa 1970. Mint, **$30.00.**

5. **Pedestal Sugar or Sherbet,** 2½" deep, 4¼" top diameter, blue & white large mottled, white interior, dark blue trim. Marked "Hong Kong 10 C.N." Circa 1980. Mint, **$30.00.**

6. **Soup Plate,** 1⅜" deep, 10¼" top diameter, blue & white large mottled inside & out, black trim. Circa 1960. Near mint, **$25.00.**

7. **Pedestal Sugar or Sherbet,** 2½" deep, 4¼" top diameter, blue & white large mottled, white interior, dark blue trim. Marked "Hong Kong 10 C.N." Circa 1980. Mint, **$30.00.**

Row 4:

1. **Cup & Saucer** (part of the set in the original box, No. 3, on this row). Cup, 1⅞" deep, 2¾" top diameter. Saucer, ½" deep, 4¾" top diameter. Black & white large mottled inside & out, black trim. Circa 1980. Mint, 2 pieces **$25.00.**

2. **Mug,** 3½" deep, 3¾" diameter, yellow & white large swirl, white interior, black trim. Circa 1960. Mint, **$30.00.**

3. **Set of Six Cups & Saucers,** in the original box, No. 1 on this row is part of this set also. Cup, 1⅞" deep, 2¾" top diameter. Saucer, ½" deep, 4¾" top diameter, black & white large mottled inside & out, black trim. Cup labeled "Made In Hong Kong." Saucer labeled "Wash In Dishwasher Or Hot Soapy Water. Do Not Scour. C.G.S. 1 International Inc. Miami, Florida. Made In Hong Kong." Box marked "C.G.S International Inc., Miami, Fla." Circa 1980. Mint, rare color, complete with box, **$175.00.**

4. **Mug,** 3⅛" deep, 3½" diameter, black & white large mottled inside & out, black trim. Circa 1980. Mint, **$20.00.**

5. **Mug,** 3⅛" deep, 3½" diameter, red & white large swirl, white interior, red trim. Circa 1970. Mint, **$30.00.**

Row 1:
  1. **Coffee Boiler,** 11" tall, 8⅝" bottom diameter, brown & white large mottled with white interior, brown trim, seamed body, rivetted spout, ears & handle. Marked "Elite Austria No. 8." Good plus, rare color, **$325.00.** **Note:** Notice the depth of color on this piece compared to the others on this row.
  2. **Dipper,** 3⅞" deep, 6⅝" top diameter, brown & white large mottled with white interior, brown trim, seamed, tubular, rivetted handle with ring for hanging. Marked "Elite Austria Reg'd S-7." Good plus, rare color, **$110.00.**
  3. **Milk Can,** 11¾" tall, 5½" bottom diameter, brown & white large mottled with white interior, brown trim, wire ears, wooden bail handle, seamless body. Marked "Elite Austria Reg'd S-7." Good plus, rare color, **$185.00.**

Row 2:
  1. **Oblong Baking Pan,** 2⅛" deep, 9¾" wide, 13½" long, including the molded handles, light blue lumpy cobblestone effect, decorated with white, brown & traces of dark blue chicken wire pattern, white interior, black trim. Molded handles, seamless body, "Duchess Ware." Good plus, extremely rare color, shape & size, **$475.00.**
  2. **Dipper,** 3" deep, 5⅜" top diameter, light blue lumpy cobblestone effect, decorated with white, brown & traces of dark blue chicken wire pattern, white interior, black trim & hollow handle with eyelet for hanging. "Duchess Ware." Good plus, extremely rare color, shape & size, **$135.00.**
  3. **Berlin-Style Kettle,** 6½" tall, 8" diameter, light blue lumpy cobblestone effect, decorated with white, brown, & traces of dark blue chicken wire pattern, white interior, black trim & ears, wire bail, seamless body. "Duchess Ware." Good plus, extremely rare color, shape & size, **$285.00.**

Row 3:
  1. **Coffee Boiler,** 12" tall, 9½" bottom diameter, brown & bluish gray large swirl inside & out, seamed body with rivetted handle, spout, & ears, wire bail handle. Near mint, rare color, **$495.00.**
  2. **Pie Plate,** ⅞" deep, 7¾" top diameter, brown & bluish gray large mottled inside & out. Good plus, rare color, **$65.00.**
  3. **Mug,** 3⅛" deep, 3⅞" top diameter, brown & bluish gray large swirl inside & out with brown trim, rivetted handle. Near mint, rare color, **$75.00.**

Row 1:

1. **Handled Sauce Pan,** 2⅞" deep, 7½" top diameter, creamy yellow with brown flecks inside & out, brown trim. Circa 1980. Mint, **$25.00.**

2. **Container,** 9⅛" deep, 6⅛" top diameter, bluish gray & white medium mottled inside & out, seamed back & bottom. Good plus, **$95.00. Note:** I am not sure about the intended use of this piece. On each side ¾" down is a hole, I would guess for hanging the container. The back seam has chipping all the way down as if it had been placed against something, much like a sap bucket would hang against a tree.

3. **Fry Pan,** 1½" deep, 10" diameter, creamy yellow with brown flecks inside & out, brown trim. Circa 1980. Mint, **$30.00.**

Row 2:

1. **Teakettle,** 5" high, 5½" bottom diameter, light blue & white large swirl with white interior & black trim, handle, & ears, wooden bail, seamless body. Circa 1940. Good plus, rare shape, **$165.00.**

2. **Sectioned Plate,** ⅝" deep, 10" top diameter, light blue & white large swirl inside & out, black trim. Circa 1960. Mint, **$35.00.**

3. **Coffeepot,** 5⅞" tall, 4" bottom diameter, light blue & white large swirl inside & out, black trim & handle, seamed bottom. Cover is attached at the top with a tin hinge & a wire that goes through the handle & folds over on each end. Circa 1960. Near mint, rare size, **$95.00.**

Row 3:

1. **Covered Straight Sided Kettle,** 4⅝" tall, 10½" diameter, yellow & white swirl inside & out with black trim, seamless body. Good plus, **$125.00. Note:** Cover handle is recessed down into the cover. Circa 1950.

2. **Coffee Boiler,** 9½" tall, 9" bottom diameter, blue & white large swirl, white interior, black trim & handles, wooden bail, seamed bottom. Circa 1940. Near mint, **$195.00.**

Row 4:

1. **Flared Basin,** 4⅜" deep, 12¾" top diameter, blue & white medium mottled inside & out. Good plus, **$70.00.**

Row 1:
1. **Oval Platter,** ¾" deep, 8" wide, 11" long, brown & white large swirl, applied over cobalt blue & white large swirl, white interior. "Redipped," Near mint, extremely rare color, shape & size, **$265.00. Note:** The redipping process was done at the factory.

Row 2:
1. **Bean Pot,** (cracker or biscuit jar). 7" tall, 6⅞" diameter, blue & white large swirl with white interior, blue trim, rivetted wire handles, seamless body. Good plus, extremely rare color & shape, **$525.00. Note:** This could be "Blue Diamond Ware," distributed by Norvell-Shapleigh.
2. **Oblong Ash Tray,** 1⅜" deep, 3¼" bottom width, 6⅛" long, green & white medium mottled with white interior. Each end has indentations for cigarettes to rest on. good plus, **$65.00.**
3. **Milk Pitcher,** 6⅜" tall, 4½" diameter, light & dark burgundy large swirl, beige interior with dark burgundy trim, seamless body. Marked "Quadruple Coated, Heavy Steel Acid Proof, Meinecke & Co. N.Y. For Hospital Use. Made In Czechoslovakia." Good plus, extremely rare color & shape, **$210.00.**

Row 3:
1. **Pedestal Shaped Bowl,** 3" high, 6" top diameter, light blue & light gray large swirl inside & out, rolled top & bottom edges, seamless body. Good plus, rare color & shape, **$185.00.**
2. **Box,** with hinged cover, 4¼" tall, 6" wide, 8" long, yellow & brown large mottled with white interior. Good plus, extremely rare color, shape & size, **$235.00.**
3. **Tube Cake Pan,** 2⅞" deep, 8½" top diameter, grayish cobalt blue & white large mottled inside & out. Good plus, rare color & shape, **$295.00.**

Row 4:
1. **Slop Bucket,** with porcelain insert & matching granite cover, 13½" tall, 10½" diameter, light blue & white large mottled. Porcelain insert is held secure inside by a bolt that goes through the bottom of the slop bucket & is tightened by a nut. Good plus, rare shape, **$210.00. Note:** This is the first slop bucket I have seen with a porcelain insert.
2. **Coffee Boiler,** 10¼" tall, 8" bottom diameter, bluish gray & white large swirl with white interior, rivetted side handle & ears, seamed body. "Lava Ware." Good plus, rare color, **$325.00.**

Row 1:
1. **Partial Set of Bowls,** small ones measure 1⅝" deep, 4" top diameter. Large bowl is 3¼" deep, 7⅞" top diameter, white decorated with red striping. Near mint, 3 pieces, **$145.00.**
2. **Oval Platter,** 1⅛" deep, 14¼" wide, 18⅛" long, white decorated with fruits, brown trim. Stamped "Made In Hong Kong." This type of ware was also advertised for sale by the "Enterprise Enamel Co." Near mint, **$95.00.**

Row 2:
1. **Sugar Bowl,** squatty shaped, 5¼" tall, 4½" diameter, solid blue with white interior, black wooden cover knob & handles. Near mint, rare shape & size, **$295.00.**
2. **Teapot,** 7" tall, 4⅝" bottom diameter. Advertised as "Vollrath Ware in new harmonizing colors," this is bisque pink pearl trimmed in deep pink pearl. The Vollrath Co., Sheboygan Wisconsin, registered U.S. Pat. Off. Copyrighted 1929 by T.V. Co. Near mint, rare color, shape & size, **$115.00.**
3. **Push-up Candlestick,** 6¼" tall, 5¼" bottom diameter, dark navy blue with fine white mottling, rivetted carry handle. A wire push-up ring fits into the slot on the side of the neck of the candlestick. This ring pushes the candle upward, & allows the candle to be used completely. Good plus, extremely rare shape, **$225.00.**

Row 3:
1. **Ruffled Bowl,** 1½" deep, 5¼" top diameter, white decorated with a green border & a silhouette of a person who appears to be sowing seeds. Near mint, **$45.00.**
2. **Fry Pan,** 1¼" deep, 6" top diameter, cream with red trim & handle. Good plus, rare size, **$95.00.**

Row 4:
1. **Teapot,** 5¼" tall, 5⅜" diameter, cream decorated with a bird & what appears to be a holly pattern. Green handle, spout, & cover knob. Cover also has a green beaded border. Green spout & thumbrest decorated with red & yellow, white interior. Marked "Elite, Made In Czecho-slovakia. Reg'd 17021." Good plus, rare color & shape, **$155.00. Note:** This pot looks as though it might have been made to commemorate the Christmas season.
2. **Serving Bowl,** 4" deep, 11" top diameter, solid brilliant cobalt blue outside with white interior that is decorated with brilliant cobalt blue flowers. Mint, rare color & shape, **$185.00. Note:** The top rim of this bowl is actually out of round. This is a very unique shaped bowl. Marked "M-0112."
3. **Covered Casserole,** 3" tall, 5" top diameter, green shading to light green with cream interior. Near mint, **$85.00.**

Row 5:
1. **Muffin Pan,** eight cup ⅞" deep, 7¼" wide, 14¼" long. Each cup measures ⅝" deep, 3" top diameter, dark brown & white fine mottled, eyelet for hanging. Near mint, **$125.00.**
2. **Washboard,** 24" overall length, 12¼" wide. Enamel surface measures 12" long, 10⅞" wide. Dark charcoal gray & white fine mottled. Metal top section is embossed "National Washboard Co. Chicago, Saginaw, Memphis. Soap Saver Trademark Registered U.S. Pat. Off. Made In U.S.A. No 197. Patent 1152766-1283148." Marked on the back side "Porcelain enamel washboard. The washing surface is made from a sheet of steel into which has been fused a coating of porcelain enamel (a composition of fine glass). It is durable, sanitary & flexible & will not rust or corrode. It is not effected by alkalies or strong washing compounds. Near mint, rare shape, **$195.00.**

Row 1:

1. **Coffeepot,** with gray coffee basket, 7¾" tall, 4⅝" bottom diameter, green & white relish type medium mottling with white interior, black handle & trim. Marked "U.S. Standard Seamless Ware." Near mint, rare color, **$135.00.**

2. **Milk Can,** 11½" tall, 6¼" bottom diameter, dark plum color with light gray & white large mottling, seamed body, wire bail handle. Near mint, rare color, **$255.00.**

3. **Lipped Preserve Kettle.** 3¼" deep, 8¼" top diameter, blue & white with some gray in the large swirl inside & out, seamless body, wire bail handle, ear for hanging. Good plus, **$85.00.**

Row 2:

1. **Lipped Preserve Kettle,** 2¾" deep, 6½" top diameter, blue & white large mottled with white interior, black trim & ears, wire bail handle-ear for hanging. "Columbian Ware." Good plus, **$130.00.**

2. **Biscuit Cutter,** 1⅞" tall, 2¼" diameter, blue & white large mottled with white interior, & black handle. The strap handle is applied through slots on top of the biscuit cutter. Columbian Ware. Good plus, extremely rare color, shape & size, **$3,250.00.**

3. **Cake Pan,** two-piece, 3" deep, 5¾" wide, 8¼" long, bright blue & white fine mottled inside & out with deeper blue trim, seamed ends. Removable oblong bottom fits in the bottom of pan snugly to prevent leakage. When the cake is baked it can be instantly removed from the pan by turning the cake pan upside down, releasing the outer section when lifting the removable bottom insert. The cake has less breakage & cools faster. "Used by good cake bakers everywhere." Good plus, extremely rare color, shape & size, **$295.00.** **Note:** One of these in a heavy, bright tin was given as a premium by the Lee Manufacturing Co. premium house in 1915.

4. **Measure,** 3⅝" tall, 2¾" bottom diameter, green veins of large mottling with a white overall lumpy effect, white interior with green trim. Marked "Elite-Austria." "Snow On The Mountain." Near mint, rare size, **$265.00.**

5. **Serving Bowl,** 3½" deep, 7¼" top diameter, green veins of large mottling with white overall lumpy effect, white interior with green trim. Marked "Elite-Austria." Good plus, rare shape, **$115.00.**

Row 3:

1. **Round Fluted Mold,** 2¼" deep, 4⅞" top diameter, dark bluish gray & white medium mottled inside & out. Good plus, **$110.00.**

Row 4:

1. **Muffin Pan,** eight cup, 1⅝" deep, 7⅜" wide, 14" long. Each cup measures 1¼" deep, 3¼" top diameter, dark plum color with light gray & white large mottling inside & out. Good plus, rare color, **$265.00.**

2. **Pudding Pan,** 3¼" deep, 10¼" top diameter, blue & white large swirl inside & out. Good plus, **$55.00.**

3. **Water Pail,** 9" deep, 11½" top diameter, cobalt blue & white large mottled with white interior, black wooden bail handle, trim & ears. Mint, rare color, **$295.00.**

Row 1:

1. **Teapot,** 8¼" tall, 5¼" bottom diameter, dark blue & white speckled inside & out. Good plus, **$110.00. Note:** This teapot is from circa 1920. I'm showing this teapot along with the other two items on this row in this category so you can compare the style & construction to the present styles. This speckled dark blue & white, along with the speckled black & white, has been produced & reproduced over a span of years.

2. **Oval Dinner Bucket,** three piece, cover, food insert & bottom. 8¼" to top of the cover handle including insert, 6⅞" wide, 9" long not including ears, black & white speckled, white interior, seamless body, wooden bail handle. Circa 1920 . Good plus, complete, **$175.00.**

3. **Child's Potty,** 4" deep, 7¼" top diameter, dark blue & white speckled inside & out. Labeled "Enameled Steel Ware Imperial Quality Metal Ware." Circa 1920. Good plus, **$35.00.**

Row 2:

1. **Handled Griddle,** corrugated bottom, ½" deep, 8⅛" diameter, black & white speckled inside & out. Circa 1960. Good plus, **$55.00.**

2. **Saucepot,** 4 qt., 5½" tall, 9⅜" top diameter, blue & white speckled inside & out. Labeled "Sauce Pot. The high tech, low care, faster cookware. Heats faster, cleans easier, saves energy, lasts a lifetime. Cooktop to table-top to refrigerator. Ceramic On Steel. 4qt. Sauce Pot. Graniteware II 6061 C.H.C. Made In U.S.A. General Housewares Corp. P.O. Box 4066. Terre Haute, Indiana. 47804. 1986." Mint, **$25.00.**

3. **Frypan,** 1¾" deep, 8½" top diameter, black & white speckled inside & out, cold handle. Circa 1920. Good plus, **$40.00. Note:** Cold handle is a handle usually constructed with an additional handle crimped over top of the original handle, three quarters of the way up, making the handle cooler to grip.

Row 3:

1. **Coffee Boile**r, 4 oz., 8¼" tall, 6⅜" bottom diameter, black & white speckled inside & out. Label reads same as No. 2, Row 2 of this page with the exception that this piece was made in 1988 by General Housewares Corp. Mint, **$35.00.**

2. **Coffee Boiler,** 12" tall, 9½" bottom diameter, black & white speckled inside & out, bottom tipping handle, black wooden bail, seamless body. Circa 1950. Good plus, **$45.00. Note:** Some black & white speckled was marked "U.S.N." on the bottom of the piece & was used in the United States Navy in World War II.

3. **Coffee Boiler,** 9½" tall, 8¾" bottom diameter, black & white speckled inside & out, wooden bail, seamed body. Circa 1940. Good plus, **$45.00.**

Row 1:

   1. **Wash Bowl,** 4⅛" deep, 14½" top diameter, green & white large swirl with white interior, cobalt blue trim, eyelet for hanging. "Emerald Ware" Strong Mfg. Co., Sebring Ohio. Good plus, rare color & shape, **$235.00. Note:** Generically called apple green & white, or kelly green & white by collectors. This wash bowl is part of a pitcher & bowl set.

Row 2:

   1. **Coffee Biggin,** including biggin with screen bottom, 4" deep, 3⅞" top diameter, 3¾" bottom diameter. Aluminum handled, fancy-perforated spreader measures 3⅜" diameter. Pot with cover, 8⅝" tall without the biggin, 5¼" bottom diameter. Green & white large mottled with white interior & green trim. Biggin is green & white large mottled inside & out. Seamed body. Near mint, rare color & shape, **$395.00.**

Row 3:

   1. **Candlestick,** with finger ring, 2" tall, 5⅝" diameter, green & white large mottled inside & out, rivetted neck. Good plus, rare color & shape, **$235.00.**

   2. **Plate,** 1" deep, 8" top diameter, green & white large mottled with white interior. Good plus, **$75.00.**

   3. **Cup,** 2" deep, 4⅝" top diameter, green & white large mottled with white interior & rivetted handle. Good plus, **$55.00.**

Row 4:

   1. **Oval Roaster,** two piece 6½" tall, 9½" wide, 14¾" long not including the handles, light green & white fine mottled inside & out, green trim & handles. Cover has self basting indentations. Good, **$65.00. Note:** The self basting indentations were designed so the liquids that formed on them while cooking would drop off and "baste" the food.

   2. **Candlestick** with finger ring, 1⅞" tall, 5" diameter, light green & white fine mottled inside & out. Near mint, rare shape, **$235.00.**

Row 5:

   1. **Wash Basin,** 3" deep, 11¾" top diameter, green & white large mottled with white interior, black trim, eyelet for hanging. Good plus, **$155.00.**

Row 1:

1. **Teakettle,** squatty shaped, 6" tall, 5¼" middle diameter, green & white large swirl, white interior, black trim & rivetted ears, seamless body, wooden bail. Mint, extremely rare color, shape & size, **$525.00.**

2. **Maslin-Style Kettle** with matching granite lid, 8½" deep, 8⅝" top diameter, green & white large swirl, white interior, black handles & trim, rivetted handles, seamless body. Near mint, rare color & shape, **$185.00.**

3. **Covered Bucket,** 4¾" high, 4⅝" diameter, green & white large swirl, white interior, black trim & rivetted ears, seamless body. Mint, rare color, **$275.00**

Row 2:

1. **Coffeepot,** 9¼" high, 6¼" bottom diameter, green & white large swirl, white interior, dark brown handle & trim, rivetted handle, seamed body. Near mint, rare color, **$395.00.**

2. **Colander,** footed, 4" high, 9⅞" top diameter, green & white large swirl, white interior, dark brown trim & rivetted handles. Good plus, rare color, **$295.00.**

3. **Teapot,** 9¼" high, 5½" bottom diameter, green & white large swirl, white interior, dark brown trim & rivetted handle, seamless body. Good plus, rare color, **$395.00.**

Row 3:

1. **Handled Skimmer,** flat, perforated, 14⅛" long to top of the handle, skimmer diameter 4¾", green & white large swirl on both sides, dark blue rivetted handle. Near mint, extremely rare color, shape & size, **$340.00.**

2. **Water Pitcher,** 9¼" to top of the lip, 6½" middle diameter, green & white large swirl, white interior, dark blue trim, seamless body. Good plus, extremely rare color, **$395.00. Note:** The rivetted handle is green & white swirl.

3. **Soup Ladle,** large, 13⅜" long, ladle 4½" diameter, green & white large swirl, white interior, blue handle. Good plus, rare color, **$225.00. Note:** The handle on this piece is a lighter blue than the handle on the skimmer on this row.

Row 4:

1. **Covered Berlin-Style Kettle,** with matching granite lid, 8" high, 11" middle diameter, green & white large swirl, white interior, dark blue trim, rivetted ears, write bail, seamless body. Near mint, rare color, **$295.00.**

2. **Pie Plate,** ⅞" deep, 9" top diameter, green & white large swirl, white interior, dark blue trim. Near mint, rare color, **$110.00.**

3. **Water Pail,** 7¾" deep, 10½" top diameter, green & white large swirl, white interior, dark blue trim, rivetted ears, seamless body, wire bail with wooden handle. Good plus, rare color, **$295.00.**

Note: I have chosen to show the various shades of greens here because collectors have a tendency to classify all greens as one color. As you can see, there are many variations. Another point of view is that people would call these greens Emerald Ware or Chrysolite especially when they do not have an Emerald Ware or Chrysolite piece to compare it to. None of these pieces is Emerald Ware or Chrysolite.

Row 1:

1. **Bread Pan,** 3" deep, 4⅝" wide, 9⅞" long, green & white large swirl with white interior, black trim. Envelope ends. Good plus, extremely rare color & shape, **$285.00. Note**: The top edge of this bread pan has a wire reinforced rolled top rim.

2. **Water Pitcher,** 7¾" tall, 5⅜" diameter, red & green large swirl inside & out, cobalt blue trim & handle, seamless body. Good plus, extremely rare color, shape & size, **$1,175.00.**

3. **Round Tube Cake Pan,** 3¼" deep, 9¾" top diameter, cobalt blue & white large swirl, white interior, black trim. Near mint, rare color & shape, **$325.00.**

Row 2:

1. **Oval Teapot,** 4¼" tall, 5¼" wide, 9" long from spout to handle, pink & green medium mottled, pink interior & black handle. Near mint, extremely rare color, shape & size, **$325.00.**

2. **Cream Can,** 7½" tall, 4" bottom diameter, blue & white large swirl, white interior, cobalt blue trim, rivetted ears, & wooden bail handle. "Blue Diamond Ware," made in the United States, distributed by Norvell-Shapleigh Hardware Co., St. Louis. Near mint, rare color & shape, **$595.00.**

3. **Bread Pan,** 3" deep, 5½" wide, 10¾" long, aqua green & white medium mottled, white interior, dark blue trim, seamed ends with wire-reinforced rolled top rim. Good plus, rare color, **$185.00.**

Row 3:

1. **Oblong Baking Pan,** with molded handles, 2¼" deep, 11¼" wide, 15¾" long, aqua green & white large swirl, white interior, dark blue trim. Good plus, rare color, **$175.00.**

2. **Body Pitcher,** 14½" tall, 8" bottom diameter, pink & white large swirl, white interior, pink trim, seamed body. Good plus, extremely rare color & shape, **$895.00. Note:**

SECTION 22
GATHERING AND CONVENTION COMMEMORATIVES AND RELATED ITEMS

You could join when registering at the annual graniteware convention, if you were not a paid member for the year. But if you were registering for the first time & paying your convention fee there was no guarantee that you would receive a commemorative. The Graniteware Association requested that you get your convention registration fees in to them by a certain date, to be guaranteed a commemorative when you came to the convention. The commemoratives were on a first-come, first served basis, because there was a required cut off as to how many would be made for the convention and the convention auction. This is one reason it is important to keep up to date on your yearly dues. The other reason is you get a very informative newsletter 4 times a year plus a roster of all the members. These items help keep you informed on what is going on in the Granite field.

The gatherings and conventions are part of our granite ware history. The commemoratives also speak of the love of granite ware & the devoted, hard working people that used their time & ingenuity to bring them to us. We can enjoy the events of the past that have been commemorated with these beautiful items. We can also pass these on to future generations of collectors, with the knowledge of how they came to be, & what they mean.

These commemorative & associated items are all from the "mother" clubs, not the regional clubs.

American Graniteware Association 1981-1985
Row 1:
1. **Commemorative 1981 American Granite Ware Association Tote Bag.** This was given to commemorate their first gathering in Downer's Grove, Ill. October 10-12, 1981. **$30.00-40.00 Note:** At this time the event was not called a convention but rather a gathering. There were approximately 60 people in attendance. The ladies that organized this event were called "Granny Granites." As we arrived they had a beautiful table set with desserts, fruits, & drinks along with "Granny Granite" to greet all of us. We also toured some to the members' homes, & Gloria Weiss, a member of the association, presented a talk on some of the history of granite ware. I also did a talk & display on the colors & shapes of granite ware. At the show & tell we all sat in a circle & unwrapped the piece or pieces we had acquired, & told of how we got the piece & perhaps the bargain we got it for. We then proceeded to a beautiful banquet with entertainment. The next morning the gathering concluded with a farewell breakfast.
2. **1983 Commemorative Trade Card, front & back view shown.** This was copied from an old "Granite Ironware" trade card. Commemorates the place & date of the Second American Graniteware Association gathering. Ann Arbor, Michigan, October 15 & 16, 1983. **$55.00-65.00.**
3. **1983 Program** for the American Graniteware Association gathering, at Weber's Inn. Program shows the breakdown of the two-day schedule. The schedule consisted of a Saturday "Early Bird" check in, brunch, welcomes, opening, Share-in, workshops, announcements, bar & hors d'oeuvres, banquet & auction, Sunday Brunch, closing meeting. **$25.00. Note:** The American Graniteware Association logo on this program was later changed to the one shown on the program on Row 2 (#2) of this page.

Row 2:
1. **Name Plate** with American Graniteware Association logo. **$10.00. Note:** These name plates were worn by members.
2. **1985 Program** for the American Graniteware Association Country Gathering at Pheasant Run. Program shows a breakdown of the 3-day schedule, which consisted of registration, sentimental journey, workshops, room sales, get acquainted time, dinner, entertainment, auction, business meetings, & so on. **$25.00. Note:** The first gathering had only 2 days, one day of activities, & Sunday brunch the second day. The second gathering had 2 days of events & farewells the third day.
3. **1985 Commemorative Trade Card,** front & back view shown. Copied from an old "Granite Ironware" trade card. This card commemorates the place & dates of the third American Graniteware Association's Country Gathering, held in St. Charles, Ill. on October 4, 5, & 6, 1985. **$55.00-65.00.**

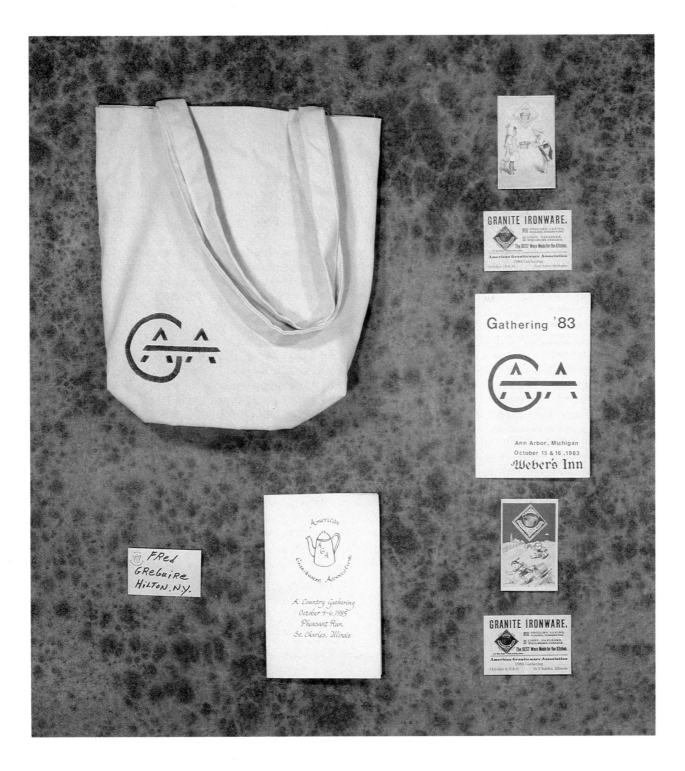

National Graniteware Society 1987 & 1988

Row 1:

1. **1987 Program** from the National Graniteware Society First Annual Convention, in Cedar Rapids, Iowa. Held on July 24-25 at the Holiday Inn. Program shows breakdown of schedule for the three days, which included Friday registration, displays, show & tell, room sales, hors d'oeuvres, & story swapping, Saturday registration, Avenue of the States (displays done by the members of the different states, each club or person choosing their own theme or using one chosen by the National Club), miniatures workshop where people brought their miniatures for display & discussion, auction consignments by members, cocktails, dinner-auction, room sales, Sunday farewell. **$10.00.**

2. **1987 Commemorative Watch Fob,** front & back view show. The teakettle is the emblem of the National Graniteware Society. Back side is embossed "1st annual convention, Cedar Rapids, Ia. July 24, 25, 1987. **$85.00-$250.00. Note:** This price range was established by what was paid at the convention auction that year.

3. **1987 Tote Bag,** brown paper, with teakettle emblem, printed "Graniteware 87." **$10.00.**

Row 2:

1. **1988 Tote Bag & Name Tag.** Bag with National Graniteware Society address stamp. **$10.00.**

2. **1988 Commemorative Pot Scrubber,** front & back view shown. Copied from an original Nesco Pot & Pan scraper. Front view reads "Nesco Pot & Pan Scraper" & shows the Nesco boy with his Royal Granite Enameled Ware. "They might imitate the ware but they can't imitate the wear." Back view; "A curve or point to fit anywhere in the pots or pans. Buy & always use Royal Granite Enameled Ware. It's easy to clean & is long lasting. The standard in kitchen utensils for over 25 years." In the center of the Nesco mark is "National Graniteware Society 2nd Annual Convention, Galesburg, Ill., July 22-23, 1988. **$85.00-135.00. Note:** This price range was also established at the convention auction that year.

3. **1988 White Nylon Pan Scraper.** Marked "Pan Scraper Nylon Hong Kong." **Note:** This was a little complimentary gift given at the convention. No price.

4. **1988 Program** from the National Graniteware Society's second annual convention in Galesburg, Ill., on July 22-23, 1988. The theme for this convention was "Christmas in July." Members brought pieces that were somehow related to the holiday. One example of this may have been a gift of granite ware that someone got for Christmas, or possibly a certain color of granite ware that would correspond to the holiday. **$10.00.**

5. **Envelope.** This is the envelope that the pot scrubber came in. Included in the price of No. 2 on this row.

Special Note: For further information write to:
National Graniteware Society
P.O. Box 10013
Cedar Rapids, Iowa 53410

Row 1:

1. **1989 "Chrysolite" Fan,** front view. Commemorative for the 3rd annual convention of the National Granite-ware Society on July 28-29, 1989. Held in Dubuque, Iowa. **$95.00-$225.00. Note:** It advertises "Almost every utensil made in tin can be had in Chrysolite enameled ware." Originally the old "Chrysolite" fans were manufactured for Hibbard, Spencer, Bartlett & Co. Chicago III. This was the jobber that sold "Chrysolite."

2. **1989 Program,** from the National Graniteware Society's third annual convention in Dubuque, Iowa, on July 28-29, 1989. The theme for the convention was "Mother Goose." Pieces were brought that related to the theme, such as child's pieces with rhymes. **$10.00.**

3. **1989 "Chrysolite" Fan,** back view, commemorating the convention. Advertising "Chrysolite Enameled Ware. First Award Paris 1900. Beautiful, pure, & acid proof, extra heavy, durable. The handsomest, most serviceable, & best finished ware yet produced. It is made of heavy steel with three coats of enamel & is absolutely pure & free from all harmful ingredients." **Special Note:** The Chrysolite fan was the color given to commemorate the National Graniteware Society convention in 1989. Four other colors were made to be auctioned off that year at the convention auction along with the surplus Chrysolite ones. **$95.00-225.00.**

Row 2:

1. **1989 Red & White Swirl Commemorative Fan,** front view. It is also modeled after the old "Chrysolite" fan. **$850.00-$1,150.00.**

Row 3:

1. **1989 Cobalt Blue & White Swirl Commemorative Fan,** back view **$225.00-$700.00. Note:** All of these fans measure 10" from the top of the fan to the bottom of the handle, 9" wide.

2. **1989 Tote Bag.** Paper stamped with National Graniteware Society's stamp. **$10.00.**

3. **1989 Blue & White Swirl Commemorative Fan,** front view. **$225.00-$550.00.**

Row 4:

1. **1989 Membership Badge.** Metal. Marked "National Graniteware Society 3rd Annual Convention. July 28-29, 1989. Dubuque, Iowa." Also has member's name & state typed in. These badges are worn at the convention. **$20.00.**

2. **1989 Brown & White Swirl Commemorative Fan,** back view . **$175.00-$300.00.**

3. **1989 Membership Card** from the National Graniteware Society. These certify that the member is in good standing for the year imprinted. **$10.00.**

Special Note: The prices for all the fans on this page were established at that year's convention auction.

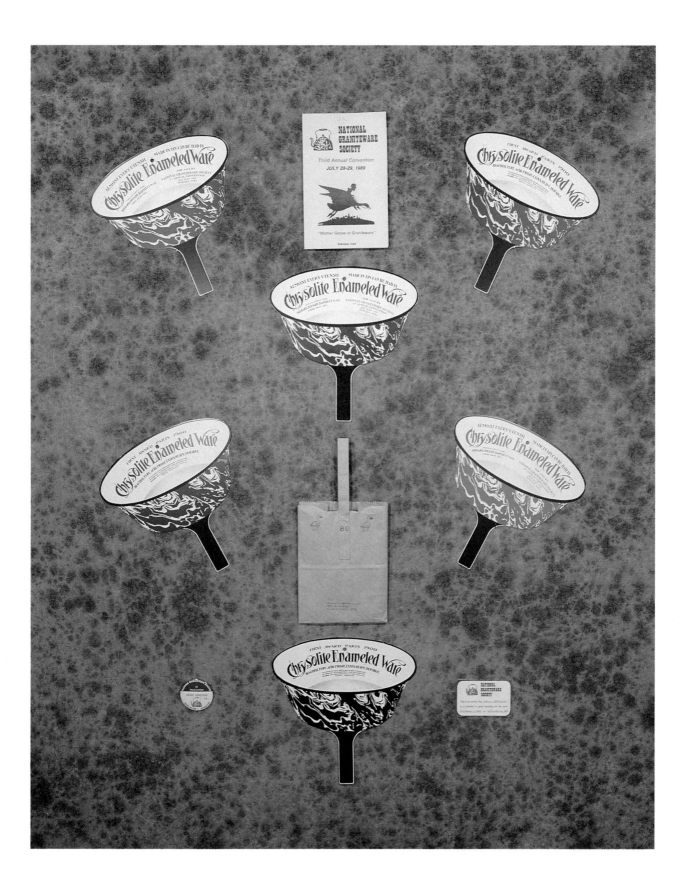

Row 1:

1. **1990 Tote Bag.** Cloth. Commemorating the National Graniteware Society's 4th Annual Convention in Terre Haute, In. on July 27-28, 1990. Price included in the commemorative No. 3 on this row.

2. **1990 Program** from the National Graniteware Society's 4th Annual Convention, Terre Haute, In. on July 27-28, 1990. The theme for this convention was a "Hoosier Salute to Graniteware." $10.00.

3. **1990 Handled Saucepan** with paper label, commemorating the National Graniteware Society's 4th Annual Convention. **$20.00-$75.00. Note:** This handled saucepan was made by General Housewares Corp., of Terre Haute, In. It also has a paper label inside that reads "Saucepan casserole 1qt. Ceramic On Steel." Black with fine white specks. The tote bag was also included as part of the handled saucepan commemorative given that year.

4. **1990 Tote Bag.** Cloth. Same as No. 1 on Row 1, except it reads "4th Annual Conventional" instead of "Convention." **Note:** These were misprinted.

Row 2:

1. **1990 Booklet,** on Columbian Enameled Ware by Suzanne Berger & Brenda Hutto. This booklet documents the Columbian Enameling & Stamping Company history as well as the granite ware they produced. This booklet was given to members present at the 4th annual convention in Terre Haute, In. **$30.00.**

2. **1990 Membership Badge.** Metal. Marked "National Graniteware Society 4th Annual Convention. July 27-28, 1990. Terre Haute, Indiana." With member's name typed in a picture of a Columbian Covered Sugar Bowl, in blue & white large swirl. **$20.00. Note:** The American flag was also a gift of that convention.

3. **Inside view** of the booklet described in row 2, #1. Showing some of the colors & shapes the Columbian Enameling & Stamping Co. made. Top left: blue & white large swirl roaster with embossed cover reading "Columbian." Lower left: 12 cup biscuit tray & biscuit cutter, large blue & white swirl. Upper right: "Onyx Ware" biscuit cutter & 12 cup biscuit tray, brown & white medium mottled. Middle: "Onyx" labeled tray, brown & white medium mottled. Bottom right: labeled Columbian gray large mottled pie plate. Other sections of the booklet show many different shapes & colors of Columbian granite ware. Also shows many of the company ads. **$30.00.**

Row 3:

1. **1991 Program** from the National Graniteware Society, 5th Annual Convention, in Springfield, Ill., on July 26-27, 1991. The theme for this convention was "Graniteware in Lincoln Land." Displays were centered around Lincoln & the log cabin. **$10.00.**

2. **1991 Commemorative A B C plate,** gray large mottled. **$55.00-250.00.** Other colors were made to be sold at the convention auction along with the surplus gray ones. Front & back view shown. Copied from an old A B C plate. Front side is embossed on the outer edge with the letters of the alphabet. Back side is stamped "The National Graniteware Society 5th Annual Convention." Cobalt & white swirl **$150.00-$250.00,** red & white swirl, **$200.00-$325.00,** brown & white swirl **$95.00-$220.00,** blue & white **$100.00-$300.00,** green & white **$100.00-$225.00.**

Special Note: Only one solid white A B C plate was made and it is in the National Graniteware Society archives. It was not sold at auction, so there is no established price. Each color made is represented in the National Graniteware Society archives.

3. **1991 A B C Membership Badge.** Metal. "Marked National Graniteware Society, 5th Annual Convention, July 26-27, 1991. Springfield, Ill." **Note:** The background on this membership badge is light gray large mottled. **$20.00.**

4. **1991 Tote Bag.** Paper, stamped with a picture of Lincoln, & the National Graniteware logo & stamp 91. **$10.00.**

Special Note: Prices for the handled saucepan, tote bag and the ABC plates were established that same year at the convention auction.

Schroeder's ANTIQUES Price Guide

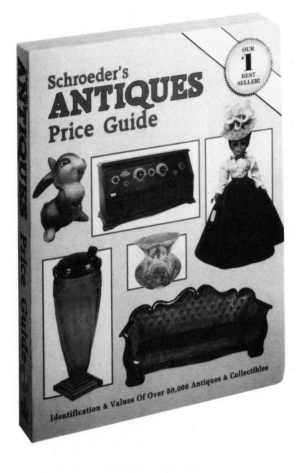

Schroeder's Antiques Price Guide is the #1 best-selling antiques & collectibles value guide on the market today, and here's why . . . More than 300 authors, well-known dealers, and top-notch collectors work together with our editors to bring you accurate information regarding pricing and identification. More than 45,000 items in almost 500 categories are listed along with hundreds of sharp original photos that illustrate not only the rare and unusual, but the common, popular collectibles as well. Each large close-up shot shows important details clearly. Every subject is represented with histories and background information, a feature not found in any of our competitors' publications. Our editors keep abreast of newly-developing trends, often adding several new categories a year as the need arises. If it merits the interest of today's collector, you'll find it in *Schroeder's*. And you can feel confident that the information we publish is up to date and accurate. Our advisors thoroughly check each category to spot inconsistencies, listings that may not be entirely reflective of market dealings, and lines too vague to be of merit. Only the best of the lot remains for publication. Without doubt, you'll find *Schroeder's Antiques Price Guide* the only one to buy for reliable information and values.

8½ x 11", 608 Pages   **$12.95**

COLLECTOR BOOKS
A Division of Schroeder Publishing Co., Inc.